Understanding Politeness

Politeness is key to all of our relationships and plays a fundamental part in the way we communicate with each other and the way we define ourselves. It isn't limited only to conventional aspects of linguistic etiquette, but encompasses all types of interpersonal behaviour through which we explore and maintain our relationships. This groundbreaking exploration navigates the reader through this fascinating area and introduces them to a variety of new insights. The book is divided into three parts and is based on an innovative framework which relies on the concepts of social practice, time and space. In this multidisciplinary approach, the authors capture a range of user and observer understandings and provide a variety of examples from different languages and cultures. With its reader-friendly style, carefully constructed exercises and useful glossary, *Understanding Politeness* will be welcomed by both researchers and postgraduate students working on politeness, pragmatics and sociolinguistics more broadly.

DÁNIEL Z. KÁDÁR is Professor of English Language and Linguistics at the University of Huddersfield.

MICHAEL HAUGH is an Associate Professor in Linguistics and International English at Griffith University, Brisbane.

Understanding Politeness

Dániel Z. Kádár

University of Huddersfield

Michael Haugh

Griffith University, Brisbane

CAMBRIDGE
UNIVERSITY PRESS

CAMBRIDGE
UNIVERSITY PRESS

University Printing House, Cambridge CB2 8BS, United Kingdom

Published in the United States of America by Cambridge University Press, New York

Cambridge University Press is part of the University of Cambridge.

It furthers the University's mission by disseminating knowledge in the pursuit of education, learning and research at the highest international levels of excellence.

www.cambridge.org
Information on this title: www.cambridge.org/9781107626942

© Dániel Z. Kádár and Michael Haugh 2013

First published 2013

Printed in the United Kingdom by Clays, St Ives plc

A catalogue record for this publication is available from the British Library

Library of Congress Cataloguing in Publication data
Kádár, Dániel Z., 1979–
Understanding politeness / Dániel Z. Kádár and Michael Haugh.
   pages   cm
Includes bibliographical references and index.
ISBN 978-1-107-03168-5 (hardback) – ISBN 978-1-107-62694-2 (pbk)
1. Politeness (Linguistics)   2. Grammar, Comparative and general – Honorific.
3. Interpersonal relations.   4. Sociolinguistics.   I. Title.
P299.H66K33   2013
306.44 – dc23   2013009545

ISBN 978-1-107-03168-5 Hardback
ISBN 978-1-107-62694-2 Paperback

Contents

Figures

Tables

Foreword

'*What* is it you are researching?? *Politeness*?!? You teach 'politeness'? You teach others how to be *polite*?! Mention 'politeness' as one of your research interests or topics you teach, and the reaction of many colleagues and friends is likely to be a mixture of incredulity, disbelief, mild condescendence and a hint of disapproval. Serious social scientists cannot possibly invest time and intellectual resources in the pursuit of what sounds like a topic for genteel conversation among **members** of a gone-by civil society inhabiting drawing-rooms and parlours!

Politeness as a topic of multidisciplinary inquiry has attracted the sustained attention of scholars for at least four decades; the effects of the **discursive turn** that has invested the social sciences have been felt in many of the recent mono-graphic studies on manifestations of (im)politeness in various social contexts, a development that is indicative of a new vitality in the field. It is against this background that this book emerges to address new and non-expert readerships and to invite them on an exploration of the conceptual and empirical richness that have come to characterize politeness studies.

If we suspend for a minute the assumptions evoked by the term 'politeness' in English, and the taken-for-granted connotations invoked by the commonsense notion of 'polite behaviour', and turn probing incredulity towards the obser-vation of everyday human interaction, a set of challenging and to date only partially answered questions begins to emerge. *Why* are we 'polite' to each other? What happens when 'politeness' is perceived to be missing? Ultimately, *what* is politeness?

In one of the rare definitions of politeness available in the English scholarly literature, Penelope Brown (2001: 11,620) observes that 'Politeness is essen-tially a matter of taking into account *the feelings of others* as to how they should be interactionally treated, including behaving in a manner that demonstrates *appropriate concern* for interactors' social status and their social relationship' (added emphasis). Almost in the same breath, Brown unambiguously states that: 'Since politeness is crucial to the construction and maintenance of social relationships, politeness in communication *goes to the very heart of social life and interaction*; indeed it is probably *a precondition for human cooperation* in general' (p. 11,620), added emphasis).

If we accept Brown's bold understanding of the hugely influential role of politeness in human interaction and, ultimately, in the construction of the social order, it is somewhat surprising that it should have taken so long for scholars to write a research-based book that seeks to examine the manifestations of this elusive yet pervasive phenomenon in a language accessible to (post)graduate readers, and which at the same time provides an innovative framework for researchers.

It is not mere chance that filling this gap in the literature has befallen two outstanding scholars of the 'new wave' of politeness studies, Dániel Kádár and Michael Haugh. Their innovative, energetic approach to politeness is the hallmark of their comprehensive book, addressing the interests of a broad-based multidisciplinary readership. Without compromising on theoretical and analytical depth, and judiciously drawing from an established tradition of dedicated scholarship, this volume has the essential qualities to become 'the' new authoritative book on Politeness published in English, and therefore accessible to readerships worldwide.

FRANCESCA BARGIELA-CHIAPPINI
UNIVERSITY OF WARWICK

Acknowledgements

We would like to express our gratitude to Andrew Winnard for inviting us to publish this volume with Cambridge University Press. We are indebted to Francesca Bargiela-Chiappini for reading the manuscript and sharing her insightful comments with us. We would like to say thanks to Francesca also for writing a Foreword for the present work. We are also grateful to the following colleagues (in alphabetical order) for their invaluable comments: Bob Arundale, Jonathan Culpeper, Saeko Fukushima, Andrew John Merrison and Sara Mills. We would like to say thanks to the anonymous referees for their insightful comments, which helped us to improve the quality of the present work. Last but not least, we are thankful to our families for their patience while we worked on this book.

We are grateful to the Hungarian blogger Szergej Tamis for permitting us to use the comic strip in Figure 3.1.

On the institutional level, we would like to express our gratitude to the Chiang Ching-Kuo Foundation for International Scholarly Exchange, for supporting our collaboration through a joint research grant (RG025-P-10).

1 Introduction

1.1 Why this book?

This book provides an overview of politeness. Politeness is a key means by which humans work out and maintain interpersonal **relationships**. Many of us have been educated how to behave politely since childhood; we only have to think about parents prescribing to their children when and how to apologise, to say 'please' and 'thank you' (at least in English), or to call (*jiao*) people by familial titles when greeting them (at least in Chinese). However, politeness is not limited to conventional acts of linguistic etiquette like formal apologies, so-called 'polite' language and address terms, although it includes all of these acts. Rather, it covers something much broader, encompassing all types of interpersonal behaviour through which we take into account the feelings of others as to how they think they should be treated in working out and maintaining our sense of personhood as well as our interpersonal relationships with others.

However, while this book relies on this broad definition of politeness, in accordance with its title *Understanding Politeness* we propose that there are in fact often multiple different **understandings** of politeness at play in discourse. Various different disciplinary and **theoretical** perspectives are necessitated, in turn, in order to tease out these multiple understandings of politeness. In this book we suggest that these various understandings offer different insights, which may at times be complementary, and so instead of singling out any one of these understandings, we aim to introduce a variety of them, with the aim of helping readers to make their way into this fascinating area. Our aim, then, is to discuss these different understandings of politeness in a systematic and organised way, with our aim being to point out interconnections between various views on and perceptions of politeness.

There is an important rationale behind authoring an overview of this field, as our aim is not just to summarise but also to provide an analytical framework by means of which one can successfully situate the analysis of politeness across time and space. Currently, politeness research is struggling with a fundamental difficulty that tends to face all work in the social sciences and humanities: namely, how to systematically analyse and describe the phenomena in

1

question without falling into the trap of overgeneralising. Politeness research has gone through several stages. Until the beginning of the twenty-first century, most politeness researchers attempted to systematise the analysis of politeness through different theoretical frameworks. However, critiques of these theories began very soon after they were first proposed, and since the 2000s these critiques have been gaining steam to the point that to talk about a scientific or theoretical understanding of politeness without consideration of the understandings of the **participants** themselves, at least in some respect, seems simply out of step with the times. Yet because of this, politeness research has been left in somewhat of a theoretical limbo. Indeed, although early theories of politeness are often claimed to be highly problematic, we have nevertheless (sometimes unwittingly) inherited many of the underlying assumptions of those first attempts at theorising politeness. And despite the numerous critiques no similar systematic account of politeness has yet been created to take their place. It is therefore perhaps not surprising that politeness researchers often continue to employ these assumptions, either as is, or in some modified form. Indeed, in the popular online encyclopedia *Wikipedia* one of the **first-wave** theories, namely, Brown and Levinson's (1987; see Chapter 2) continues to be equated with 'politeness theory' as if there were no other valid perspectives in existence (see: http://en.wikipedia.org/wiki/Politeness_theory). From the perspective of many, this lack of a systematic theoretical approach to politeness is understandable and even acceptable. As Mills (2011a) argues, it is not a pre-evident objective that we need to systematically describe linguistic politeness, which is by its very nature diverse and **contested**, while Watts (2005) questions whether a theory of politeness is even possible. And yet an account of politeness, especially a book on politeness, cannot function without being able to determine what politeness involves, how it arises and how understandings of it can vary between individuals and across various social groups.

We argue that if there is such a thing as politeness it goes beyond the boundaries of language, and so an overview of how we can analyse politeness – like the one provided by this book – necessitates a multidisciplinary approach that goes beyond the boundaries of traditional linguistic pragmatics and sociolinguistics, drawing also from insights into politeness that can be gained from work in semantics, corpus linguistics, historical linguistics and pragmatics, phonetics and phonology, conversation analysis and ethnomethodology, sociology, (intercultural) communication, cognitive science and psychology and so on and so forth. This means we need to observe politeness as a **social practice**, and to bring together first-order (language **user**) and second-order (language **observer**) understandings of it. We also need to capture the pervasiveness of politeness, which is more often than not noted for its absence rather than for its presence. This is very much in accordance with recent arguments in the field that call for research that explores politeness from multiple perspectives through interdisciplinary analyses by reflexively aware researchers (Haugh, Kádár and Mills 2013). Developing an understanding of politeness as social practice reflects this fast-growing body of research, which offers more credible alternatives to the traditional politeness paradigm in two key ways.

First, it allows for a much more nuanced range of approaches and methodologies to be drawn upon in furthering our understanding of politeness. We build here on the well-known first-order/second-order distinction in politeness research (see Chapters 3, 4 and 5) in proposing a framework that helps readers situate different perspectives on politeness, and see how they can be integrated into a more holistic approach to the analysis of politeness. Instead of defining **first-order politeness** as simply reflecting 'commonsense' or 'lay' perspectives, and **second-order politeness** as reflecting 'scientific' perspectives, we argue that any productive understanding of politeness is necessarily rooted in both, consistent with well-developed understandings of social practice in ethnomethodology and related fields. We propose a framework that breaks down different ways of understanding politeness into distinct perspectives, and which should, therefore, be useful for those approaching the complex field of politeness for the first time. In essence, our claim is that politeness can be analysed from the perspective of both participants (versus **metaparticipants**) and **emic** or 'insider' (versus **etic** or 'outsider') understandings (which are both first-order *user* perspectives), as well as from the perspective of analysts (versus lay observers) and theoretical (versus **folk-theoretic**) understandings (which are both second-order *observer* perspectives). These terms and the perspectives that they imply will be introduced in detail in Part I. Crucially, we do not place any inherent greater value on any one of these perspectives, but rather argue that *all* of these can in principle contribute to a holistic understanding of politeness.

Second, it allows us to go beyond the traditional focus on linguistic manifestations of politeness behaviour. We claim that a systematic presentation of politeness cannot ignore what has often been treated as something 'remaining' for future work because politeness permeates the very ways in which people interact: it is more than simply the use of linguistic **forms**. We only need to consider **rituals** (Kádár 2013) and the relationship between language and the senses (see Levinson 2003) or the rise of multimodal forms of computer-mediated interpersonal communication, for instance, to see that politeness often manifests itself as a social behavioural phenomenon beyond the boundaries of language. This broader focus is reflected in the wide range of data we use to illustrate and exemplify points in this book, which will include not only analyses of spoken face-to-face interaction, but also other modalities and modes, including various forms of **computer-mediated communication** (CMC) as well as different types of historical texts such as letters and invitation cards.

Our model of politeness as social practice also integrates various perceptions of politeness, thereby acknowledging the different worldviews they inevitably encompass. In accordance with our claim that politeness is a social practice rather than a simple manifestation of language usage, we argue that politeness, as with any other practice, has to be described with reference to **time** and **space**. The concept of time underpins the claim that any understanding of politeness always arises relative to time, and so politeness in ongoing and historical interactions is necessarily interlinked. Our argument is that while politeness in interaction involves an understanding in the here-and-now, this here-and-now can also be understood in the sense of a current moment of talk being constrained and afforded by prior and subsequent talk. Furthermore, in many cases politeness does not come into existence simply through what is said in the moment, as many **social actions** and **pragmatic meanings** that are understood in locally situated contexts in fact follow pre-existing (often formalised) patterns. Finally, certain manifestations of politeness are historically situated, and so should be properly analysed in retrospection to trace how understandings of politeness in the here-and-now can never be totally divorced from understandings in the there and then. The importance of time should not be underestimated because these different temporal occurrences of politeness necessitate different conceptual and methodological approaches. For example, projecting an analysis of what took place diachronically from a synchronic perspective (or vice-versa) is problematic because such an approach may inadvertently decontextualise diachronic manifestations of politeness (see Chapter 8).

The concept of space here refers specifically to social space, which operates with reference to time, given that there is no space without time. Space in our understanding refers to the relationship between the individual and the society in which he or she lives, and thus provides a suitable grounding for the analysis of politeness with reference to cognition and culture. A linguistic phenomenon like politeness is an example *par excellence* of a social phenomenon that emerges through the ongoing, interlinked interactions of individuals. Just like language, then, we cannot trace politeness to any one single **person** or group of persons, but rather to the self-organising and **emergent** properties of the complex systems that form through ongoing interactions between persons over time and social space.

To sum up, it is hoped that the framework we offer here for analysing the multiple understandings of politeness, which inevitably arise when politeness is understood as social practice, and the conceptual links to time and social space we are making in grounding the analysis of these practices, will provide a working model by means of which the reader can approach politeness in different languages and contexts, without falling into the trap of overgeneralising. A treatment of politeness as arising from particular behaviours or linguistic forms can lead to overgeneralisations and even stereotyping. Approaching politeness as social practice, on the other hand, means that politeness can be systematically theorised and analysed within a wider research framework.

It is pertinent to note that, perhaps like any other book, the present volume has its limitations. Most importantly, we are primarily focused here on politeness. It can be observed that since the 2000s politeness researchers have increasingly recognised the importance of studying both politeness and impoliteness, and various frameworks (for example, Culpeper 2011a) have been exclusively devoted to the latter area. It has even been suggested that they require distinct theoretical frameworks. However, we are doubtful that it is really possible, in the final analysis, to talk about impoliteness without implicitly invoking politenesss, and vice-versa. For that reason, while much of our discussion focuses on instances where politeness is involved, we nevertheless draw from data that also include impoliteness phenomena. Indeed, in many instances the two are intertwined to the point that it makes little sense to rigidly separate them. In any case, it is our view that to focus exclusively on 'politeness' or 'impoliteness' ignores the multitude of other kinds of understandings vis-à-vis politeness that evidently arise in interaction. In some instances, something might be considered to be *mock* polite or *mock* impolite by participants. And it does not stop there. If asked for particular evaluations, participants may start talking about something being 'not polite' or 'not impolite', or 'neither polite nor impolite', 'overpolite' and so on and so forth. One wonders where such evaluations fit in if politeness and impoliteness are treated as completely distinct areas of theorisation. When we talk about politeness in this volume, then, we mean politeness as it is inevitably contextualised relative to impoliteness, mock politeness and the like by participants themselves.

1.2   Contents

The present book has three parts. Part I, 'Theoretical framework', is comprised of four chapters which give the reader an account of previous research on the field of politeness, and in which we introduce our analytical framework. Chapter 2 'The roots of politeness research', overviews the history and concepts of politeness research from its beginnings in the 1970s until the so-called recent discursive turn in the 2000s. We suggest that, like many other scholarly fields with history, politeness research can be metaphorically described as a tree. Current theories of politeness have been influenced by earlier models, which benchmarked the birth of the field, and indeed many of the underlying assumptions and concepts in those first-wave approaches to politeness continue to exist in various guises in more recently developed frameworks.

Chapter 3, 'Recent developments in politeness research', introduces more contemporary approaches to the study of politeness, from the 2000s onwards, an area that has generally been missing in most accounts of politeness in books on pragmatics to date. The new wave of research in this period is often referred to in the field as the 'discursive' turn, which was kick-started by Eelen's (2001) influential monograph, and subsequently grounded in important monographs by Watts (2003) and Mills (2003). The discursive turn brought with it various important changes in the field, including, to mention just a few, an increasing reliance on longer fragments of authentic discourse (e.g. Watts 2003), and the exploration of (im)politeness as an interactionally constructed phenomenon (Locher 2004; Haugh 2007a). A focus on participants' understandings of politeness and a greater awareness of the analyst's role in elucidating these thus emerges as a key contribution of recent scholarship.

Chapter 4, 'Politeness as social practice', introduces an approach to understanding politeness as ultimately located in evaluations of social actions and meanings by persons that are situated relative to both time and social space. It is suggested that politeness constitutes a social practice because it involves evaluations that (implicitly) appeal to a **moral order**: a set of expectancies through which social actions and meanings are recognisable as such, and consequently are inevitably open to moral evaluation. It is proposed that, when understood in this way, politeness can be approached from the perspective of a number of disciplines and employ a wide range of methodologies. While various influential concepts and approaches have been proposed (see Chapter 3), there is not yet a clear overarching theoretical framework in which to situate these different understandings or perspectives. Theorising politeness as social practice enables us to account for the inherent diversity in understandings of politeness, without an appreciation of which we are likely to form essentialised or overgeneralised views on politeness.

Following Chapter 4's train of thought, Chapter 5, 'Understandings of politeness', explores the understandings of different users on politeness from various disciplinary perspectives by observers, including researchers who are aware of their own evaluations vis-à-vis those of the participants. Building on the overviews of traditional and more recent approaches to politeness in the previous chapters, we propose a framework that situates understandings of politeness relative to four key loci of understanding. It is suggested that the way in which the first-order/second-order distinction is generally drawn between participant and scientific understandings masks other important distinctions. Starting from the basic idea that the first-order/second-order distinction involves a distinction between *user* and *observer* understandings of politeness, it is proposed that there are in fact four key loci of understanding vis-à-vis politeness:

  (i) participant/metaparticipant understandings (first-order)
 (ii) emic/etic conceptualisations (first-order)
(iii) analyst/lay-observer understandings (second-order)
(iv) theoretical/folk-theoretic conceptualisations (second-order)

This framework allows readers to approach politeness from one perspective (or more) with greater awareness of what such a perspective offers as well as its natural limitations.

The three chapters in Part II, 'Politeness and time', are centred on how understandings of politeness inevitably arise relative to time. We focus on how such understandings can span different temporal settings, namely, the ongoing here-and-now in interaction (Chapter 6), the there-and-then projected into here-and-now through **recurrence** (Chapter 7) and the there-and-then historically situated in its own right (Chapter 8). Chapter 6, 'Politeness in interaction', argues that understandings of politeness, impoliteness and so on are co-constructed by two or more participants over the course of an interaction. To be co-constructed means that not only the speaker but also other participants can influence the *trajectory* of social actions/meanings and the evaluations of politeness they reflexively occasion as they develop in interaction. The upshot of this is that politeness must be analysed as situated in interaction, although it is important to note here that we conceptualise interaction not as isolated moments of the here-and-now but rather as inextricably linked to understandings of politeness in the there-and-then. In Chapter 6 we thus consider more deeply the various ways in which interaction in this broader sense, whether it be direct or mediated, both constrains and affords understandings of politeness.

Chapter 7 'Politeness, convention and rituality', examines **conventions** and rituals, and it introduces a concept of time that differs from that in Chapter 6. If we put politeness on a time scale, it can be argued understandings of politeness localised in a particular interaction involve an interlinking cycle of participant action and reaction, albeit drawing from a certain underlying set of moral expectancies. However, understandings of politeness are not always completely localised in this way: they can be formalised and pre-determined. Indeed, many contexts do not necessitate such localised understandings. A formal interaction between political leaders, for instance, represents a context in which understandings of politeness are less localised given the interactants are expected to follow certain (often scripted) **expectations**. In such contexts politeness tends to clearly follow certain underlying **schemata**: an organised pattern of thought and behaviour. These schemata reduce uncertainty in the formation and interpretation of linguistic politeness, due to the simple reason that by relying on them the interactants can invoke pre-existing ways of communicating and interpreting politeness. It can be argued that understandings of politeness drawing from such schemata represent a kind of pre-existing interpretive framework for understandings of politeness in the here-and-now.

Chapter 8, 'Politeness and history', argues for the **relativity** of politeness by examining understandings of politeness in historically situated interactions. Through exploring the notion of **historicity**, we argue that what we mean by 'historical' must be interpreted broadly, as historical interactions can include interactions that occurred a millennium before or just a few days ago (given we do not normally have access to prior interactions with the same mindset as we had at the time of their occurrence). An analysis which is based on this broad definition of 'historical' can include various data types. For example, an email written some time ago can be regarded as 'historical' as a medieval codex. In terms of politeness and time, **historical politeness** constitutes the realm of there-and-then. Examining this there-and-then necessitates a specific approach, as the mindsets of interactants who communicated with each other before our time are often not readily accessible to us.

Finally, Part III, 'Politeness and social space: from mind to society', comprises three chapters which analyse the relationship between politeness and social space, spanning the realm of the individual to society and culture. Chapter 9, 'Politeness and metapragmatics', focuses on the study of awareness on the part of ordinary or lay observers about the ways in which they interact and communicate with others. It is argued that without systematically analysing the ways in which participants themselves generally conceptualise their own behaviour, we are not able to understand the social practices through which politeness arises. A focus on different forms of **metapragmatic awareness** also allows us to go beyond idiosyncratic understandings and to analyse the moral order that underpins politeness as social practice as an object of study in its own right.

Chapter 10, 'Politeness, cognition and emotion', overviews the key cognitive-state processes that have been held to underpin politeness from the perspective of individual cognition (**subjectivity**) and how it is interlinked with that of others (**intersubjectivity**). We focus, in particular, on notions that feature in sociocognitive or psychological accounts of politeness, such as attitude, **inference**, **intention**, as well as making links with Chapter 9 on metapragmatics. We conclude by arguing that politeness not only involves **rationality** and states of mind, as originally assumed in pre-2000 theories (or **first-wave approaches** to politeness, see Chapter 2), and indeed in much of the work on politeness to date, but is in fact inherently emotive.

Chapter 11, 'Culture, identity and politeness', examines the notion of culture from a critical perspective. We argue that in order to go beyond **essentialist** views on culture, one needs to analyse culture as a culturally constructed rather than an inherited property. Culture is inevitably construed as part of one's **identity**, and because of this it is relative to the individual's perception of her or his identity, even though this is also influenced by one's perceptions of norms. One's cultural identity is worked out primarily through the practices of **association** and **dissociation**: interactants take on certain cultural identities and refuse other ones in localised interactions. In discourse, then, culture can be used as a so-called **discursive resource**: it is invoked in order to gain the upper hand in an interaction or to focus on difference as opposed to similarity amongst persons, and in this sense also inevitably involves understandings of politeness and the like.

Chapter 12, 'Conclusion', briefly summarises the contents of the previous chapters and then discusses our views on the future direction of politeness research. The Conclusion is followed by a Glossary, an annotated list of the most important technical terms in politeness research.

1.3   Features

The present research-based volume is written for advanced readers and above who have a command of at least some key notions in pragmatics, such as the importance of context for understanding meaning, including meaning beyond what is said (for a useful introduction to basic concepts in pragmatics see, for example, Culpeper and Haugh, forthcoming). This book is thus primarily designed for academic readers wanting to brush up their understanding of the field in which they work, as well as senior undergraduate and postgraduate students who intend to make their way into linguistic politeness research.

While this book aims to propose a model for researchers, it is also meant to have educational value, and it thus includes a number of reader-friendly features. Along with the previously discussed innovative approach of treating politeness from multiple perspectives, we provide recommended readings in the form of annotated titles at the end of each chapter. Key concepts in the annotated Glossary are highlighted in bold on the first instance of their use, and thence in italics along with other key terms. In relation to data, we draw from a variety of different data types, including naturally occurring face-to-face conversational and CMC data, textual data and extracts from films. It is hoped that studying politeness arising in these different data types will provide insight for the reader into the diversity of politeness phenomena. Every chapter in Parts II and III thus also includes exercises at the end, by means of which readers can work through how one might analyse politeness in different types of discourse.

Part I

Theoretical framework

2 The roots of politeness research

2.1 Introduction

Like many other scholarly fields with a history, politeness research can be metaphorically described as a tree. Current theories of politeness have been influenced by earlier models which benchmarked the birth of the field. Indeed, earlier models continue to have an influence on the way in which politeness is described and studied, either directly, as some of these models continue to be used by researchers, or indirectly, as many of the approaches that have been subsequently developed clearly position themselves as counter or alternatives to these early theories. Using the tree analogy, earlier models of politeness are akin to the roots: they provide the fundamental starting point for understanding the field. In this chapter we will refer to these early models, following Jonathan Culpeper (2011b), as **first-wave approaches**. However, rather than reviewing the entire history of their development and reception in the field, we will concentrate on highlighting the key theoretical and methodological *assumptions* underlying these first-wave approaches.

In general, the first-wave approaches aimed to model politeness on a somewhat abstract, theoretical level. This reflects the way in which scientists usually approach hitherto unknown realms: they tend to rely on theoretical models, even though they maintain that the model is an abstraction of reality, and not the reality itself. Accordingly, it is an implicit assumption in all first-wave approaches that linguistic politeness can and should be modelled in abstract terms. While these various approaches differ in their detail, they all build on the seminal work of the language philosopher Herbert Paul Grice (1989[1975]) on **pragmatic meaning**, in particular, the so-called **Cooperative Principle** (CP), as the underlying conceptual basis of the models proposed.

According to Grice, interactants figure out what others are meaning, although not necessarily saying, in a principled way, based on normative expectations about communication. These normative expectations were summarised in the CP, which he formulated as follows:

Make your conversational contribution such as is required, at the stage at which it occurs, by the accepted purpose or direction of the talk exchange in which you are engaged. (1989[1975]: 26)

The basic idea is that we all have expectations about the kinds of things people will say, how they will say things, how specific we need to be, the order in which things are said, and so on, when engaging in talk. The CP was further elaborated in the four *conversational maxims*: *quality* (the expectation that one will be truthful), *quantity* (the expectation that one will supply the right amount of information), *relevance* (the expectation that the information provided will be relevant) and *manner* (the expectation that information will be clear). Conversational maxims are not rules, however, as speakers who interact do not necessarily need to follow them. Instead, Grice's claim was that a speaker can make available a pragmatic meaning (i.e. something beyond what is said) through the normative expectation that he or she is observing the CP overall, and either observing or not observing specific conversational maxims in order to maintain the former assumption. The maxims can thus be violated in various ways in Grice's framework, but one of the most common ways of not observing them is through what Grice labelled *flouting*.

In example (1), Homer, a protagonist of the renowned cartoon *The Simpsons*, and his father are talking at a certain Bea's funeral after Grampa missed saying goodbye to Bea (a friend of Grampa's) because of Homer. Grampa implies that he does not want to talk to Homer and that he does not accept Homer's apology by markedly flouting what Grice defined as the quality maxim ('do not say what you believe to be false').

> (1) Homer: I can't tell you how sorry I am, Dad.
> Grampa: Is someone talking to me? I didn't hear anything.
> Homer: Oh no! Dad's lost his hearing!
> ('Old money', *The Simpsons*, Season 2, Episode 17, 1991)

It is quite evident that Grampa *can* hear what Homer is saying (although Homer, being Homer, thinks otherwise). In order to maintain the assumption that Grampa is observing the CP, then, something must be implicated, an inference that is strengthened by Grampa pointedly saying something he obviously does not believe to be true. In flouting the quality maxim by pretending he cannot hear Homer's apology, Grampa thereby implicates that he does not want to listen to Homer. This, in turn, indicates that Grampa does not accept Homer's apology and remains upset and angry about what has happened.

Grice's approach to meaning was focused primarily on information: the *propositional content* of what is said, implied and so on. However, he acknowledged, in passing, that the CP could be maintained with reference to other kinds of maxims, including the expectation that the speaker will 'be polite' (Grice

1989[1975]: 28). The idea was that such a maxim could rise to other kinds of pragmatic meaning relating to moral issues such as politeness. For example, when delivering bad news such as failing an exam, the speaker is likely to introduce this news in an indirect way, using formulations such as 'I am sorry to be the bearer of bad news but...' instead of directly saying 'You have failed.' In this way, the speaker flouts the maxims of quantity (i.e. saying more than what is needed) and manner (i.e. not being as clear as possible) in order to implicate that he or she is being polite. Although Grice himself did not develop these ideas any further, it was assumed in all first-wave approaches to politeness that it was possible to model politeness based on this Gricean framework. That is, the hearer can infer that the speaker has flouted one or more of the maxims in order to implicate that he or she is being polite, instead of flouting them in order to be 'uncooperative' and, vice-versa, the speaker can assume that by flouting one or more of the maxims the hearer will infer that he or she is being polite.

In order to illustrate how this Gricean conceptualisation operates, let us analyse the brief interaction in example (2):

> (2) Medway drew closer. Halting, she fixed him with respectful eye and extended the cigar-stump between dainty fingers.
> 'Would you be requiring this any further, sir?'
> 'Eh?'
> 'You left it in moddom's room, and I thought perhaps you would be needing it.'
>
> (P. G. Woodhouse, *Hot Water*, Chapter 8, 1963)

In this brief example, cited from the British author P. G. Woodhouse (1881–1975), the maid's style represents traditional British **indirectness**, which is often associated with politeness. Upon returning a cigar-stump to a guest who has left it in her lady's room, the maid flouts the maxim of manner: instead of making a clear statement such as 'You have left your cigar-stump in the room and I have brought it back to you,' she inquires indirectly as to whether the guest, an American senator, still requires it. This implicature seems to invoke the power difference triggered by the hierarchical social relationship between a high-ranking guest and a maid, a point which is reinforced by the use of the deferential form of address 'sir'.

The most influential first-wave theory of politeness was introduced in the monograph *Politeness: Some Universals in Language Usage*, written by Penelope Brown and Stephen C. Levinson (1987).[1] Brown and Levinson's framework aims to model politeness as implicated through forms of linguistic behaviour that flout the conversational maxims in order to avoid conflict. This framework has still has an unprecedented status both within and outside the field of pragmatics. In fact, even now, when politeness is discussed in other areas of linguistics as well as disciplines such as social and anthropological studies, Brown and Levinson's approach continues to be regarded as *the* definitive work on linguistic politeness, a point which is evident from it being referred to as 'politeness theory' in many circles as if there were no other plausible approach to theorising politeness. It is for this reason that in the following overview of the conceptualisation of linguistic politeness in first-wave approaches, Brown and Levinson's framework will occupy a predominant position, though we will also make reference to other frameworks in the course of our discussion.

2.2   Concepts

Universality

A central concept in first-wave approaches is the notion of **universality**. Universality refers to the claim that linguistic politeness can be systematically described across languages and cultures using the same underlying theoretical framework. The idea of describing manifestations of language and language usage through universal parameters is not at all unique to theories of politeness. It appears, perhaps most representatively, in the work of the linguist Noam Chomsky (e.g. 1957, 1965) on so-called Generative Grammar. The theory of Generative Grammar claims that it is possible to develop theoretical descriptions of syntactic properties of a language through abstraction and by means of data focusing on the underlying competence of speakers rather than actual performance. As Chomsky notes,

a grammar is based on a finite number of observed sentences (the linguist's corpus) and it 'projects' this set to an infinite set of grammatical sentences by establishing general 'laws' (grammatical rules) framed in terms of such hypothetical constructs as the particular phonemes, words, phrases, and so on, of the language under analysis. (1965: 1)

The idea of hypothetical models based on datasets limited to **utterances** was adopted by pioneers of politeness research who were heavily influenced by Chomsky's thinking. As a pragmatic answer to the grammatical parameters studied by adherents of Generative Grammar, first-wave politeness theorists echoed Chomsky's claims in proposing that politeness, which is a means of avoiding conflict, largely operates through flouting universally applicable Conversational Maxims.

The idea of universality appeared first in the framework of Robin Lakoff (1973, 1977), which represents perhaps the earliest attempt to theorise politeness. Lakoff argues that politeness has 'rules', just as the CP has maxims. These rules include the following: 'Don't impose' (Rule 1), 'Give options' (Rule 2) and 'Make *A* feel good, be friendly' (Rule 3) (Lakoff 1973: 298). The conversational maxims are flouted when these rules are observed, as one is acting according to the normative expectations associated with the Gricean maxim 'Be polite.' Lakoff claims that politeness behaviour can be described universally, and the basic difference among cultures is that they put more emphasis on one of these rules than on the others. For example, people from Asian cultures were claimed by Lakoff to be more likely to act deferentially when being polite (Rule 1), while in Australian culture the **strategy** of camaraderie (Rule 3) was claimed to dominate.

A claim to universality is also present, although in a less explicit form, in the framework of politeness maxims developed by Geoffrey N. Leech (1983). While Leech makes an argument that politeness operates variably in different cultures or language communities, he nevertheless claims that a uniform binding factor behind culturally different manifestations of politeness behaviour is their overall function of cooperative conflict avoidance. Leech's theory describes politeness as a means to avoid conflict, which operates via decreasing the cost and increasing the benefit for the hearer, while increasing the cost and decreasing the benefit for the speaker. That is, the less the action proposed in an utterance 'costs' and the more 'benefit' it brings to the hearer, the more polite it becomes. For example, 'Make the sandwiches' is less polite than 'Have another sandwich' because the former implies a cost to the hearer (i.e. he is requested to do some work), while the latter involves something of potential benefit to the hearer (i.e. something is offered). Politeness is, according to Leech, a means of symbolically decreasing the cost incurred or the benefit accrued to the hearer. For instance, the form 'Would you mind making some sandwiches?' is a **symbolic** expression of the speaker's intention to decrease the cost to the hearer, and the hearer is assumed to be able to infer this intention based on the assumption that he is maintaining the Politeness Principle (i.e. 'Be polite'). On the analytic level, then, Leech's theory describes the politeness value of an utterance by means of a 'cost–benefit scale': a scale which represents the cost–benefit value of actions.

Universality is also a key notion in Brown and Levinson's framework. In a similar manner to other first-wave approaches, Brown and Levinson claim that politeness universally functions as a means of conflict avoidance, and even though the ways in which it manifests itself differ across languages and cultures, underpinning it are exactly the same operational assumptions. These include, most importantly, a so-called universal notion of **face** and the assumed universal applicability of rationality in theorising politeness, two points to which we shall now turn.

Face and rationality

The concept of face as a technical term is derived from work in sociology and anthropology (see below) and, according to Brown and Levinson, consists of two specific kinds of desires ('face-wants') attributed by interactants to one another: the desire to be unimpeded in one's actions (negative face), and the desire to be approved of (positive face). According to Brown and Levinson, some acts intrinsically threaten face. For example, a request is said to threaten negative face, while a criticism threatens positive face. Politeness arises through strategies that minimise the threat to face when such an act, which is labelled a *face-threatening act*, occurs, thereby avoiding conflict. Politeness strategies can be directed at either (1) the hearer's negative face, as when the speaker avoids presuming, coercing, personalising, and emphasises the hearer's status; or (2) the hearer's positive face, as when the speaker claims common ground with the hearer, conveys that they are co-operators, and when he fulfils a want of the hearer and so on. The former is termed **negative politeness**, while the latter is termed **positive politeness**.

The notion of face is claimed to allow for politeness to be modelled universally, because it helps the researcher to make distinctions between cultures and smaller groups of language users according to whether they prefer politeness that appeals to the other's positive face or negative face; that is, so-called 'positive politeness' and 'negative politeness' cultures (see Chapter 11 for an alternative to this view). It is important to note, however, that positive and negative politeness reflect **preferences** rather than hard-and-fast rules, as they can differ across situations, even though cultures are claimed to have a preference for either negative or positive politeness patterns overall. According to Brown and Levinson,

the bare bones of a notion of face which (we argue) is universal, but which in any particular society we would expect to be the subject of much cultural elaboration. (1987: 13)

One key debate in politeness research has centred on whether this claimed universal notion of face does actually allow for cultural elaboration or is too tightly bound to a view of interaction as arising between independent, autonomous individuals who are fully rational.

Influenced by Brown and Levinson's theory, the assumed connection between politeness and face has become axiomatic in the field over time, to the point that it now seems impossible to talk about politeness without examining the notion of face. This assumption is rooted in a specific interpretation of the practices by means of which face is maintained. These practices were originally termed **facework** by the renowned scholar Erving Goffman, who first introduced the notion of face into academic discourse. However, it is worth noting that in Goffman's original work, facework actually refers to 'the actions taken by a person to make whatever he is doing consistent with face' (1967: 12). Facework thus includes a wide variety of practices, including among others so-called *corrective* facework and *avoidance* facework. Early theories of politeness gave pre-eminence to these forms of facework, but in doing so excluded many other aspects of facework originally noted by Goffman.

The second key universalistic assumption made in Brown and Levinson's theory of politeness centres on the notion of **rationality**. Face is claimed to be a universal property of the human psyche because human beings are, for the most part at least, considered to be rational. Rationality means that whenever a certain form of politeness is chosen to address the hearer's face needs, the speaker is making a rational choice to observe the 'face-wants' of the hearer. Brown and Levinson argue that rationality means 'the application of a specific mode of reasoning . . . which guarantees inferences from ends or goals to means that will satisfy those ends' (1987: 64). Essentially, this means that in order to get things done without creating unnecessary conflict it is rational to respect the face-wants of others, and thus we reason about the behaviour of others based on this assumption of rationality. This means–ends conceptualisation thus directly incorporates the Gricean CP into Brown and Levinson's framework: it is claimed that an implicature of politeness arises when a conversational maxim is flouted because it is rational for the hearer to believe that the speaker is acting politely when flouting this maxim, and it is also rational for the hearer to maintain the assumptions inherent in the CP in doing so (i.e. to interpret flouting as politeness, at least in some instances).

Rationality plays a key role in universalistic theorisation because it helps the analyst to systematise what appears to be endless variation in linguistic behaviour. A major challenge facing politeness researchers is to account for the ways and extent to which politeness behaviour changes across various contexts. A key claim in first-wave approaches to politeness is that this ever-fluctuating phenomenon becomes easier to capture and model if its production is described as resulting from a rational means–ends process, which follows certain societal norms. Brown and Levinson argue that such contextual variation can be systematically accounted for by means of three social variables, namely, relative power (P), social distance (D) and ranking of imposition in that culture (R). Speakers are claimed to be sensitive to these variables due to socialisation processes: e.g. we are educated since our childhood to employ rational means–end reasoning to choose politeness strategies according to these social factors (see more on 'strategy' later in this chapter). Consequently, on this view, since these variables are held to influence the rational choice of politeness strategy, it becomes possible for the analyst to systematically describe politeness in any interaction simply by 'calculating' the contextual effects of these variables.

Universality versus culture-specificity

Universality is a common scholarly concern in the social sciences. The emphasis on identifying universals in relation to politeness can create problems, however, in that it inevitably involves foregrounding *outsider* or etic perceptions of politeness and it ignores culture-specific, *insider* interpretations of what counts as polite. Although the **etic** description of politeness-related phenomena is a seemingly reasonable standpoint to take, universality is a very ambitious claim because it downgrades or even bleaches out these insider or **emic** differences in understandings of politeness. The notions of face and rationality as described by Brown and Levinson, for instance, reflect specific understandings of the human psyche which do not apply in every culture and society, at least not in the way they are interpreted in these universalistic frameworks. It thus may not be surprising that the claim to universality, in spite of the great popularity it garnered after its appearance, has been criticised and even rejected by scholars who have come from cultures in which the aforementioned notions differ from their Anglo-American counterparts.

In fact, the universalistic Brown and Levinsonian framework has provided a rich soil for inquiries which have applied the universal claims of first-wave approaches to culturally situated data. Several scholars have attempted to describe cross-cultural differences in terms of the universalistic notions of face and rationality. The most representative research among these inquiries has been undertaken by the Greek scholar Maria Sifianou (1992), who has explored cross-cultural differences between British and Greek politeness phenomena. Her analysis illustrated that the British tend to prefer politeness strategies that appeal to the hearer's negative face, and the Greeks tend to prefer to appeal to the hearer's positive face. This is a noteworthy finding because it contributes to deconstructing common stereotypes, according to which the British are held to be more polite than the Greeks. As Sifianou reveals, the situation is simply that approaches that appeal to the hearer's negative face are more popularly associated with politeness than their positive-face counterparts, and this is why various lay observers claim that the British are more polite than the Greeks. According to Brown and Levinson's view, then, there can be no objective verification of the view that one nation is more polite than another.

However, many researchers who have an interest in emic concepts and 'insider' perceptions of linguistic politeness have refuted claims to universality in first-wave approaches to politeness. They have claimed, instead, that politeness is an inherently *culture-specific* phenomenon. A major point in these criticisms was that rationality, as it is understood in the universalistic frameworks, reflects a modern Western interpretation of rational behaviour as an *individualistic* form of action. One of the most influential critiques has come from the Japanese sociolinguist Sachiko Ide (1982, 1989), who criticised the universalistic model primarily because it relies on the idea that politeness comes into existence as the speaker flouts conversational maxims through the means–ends reasoning of individuals. Drawing from the Japanese emic notion of *wakimae* 弁え (lit. 'discernment'), Ide (1989) argues that in Japanese one's behaviour is judged to be polite when one discerns the appropriate communal norm, and that this overrides pure individual rationality. The operation of 'discernment' can be illustrated by the examples (3) and (4).

(3) * Sensei-wa kore-o yonda.
　　'The professor read this.'

(4) Sensei-wa kore-o o-yomi-ni-natta.
　　'The professor read[Hon] this.'

　　　　　　　　　(adapted from Ide 1989: 227, underscore added)

These are both references to a lecturer's activity (i.e. that he has read some material) by students. However, example (3) is claimed to be improper in Japanese communication, irrespective of context, because students are expected to use an elevating honorific inflection when referring to a lecturer (i.e. *oyomi-ni-natta* instead of *yonda*), who is their social superior, as seen in example (4). In other words, in Japanese the use of honorifics and other formal forms of politeness is not necessarily bound to what universalistic frameworks describe as rational individual choices in relation to achieving certain goals or ends, but rather to patterns normatively expected in certain situations and hierarchical relationships. According to Ide, then, the Japanese tend to perceive the so-called rationality of politeness as a means to fulfil communal rather than individual strategic goals, even if these two goal types may coincide. The **culture-specificity** of politeness thus poses a serious challenge to universalistic claims, particularly in cultures which emphasise communality and normativity over individuality and agency.[2]

Universalistic rationality is problematic in certain cultural settings also because it is described as an other-oriented phenomenon, in the sense that a choice of a certain form of politeness depends on the estimation of the hearer's face-wants. Nevertheless, as Ide demonstrated, politeness is often a form of self-display because 'discerning' appropriate behaviour in interaction, from an emic perspective, shows verbally one's sense of place or role in a given situation according to social conventions. The appropriate use of Japanese honorifics can signal the speaker's relative rank in a given interaction just as much as being a form of other-oriented politeness. In fact, even the omission of honorifics and other formal forms signals a relative stance on the part of the speaker, and because of this there is no 'politeness-neutral' situation in Japanese interactions.

The claim to universality has also been criticised with reference to the notion of face. The two perhaps most influential criticisms of face as a universal notion were written by two Chinese researchers Yueguo Gu (1990) and LuMing

Mao (1994). It is perhaps not coincidental that it was East Asian scholars who revisited face because this notion originates in Chinese, even if western anthropology and sociology has transformed it into an etic term.

Gu, in a similar way to Ide, applied an emic term, *mianzi* ('face'), to draw attention to the inappropriateness of applying individualistic universals to communalistic societies and cultures. As Gu argues, Brown and Levinson's theory fails to describe Chinese politeness behaviour because in the Chinese cultural context, face is a *societal* rather than a psychological property. That is, while in Brown and Levinson's approach, face is a private property of the individual and consequently choices of politeness strategies are bound to the psychology of individuals, in China *mianzi* is a social and consequently shared phenomenon. Naturally, different perceptions of face necessitate different practices of politeness, which explains cross-cultural differences in terms of politeness behaviour. For example, Gu illustrates that the Chinese traditionally tend to express politeness by denigrating themselves and elevating their speech partners.

Mao's description of Chinese face accords with that of Gu in that he also draws attention to the communal value of Chinese face, pointing out that in China group harmony is privileged over individual freedom. Therefore, to be a respected **member** of a society means to be included in a group, rather than emphasising one's independence as an agentive individual. This focus on relationality blurs the difference between 'negative' and 'positive' face as described by Brown and Levinson because negative face implies that persons are distinct, autonomous individuals rather than relationally involved, interdependent individuals. Mao also argues that emic notions of face should not be neglected, all the more because in Chinese there is a rich **metalanguage** of face-related notions.

Speech acts and indirectness

In its formative period, politeness research was heavily influenced by the notion of **speech acts**. The notion of speech act is a concept that arose out of the work of the language philosophers John L. Austin (1962) and John Searle (1969, 1975) on the performative function of language. The performative function means that language is used to do things like requests, offers and invitations, rather than simply being a means of delivering information. For example, although the sentence 'It's hot in here' can be a simple statement, or *locutionary act* as it is called in the field, it can also be understood as a request to open the window, which is its communicative function, or what is termed an *illocutionary act*. Speech acts tend to have outcomes in the real world when the hearer reacts to them: that is, they accomplish *perlocutionary acts*. For example, the window is likely to be opened as a result of the indirect request above. Speech acts function according to the so-called *felicity conditions*, which refer to real-world conditions that must be met in order for a particular speech act to be regarded as (felicitously) intended in a particular communicative setting.

The concept of speech act has proven to be a powerful explanatory notion in politeness research. This is partly because various speech acts such as requests and apologies are commonly associated with acts of politeness, and so focusing on these speech acts made it possible to describe a certain aspect of linguistic politeness in a relatively systematic way. The renowned Israeli researcher Shoshana Blum-Kulka (1987) conducted extensive research on apologies and their relationship with politeness, and apology research continues to exist as a relatively independent subfield within politeness research.

A further reason why speech acts have been extensively studied is that they explain the function of communicative **indirectness**, a claim originally made in passing by Searle (1975). That is to say, there are many speech acts that attain their illocutionary, and thus perlocutionary, effects indirectly, as we saw in the above example of a request arising through saying 'It's hot in here.' The notion of indirect speech acts fits nicely with the claim that politeness serves to avoid conflict by minimising imposition. The felicity conditions of indirect polite speech acts can also be explained with reference to the Gricean CP: the hearer is expected to interpret the speaker's 'indirectness' as an expression of polite intention. In other words, in being made indirectly they trigger implicatures of politeness. To provide a simple example, a request can be made more indirect by using the mitigating strategy of *hedging*: using forms such as 'would you mind' or 'I was wondering if' before making a request. Indirect hedging does not change the content of the request and ideally the hearer understands that the question is not to be understood at the level of its potential direct locutionary force but rather with reference to its indirect illocutionary force: the speaker is not inquiring about the hearer's state of mind but simply wants something. On the other hand, the hearer will also perceive that the speaker used this indirect approach in order to decrease the impact of the request on the hearer's negative face, and through flouting the conversational maxims will understand the speaker is being consistent with the overall CP via an implicature of politeness.

However, despite its prominence in first-wave approaches to politeness, the notion of the indirect speech act is one that continues to generate disagreement in the field, particularly as to whether it can be successfully operationalised in examining politeness across different languages. One reason for this ongoing debate is that the notion of indirect speech acts is closely tied to the notion of grammatical mood. In English, at least, there are generally assumed to be three major grammatical moods or sentence types that are associated with speech acts: indicative, interrogative and imperative. The basic idea is that a direct speech act arises when the grammatical mood prototypically associated with the speech act is used, while an indirect speech act arises when another

Table 2.1 *Sentence types and speech acts.*

Sentence type	Example	Speech act
Imperative	Pass me the salt.	Direct request
Interrogative	Could you pass me the salt?	Indirect request (via question)
Indicative	This could do with a little salt.	Indirect request (via assertion)

grammatical mood is employed. We can see how this works in relation to requests in Table 2.1 below.

Essentially, when there is a 'mismatch' between the grammatical mood and the illocutionary point of the speech act we are dealing with a case of an indirect speech act. Thus, a direct request is accomplished via the imperative mood, while an indirect request is accomplished via the interrogative or indicative. A more general way of putting this is that an indirect speech act arises when one illocutionary act is performed by means of performing another. In the case of 'It's hot in here', two illocutionary acts arise, one which is direct (i.e. an assertion that is it is hot), and one which is indirect (i.e. a request that the hearer do something about this situation of being hot).

Another point that we might notice about the two examples of indirect requests in Table 2.1 is that the second example ('This could do with a little salt') seems more indirect than the first example ('Could you pass me the salt?'). In terms of politeness, then, it is widely held, following the work of Blum-Kulka and colleagues on speech acts across cultures, that the speaker can choose among various degrees of (in)directness when formulating a speech act (Blum-Kulka *et al.* 1989). The three basic categories of (in)directness are direct, conventionally indirect and non-conventionally indirect. A direct speech act is where the grammatical mood and speech act are in accord: for example, a request is syntactically marked as such through the imperative mood. A conventionally indirect speech act is where particular expressions have become conventionally associated with the act in question, for example, a request can be marked as such through modal expressions like 'can/could you . . .', 'would you . . .' and so on. Finally, a non-conventionally indirect speech act is where the target of the speech act is not made explicit. In the example above, 'This could do with a little bit of salt', the target action of 'passing' is not mentioned. If the target object were to be not mentioned as well, 'this is a little bland', this would make the speech act even more indirect on this view.

A number of approaches in the first wave made the strong claim that the more indirect a speech act is, the more polite it will be. This is most apparent in Brown and Levinson's distinction between 'on record' and 'off record' politeness

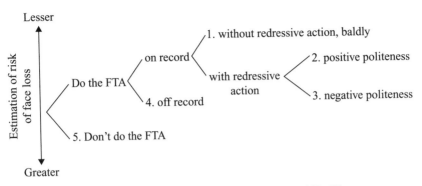

Figure 2.1 Types of politeness strategy (Brown and Levinson 1987: 60).

strategies. Being 'off record' implies that some aspect of the target of a speech act such as a request is not explicitly mentioned, and so the hearer's face is not threatened through what is said. A speech act can be accomplished off record in a non-verbal way, as for example when at a dinner table one only looks at a piece of cake instead of requesting it. It can also be accomplished off record through implying a request to have some cake without clearly referring to it; for example, where one hints that one would like some cake by saying something like 'Gee, I'm still a bit peckish.' Although off record indirectness is certainly useful, it cannot be applied in every context, and so often the interactants go 'on record': the illocutionary point of the speech act has a clear mention in the utterance in question. Brown and Levinson distinguished between three strategies for accomplishing speech acts on-record: bald on-record, positive politeness and negative politeness. For example, to return to the different sentence types (outlined in Table 2.1) through which requests can be accomplished, the piece of cake can be requested directly through a bald on-record strategy ('Gimme that cake!') or accomplished using various different positive and negative politeness strategies. By its very nature, positive politeness is held to involve a lesser degree of indirectness than its negative counterpart, as the former assumes closeness between the speaker and hearer, even though it is not fully direct (cf. bald on-record). For example, a positively polite dinner table sentence like 'Would you gimme that cake?' follows the pattern of a question, even if its illocutionary function is not questioning, and so is in some respects indirect. However, a negatively polite counterpart of this request such as 'I was wondering if you could perhaps give me some of that cake, please?' is generally regarded as more indirect. The various degrees of (in)directness of speech acts are represented in Figure 2.1, which reproduces Brown and Levinson's (1987: 60) summary of politeness strategies.

However, it has become clear that the relationship between politeness and indirectness is not as straightforward as initially claimed in first-wave approaches to politeness. For instance, in a seminal study on this issue, Blum-Kulka (1987) demonstrated that a more indirect speech act is not necessarily interpreted as more polite in Israeli interaction, a finding that has subsequently been extended to many other languages. As a matter of course, then, it is not always considered more polite to make a request or indeed any kind of speech act more indirectly. We only have to think about the relationship between close friends, where indirectness might be evaluated negatively, to appreciate this point. Politeness by its nature necessitates some degree of indirectness in many cases as an absolutely direct form could imply that no politeness strategy is being employed, but the actual degree of indirectness is a matter influenced in large part by the context. That is, speech acts necessitate varying degrees of (in)directness in different interactional situations, depending on the relationship between the interactants, as well as depending on the type of imposition that the speech act involves (see Figure 2.1).

Forms and strategies

We have inherited from first-wave approaches to politeness a general tendency to describe linguistic politeness as a system of forms and strategies. A **form** is broadly defined as a meaningful unit of language, such as a morpheme, word, phrase or sentence. A focus on politeness forms thus entails an analysis of the linguistic structures by which politeness is conventionally accomplished. A **strategy**, on the other hand, is broadly defined as a plan or series of moves for obtaining a specific goal or result. A focus on politeness strategies thus presumes that speakers have particular goals in mind, and employ rationale means-to-ends reasoning to formulate a series of moves in order to achieve that goal in a way that is considered 'polite', and that hearers must employ ends-to-means reasoning in order to figure out what that goal might be, as well as recognising the speaker's polite intention. In other words, when the speaker's underlying plans or series of moves are recognisably oriented to a politeness maxim or the hearer's face, we are dealing with politeness strategies.

Linguistic forms of politeness have been studied by both Western and East Asian researchers. The former were predominantly interested in terms of address and pronominal forms, while the latter focused on honorific forms, including self-denigrating and other-elevating forms of address, humble and deferential verbal forms, and other aspects of honorific language. Perhaps the most influential study on the polite usage of Western terms of address was written by Roger Brown and Albert Gilman in 1960. Brown and Gilman examined the duality of the so-called T/V pronominal distinction, namely the finding that in certain languages there are 'respectful' (V, derived from the French *vous*) and a 'plain' (T, derived from the French *tu*) pronominal forms. Their claim was that the choice of a T or a V form is governed by the social factors of 'power' and 'solidarity', depending on the relationship and the culture of the speakers. Brown and Gilman's study has generated extensive descriptive research on the systems of deferential and 'plain' pronouns across languages. Brown and Levinson subsequently integrated T/V theory into their framework by associating respectful term of address forms with negative politeness and plain term of address forms with positive politeness.

East Asian scholars have studied honorific forms throughout history. A study which has had strong influence on modern linguistics is the book by Susumu Kuno (1973), which describes Japanese honorifics from the perspective of generative linguistics. The Japanese pragmatician Yoshiko Matsumoto (1989) also used Japanese honorifics to illustrate the complexity of the applicability of the T/V distinction in Japanese, as honorifics in fact have multidimensional applications. This means that instead of operating within a duality of deference and non-deference, Japanese provides many registers, spanning from humble to deferential, which are accomplished by means of a range of different honorific forms. Japanese scholars have thus been predominantly critical of universalistic frameworks of politeness (e.g. (Ide 1989).

The term *strategy*, which figures most prominently in Brown and Levinson's framework, refers in that model to the various ways the potential face-threat arising from a speech act, which the speaker wants to accomplish, is reduced in order to save the hearer's face. For example, off-record politeness strategies include giving hints, communicating via presuppositions, or using metaphors and rhetorical questions. On-record positive politeness can be realised by means of strategies such as seeking agreement, avoiding disagreement, making jokes and presupposing shared knowledge with the hearer. On-record negative politeness can come into existence via strategies such as giving deference, emphasising the speaker's want to not impinge on the hearer, and by making one's speech impersonal.

An important rationale behind the idea of strategies is that they help to describe the diverse ways in which politeness is conveyed in communication in a systematic way. Furthermore, the view that various forms of politeness are chosen in order to strategically cope with certain interpersonal situations provides an analytic explanation as to why a particular form of politeness is preferred in a given setting. To provide an example, Brown and Levinson note that the positive politeness strategy 'seeking agreement' involves looking for those aspects of topics on which it is possible to agree and sticking to them. This explains why people appraise only a slice of reality, as, for example, when one compliments a neighbour on his new car by saying 'Isn't your new car a beautiful colour?' Obviously, if the speaker finds the hearer's car to be ostentatious or overly pollution-producing, it is strategic to refer positively to a part of it which he or she finds acceptable, like its colour, instead of appraising the whole object.

One difficulty for the strategy model, however, resides in its descriptive nature: one can only capture the most representative techniques of politeness in a certain language or culture, and such a description may not apply to politeness in other languages and cultures, as various criticisms of first-wave universalistic frameworks have made clear. Furthermore, a strategy is a behavioural rather than a formal aspect of language usage, one consequence of which was that linguistic forms associated with politeness were relatively neglected in early universalistic theories.

As the present description has illustrated, first-wave approaches represented politeness as a duality of strategies and forms. This duality reflects a conceptual stance: namely, that politeness is perceived in these frameworks as the speaker's 'product', an isolated and 'measurable' unit which is produced by the speaker and interpreted by the researcher in light of contextual factors. As we argue in Section 2.3, these conceptual assumptions are also reflected in the methodologies of first-wave approaches to politeness.

2.3   Methodology

Utterance-level analysis

In the field of pragmatics, the expression **utterance** refers to the smallest unit of communication. Unlike units in descriptive linguistics, which traditionally span from a morpheme to a sentence, an utterance is not defined by its size but rather with respect to its function: it is a communicative unit produced by a single speaker. For example, the exclamation 'Huh?', the expression 'Pardon me?' and a longer piece of monologue are all, potentially, utterances. First-wave approaches describe politeness at the utterance level due to the aforementioned conceptual stance of observing politeness as the speaker's product. An utterance-level analysis facilitates the identification of politeness forms and strategies because when they are relatively isolated vis-à-vis utterances, the function of strategies and forms tends to be easier to generalise about, while in longer stretches of interaction the function of politeness forms and strategies tends to become more complex. A focus on the utterance level does not in principle exclude analysis of longer interactions such as dialogues. A set of utterances can, in fact, be studied through this approach; it is simply that the analyst has an interest primarily in the utterances, themselves, rather than in the relationship between the utterances, and the wider discursive context. To explain this point further, let us consider the brief dialogue in example (5).

(5) A: I had a flat tyre on the way home.
    B: Oh God, a flat tyre!

                                                  (Brown and Levinson 1987: 113)

Brown and Levinson cite this interaction as a representative example of the positive politeness strategy of repetition: when the hearer repeats part or all of what the speaker has just said in order to seek agreement. The question emerges as to how it is possible to regard this dialogue as an example of politeness, considering that these utterances could mean something different. For instance, it could be that A is the wife of B, and the latter utters 'Oh God, a flat tyre!' as an ironic reference to A's inability to change wheels. The answer is simple: studying politeness at the level of utterances requires us to examine the regular, routinised use of polite utterances which, in turn, presupposes default interpretations.

Elicited data

The focus on the utterance level brought along with it certain preferred methods of data collection in first-wave approaches to linguistic politeness. In order to obtain data which are as illustrative as possible, various studies use carefully selected pieces of either (allegedly) **naturally occurring data** or, more often than not, **elicited data**. Naturally occurring data are utterances that arise in *spontaneous* interaction, while elicited data are utterances that arise in discourse or interaction facilitated through *intervention* by the researcher. Many researchers set out with the methodological assumption that certain naturally occurring utterances can and must be excluded from the analysis on theoretical grounds. In practice this means, for example, that the analyst can ignore an utterance that deviates from what is defined as the standard usage of politeness. The idea that certain manifestations of language usage are 'improper' originates in Chomsky's Generative Grammar (see above), which, at least to some extent, has influenced the thinking of early theorists of politeness. In generative studies, syntactic structures that deviate from grammatical rules are described as 'non-well-formed' and so are excluded from the analysis. The idea of 'well-formedness' appears, for instance, in Lakoff's study when she argues that in politeness research 'we should like to have some kind of pragmatic rules, dictating whether an utterance is pragmatically well-formed or not' (1973: 296). While other first-wave approaches were less explicit in making such claims, they nevertheless also assume an underlying criterion of pragmatic well-formedness in that they present canonical examples of politeness strategies in their analyses. In other words, by presenting a particular piece of data as an example of a particular politeness strategy one is implicitly assuming the utterance in question is pragmatically well-formed (i.e. would be accepted by other competent speakers as a canonical instance of politeness).

'Well-formed' politeness data can either be naturally occurring, which implies that the researcher collects them from datasets, or they can be elicited, as we have briefly mentioned. Elicitation refers to methodologies by means of which researchers can obtain data directly from the speakers, according to criteria that suit the research project's specific objectives. These methodologies aim to vouchsafe for the given dataset's 'well-formedness'. For example, a pragmatic research project dedicated to analysing polite lexemes, which was conducted in the 1970s, instructed informants to ignore contexts, in order for the researchers to obtain 'standard lexical context' for the forms studied.[3] In linguistic politeness research, data can be elicited through various methodologies, including **discourse completion tasks/tests** (DCTs), **questionnaires/surveys** and **interviews**.

A DCT refers to a one-sided situational role play designed by the researcher. DCTs include situations by means of which the analyst can observe the ways in which a 'polite' speech act is performed. For example, a typical DCT that elicits data on speech acts, in this case apology, might consist of several questions along the lines of example (6).

(6) You are late to a meeting and have made others wait for you. Your colleague asks: 'Where have you been?' You respond: _____

DCTs allow researchers to investigate correlations between forms and strategies that informants report they would use, and various sociological and linguistic variables. For example, example (6) can be modified to address the influence of rank, gender, frequency of interaction and so on, simply by altering the first sentence in the following way:

You are late to a *weekly* meeting with your *female section head* and have made others wait for you.

Changing the details of a given question pattern helps researchers to examine the sociopragmatic **variability** of speech acts. Perhaps the most representative work on the use of DCTs to elicit politeness-related speech act data has been compiled by a team of three pragmaticians, Shoshana Blum-Kulka, Juliane House and Gabriele Kasper (1989), who utilised this kind of elicited data to analyse politeness forms and strategies across cultures.

Along with DCTs, which focus on how speakers produce certain utterances, there are other, more general tools, such as questionnaires/surveys, which aim to measure the speaker's evaluation of certain forms of politeness. A typical questionnaire/survey would, for example, ask the informant to evaluate the politeness value of a request utterance like 'Could you please lend me a pen?' on a scale. Ethnographic interviews are another tool, by means of which the analyst can elicit information from the informant in a less structured or formally bound way, by requesting, for instance, that the informant comment on a certain politeness-related topic.

All of these approaches aim to generate data about the production of speech acts that are specified in the research design: they are designed to elicit and describe linguistic features, such as directness versus indirectness of a specific speech act. An important rationale behind adopting these methodologies is that they have enabled, and continue to enable, researchers to build up extensive databases relatively quickly and without, perhaps even more importantly, generating analytical complexities. This latter practical aspect is an important reason behind the lasting popularity of these various methodologies for eliciting data. Although in the current age of the internet it often only takes a few clicks for the researcher to search within large databases of **naturally occurring data**, it continues to be difficult to identify speech acts in these databases. This is because database searches are usually based on lexical items, and although speech acts like requests and apologies may involve some typical expressions such as 'please' and 'excuse me', they can be expressed in many alternative ways. Obviously, this is not an issue in the case of elicited data.

However, one key challenge facing approaches that elicit data for politeness research is the issue of *validity*. It is now well established in pragmatics that what informants report they might say when data is elicited and what they actually say in naturally occurring interactions are not always the same. This is because it is difficult to establish with any great certainty whether informants are recalling what they have said or predicting what they might say. There is also the possible influence of social desirability effects: informants wanting to be seen to be saying the 'right' thing, or wanting to think of themselves as the kind of person who says the 'right' thing.[4] Another problem is that elicited data tend to remain at the level of utterances. For an utterance-based analysis this is not in itself a problem, but if the aim is to investigate the relationship between utterances and the wider discursive context, then clearly this is a problem. Methods for eliciting longer interactions, in particular role plays, have consequently been employed more frequently in recent years in studies using first-wave theories of politeness. However, role plays still face the problem of establishing the validity of the dataset given it is elicited rather than naturally occurring. It is thus now considered prudent to triangulate elicited data with data collected through other methods.

Observer coding

The above-discussed methodologies of data collection also presuppose reliance on a certain analytical stance, namely **observer coding** of linguistic forms and strategies vis-à-vis politeness. This essentially includes cases where 'a category system is established in advance on the basis of theory or research, and the analyst decides which category applies to each utterance/behaviour' (Arundale 2010a: 152). The question thus arises as to what exactly is being coded. As the sociologist Thomas P. Wilson (1970) points out, there are essentially two ways in which we construct our interpretations of interactions involving human beings. On the one hand, we may limit our understanding to our own perspective or understanding of the interaction under study. This is generally termed the *analyst's perspective*. On the other hand, we may attempt to also include within this interpretation the perspectives or understandings of the participants themselves as they are engaged in that very same interaction. This is generally termed the *participant's perspective*. The problem then arises as to how we might systematically examine these perspectives. Observer coding is the most common method of systematising the analyst's perspective on social phenomena.

While all first-wave approaches to politeness rely on observer coding, Brown and Levinson's framework is an example *par excellence* of an approach to politeness grounded in observer coding. Explicit definitions of various types of politeness forms and strategies are formulated in the theory itself. The main job of the analyst is thus first to assemble a dataset, second to apply these definitions to categorise the data at hand, and finally to interpret what this coding of the data might mean. For example, a prototypical study that has been carried out in the context of the first-wave politeness paradigm has involved first collecting two datasets of a particular speech act for the purposes of comparison (e.g. requests in English and Japanese), then using Brown and Levinson's framework to code the utterances in these datasets vis-à-vis different kinds of politeness forms and strategies and, finally, interpreting the relative frequency of the different forms and strategies in the two datasets vis-à-vis general orientations to positive and negative face. Often statistical techniques are applied to establish whether differences in the frequency of forms and strategies are (statistically) significant.

The application of statistical tests and, in some cases, including measures of the reliability of coding of data, certainly affords the analysis a veneer of scientific credibility. However, a very significant question facing such studies is just what are we coding and thus counting? Any coding system that is not tied in some way to the understandings of the participants themselves is in danger of generating analytical artifacts. Essentially, what this means is that we are coding and counting up phenomena that do not reflect what is actually going on in those interactions, at least not from the perspective of the participants themselves. The upshot is that while observer coding is very strong on *reliability* in that it generates analyses that can be replicated, the *validity* of the analyses it generates is much more open to question: particularly the validity of the coding system across languages and cultures from an emic perspective. The consensus in the field now seems to be that while Brown and Levinson's theory, in particular the notions of positive and negative face, generate relatively sound (and thus valid) analyses when applied to the examination of politeness in Anglo-English interactions[5] (e.g. British English, American English, Australian English, New Zealand English and so on) and perhaps even some other western European languages and cultures, its validity vis-à-vis the coding of politeness phenomena in other languages and cultures around the world is much more problematic. It is most telling that when defences of Brown and Levinson's theory are mounted from the perspective of other languages, such as Japanese, they invariably do not address the validity of the notions of positive and negative face, but rather appeal to the sociological variables of power and distance. In our view, then, this means that observer coding grounded solely in Brown and Levinson's framework is just as likely to be generating analytical artifacts as it is to be generating meaningful cross-cultural analyses, a point we will return to in Chapter 11.

2.4   A sample analysis

In what follows, let us analyse example (7) in order to illustrate how early theories can be employed in examining politeness phenomena. In doing so, we wish to highlight not only what light they can shed on politeness, but also what is neglected in such analyses. We have deliberately chosen an example from English here because the validity of first-wave approaches is much less in question in the case of Anglo-Englishes compared to data from other languages. Nevertheless, as we shall see, there is still much that is left open to question in this kind of analysis.

> (7) Archie: All right, all right, I apologise.
>   Otto: You're really sorry.
>   Archie: I'm really really sorry, I apologise unreservedly.
>   Otto: You take it back.
>   Archie: I do, I offer a complete and utter retraction. The imputa-
>   tion was totally without basis in fact, and was in no way
>   fair comment, and was motivated purely by malice, and
>   I deeply regret any distress that my comments may have
>   caused you, or your family, and I hereby undertake not to
>   repeat any such slander at any time in the future.
>   Otto: Okay.
>   (*A Fish Called Wanda*, 1988)

This interaction takes place between the assassin Otto West and the lawyer Archie Leach, as Otto dangles Archie out a window to make him apologise for a claimed offence (although it was Otto in fact who offended Archie).

From a Brown and Levinsonian perspective, Archie's utterances employ negative politeness strategies in formulating this apology speech act. On the one hand, he uses several routine forms of apology, including 'I'm really sorry' and 'I offer a complete and utter retraction', in order to formalise the speech act. On the other hand, he also utilises various politeness strategies, such as 'The imputation was totally without basis in fact', which Brown and Levinson (1987: 68) define as a strategy for 'indicat[ing] that he [the speaker] regrets doing a prior FTA [face-threatening act]', as well as the strategy of making a joint promise of forbearance and apology when uttering 'I hereby undertake not to repeat any such slander at any time in the future.' The occurrence of these negative polite politeness strategies in accomplishing this apology is in accordance with the immediate contextual requirements. Considering the relative power between the interactants (Archie is being hung out of a window and it is Otto who is deciding on his fate), it is clearly rational for Archie to be attempting to appeal to the other's face.

This analysis, however, leaves a number of questions open. Most importantly, one wonders whether Archie's politeness is appropriate in the present form. If yes, for whom is it appropriate? That is, even though Otto might take Archie's utterances as proper and thus sufficiently polite forms of apology, we have to keep it mind that it is not so much him as *we*, the audience of the film, who need to decide on the appropriateness of these manifestations of apology. The question, then, is whether we evaluate them in way similar to Otto.

If we perceive an apology to be an inherently polite speech act, Archie's utterances are of course polite (in fact, extremely polite). On the other hand, the wording of his apologies – Archie, as a lawyer, uses super-formal language, which does not seem to fit with a situation where he is begging for his life – suggests that we need to examine the personality and states of mind of the interactants, the history behind this interaction, the comedy genre in which this interaction takes place, and other contextual factors, in order to understand what is exactly going on in this interaction vis-à-vis politeness. In Chapter 3 we will start to address a number of these issues.

2.5   Summary

The theories of politeness studied in the present chapter, in particular the Brown and Levinsonian framework, have dominated the field for three decades since the late 1970s. At the beginning of this chapter we defined early theories as the 'roots' of politeness research. Although in Chapter 3 we will discuss frameworks that not only criticise these first-wave theories, but also approach the theorisation and analysis of politeness from new angles, we nevertheless maintain that the theories discussed here constitute the basis of the field. In that sense they cannot be disregarded as outdated, because many of the underlying assumptions embodied in these first-wave approaches continue to exert a very strong influence on the field. Indeed, not only do Brown and Levinson's theory and other first-wave approaches continue to be widely cited, both in other areas of linguistics such as language teaching, and in other major fields in the social sciences, such as psychology, sociology and anthropology, but the notions of rationality, face, speech acts, observer coding and other related assumptions still influence the way in which many researchers theorise linguistic politeness.

2.6   Key readings

A chapter by Culpeper (2011b), 'Politeness and impoliteness', provides a detailed but comprehensible, and indeed very useful, overview of the history of linguistic (im)politeness research. It is recommended particularly to those who have interest in both politeness and impoliteness.

Earlier papers by Bruce Fraser (1990) and Kasper (1990) offer more technical but illuminating summaries of approaches to politeness that were developed in the first wave of approaches. A noteworthy characteristic of these studies is that, as far as we are aware, they constitute the first critical overviews of the field to be published.

Finally, Chapters 2 and 3 of the monograph *Politeness* by Watts (2003) provide a very detailed critical retrospection of the development of, and key topics in, politeness research. These chapters are recommended primarily to those who intend to pursue further studies in the field.

3 Recent developments in politeness research

3.1 Introduction

The field of politeness research has increased in scope and diversity since the beginning of the second millennium. In the past decade, certain critical ideas on linguistic politeness which had been latent in the field for some time, such as the importance of making a distinction between lay and technical understandings of politeness, have been combined with a far-reaching methodological shift towards examining politeness situated in discourse and interaction. This methodological shift in politeness research is often referred to in the field as the discursive turn.

It is often argued that the discursive turn started with the publication of Gino Eelen's (2001) *A Critique of Politeness Theories*, a monograph which in some sense has become as influential as Brown and Levinson (1987) (see Chapter 2). Eelen's (2001) work, in turn, has its roots in an earlier edited collection by Watts, Ide and Konrad Ehlich (1992a). However, while enormously influential amongst politeness researchers, the impact of this work has not yet reached the stature of the first-wave approaches since, as was argued in Chapter 2, thus far no theory has been able to significantly dent the popularity of Brown and Levinson's framework across various disciplines. Furthermore, Eelen did not attempt to elaborate a framework *per se*, but instead was engaged in a **self-reflexive** exercise, essentially focusing on a critique of theoretical and methodological issues in the field. Yet while Eelen's book did not, like Brown and Levinson, create a theoretical paradigm for examining politeness, it successfully drew attention to the need to devote greater attention to the participants' perspective in studying linguistic politeness. This focus on the participant has become a cornerstone in the major body of post-2000 politeness research.

The examination of longer stretches of interaction has a number of important implications. Perhaps most importantly, it necessitates examining the behaviour of both the speaker and the hearer. As illustrated in Chapter 2, in first-wave approaches to politeness research, the focus was predominantly on the speaker. However, insofar as we analyse politeness in interactions between speakers and hearers, it becomes necessary to examine the discursive effect of an utterance. Eelen put this point in the following way:

in everyday practice im/politeness occurs not so much when the speaker produces behaviour but rather when the hearer evaluates that behaviour. (2001: 109)

Although this view will be challenged to some extent in Chapter 4, since it goes without saying that interactions are co-constructed by both the speaker and the hearer, Eelen's main argument that there needs to be a greater focus on evaluations of politeness, not simply linguistic forms and strategies used by speakers, is one that has been enormously influential.

The most important rationale behind examining politeness in longer stretches of interaction is that when considered in the wider context in which they arise, seemingly clear usages of politeness turn out to be rather complex. For example, let us revisit an excerpt we discussed previously in Chapter 2:

(1) Medway drew closer. Halting, she fixed him with respectful eye and extended the cigar-stump between dainty fingers.
'Would you be requiring this any further, sir?'
'Eh?'
'You left it in moddom's room, and I thought perhaps you would be needing it.'
(P. G. Woodhouse, *Hot Water*, Chapter 8, 1963)

In Chapter 2 we argued, following the key principles of first-wave approaches to politeness, that this interaction between a high-ranking guest (an American senator) and a British maid (Medway) represents a clear usage of politeness, which comes into operation due to rank and consequent power differences. That is, it constitutes a prototypical instance of 'negative politeness', in Brown and Levinson's sense. This conversation functions very well as a representative example if we pick it out from its immediate discursive context. However, the transparency of the interpretation of this interaction as involving a straightforward case of politeness becomes problematic if the conversation is placed in a wider context: if we examine (a) contextual factors and the interactional relationship between the interactants, as well as (b) the way in which the interaction itself is constructed.

In regard to (a), although Brown and Levinson's framework does not ignore context completely, it encourages the analyst to examine only basic contextual factors without analysing the interactional history behind a certain conversation. For example, in the case of example (1) it is important to know that Senator Opal is a guest in a chateau in France, and his hostess is blackmailing him with a document that may end his career. The Senator attempts to search the hostess' room in her absence to find and steal the document, and although this attempt turns out to be unsuccessful, the Senator believes, until he meets the maid, that he was at least unseen. Thus, although the conversation could be explained as a typical instance of negative politeness, if one observes the wider discursive context another plausible explanation becomes evident. That is, the Senator has been caught in a criminal act, and his abrupt response may not so much be due to his powerful position but perhaps arises simply out of shock. Looking at this point from another angle, although the Senator's social rank could imply interactional power, in this specific context he is not at all powerful. It is Medway who holds power, and this twist in their power relationship affords further interpretative possibilities for her utterances, which may be just as much menacing as deferential.

This latter point becomes evident if we read the subsequent conversation between Senator Opal and Miss Medway; that is, if we analyse how the interaction unfolds.

> (2) A great deal of Senator Opal's effervescence evaporated. An almost automatic and unconscious smoker, he had forgotten that he had been half-way through a cigar when he embarked on that search of his. A well-defined feeling of constriction in the muscles of his throat caused him to utter a faint sound like the gurgle of a dying duck.
> 'You weren't there!'
> 'Yes, sir.'
> 'I didn't see you.'
> 'No, sir.'
> The Senator cleared his throat noisily. There were several questions he would have liked to ask this calm-bowed girl, but he felt that asking would be injudicious. The salient fact, the one that must be dealt with immediately, was that she had seen him nosing about the Venetian Suite. Where she had been concealed was a side issue.
> 'H'r'r'mph!' he said awkwardly.
> Medway awaited his confidences with quiet respect. And yet, the Senator asked himself as he gazed into it, was the eye of hers quite so respectful as he had supposed? A demure girl. Difficult to know just what she was thinking.
> 'I dare say,' he said, 'it seemed a little strange to you that I should be in Mrs Gedge's room?'
> Medway did not speak.
> 'The fact is, I am a man with hobby. I am much interested in antiques.'

Medway remained quiescent.
'An old place like this . . . a historic old house like this . . . a real old-world Château like this, full of interesting subjects, is – er – interesting to me. It interests me. I am interested in it. Most interested. It – er – interests me to – ah – potter around. I find it interesting.'
A fly settled on his snowy hair. Medway eyed it in silence. He cleared his throat again. He was feeling that he would have to do a little bit better than this.

(P. G. Wodehouse, *Hot Water*, Chapter 8, 1963)

Example (2) illustrates that (i) Miss Medway's previous utterances are indeed more menacing than negatively polite, but (ii) this is a complex point, because from an interactional perspective, polite utterances are open to interpretation by the interactants, and so various meanings and evaluations can potentially emerge over the course of an exchange (see Chapters 4 and 5 for more on emergence). For instance, the section:

Medway awaited his confidences with quiet respect. And yet, the Senator asked himself as he gazed into it, was the eye of hers quite so respectful as he had supposed? A demure girl. Difficult to know just what she was thinking.

illustrates that although Miss Medway acts according to the norms of appropriateness – and thus that her silence would imply deference in many contexts – in this specific setting it is not necessarily polite: it is open to interpretation by the hearer (i.e. Senator Opal) as menacing.

As we can see, then, the discursive turn, by looking into longer stretches of interaction, starts to paint a much more complex and nuanced landscape for analysing politeness than was represented in first-wave approaches. In what follows, we will overview the main concepts and methodologies underlying broadly discursive approaches to politeness. It is pertinent to note that in this discussion Eelen (2001) will play a central (but not exclusive) role, in a somewhat similar way to our focus on Brown and Levinson (1987) in Chapter 2.

3.2   Concepts

First-order versus second-order politeness

As discursive approaches have gained increasing traction in politeness research, more and more scholars have become interested in the self-reflexive question of just how we should conceptualise linguistic politeness. As various researchers have argued, a basic problem in first-wave approaches is that they rest on an

Figure 3.1 Szervusz üdvözöllek [Hello and welcome] by Szergej Tamis (http://udvozollek.blogspot.co.uk).

analytic standpoint that implicitly favours the analyst's view over that of 'lay' people. One consequence of this is that theories such as Brown and Levinson (1987) can only accept certain usages of politeness as 'proper' ones given it essentially prescribes what counts as positive and negative politeness, and so inadvertently dismisses other interpretations as due to indiosyncracises on the part of individuals. In other words, data produced by 'laymen' go through a scholarly sieve, and if certain pieces of data do not conform with the theory they are regarded as inappropriate. While this approach is understandable in the light of the assumptions prevalent in pragmatics at the time (see Chapter 2), it is problematic in the sense that a selective treatment of data raises the very real question of whether we are studying the interactants' linguistic behaviour and their understandings of politeness, or rather our (i.e. the researchers') own understanding of politeness. This is because the selective treatment of data in itself reflects a certain perception of politeness, namely, the researcher's perception.

The problematic nature of dismissing certain perceptions of politeness can be illustrated by Figure 3.1, from a Hungarian comic:

(3) Frame 1: 'My heartfelt greetings, Mr Department Chair', 'At your service.'
     Frame 3: 'Mother fucker.' 'Prick.'

In the first frame of the cartoon, which represents an imaginary workplace interaction, both interactants utilise lexical items that are generally categorised by semanticians as old-fashioned polite expressions. Perhaps most importantly, the second speaker's form 'Szervusz üdvözöllek' (lit. 'At your service, greetings') is often represented as a traditional and rather conventional jovial greeting in Hungarian. However, this cartoon in fact ridicules the insincerity of such conventional greetings at workplaces, as becomes apparent in frame 3, and through this it becomes obvious that there is a certain perception of such Hungarian forms that contradicts their normative perception as traditional lexical **repre-sentations** of politeness. If one dismisses this alternative perception on any grounds – e.g. the interactants in the cartoon cannot represent proper language usage due to the low level of civility (swearwords are used here) – they will automatically dismiss various important alternative pragmatic implications of such forms, such as being interpreted as 'outdated' and 'insincere'.

This problem motivated researchers to distinguish between two different perspectives on politeness, the distinction between so-called **first-order** and **second-order politeness**. The terminology of first-order and second-order is used in various fields of linguistics, as well as other areas. In general, a first-order conceptualisation refers to the way in which a phenomenon is perceived by its users, while second-order describes a more abstract, scientific conceptu-alisation of the given phenomenon. In relation to politeness, as Watts, Ide and Ehlich first argued, **first-order politeness** involves 'commonsense notions of politeness' (1992b: 3): the 'various ways in which polite behaviour is perceived and talked about by members of sociocultural group' (1992b: 3). Second-order politeness, on the other hand, is a technical term 'within a theory of social behaviour and language usage' (1992b: 3): the way in which politeness is defined and conceptualised by theorists. For example, the anthropologist William Foley (1997: 270) defines politeness as 'a battery of social skills whose goal is to ensure everyone feels affirmed in a social interaction'. While this is a useful definition, it is obvious that it is a technical description, and if a man or woman on the street were asked to provide a definition he or she would provide a quite different description.

As alluded to above, while first-order and second-order perspectives involve conceptualisations of politeness, the first-order perspective also reflects certain practices. In the case of example (3), there is a standard and a non-standard practice of usage of the forms in frame 1: in other words, there are different first-order practices at play here. On the one hand there is the use of these forms sincerely as a traditional and rather conventional jovial greeting. On the other hand, there is the use of these forms to highlight the apparent insincerity or outmoded nature of this practice.

From this point, we can note that there are further important nuances in the way in which the first-order and second-order perspectives are interpreted in different discursive theories of politeness. The most important one among these differences is that while, according to Watts *et al.* (1992b; see above), first-order politeness is a commonsense or lay conceptualisation of politeness, Eelen (2001) argues that it is not just a concept talked about by people, but is also a phenomenon inextricably linked to their behaviour. First-order politeness is thus a mixture of politeness as a lay concept of which speakers are con-sciously aware, and politeness in practice, which is implicit only in discursive practices, and thus at times people are not necessarily consciously aware of it.

Second-order politeness, on the other hand, is a theoretical construct, a term within a theory of social behaviour and language use. In some cases, politeness comes under a broader technical notion. For example, the intercultural expert Helen Spencer-Oatey (2008[2000]) uses the term 'rapport management', while Watts (1989, 2003) proposes the notion of 'politic behaviour'.

The distinction between first-order and second-order politeness also echoes differences in the assumptions underlying research on politeness. Research based on first-order notions of politeness proceeds on the assumption that differences in the forms and strategies that give rise to politeness reflect divergences in the ways in which politeness itself is conceptualised in different cultures. In contrast, it is often assumed in research based on second-order notions of politeness that politeness is essentially conceptualised in the same way across cultures, and that differences in politeness forms and strategies are simply a reflection of divergences in the relative weight placed on the various structures that constitute different languages and the norms governing the usage of those structures.

As the discussion in Chapters 4 and 5 will illustrate, the relationship between first-order and second-order politeness needs to be teased out further in a somewhat more complex way than indicated in the present discussion. However, at this point it can be argued that in general the drawing of the first-order/second-order distinction has given a pivotal boost to the field, as it has challenged the dominance of inadvertently prescriptive approaches to politeness, which accepted only certain usages of politeness as 'appropriate'.

Variability and contestedness

As the politeness theorist and gender researcher Mills (2003) argues in her seminal monograph on politeness and gender, politeness is always subject to variability. While it was implicitly assumed in first-wave approaches to politeness that people within the same cultural group would have the same interpretations of a given utterance as polite (or impolite) – for instance, when the perceptions of members of the same cultural group are examined empirically – they are not always the same, a point first noted by Eelen (2001). In fact, there can be significant variability in the ways in which members from the same group evaluate the very same event vis-à-vis politeness, as Haugh (2010a) demonstrates, for instance, in an analysis of evaluations of an email sent by a lecturer to an international student that entered the public domain when the said lecturer was dismissed. In a sense such variability should not come as surprise to us. After all, the idea that 120 million Japanese or 310 million Americans would all agree about what counts as 'polite' in their respective societies is rather preposterous even when considered on first principles (i.e. based on what the ordinary user might observe). Yet it is worth reiterating that this is an implicit claim in first-wave approaches where Japan is characterised as a 'negative politeness culture' and the US is claimed to be a 'positive politeness culture' (see Chapter 11 on the problematic aspect of 'culture' as a prescriptive notion). What this variability means is that no preconceived assumptions can be straightforwardly applied to the analysis of linguistic politeness in naturally occurring data, without a careful examination of the details of situated contexts. What close examination of real-life interactions reveals is that the perceived social order – and consequently normative usage of so-called politeness forms and strategies – is often violated in real interactions. In this sense variability is closely interwoven with the first-order and second-order distinction, as it implies that 'local' (first-order) perceptions of politeness, must be incorporated into scholarly and technical (second-order) descriptions. In order to illustrate the function of variability in politeness practices in terms of how we map out positions in relation to interactional power, Mills (2003: 174–5) discusses the example of an older white, working-class female server at a coffee bar who openly defied all the behavioural norms of university academics, but the latter nevertheless tolerated her behaviour in spite of her 'low' position in the university hierarchy. As Mills concludes,

> She had a fairly 'low' position in the university hierarchy, and yet she simply flouted all of the linguistic 'rules' of interaction of how one should behave with senior staff. Thus, positions of power mapped out by one's role in an institution may not relate directly to the interactional power that one may gain through one's access to information, one's verbal skill, or one's display of care and concern for other group members.

Variability has two-fold implications: apart from questioning the absolute validity of norms of linguistic politeness due to interactants' potential opposition to this perceived order, as in the case above, it also means we should as analysts question the validity of cases, which seem to neatly fit into a certain second-order conceptualisation of politeness. In other words, even in cases in which the interactants behave exactly according to the researcher's **expectations** vis-à-vis a particular theoretical framework, one still needs to be cautious as the interactants may have myriads of reasons for behaving in that way. Thus, it is dangerous to make claims about the interactants' politeness behaviour without a detailed contextual analysis, as the motivating factor behind a certain form of behaviour might be entirely different from what we normally assume (as Chapter 8 on history illustrates, this is markedly the case in interactions which took place a long time ago). While this may seem to be an overly cautious standpoint, it cannot be ignored because politeness, by its very nature, is what Eelen (2001) originally termed *argumentative*, but which might be more straightforwardly described as **contested**.

Example (4) illustrates the contested nature of politeness. It comes from a nineteenth-century cross-cultural epistolary interaction between two intellectuals from China and Japan.[1] The extract is from a letter written in Classical Chinese by Kotaro Munakata (1864–1923), a sinologist and secret agent of the Japanese government, to the renowned Chinese intellectual Wang Yiwu (1842–1917). Munakata, who had an excellent command of this language, starts with the following words (sections of interest are squared in the Chinese text and underlined in the English translation):

(4) 王益吾⬜大宗師⬜ ⬜閣下⬜:
⬜僕⬜日本之處士。少小讀聖賢之書。⬜竊慕⬜ ⬜貴國⬜ ⬜名教⬜之隆。人物之盛。負笈泛海。轉遊於吳楚燕趙之間。五年於茲矣。...⬜竊恐⬜ ⬜唐突晉謁⬜。或⬜失禮於長者⬜。故此⬜謹修⬜短牘。

[To His Excellency Wang Yiwu, the Great Scholar:
This humble servant is a reclusive scholar of Japan who learnt the books of the sages from youth. I humbly envied the grandiosity of your great country's renowned Confucian teachings, the prosperity of [outstanding] personae, and so I left my home to study [in China], and until the present day I have travelled in the country for five years . . . I humbly am afraid that I will be brusque when attending an audience [i.e. visit you], or that I will violate the etiquette in front of your high-ranking person, and thus I solemnly write this brief letter].

(Mills and Kádár 2011: 22)

Example (4) is representative of the style of the letter as a whole. For experts of Chinese politeness, an interesting feature of the work is that the author applies an overtly deferential style. Whilst the genre of historical Chinese private letters presupposes the use of deferential lexicon, this letter is heavily loaded with such forms. The excerpt, which does not even include the formal opening, contains as many as eight honorific expressions, alongside some discursive techniques of self-denigration (such as the author's symbolic claim that his letter is brief, which contrasts markedly with its actual length). When reading this work initially, it is possible to assume that these features are due to intercultural differences between Chinese and Japanese politeness. This seems to be confirmed by modern empirical research: many case studies suggest that the Japanese can be more indirect and formal than the Chinese, which would explain Munakata's application of an extensive number of honorific forms. However, this interpretation is rooted in a pre-existing, scientific (second-order) understanding of present-day Chinese and Japanese politeness behaviour, and if we adopted it without looking at the context and other particulars of this historically situated interaction, we would unwittingly project it on the data without understanding the full implications of its appearance here. In fact, an analysis of this work has shown that contextual factors made it prudent for Munakata to be deferential: he was asking a favour from and wanted to establish a working relationship with Wang, who was considerably more highly ranked than himself. If one examines the letters of native Chinese authors it becomes evident that in similar contexts and interpersonal relationships, native Chinese authors also used honorifics. Thus, although Munakata's style is considerably more deferential than on average, his letter nevertheless is consistent with practices of Chinese in similar situated contexts. In fact, there is not any clear evidence that Munakata's style is due to his cultural background. Furthermore, if his cultural background was manifested in his style, one would to have to assume that there is an influence from Japanese in this text. However, some of the honorific items used in this letter actually suggest the opposite: Munakata, having an excellent command of Classical Chinese, applied a style exempt from Japanese influence. In sum, although on the basis of an alleged difference between present-day Japanese and Chinese politeness it might appear easy to argue that, in this example, Munakata follows a Japanese polite speech style, on closer examination we can observe that there is no evidence to support such a claim, or even the idea that Japanese and Chinese politeness systems really differed in terms of the perceived norms of indirectness/deference at the time of this interaction.

In sum, variability and contestedness are always potentially relevant to the analysis of any given piece of data. After theorising more carefully the reasons for the variability and contested nature of understandings of politeness in Chapters 4 and 5, we will revisit such issues in relation to culture in Chapter 11.

Beyond culture as the unit of analysis

As Eelen explains, first-wave approaches tended to use **units of analysis** focused at the level of languages, societies or cultures, instead of analysing politeness behaviour at the level of localised individuals and smaller groups. Most commonly they adopted culture as the key notion for explaining differences in politeness forms and strategies. In Brown and Levinson's (1987) universalistic framework, cultures are categorised into positive and negative politeness cultures, depending on their broad preference for mitigating face-threatening acts either by negative or positive politeness strategies. However, this broad reliance on culture results in some degree of terminological fuzziness. As Eelen notes,

in Brown and Levinson's discussion of 'cultural variation' ... the terms 'culture', 'society' and 'group' are used interchangeably. Sometimes the term 'subculture' is also encountered, although it is not clear how it relates to the other three. (2001: 159–60)

Furthermore, as we discussed in Chapter 2, many early critiques of the Brown and Levinsonian framework appealed to a notion of culture-specific politeness in order to decompose the universalistic framework, and so they, similar to Brown and Levinson, adopted a broad and thus vague definition of culture. The problem with this broad and vague notion is that it is inherently normative, an **essentialist** approach to culture and politeness, which presupposes that members of a certain culture tend to share these claimed values (see Chapter 2). This concept has often been criticised by discursive scholars. For example, the Japanese expert Naomi Geyer (2008: 65) argues that – if we want to retain culture as a unit of analysis – we need to adopt methodologies that observe culture as an interactionally constructed notion rather than as an inherited property.

However, the question may rightly emerge as to *why* we should get rid of generalisations. After all, if the majority of Japanese behave in one way, and the majority of Americans in another way, does it make sense to refrain from comparing general trends? However, while this point might be tempting, critical research reveals that even in terms of major patterns of politeness there are large-scale differences within a single culture. While culture will be analysed in considerable detail in Chapter 11, let us discuss a simple case to illustrate this point.

Consider, for instance, the politeness norms associated with so-called 'blunt Yorkshiremen', where there are recognisable regional norms that are quite distinct from the wider cultural norms (see Kádár and Mills, forthcoming). On the basis of stereotypical thinking about themselves, many Yorkshiremen feel enabled to speak in a way which, if used by people from other regions in the UK, might be considered impolite or overly direct. However, within Yorkshire, there is a pride in using certain speech styles which are classified by speakers as 'plain speaking' or 'speaking your mind' and are thus not considered impolite. Use of these speech styles is valued for the sense that it gives of a strong regional **identity** for certain groups of people within the county, and this speech style seems to transcend some of the class boundaries within the region. In Yorkshire, what are seen as 'soft Southern ways', epitomised by so-called negative politeness strategies, are often characterised as affected and undesirable. This illustrates that it is difficult to make general claims about a single culture, and thus culture is often a problematic unit of analysis. If we follow culture-specific generalisations and describe the British as a negative politeness culture, for instance, the question emerges as to how to describe the blunt behaviour Yorkshire people without disqualifying them as British.

Due to this problem, discursive theorists have proposed alternative units of analysis. The perhaps most important one among these units is the so-called **community of practice**, developed by the educational theorist Etienne Wenger (1998). This notion will recur in the present volume and will be discussed in some detail in Chapter 7, so at this point it will only be briefly noted that a

community of practice refers to a group of people, who are brought together
through engagement in a joint (often but not always professional) activity
or task. The notion of community of practice has become very popular in
discursive approaches to politeness research, as this notion allows researchers
to analyse politeness in a relatively contextualised way. As Wenger notes,

Communities of practice exist in any organization. Because membership is based on
participation rather than on official status, these communities are not bound by organizational affiliations; they can span institutional structures and hierarchies. (1983: 3)

In spite of the advantages of this notion, its value is somewhat limited because
it presupposes a specific contact between interactants focused on a common
task or activity. That means there are many interactional relationships that do
not fall under the category of community of practice (see Mills 2011b).

It is pertinent to note that in this book, as the following chapters will make
clear, we devote particular attention to politeness as it is constituted in **relational
networks**. Relational networks are sets of intersecting social links between
persons that collectively form the basis of an identifiable group for those persons who constitute the relational network in question (see Milroy and Milroy
1992 on 'social' networks). The politeness theorist Watts (2003) suggests that
relational networks can be either **emergent** or *latent*. An emergent relational
network is one where such social links are maintained, reactivated or changed
through interaction, while a latent relational network is one that is objectified by
persons that constitute that network (i.e. one they talk about as if it had a 'real'
existence independent of interaction). Relational networks are a useful level of
analysis in relation to politeness for two reasons. First, they allow us to study
politeness in a contextualised way, but in more settings than communities of
practice. Second, they help us to examine so-called cultural practices, as it can
be argued that a culture is constituted through multiple intersecting networks
of more localised relational networks (see e.g. Chapter 7), thereby avoiding
overgeneralisations.

It should be also noted, however, that no unit can capture every interactional
relationship, and so a self-reflexive analysis should avoid claiming that a given
unit is suitable to every analysis. Indeed, while, post-2000 theories of politeness
have devoted more attention to localised, individual politeness behaviour – one
of the most important units of analysis is regarded to be the **individual** – other
units such as communities of practice, social groups, sub-cultures, cultures and
societies still continue to be used. However, given the difficulties faced when
dealing with larger, more diffuse groups, many researchers tend to utilise these
units carefully, often using fairly nuanced definitions. Accordingly, while in this
book we will address other units of analysis including culture (see Chapter 11),
we will do so largely through the lens of the concept of relational networks.

Politeness as situated: contexts, text types and genres

As Haugh, Davies and Merrison argue,

As a pragmatic and sociolinguistic concept im/politeness has always been seen as dependent on context. This situatedness comes in many forms. It can involve considering contrasts (across cultural groups, languages, dialects or genres), but this is not essential. The in-depth study of politeness phenomena within a particular setting – such as educational, medical, or legal settings – can also deepen our knowledge of how im/politeness functions, and contribute to the theorising of the discipline. The text type within which the communication is situated (e.g. computer-mediated discourse, media discourse, advertising texts) also affects (and thus tells us more about) the functions of im/politeness. (2011: 1)

In post-2000 thinking, the claim that politeness is situated relative to contexts, text types and genres has gained prominence (see also Blitvich 2009). Various scholars argue that no prediction can be made about the interactional effect of a certain form of politeness because both the function and the interpretation of an utterance depend on its context (see the first part of the present section), as well as the text type (e.g. email versus letter) and genre (e.g. personal versus work-related email) in which it occurs.

In order to illustrate this point, let us cite an online interaction in Chinese, which has been analysed by Kádár, Haugh and Chang (2013):

> (5) 台湾同胞们, 请看帖子!
> Post 1 (疯狂海军 07/19/2010 02:30:25):
> 本是同根生, 相煎何太急!
> 各位台灣同胞! 請你體諒我們大陸玩家! 我們視你們為兄弟姐妹, 你們何故要傷害我們呢?
> 不說政治的話題, 說說歷史! 你知道在遙遠的歷史我們本是一個祖先? 我們都是炎黃的子孫後代! 為何不團結一起呢? 高麗棒子在我們教訓他們, 但是他們分開了何必要重言自己的同胞們呢? 我們都是一家人, 從過去到現在都是! 我們要團結不能被外人的搗鼓導致我們的分裂! ～台灣的兄弟姐們! 我們永遠都是一家人! 以後可不能因為一點小事就這樣惡言傷人了! 團结一致, 共同游戏!
>
> Post 3 (Deltablue 2. 07/29/2010 07:14:29):
> 「本是同根生」「各位台灣同胞」「本是一個祖先」「都是炎黃的子孫」「我們都是一家人, 從過去到現在都是」
> 在我看來全部是「文化侵略」
> 我們不希望在遊戲上談論「政治」「兩國(岸)關係」 這種「文化侵略」 也別來了 好嗎??
>
> [Taiwanese compatriots, please read this post!
> Post 1 (Fengkuang Haijun [Insane Navy]):

We have the same national roots, so why we should shoot on each other so quickly?
[All Taiwanese compatriots! Please forgive us mainland Chinese players! We are your brothers and sisters, why should you harm us? This is nothing to do with politics, it is all about history! Don't we have the same ancestors? We are the descendants of the Mythical Emperors! Why don't we unite? Let us give a lesson to those [South] Korean hoodlums who cannot unite with their compatriots [i.e. North Koreans]. We are members of the same family, from ancient times until present. We should unite and not allow outsiders to divide us! ~ Taiwanese brothers and sisters! We will always be a family! From now on we should not insult each other because of small matters. Let us unite and play together!

Post 3 (Deltablue 2.):
'Have the same national roots', 'all Taiwanese compatriots', 'have the same ancestors', 'the descendants of the Mythical Emperors', 'we are members of the same family, from ancient times until present'
In my view these are all terms of 'cultural aggression'.
Keep out 'politics' and 'cross-Strait' and all this kind of 'cultural aggression' from our game, will you?]

The interaction in example (5) took place on a thread on the online game 'battle.net's' discussion board relating to the simulated battle 'Decisive Battle for the Senkaku Islands', which is an island chain claimed by Taiwan, Japan and Mainland China. Importantly, while battle.net is a multilingual and multicultural game website, and is officially politics-free, players sometimes do discuss real political matters on the discussion board on this website, although such 'hostilities' do not generally stir metapragmatic debates or generate wider attention.

Example (5) illustrates the contextual and the generic situatedness of linguistic politeness, as well as the fact that politeness cannot be predictively described even in single language settings (this interaction takes place between native speakers of Chinese). In order to understand what is happening in this interaction, it is pertinent to note that there are political tensions between Mainland China (People's Republic of China) and Taiwan (Republic of China), which originate in China's claim that Taiwan is part of China, and Taiwan's (current) refusal of this claim. In example (5), the Mainland Chinese player Fengkuang Haijun's call to Taiwanese players – to 'unite forces' with Mainland Chinese players both in the game and in discussions relating to the game – seems to be spontaneous. Fengkuang Haijun claims his post has 'nothing to do with politics', and he also attempts to 'give face' to the Taiwanese players by performing a collective apology on behalf of Mainland Chinese. However, his posting is received in an extremely critical way by other players, apparently because his post (e.g. 'Taiwanese compatriots', 'Why don't we unite?', etc.) implicitly conveys China's claim of sovereignty over Taiwan, and in this way is perceived as a threat towards the claimed identity of Taiwanese players. In other words, although in many other contexts such expressions would be interpreted as markers of politeness, they do not function in this way in the present context. Altogether six players responded to this post, with all of them being critical (although due to space constraints we only cite one response). The Taiwanese player Deltablue evaluates Fengkuang Haijun's attempts to project association with the Taiwanese as a form of 'cultural aggression', and he also reminds him that in the present genre his seemingly polite behaviour is not acceptable, as this specific site should be politics-free. This latter point illustrates that context and genre often function together in giving rise to evaluations of a certain form or strategy vis-à-vis (im)politeness.

Face and relationships

One important development in post-2000 politeness research has been the increasing focus on interpersonal relationships, or what has been broadly termed the **relational shift** in politeness research. Indeed, it is striking that almost without exception every approach to politeness that has been proposed in the past ten to fifteen years has had an explicit focus on relationships in some shape or form, albeit with a variety of different terms being used, ranging from 'rapport management' and 'relational practice' through to 'relational work' and 'relating'. Some of these approaches have remained more closely aligned with the underlying theoretical commitments of first-wave approaches to politeness, such as Spencer-Oatey's (2008 [2000]) *rapport management theory* (dealing with 'rapport management'), or Holmes and colleagues' (e.g. Holmes, Marra and Vine 2012) *neo-politeness theory* (dealing with 'relational practices'). Other approaches have been more firmly situated within a broadly discursive approach, such as Locher and Watts' (2005) *theory of relational work*, or Arundale's (2006, 2010b) *face constituting theory* (dealing with 'relating'). As Spencer-Oatey notes in a useful overview, what all these approaches have in common is 'a central focus on interpersonal relations, rather than, as with traditional models of politeness, a central focus on the individual performing "politeness", which is then correlated with interpersonal relations as variables' (2011: 3565). It is clear, then, that politeness is conceptualised as part of a much broader interpersonal tapestry albeit, we would maintain, an important part of that tapestry.

A second, largely parallel development in post-2000 politeness research has been the rise of research focusing on face as a topic in its own right, or what might be characterised as the increasing separation of face and politeness research. While first-wave approaches to politeness, particularly Brown and Levinson's (1987) theory, treated face as inseparable from politeness, this stance has been increasingly challenged in the past decade. While it is now well accepted that not all facework amounts to politeness *à la* Brown and Levinson, as was convincing argued by Watts (2003) in his overview of politeness research, there have been a number of edited collections in recent years dealing with face as an important topic in its own right (Bargiela-Chiappini and Haugh 2009; Haugh and Bargiela-Chiappini 2010). The argument being made is that face and politeness should be disentangled from each other such that they constitute important areas of research in their own right (Haugh 2013a).

Let us consider for a moment example (6), which is from the American comedy series *Everybody Hates Chris*. Here, Chris is trying to convince his parents, Rochelle and Julius, to buy some new clothes for him to wear to the school photo day. He has been complaining that he has to wear his younger brother's old clothes.

(6) Chris: Well, can I please wear something else?

Julius: As long as I don't have to pay for it.

Rochelle: Just find something to wear and I'll take a look at it, okay?

Chris: I don't have anything special.

Julius: When I was a kid we didn't need any special clothes. Just having clothes was special.

Narrator: *The only way I was going to get my mom to spend money on me was if not doing it would embarrass her.*

Chris: Mom, I'm the only black kid in the whole school. They already think I'm a crack baby. Wearing this sweater they'll probably think we're on welfare.

Rochelle: Who said we were on welfare? Be home from school on time tomorrow. We're gonna go shopping.

Julius: I thought you said we didn't have the money?

Rochelle: Oh, I'll get it. Not havin' people think we on welfare.

('Everybody hates picture day', *Everybody Hates Chris*, Season 1, Episode 13, 2006)

After Chris pleading to wear something other than what his mother had picked out, his father indicates that he is not allowed to buy anything new. His mother only suggests that he find something else (i.e. something he already owns or can borrow from his brother). It is at this point that the narrator (the grown-up version of Chris) comes up with a strategy, namely, alluding to the potential embarrassment or threat to his family's and thus his mother's *face*, if people were to think they are too poor to buy new clothes. Rochelle reacts strongly to this potential face threat, and decides they will buy new clothes for Chris in spite of protests from Julius. However, despite the obvious salience of face in this interaction, it is quite clear that evaluations of politeness (or impoliteness) are not at issue here. Rochelle does not decide to get new clothes for Chris because it would be polite to do so, but because she wants to avoid having others think badly of their family. In other words, she wants to protect their face.

It is evident from example (6), then, that face and politeness need to be carefully disentangled. However, this suggests that other alternative metaphors for explaining politeness need to be sought. This is a theme which will reoccur in various guises throughout the remainder of this book, and to which we will explicitly return in Chapter 12.

3.3   Methodology

Naturally occurring interactions

As we illustrated briefly in Section 3.1, a fundamental difference between first-wave theories and post-2000 discursive theories of politeness is that the latter focus more on the participants' perspective. For example, as the discursive researchers Locher and Watts argue,

> We consider it important to take native speaker assessments of politeness seriously and to make them the basis of a discursive, data-driven, bottom-up approach to politeness. (2005: 16)

Here, 'bottom-up' means that theories of politeness should be built up relying on the participants' perspective, instead of creating theories first and then using them to analyse interactions.

Due to this methodological change, certain methodological approaches, such as eliciting data with the aid of DCTs (see Chapter 2), have been treated as less important in this research, and more attention has been given to naturally occurring data. The importance of naturally occurring data was emphasised by Eelen, who noted that we need to examine more:

> examples of actual (im)politeness evaluations, but due to the situational embeddedness and argumentativity of politeness, they would have to derive from natural settings and occur spontaneously, as elicited evaluations and/or an experimental setting introduce particular social aspects and motivations that warrant their classification as separate social practices. This points towards the need for real-life spontaneous conversational data. (2001: 255)

Naturally occurring data is in fact a broad category, and it allows researchers to focus on a wide variety of datasets, as well as to rely on different ways of recording. As Grainger's (2011) study of politeness illustrates, however, a naturally occurring conversation does not necessarily always need to be audio- or video-recorded: the researcher can, for example, reconstruct a previous interaction from memory. One advantage of this is that it can provide extra insight into the thoughts and feelings of participants beyond what emerges in the interaction itself given the researcher has access to at least his or her own thoughts at the time. The disadvantage, of course, is that the interaction is not as open to inspection by other researchers to the same extent as recordings, and it may also be subject to inadvertent interpretation by the researcher in the very recalling of it. For this reason, the overwhelming tendency is for naturally occurring interactions to be recorded and transcribed for analysis. The main difference, then, is in the level of detail found in those transcriptions.

Although discursive approaches focus more on the participants' perspective, it is sometimes complemented with observer coding (see Chapter 2). In fact, post-2000 researchers are not at all unanimous in the way they conceptualise politeness or in their mode of analysis. Certain theories such as Marina Terkourafi's (2001, 2005) frame-based approach continue to emphasise the role of theory in interpreting manifestations of linguistic politeness. Nevertheless, almost every approach is united in its commitment to analysing politeness in naturally occurring data.

Data types

In discursive approaches to politeness certain data types have gained particular attention alongside naturally occurring face-to-face interactions, either because they reveal information about the hearer's evaluation, or because they shed light on certain aspects of politeness in interaction, which has been largely ignored in first-wave approaches.

CMC is one of the most noteworthy and most popular data sources in discursive research. According to Locher (2010: 3–4), this is due to three reasons. First, online language usage tends to develop its own set of norms given the diversity in text type, genre and communities of practice involved (see also example (5) above). Thus, online etiquette, or so-called netiquette, affords a significant amount of data for studying variability in norms of politeness. Second, politeness can arise in different ways in online interactions given the various possibilities for public and ostensibly private interactions to merge online, and the potential for much larger audiences than generally found for private face-to-face interactions (even multiparty ones). Third, online interactions provide a unique channel for interaction, due to their multimodal nature (see more on **multimodality** in Chapters 6 and 8). That is, in CMC a given message is conveyed through different channels, which results in specific, online designs of polite messages (e.g. the use of emoticons in emails).

Another important data source in discursive research has been provided by historical texts. Although **historical politeness** will be studied in detail in Chapter 8, it is pertinent to note here that historical interaction has stirred interest in post-2000 politeness research due to its explanatory power. As historical experts Kádár and Culpeper argue,

studying historical (im)politeness is of bi-directional importance: by examining the past, the usage of politeness language today can be placed in context; by examining the present, politeness language usage of the past can be placed in context. (2010: 13)

In other words, the examination of diachronically situated politeness can explain certain peculiarities of contemporary politeness usage, and as such it aids researchers to critically revisit certain prescriptive assumptions, which are based on contemporary understandings of linguistic politeness.

The prosodic and **paralinguistic features** of politeness and impoliteness were often mentioned in pre-2000 research, but it is only in recent years that in-depth research on this topic has actually been undertaken. Arguably the most representative study on this theme was conducted by Culpeper (2005, 2011c) who examined the **prosody** of impoliteness rather than politeness, although these findings are relevant to politeness research as well. As Culpeper argues, prosody is an important way of giving rise to (im)politeness, and so it is essential to examine the prosodic features of interactions. Although Culpeper utilises instrumental approaches to examine prosody, it is important to note that prosody is a communicative channel which can be studied in other ways as well; for example, simply by denoting or describing relevant parts in transcribed interactions. Indeed, in the field of conversation analysis (see Schegloff 2007a for an overview), transcripts generally include details of hearable prosodic and paralinguistic features of talk.

Institutional discourse is another important data type, as it provides information on the relationship between power and politeness, as well as the usage of politeness as a tool to enforce or redistribute power. For example, courtroom interactions, which have been analysed in depth by Sandra Harris (2011), provide a noteworthy case of the usage of (im)politeness in power-dominated settings. Courtroom interactions are highly regulated, which means that the powerless (e.g. the witnesses) cannot directly oppose the powerful (e.g. by keeping silent). It is for exactly this reason that skilful usage of politeness, as well as covert impoliteness, can become a key means to challenge the powerful and redistribute power.

The above-discussed data types are all naturally occurring, in the sense that 'they are simply there for the researcher' to record and analyse them. There is, however, another type of data in discursive research, which is elicited, namely, **post-recording interviews**. Certain researchers, most representatively Spencer-Oatey (2008 [2000]), conduct interviews with the participants of an interaction after the occurrence of the given interaction, in order to reconstruct their states of mind during the interactions. Post-recording interviews are in some sense naturalistic because, unlike in DCTs, the participants of the interview can freely talk about the way in which they experienced an interaction.

3.4   A sample analysis

Let us now look at example (7): a brief sample from a popular work written by British journalist Lynne Truss (2005), which was analysed in detail by Mills and Kádár (2011). The point we want to make is that the journalist's claims are quite problematic from the perspective of post-2000 politeness research.

> (7) Good morning madam.
> Good morning sir.
> How may we help you?
> I would like some tomatoes/eggs/postage stamps please.
> Of course. How many tomatoes/eggs/postage stamps would you like?
> Seven/five/twelve, thank you.
> That will be six/four/two Euros. Do you have the exact money?
> I do.
> Thank you madam.
> Thank you sir. Good day!
> Good day!
> Now the amazing thing is, this formal and civil exchange actually represents what happens in French shops. French shopkeepers really say good morning and goodbye; they answer questions; they wrap things ever so nicely; and when it's all over, they wave you off like a near relation.

This example represents the French as polite people through the example of an imagined conversation in a shop. Truss compares the French with the British who – in Truss' view – are becoming a 'rude nation'. Such a description is problematic from the perspective of discursive theorisation of politeness for several reasons. First, it is constructed (textbook-like) and not naturally occurring data, and so we lack evidence as to whether such an interaction would occur in real-life in this way. Second, as this chapter has argued, politeness by its nature is subject to contestation due to its inherent variability, and so it can be argued that whilst certain French employees may communicate in such a deferential way, this is definitely not a register that characterises the speech style of *every* French employee. Third, this description represents a case where politeness is represented according to the researcher's normative view, and it lacks acknowledgement of the first-order and second-order distinction between participants' and researchers' understandings of politeness, which gained prominence in post-2000 politeness research.

3.5   Summary

Although this chapter is dedicated to examining discursive theorisations of politeness, it is important to emphasise that there are other competing approaches in the field. And while we aimed to show the most important features of discursive research, it should be emphasised again that discursive research is not at all homogeneous.

There are various challenges in applying post-2000 theories, particularly in the case of the discursive approach. Overall, there are various theoretical claims and methodologies, which have been discussed here, but no clear overarching theory that has reached the level of influence of Brown and Levinson's (1987) theory has yet emerged. The most intriguing question for contemporary politeness research, then, is how we can integrate these theoretical concepts and methodological approaches into a coherent and integrated theoretical framework.

3.6   Key readings

The short introduction by Kádár and Mills (2011) provides an overview of the main concepts and objectives of discursive politeness research.

A more elaborate description can be found in Mills (2011a), which goes into a more detailed discussion of terminological and other theoretical and methodological issues in discursive politeness research. This work is a key reading for those who intend to work using the discursive approach.

The paper by Locher and Watts (2005) offers another useful summary of some of the main tenets of the discursive approach to politeness. This is another key reading for those who intend to work using the discursive approach.

Haugh (2007c) offers an early self-reflexive critique of discursive approaches, focusing in particular on the difficulties inherent in reconciling the theoretical claims of discursive approaches with their reliance on assumptions inherited from first-wave approaches to politeness. It is proposed that a truly discursive approach to politeness must inevitably be informed by research and methods in conversation analysis and ethnomethodology.

Finally, a paper by Pilar Blitvich (2010) offers a useful reflection on issues facing researchers more generally in the post-Brown and Levinson era of politeness. Alongside outlining a genre-based approach to impoliteness that arguably complements other discursive approaches, Blitvich considers various outstanding issues, including the place of speaker intentions, norms, face, identity, emotions, and terminological debates that continue to dog the field.

4   Politeness as social practice

4.1   Introduction

One of the most important findings in politeness research to date is that politeness does not reside in particular behaviours or linguistic forms, but rather in *evaluations* of behaviours and linguistic forms. This means that politeness is always situated: in particular institutional, interpersonal or public contexts, in certain interaction types or genres, as well as in particular relational networks. It also means that politeness is crucially dependent on the understanding of the participants themselves. Another key finding has been that evaluations of politeness can vary across individuals, even when they are – at least nominally – from the same social group. This variability, and the moral implications of such evaluations, means that politeness is inherently *argumentative*. In other words, people don't always agree about what is polite, impolite and so on.[1] And not only that, these evaluations can have significant consequences for the parties involved.

Consider example (1), which is from the movie *The Social Network*. Mark and Erica have been talking about Mark's 'obsession' with getting into a 'final club' (i.e. an undergraduate social club) at Harvard University.

(1) Mark: I want to try to be straight forward with you and tell you that I think you might want to be a little more supportive. If I get in I'll be taking you to the events, and the gatherings and you'll be meeting a lot of people you wouldn't normally get to meet.
Erica: You would do that for me?
Mark: We're dating.
Erica: Okay, well I want to try and be straightforward with you and let you know that we're not any more.
Mark: What do you mean?
Erica: We're not dating any more, I'm sorry.
Mark: Is this a joke?
Erica: No, it's not.
Mark: You're breaking up with me?

Erica: You're going to introduce me to people I wouldn't normally have the chance to meet? What the fff – What is that
supposed to mean?

Mark: Wait, settle down.

Erica: What is it supposed to mean?

[omitted section]

Mark: All I meant is that you're not likely to, currently, I wasn't
making a comment on your parents – I was just saying you
go to B.U., I was stating a fact, that's all, and if it seemed
rude then of course I apologise.

Erica: I have to go study.

Mark: You don't have to study.

Erica: Why do you keep saying I don't have to study?!

Mark: Because you go to B.U.! ((pause))
Do you want to get some food?

Erica: I'm sorry you're not sufficiently impressed with my education.

Mark: And I'm sorry I don't have a rowboat so we're even.

Erica: I think we should just be friends.

Mark: I don't want friends.

Erica: I was being polite, I have no intention of being friends with
you.

(*The Social Network*, 2005)

It is quite apparent here that Erica has been offended by Mark's remarks at
the beginning of this excerpt. This offence arises from what he has implied
by saying that she'll get to meet a lot of people she wouldn't normally get
to meet if he gets into a final club, namely, that she is not as good as those
people. Erica initially responds sarcastically before going on to say she does
not want to continue dating him. She then explicitly holds him accountable
for what he has implied by asking him 'what is that supposed to mean?',
displaying her apparent anger at his remarks through the prosodic contour of
her responses, as well as through an incompletely uttered 'what the fuck?' It is
obvious that Mark has implied something about Erica, casting her as someone
of a lower social level (than him). What is most interesting is that Mark initially
seems oblivious to the potentially offensive implications of his remarks. As it
becomes obvious to him that Erica is indeed offended, he moves to clarify what
he meant and to apologise. However, his apology is qualified in that he only
recognises that she might have thought he was being 'rude', but he maintains his
'intended' meaning: that she will get to meet better people than those at Boston
University (B.U.) is simply a 'fact', and thus presumably not offensive. Erica,
however, does not accept his apology, and says she wants to leave and that they

should just be 'friends'. When Mark responds that he is not interested in being friends with her, Erica claims that what she really meant was that she no longer wants to date him, and that talk of being friends was just for the sake of being 'polite'.

In this brief excerpt, then, Mark and Erica have not evaluated his initial remarks in the same way. On the one hand, Erica is upset and offended and moves to break up with Mark. On the other hand, Mark is initially oblivious to the offensive implications of his remarks, and then maintains they are only potentially offensive because Erica 'misunderstood' him. They also do not have the same understanding of what Erica means by saying that they should just be 'friends'. For Erica, this is a 'polite' way of breaking up with someone because it draws from a recurrent practice or convention for doing just that, a point which Mark appears to miss. Even between two people from the same culture (mainstream white Americans), with a similar background as college students in the north east of the US, engaging in a joint activity (dating), then, there is no apparent agreement about what is polite or rude. The perceived rudeness or offensiveness of Mark's remarks from Erica's perspective has very real-world consequences in that it leads to the end of their relationship, although Mark is apparently left somewhat bewildered as to why she is so offended. Of course, we, the audience, are positioned to judge Mark as the 'strange' one who does not know how to interact appropriately with girls. But there's no guarantee, even though it is likely, that everyone watching this scene would evaluate Mark's behaviour in the same way. We as the audience know what we are supposed to think of Mark, but that does not mean that is what everyone really does think. After all, what we think of the fictional character Mark may be influenced by what we think of the real living person he is supposed to be based on (Mark Zuckerberg, the founder and CEO of Facebook).

There are at least two points that follow from examining example (1). First, we can see evidence of variability and argumentativity in evaluations of politeness on two levels here: on one level, between Mark and Erica; on a second level, between the audience and the writers or creators of this film. This is important to note, because when we are studying politeness we are in many cases like an audience. We're not in the same position as the participants themselves in evaluating particular situated behaviour as polite, impolite and so on. We as analysts thus need to distinguish our own evaluations of politeness (which follow from forming our own understandings of an interaction), and those of the participants themselves, a point which has been emphasised in the distinction between first-order and second-order understandings of politeness (see Chapter 3). Second, it is obvious not only from what Erica says and implies here, but also from Erica's facial expressions and tone of voice (if you watch the actual clip from the movie), that she has been offended by Mark's remarks. In other words, evaluations of politeness do not reside only in what people say.

They are more often than not embodied in prosody, facial expressions, gestures and the like. Any examination of politeness must therefore at least recognise that it is very often multimodal in nature, even if analysts choose to restrict their analysis to primarily linguistic aspects of discourse and interaction.

These two key points have led to calls to explore the understandings of different participants on politeness from various disciplinary perspectives. Yet while various influential concepts and approaches have been proposed, as we discussed in Chapter 3, there is as yet no clear overarching theoretical framework in which to situate these different understandings or perspectives. In this chapter and the next, we move to offer just such a framework. We begin by outlining an approach, building on the idea that politeness is an evaluation of (verbal and non-verbal) behaviour, which conceptualises politeness as a form of *social practice*. We suggest that any examination of politeness must begin by appreciating that such evaluations are necessarily tied to *social actions* and *meanings* that are recognisable to participants in situated contexts, not 'behaviours' or 'linguistic forms' *per se*.[2] In Section 4.2, we begin by exploring the nature of interpersonal evaluation, and how it lies at the core of our understanding(s) of politeness. We then explain what we mean by social actions and meanings, and why we think politeness is ultimately tied to these as recognisable forms of social practice. In Section 4.3, we discuss how politeness as social practice needs to be situated relative to different understandings of *time*, and the different understandings of social *space* that underpin these evaluative moments of politeness. In Chapter 5, we will then outline a framework for situating these various perspectives on evaluative moments of politeness, suggesting that we need to appreciate there are inevitably multiple ways of understanding politeness.

4.2   Politeness and interpersonal evaluation

While it is widely accepted that politeness involves some kind of evaluation or attitude, as we discussed in Chapter 3, the notion of evaluation itself has not been carefully theorised in politeness research. Apart from a few important exceptions, such as in the work of Mills (2003) on gender and politeness (see Chapter 11), interpersonal evaluations have been remarkably understudied. While Eelen (2001), for instance, was emphatic in arguing that (im)politeness always involves evaluative moments, he did not offer any clear theorisation of interpersonal evaluations as such. To a large extent it has been simply taken for granted that evaluations by speakers and hearers – however they might be understood – are what give rise to politeness, impoliteness and the like.

Any attempt to understand interpersonal evaluations in relation to politeness must, however, start by considering a number of complex issues. These include questions relating to:

- the *scope* of interpersonal evaluations (i.e. what constitutes an *interpersonal* evaluation?)
- the *source* of interpersonal evaluations (i.e. who does the evaluating?)
- the *temporal locus* of interpersonal evaluations (i.e. how and when do interpersonal evaluations arise?)
- the *normative* basis of interpersonal evaluations (i.e. on what moral grounds do interpersonal evaluations arise)
- the *sociocognitive* locus of interpersonal evaluations (i.e. how do social and cognitive processes intersect in giving rise to interpersonal evaluations?)

In this section, we will start by focusing on just the first question. The other issues will be addressed in subsequent sections of this chapter, and the chapters that follow.

We can start to tease out what we mean by interpersonal evaluations by first considering how *evaluation* and *attitude* are ordinarily defined. According to the Merriam-Webster Online Dictionary (www.merriam-webster.com, 2012), an evaluation is broadly defined as the action of 'judg[ing] the value or condition of (someone or something) in a careful and thoughtful way', while an attitude is defined as 'the way you think and feel about someone or something' or 'a feeling or way of thinking that affects a person's behaviour'. Evaluations and attitudes are thus closely related in that 'the act of judging or assessing a person or situation or event' (an *evaluation*) is thought to generate ways of thinking and feeling about those people, situations and events (an *attitude*). An *interpersonal* evaluation or attitude is restricted to appraisals or assessment of persons, or our relationships with those persons, which influence the way we think and feel about those persons and relationships, and consequently sometimes what we do.

From a lay or folk understanding of *evaluation* and *attitude*, then, we can draw out four key dimensions of interpersonal evaluations:

(i) persons and relationships
(ii) categorisation
(iii) valency
(iv) normative frame of reference

In other words, interpersonal evaluations involve casting persons and relationships into certain valenced categories according to some kind of perceived normative scale or frame of reference.

What makes interpersonal evaluations interpersonal in the first instance is that they are directed at **persons** and **relationships**. A *person* can be conceptualised as an individual in a social environment, and is thus a socially defined concept. This allows for the fact that while biologically we are all cognitively autonomous individuals, persons in an interpersonal sense are conceptualised differently across different social groups. For example, in some societies a person is conceptualised as an independent monad (an independent social unit). In other societies, a person is conceptualised as a node located in a web of interpersonal connections. In other words, one cannot talk about one individual without considering those close to him or her. These two understandings of 'person' reflect different ways of conceptualising persons amongst mainstream Anglo-North Americans and Chinese respectively. But there are many variations on this theme across different kinds of social groups. In other words, there is an important link between the conceptualisations of persons and the relational networks through which they are constituted (see also Chapter 11). A *relationship*, following Arundale, can be conceptualised as 'establishing and maintaining of connection between two otherwise separate individuals' (2010a): 138). Once again, this allows for the different ways in which connection and separation themselves can be understood across various social groups. Most importantly, these different conceptualisations of persons and relationships are highly consequential for understanding interpersonal evaluations. For example, in some cases, how one person is evaluated does not impact on those with whom he or she is closely connected. In other cases, evaluating one person can also entail evaluations of other persons with whom he or she is closely connected. At the core of interpersonal evaluations, then, lie our conceptualisations of persons and relationships.

Categorisation naturally involves categories. But what do we mean by *categories* in an interpersonal sense? In summarising work by the ethnomethodologist Harvey Sacks (1992) on membership categorisation analysis, Emanuel Schegloff defines categories as

the store house and the filing system for the common-sense knowledge that ordinary people – that means *all* people in their capacity as ordinary people – have about what people are like, how they behave, etc. This knowledge is stored and accessed by reference to categories of member/person. (2007b: 469)

To this, we would add categories of relationship. Categorisation thus involves commonsense or ordinary knowledge we have about persons, and how we expect them to behave in the context of those relationships. This goes beyond prototypical persons (such as babies and mothers) to include specific persons (such as 'my son' or 'my wife'). For example, in some societies persons are expected to apologise for transgressions on the part of other persons with whom they share a close familial relationship (not only children, but also partners and the like), while in others they are not obligated to apologise (although they may of course do so).

Interpersonal evaluations involve not just any kind of categorisation, but rather categorisations that are valenced. **Valency** is generally thought to be positive when it involves attraction and negative when it involves aversion. In some cases it may be neutral when it involves neither attraction nor aversion. Valency thus refers to various scales ranging from good to bad, appropriate to

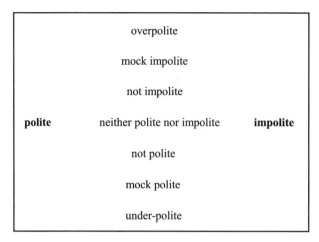

Figure 4.1 Politeness-related evaluators in English.

inappropriate, like to dislike and so on. This means that valency is inevitably emotively charged. Some person or relationship categories, such as babies or mothers, can be positively valenced (although a particular mother might be valenced negatively for some individuals), while others are generally negatively valenced, such as criminals or arseholes (although once again particular categorisations of individuals might be valenced positively). In relation to politeness, there is also a range of valenced categorisations, some of which are represented in Figure 4.1. Here we have summarised just some of the possible politeness-related **evaluators** (at least in English in the first instance).[3] The point we are trying to make here is that there are a lot of ways of evaluating that do not fall straightforwardly into being labelled either 'polite' and 'impolite'. These include being 'overpolite' or 'under-polite', 'mock impolite' or 'mock polite', 'not impolite', 'not polite' or 'neither polite nor impolite' and many other gradations between. When we talk about politeness in this book, then, we are referring to this whole range of possible politeness-related evaluators. What is important to note, however, is that these evaluators are not consistently valenced as either positive, negative or neutral. While 'polite' is often thought to be positively valenced, and 'overpolite' to be negatively valenced, these valencies can be reversed in specific, situated interactions.

Consider the following experience of a politeness scholar visiting Britain who was having trouble getting a drink at a local pub. After failing to get the barman's attention through various attempted 'sorries', 'excuse-mes' and 'pardon-mes', a local told him that he needed 'cut the crap' and simply 'state loudly and clearly what [he] wanted'. At that point he was immediately served.

(2) As the evening progressed I got to talk to my saviour, whose name was Andy.
I explained what I did for a living, and that I was on my way to Lancaster to begin my study on politeness in the BNC. He proceeded to give me his own theory on politeness: to him it was just another form of dishonesty, either used by 'wankers' who did not dare deliver a straight and honest message (he was probably indirectly referring to me and my rather pathetic attempts to order a drink), or by 'slimy bastards' whose mild manners concealed some devious ulterior motive.
He was, on the whole, rather suspicious of polite people.

(Deutschmann 2003: 23–4)

While example (2) is just an anecdote, it does illustrate that being evaluated as *polite* is not necessarily always a good thing. In particular, it illustrates how evaluations of what counts as *polite* can relate to (perceived) membership in different social classes (see Chapter 11). Thus, while it might be tempting to intuitively position some of these other evaluators as lying closer to either the 'polite' or 'impolite' evaluators, or as inherently positively or negatively valenced, we have not done so here simply because the valence of all of these evaluators is very often determined through the locally situated evaluative moments in which they arise. It also allows for the inevitable differences in the *content* of analogous 'politeness' evaluators across languages and social groups (see Chapter 9).

The final key dimension of interpersonal evaluations is that they involve some kind of **normative frame of reference**: the perception that others from the same social group would evaluate a person or relationship in the same way. While politeness research has traditionally located normative understandings at the level of society or culture, there has, more recently, been a move to locate them relative to more tightly focused social groups. Here we take this a step further. We suggest that normative understandings can be situated relative to *any* social unit, ranging from dyads and relatively closed relational networks (such as families or groups of close friends), through to a localised grouping such as a workplace or community group, through to larger and thus inevitably more diffuse societal or cultural groups. We are not claiming that all these different social units are equally influential in evaluative moments of politeness. Rather, we are pointing out that evaluations of politeness involve not only a high level or abstract societal or cultural frame of reference (see Chapter 11), but can also involve the relational histories of those persons (or groups of persons) involved. We will explore these issues further in Chapter 5.

Figure 4.2 Politeness and evaluation. (*Peanuts* ©1965 Peanuts Worldwide LLC. Distributed by UNIVERSAL UCLICK. Reprinted with permission. All rights reserved.)

4.3 Politeness and social practice

In this section, we extend the idea that politeness arises through *evaluations* of behaviours and linguistic forms by proposing that politeness is itself a kind of social practice. Let us begin by considering the interaction from the comic *Peanuts* in Figure 4.2. Obviously Charlie Brown is offended by Lucy's questions here, as he explicitly labels her remarks as 'rude'; more specifically, he implies that Lucy herself is 'rude' in making these remarks. But what gives rise to this evaluation? Why does Charlie Brown think her questions are 'rude'?

The answer lies, in part, in the last frame of Figure 4.2. Lucy ponders on the fact that in her experience criticising others inevitably leads to being criticised by those others. In doing so, she attributes Charlie Brown's evaluation of her questions as 'rude' to his perception that she was *criticising* him. In asking 'Why do you suppose you do this?', Lucy is not only casting Charlie Brown as someone who 'talks loudly' but also implying that this is not a good thing. In other words, she implies that he sometimes talks too loudly when he gets excited, and criticises him for it. This criticism is a form of **social action**. It is an understanding of what Lucy is *doing* through this talk that is jointly formed by her and Charlie Brown through the course of this interaction. The criticism, in turn, is necessarily directed at something, some kind of *information* or *object*, and arises through particular types of **meaning representation**, here involving both *what is said* ('You have a tendency to talk loudly when you get excited, don't you Charlie Brown?) and *what is implied* (something like 'you talk too loudly' or 'it's annoying') (see Chapter 2). The latter is a form of **pragmatic meaning**, that is, where Lucy is held to be committed to or accountable for meaning something by what she has said (see Haugh 2013b). In other words, we can see that Charlie Brown is offended by Lucy's criticism and that Lucy is aware of this offence as arising due to this perceived criticism. It is thus the social action of criticism and the content of that criticism (i.e. the associated pragmatic meaning), that here occasions an evaluation of 'rudeness' on Lucy's part in Charlie Brown's view.

However, not only do social actions and meanings lead to, or occasion, evaluations of politeness, impoliteness and so on, but such evaluations may themselves occasion evaluative social actions and meanings. Lucy herself points this out when she bemoans that 'we critical people are always being criticized!' In other words, Charlie Brown's interpretation of her remarks as criticism, and his evaluation of this criticism as 'rude', occasions, in turn, an evaluative social action on his part: namely, an implied criticism of Lucy as someone who asks 'rude' questions. There's no evidence here as to whether Lucy evaluates Charlie Brown's criticism of her as 'rude' or at least 'not polite', but she may well do so.

Politeness is a social practice in one sense, then, because it involves evaluations *occasioned* by social actions and meanings that are *recognisable to participants*. In some cases, these evaluations may also be *reflexively occasioned*. In saying these social actions and meanings are 'recognisable to participants' we are alluding to the fact that social actions and meanings necessarily draw on normative practices, ways of formulating talk and conduct that are understood by participants as doing and meaning certain things. In other words, we know – not only Charlie Brown and Lucy but also we the readers – that Lucy is criticising Charlie Brown here because asking someone for an account of a habitual behaviour on their part is a recognisable practice for criticising others (at least in English, although not necessarily in other languages). What is meant here by 'reflexively occasioned' is that not only can evaluations of politeness and the like be occasioned by social actions and meanings, but also that evaluations of politeness and so on may in themselves occasion evaluative social actions and meanings.

However, an analysis of politeness as social practice does not end there. The answer as to why Charlie Brown thinks her questions are 'rude' also lies, in part, in the way in which Charlie *formulates* his response to her question. He first responds that he does not know, and then offers an account for this lack of a specific answer; namely, that he has never been asked such a question, thereby indicating he has never thought about it before. The specific formulation of this account is important in two ways. First, he uses the account to *categorise* the prior criticism as 'rude'. Second, he formulates it at a more *generalised level* in saying that no one has ever criticised him like that before because they are not 'rude enough'. In generalising this categorisation of the criticism as 'rude' in this way, Charlie Brown is implicitly appealing to broader norms, namely, what everyone knows: criticising people in this way is 'rude'. This generalised level of the formulation of his account contrasts with the specific, locally situated context of Lucy's question. There is thus an implied contrast between Lucy and 'everyone else'. If others are not 'rude enough' to say such things, then this implies Lucy herself is rude. Importantly though, in formulating this categorisation at a more generalised level, Charlie Brown is implicitly claiming this is common, everyday knowledge (in the sense that everyone knows that). In other words, Charlie Brown's evaluation of Lucy's criticism of him as 'rude' is not just his own idiosyncratic evaluation, but rather is one rooted in a broader **moral order**. We know this because we, the readers, can also readily understand how Charlie Brown is evaluating Lucy's initial remarks here.

The moral order refers to what members of a sociocultural group or relational network 'take for granted', or what the ethnomethodologist Harold Garfinkel (1964, 1967) referred to as the '"seen but unnoticed", expected, background features of everyday scenes' (1967: 35–6). This background to interpretation and evaluation is not just a matter of common knowledge, but lies at the core of what social actions and meanings members think are appropriate/inappropriate, good/bad, polite/impolite and so on. It is not simply that we tend to expect certain things in the talk and conduct of others and ourselves in interaction, but that members regard such 'familiar scenes of everyday affairs' to be familiar scenes 'because it is morally right or wrong that they are so' (Garfinkel 1967: 35). An evaluation of politeness or impoliteness thus always involves an implicit appeal to the moral order, or to be more accurate, an appeal to a moral order perceived to be in common amongst two or more participants by at least one of those participants.

Another crucial point that Garfinkel made is that the 'seen but unnoticed' expectations that constitute that moral order are both 'socially standardised and standardising' (1967: 36). This means they are not simply norms that somehow afford or constrain the behaviour of members, but rather are the means by which one makes a claim to be a member of society in the first place. In other words, not only do practices depend on these expectations in order to be recognisable to members and thus accessible as interpretative resources, but also that as members continually engage in such practices in their everyday interactions they both sustain the moral order, and over time act to change it. Most importantly, Garfinkel did not regard these 'seen but unnoticed' expectations as something to be simply assumed by the analyst, but rather something that constitutes an important object of study in its own right. This is because, while members are demonstrably 'responsive to this background', since they are generally taken for granted, such expectations are very often difficult for members to explicitly articulate.

Garfinkel started work on exploring this underlying moral order through his now infamous 'breaching experiments', a method whereby one starts with familiar scenes and asks 'what can be done to make trouble' (p. 37) in order to tap into the 'seen but unnoticed' expectations of the moral order. For instance, example (3) was reported by one of his students, who was asked to observe and note down responses when they pressed others for further clarification of standard, commonsense remarks or questions.

>(3) S: How are you?
>
>E: How am I in regard to what? My health, my finances, my school work, my peace of mind, my . . . ?
>
>S: ((red in the face and out of control)) Look! I was just trying to be polite. Frankly, I don't give a damn how you are.
>
> (Garfinkel 1967: 44)

Responses to someone questioning these commonsense activities were often remarkably extreme, as seen in example (3). To question the 'commonsense-ness' of such remarks or questions was regarded by the unwitting participants in the experiments as questioning the very basis of their social reality, and was thus treated as a moral transgression. It is interesting to note that the 'how are you?' routine is treated here as a matter of 'just trying to be *polite*', thereby also alluding to a certain lack of sincerity in asking the question but not seeking a full and extended response from the addressee, although notably not a lack of sincerity in regard to the relational implications of the routine. In other words, what example (3) indicates is that commonsense expectations in relation to the 'how are you?' routine are that it is not necessarily intended to elicit extended or detailed responses, but rather that it meets expectations of what counts as *polite* within the context of this particular moral order.

Other useful insights into the moral order – at least in mainstream white American society at that time – were found from breaching experiments where students were asked to act out the assumption they were boarders in their own homes. Once again, in breaching expected, background features of everyday scenes, the students quite often occasioned rather vitriolic responses. Garfinkel reported that:

family members were stupefied. They vigorously sought to make the strange actions intelligible and to restore the situation to normal appearances. Reports were filled with accounts of astonishment, bewilderment, shock, anxiety, embarrassment, and anger and with charges by various family members that the student was mean, inconsiderate, selfish, nasty, or impolite. Family members demanded explanations. (1967: 47)

In example (4), an exchange reported by a student, his father attempted to normalise his son's previous actions by offering a plausible account for it.

>(4) Father: Your mother is right. You don't look well and you're not talking sense. You had better get another job that doesn't require such late hours.
>
>Son: I appreciate the consideration but I feel fine and just want a bit of privacy.

Father: I don't want any more of *that* out of *you* and if you can't
treat your mother decently you'd better move out!

(Garfinkel 1967: 48)

The son's rejection of his father's attempt to normalise their relationship through
continuing to respond to his father as if he were the landlord is treated as a
serious moral transgression by his father. What is notable here is that ostensibly
polite behaviour, at least what would be regarded as *polite* if one were a boarder
at that time, is treated as highly offensive by his parents (although, of course,
not every family responded in exactly the same way).

Politeness thus does not involve just any kind of (idiosyncratic) interpersonal
evaluation, but one that is rooted in the practices that constitute the moral
order of those members. It is in this second sense that politeness can also be
conceptualised as a social practice. In other words, politeness can be captured as
social practice because (1) evaluations of politeness are (reflexively) occasioned
by social actions and meanings that are recognisable through the fact they are
practices in themselves, and (2) evaluations of politeness involve appeals to a
moral order, not idiosyncratic standards. Yet in implicitly involving an appeal to
the moral order, and the practices that give rise to it, evaluations of politeness
are thereby open to dispute, because members of different groups, or even
members of the same group, do not necessarily always perceive the moral
order in the same way.

Take the case of moral basis of 'complaining', for instance. Complaining
about third parties (in English at least) is prototypically associated with evaluations of impoliteness in that it orients to some kind of 'impropriety' on the
part of the target of the complaint. As the conversation analyst Paul Drew
points out, 'an instance of conduct is not self-evidently, intrinsically, or inherently morally reprehensible as being a transgression, impropriety, offense, fault,
insult, unjustified accusation' (1998): 322). A complaint about others thus generally involves talk where the moral character of the conduct (whether it be
verbal or non-verbal) is constituted through that talk itself. Therefore, in order
to find fault in others – and so build grounds for making a complaint – the
speaker needs to invoke some kind of 'normative standard(s) that the other's
behaviour has transgressed' (p. 303). This means that complaints about others
involve implicit appeals to the moral order. It is this appeal to the moral order
that underlies the prototypical assumption in the case of complaints about
the conduct of others that the 'complainable impropriety involves a kind of
rudeness or offensiveness' (p. 303).

Consider the interaction in example (5), where Lisa is offering an account
for why she does not want to pick up Edna to take her to church this week. The
example begins with the formulation of a complainable, that is, a matter about

which a complaint can be made, namely, that Edna asked Lisa to take her home straightaway thereby forcing Lisa to make an extra trip.[4]

> (5) (Three friends, Bob, Lisa and Tom are talking while playing computer games and studying)
> 24 Lisa: like last week she made me take her home straightaway after the service. So I had to leave and then c[ome back.]
> 25 Bob: [Come back.]
> 26   (brief pause)
> 27 Tom: Oh
> 28 Lisa: And just- she's just really doesn't think of anyone but herself.
>   . . .
> 37 Lisa: She's just really oblivious to social etiquette.
> 38 Tom: Oh yeah.

Having formulated the complainable, Lisa then makes a recognisable complaint (that she 'doesn't think of anyone but herself') by implying that Edna does not think of others, or, in other words, does not show consideration for others. What is notable about this complaint is that it is formulated, just like Charlie Brown in Figure 4.2, at a more generalised level than the locally situated context of the complainable. In being formulated in this way, Lisa invokes an aspect of the moral order, namely the understanding of members that 'not thinking of anyone but oneself' is a bad thing, and members should know this. Lisa subsequently categorises this impropriety as a breach of 'social etiquette' in casting Edna as someone who is 'really oblivious to social etiquette', and thus 'not polite' or even 'impolite'. Notably, while the other participants do not strongly *align* with Lisa's complaint here by making some kind of assessment, and nor do they express strong agreement (i.e. *affiliate*) with her stance that Edna's behaviour constitutes an impropriety that reflects her lack of understanding of 'social etiquette', they do not challenge it either. In other words, it is tacitly accepted by Tom and Bob as consistent with their understandings of the underlying moral order to which Lisa's complaint appeals. Here we can observe an instance of a social action (a complaint) and meaning (the object of that complaint) being occasioned by a prior evaluation of someone else's conduct, namely, a breach of social etiquette. In other words, the complaint is occasioned by a prior evaluation of someone's behaviour as 'not polite' or even 'impolite'.

Of course, no social action or meaning occasions evaluations of politeness, impoliteness and so on as a matter of course. Complaining is not always about improprieties or breaches of etiquette. In some cases, complaining about things (whether about events, situations or even other people) can even play a part in establishing a sense of relational connection between participants. In example (6), in which two female neighbours are engaging in a form of 'mutual complaining', the complaints actually offer the other person a chance to affiliate with the complaint by expressing their concern or empathy for the person doing the complaining.

(6) June: Hi, how are you doing?
    Mary: Boy, can you believe how hot it's been?
    June: Amazing, isn't it? And I'm just returning from a four-mile walk. Look at me. ((pointing to perspiration on shirt))
    Mary: I've had such a bad headache since the beginning of this heat wave, and my allergies don't help things much.
    June: Yeah, I can imagine how that feels.

(Boxer 1993: 106)

In engaging in a sequence of complaining followed by affiliating with the complaint where they swap the roles of the one complaining and the one aligning with the complaint, June and Mary are implicitly invoking the moral order. This time, however, the expectation that the other person will affiliate with the complaint involves a specific practice, namely, expressing empathy or concern. Since not responding with such an expression of empathy or concern is a morally accountable matter – that is, it would presumably be 'not polite' to withhold a display of empathy or concern – it is evident that these mutually complaining sequences can occasion evaluations of politeness, although the participants do not explicitly comment as such. Thus, as Haugh (2007c) argues, evaluations of politeness can arise through the adjacent placement of expressions that display reciprocation of concern. The mutual complaining in example (6) thus arguably occasions 'seen but unnoticed' evaluations of politeness (see also Chapter 9).

Our conceptualisation of politeness as social practice – as an evaluation that is (reflexively) occasioned by social actions and meanings – does not preclude a focus on the various forms that have remained an important area of concern in politeness research (see Chapters 2 and 3). Consider the case of requests prefaced with 'I wonder'-derived expressions (e.g. 'I was wondering if', 'I wonder if'). In a careful study of requests in telephone calls, the conversation analysts Traci Curl and Drew (2008) show that requests formulated using modal verbs (e.g. *could you, would you*) treat the speaker's request as non-contingent, meaning the necessary conditions for granting the request are already met so the request is unproblematic. *I-wonder*-prefaced request formulations, on the other hand, are understood as orienting to specific *contingencies* that might be associated with granting the request. If we compare examples (7) and (8) below, we can see that while the modal verb *could*, which is typical of requests in English, appears in both, in the case of example (8), the *I-wonder*-prefaced request involves a clear orientation to the contingencies of granting that request.

> (7) Field SO88:2:8:1
> 1 Lesley: Hello?
> 2   (0.3)
> 3 Gordon: It's Gordon.
> 4 Lesley: oh Gordon. Shall I ring you back darling,
> 5 Gordon: Uh no y- I don't think you can,
> 6   (0.3)
> 7 Gordon: But uh just to (0.3) say, could you bring up a
> 8   letter. When you come up
> (adapted from Curl and Drew 2008: 137)

> (8) Field:2:2:1
> 1 Lesley: and ordered a book [and you said you'd hold
> 2 Jon: [yeah
> 3 Lesley: it for me
> 4   And I was supposed to be coming in around Easter
> 5   well I haven't managed to get in and I wonder if you
> 6   could send it to me if you've still got it
> (adapted from Curl and Drew 2008: 141)

In example (7), Gordon's request is non-contingent in that he does not orient to any particular pre-conditions – or what are termed 'felicity conditions' in speech act theory (Chapter 2) – for making a request that is not yet fulfilled. In other words, there is nothing in the formulation of Gordon's request to indicate that he thinks there is any reason why Lesley cannot grant it (albeit not immediately). However, in example (8), where Lesley is calling up a bookshop to request they send a book out to her that she previously ordered, the *I-wonder* prefacing constitutes a kind of discursive resource (Thornborrow 2002) for making requests. That is, a pre-existing pattern used in recurrent ways that are recognisable to members (see more on these patterns in Chapter 7), by which she indicates an orientation to contingencies that may make granting the request difficult or even impossible, including the book no longer being there. In doing so, she avoids making an implicit claim to having an *entitlement* to have this request fulfilled in contrast to Gordon's request in example (7). In other words, Lesley displays her lack of entitlement to have this request granted by orienting to the contingencies of granting through *I-wonder*-prefacing her request. In this sense, she is invoking the moral order in that entitlements are associated with interpretations of the *social relationship* that holds between persons – in this case, between herself and the person working in the bookshop,

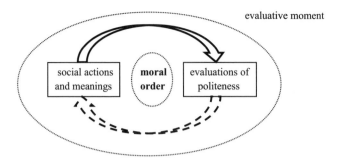

Figure 4.3 Politeness as social practice.

Jon. In other words, by formulating her request in this way using this particular discursive resource, Lesley is implicitly evaluating her relationship with Jon as requiring caution in displaying entitlements. In displaying a lack of entitlement in this case of requesting she is thus occasioning an interpersonal evaluation of politeness vis-à-vis their ongoing relationship.[5]

We have thus far claimed that politeness constitutes a social practice in two key ways. On the one hand, politeness involves evaluations which are occasioned by social actions and meanings that are recognisable through the fact they are practices in themselves. These evaluations also have the potential to reflexively occasion evaluative social actions and meanings. In other words, social actions and meanings may themselves be occasioned by such evaluations. On the other hand, politeness involves implicit appeals to the moral order, which is constituted through practices by which social actions and meanings are made recognisable as 'familiar scenes of everyday affairs' and thus open to moral evaluation (e.g. as good/bad, appropriate/inappropriate, polite/not polite, impolite/not impolite and so on). This view of politeness as social practice that arises through evaluative moments is summarised in Figure 4.3.

In treating politeness as a social practice, then, we have made the point that we do not think something or someone is polite, impolite and so on because of a particular behaviour on their part, or because they have used a particular linguistic form *per se*. Instead, it is because we evaluate the *social action or meaning* we interpret as arising through this (embodied) talk and conduct as polite, impolite and so on. The content of these evaluations, and the social actions and meanings through which they arise (and they themselves give rise to), should thus be the starting point for empirical studies of politeness.

4.4   Politeness and time

In characterising politeness as a social practice it is clear that it needs to be situated, first of all, relative to time, a concept that we treat in the present volume as critical for situating understandings of politeness. It is important to understand that in doing so, however, there are different ways of understanding time. In this section, we introduce different perspectives on conceptualising time that are particularly salient to understanding politeness as social practice. The first understanding of time relates to the **here-and-now** of an evaluative moment of politeness, as captured in Figure 4.3: how particular social actions and meanings are evaluated vis-à-vis politeness in the very moment in which those social actions and meanings arise through interaction. This will be subsequently contrasted with time in the sense of the there-and-then.

It is important to appreciate, however, that even a basic conceptualisation of time in the here-and-now necessarily involves more than one way of perceiving time. In politeness research to date, time in the here-and-now has generally involved an understanding of time as **punctuated**. In other words, politeness has been treated as a discrete, independent evaluative moment on the part of either the speaker or the hearer. In practice, this involves evaluating each utterance or turn at talk vis-à-vis politeness.

However, time in the here-and-now can also be understood in the sense of a current moment of talk being constrained and afforded by prior and subsequent talk, or what Garfinkel calls the 'retrospective–prospective sense of a present occurrence' (1967): 41). On this view of time, evaluations of a particular utterance of turn at talk vis-à-vis politeness are invariably situated relative to prior evaluations and those evaluations that follow. Inevitably those evaluations that arise contiguously – that is, adjacently – tend to be most tightly interlinked, but the retrospective–prospective sense of a present occurrence can, of course, go beyond adjacent turns at talk. This is an understanding of time in the here-and-now as **emergent**.

To better understand what we mean by these two senses of time in the here-and-now – namely, time as punctuated and time as emergent – consider example (9). Michael (one of the authors of this book) is staying at Sirl's house on holiday in London and Michael is going out sightseeing that day. Sirl and Michael have just met outside the bathroom in the morning.

> (9) 1 S: What time are you leaving this morning?
> 2 M: Oh, in about an hour I suppose. Are you in a hurry to leave?
> 3 S: No, no. Just asking.
> 4   (2 second pause)
> 5 M: Would you like to use the bathroom first?
> 6 S: Yeah, sure, if you don't mind.

(adapted from Haugh 2007a: 94)

Sirl's initial inquiry in turn 1 might be interpreted as a pre-request in that it constitutes a preparatory condition for making a request to use the bathroom first, and Michael subsequently leaves open the possibility that Sirl may wish to make such a request in turn 2 in his response. Sirl's utterance in turn 1 is therefore open to evaluation as 'polite', since he is orienting to high contingency and relatively low entitlement in making a request: recognising it is a matter of delicacy for Sirl to request outright to use the bathroom first given he is the host. Michael's response is also open to evaluation as 'polite', through an adjacent display of an orientation to the currently invoked contingencies of making that request. However, Sirl does not go on to make the request to use the bathroom in turn 3. Instead, he treats his first utterance as simply a request for information. Sirl's second utterance (in turn 3) is also open to evaluation as 'polite' given he appears to abandon the request to use the bathroom first, apparently in a display of deference to Michael (who implied he might be in a hurry to leave given he has raised this as a specific contingency). However, the marked pause after Sirl's counter-response indicates that something has been left unsaid. In turn 5, Michael thus makes an offer to Sirl that he use the bathroom first, thereby treating Sirl's utterance in turn 1 as being 'pre' to soliciting an offer from Michael to use the bathroom first. In other words, Michael reinterprets Sirl's first utterance as attempting to get Michael to offer that Sirl use the bathroom first, and so this plausibly counts as an instance of soliciting an offer rather than requesting. In making a pre-emptive offer, albeit a couple of turns late, this utterance is open to evaluation as 'polite', given it reciprocates concern for Sirl's position as a host unwilling to ask a guest to wait for the bathroom. The subsequent acceptance of this offer by Sirl in turn 6 ratifies Michael's retrospective interpreting of this prior turn. Since soliciting an offer orients to a lower degree of entitlement, this turn is also open to evaluation as 'polite'. From the perspective of a punctuated view of time, then, each turn at talk here is plausibly open to evaluation as 'polite'.

However, when considered from the perspective of time as emergent, a somewhat different analysis of evaluations of politeness arises. The critical moment here is when Sirl pauses in turn 4. Through this interactionally marked pause Sirl indicates his possible dissatisfaction with Michael's response in turn 2. In other words, while Sirl *says* he does not want to use the bathroom first, he *implies* (through pausing) that in fact he may indeed want to use the bathroom first. By not *saying* he wants to use the bathroom, he avoids being held accountable for requesting to use the bathroom. This leaves Michael with the option of either pretending to not notice this implication (which could be evaluated as 'impolite' or at least 'inattentive' to the needs of Sirl), or responding to it by pre-emptively offering that Sirl use the bathroom first. In other words, Michael is left with the choice of looking potentially impolite, or having to let Sirl use the bathroom first without Sirl needing to be held accountable for making such a request. The question, then, is whether soliciting an offer in this way is 'polite'. From Michael's perspective, at least, it was 'not polite', largely because acknowledgement of the high contingency/low entitlement of a request to use the bathroom first was ultimately by-passed through the course of this sequence by securing a pre-offer from Michael. The emergent evaluation of the social actions and meanings that ultimately arose here as 'not polite', at least on Michael's part, is not consistent with the punctuated evaluations of each social action and meaning as 'polite' in the above analysis. This contradiction, however, is part and parcel of this particular interaction, because it was this inconsistency that generated the sense of interactional 'jarring' or 'dissonance' (even possibly prototypical 'passive aggressive' behaviour) at play here. We can thus view time in the here-and-now in both ways: either as punctuated points on a continuum or as interleaving spans across a continuum. We will discuss this point in further detail in Chapter 6 when we examine politeness in interaction more closely.

Of course a particular evaluative moment of politeness – or interlinked set of moments – does not arise in a vacuum. It is invariably located vis-à-vis other evaluative moments over time. In other words, we can understand time as **historicity**: the ongoing linking of the here-and-now with the **there-and-then** (i.e. over time), as well as the there-and-then in its own right (i.e. back in time).

There are two main ways in which evaluative moments in the here-and-now are connected with evaluative moments in the there-and-then. First, an evaluative moment of politeness in the here-and-now draws from recurrent evaluative moments of politeness vis-à-vis the moral order. This means that the border between here-and-now and there-and-then is porous because an understanding in the here-and-now is dependent on understandings established through the there-and-then. Many social actions and meanings that are understood in locally situated contexts in fact follow pre-existing patterns. Recall, for instance, Erica's 'I think we should just be friends' in example (1) above, which draws from a recurrent practice people use when breaking up an intimate relationship. It is exactly due to the conventional nature of this utterance that many of us find Mark's reaction to it to be humorous (it seems that Mark belongs to a small minority for whom Erica's utterance does not politely imply that she is breaking up with him). When such utterances are deployed in the here-and-now, the interactants invoke understandings that they have created in the past and so are in some sense 'continuously there'. In other words, we need to see time as also involving a recurrent here-and-now: practices by which social actions and meanings arose in the past there-and-then can be invoked in the here-and-now. Erica's social action of breaking up in example (1) is clearly conventional, and so it represents a situation where an understanding from the there-and-then is embedded in the understanding in the here-and-now of an interaction.

It is important to note, however, that not every utterance is recurrent to the same degree. In other words, the degree of conventionality of an utterance lies on a scalar continuum. Whenever we act according to the moral order we appeal to pre-existing understandings; the main difference between emergent and recurrent understandings is that the latter arise through invoking the there-and-then. Understandings in the here-and-now are thus always potentially subject to influence from understandings in the there-and-then. Certain usages of politeness can become preferred by a society or a relational network within a society, and through recurrence they can become formalised, a process defined as, and extended to **ritualisation** by Kádár (2013). We will discuss these points in further detail in Chapter 7 when we examine politeness and its relationship with convention and ritual.

Second, an evaluative moment of politeness in the here-and-now can interlink with other evaluative moments of politeness vis-à-vis the **relational history** of those participants. After all, an interaction can be conceptualised not only as sequential, adjacently placed turns of talk (the prototypical sense of interaction in the here-and-now), but also as 'turns in an ongoing exchange interspersed with "pauses" of minutes, hours or days' (Sifianou 2012: 1561). We often evaluate (and expect others to evaluate) social actions and meanings in the light of happenings that took place in the past. Indeed, there is a distinct form of politeness which comes into operation through this sense of historicity: its operation presupposes relational history (see Chapter 7).

Relational history forms an important link between the past and the present, as historicity influences evaluations in the here-and-now. It is important to note, however, that historicity has yet another interpretation: there are interactions that are reported to have taken place in the past. Past has a relative value here in the sense that for interactions that are reported, as opposed to those that take place in front of our eyes, it is simply a matter of relativity whether they took place just a few days earlier or centuries ago. We can thus also talk of evaluative moments existing in the there-and-then in their own right, as, for example, in talk about the relational history of people who interacted some time ago in the past. This has its own analytical challenges, which are further discussed in Chapter 8. It is also worth pointing out that relational histories can also play out across relational networks, a perspective we explore further in Chapter 9. However, at this point we only need to note that not only are evaluative moments in the here-and-now connected with evaluative moments in the there-and-then in these two main ways, but also that evaluative moments arise in the there-and-then in their own right.

4.5   Politeness and social space

In characterising politeness as a social practice it is clear that it also needs to be situated relative to space; or, to be more precise, social space. The notion of **field** (*ba* 場 in Japanese; *chang* 場 in Mandarin Chinese) is rather useful in representing what we mean by the social space in which politeness is necessarily always situated. It was first introduced into academic theorisation by the Japanese philosopher Kitaro Nishida (1949), and has since found resonance with the study of complex systems in biology, quantum physics and cognitive science (Ohtsuka 2011; Shimizu 1995). A field in Eastern philosophical thought is essentially a dynamic relational network, which is not only imbued with its own historicity, given that there is no space without time, but is also imbued with ongoing interaction and emerging relationships. These relational networks vary from ongoing relational networks imbued with considerable relational history such as intimate dyadic relationships, families, neighbourhoods, schools and communities, to groups or teams in institutional or organisational environments where relational histories and historicity intersect, through to larger, more diffuse relational networks labelled variously as nations, societies and cultures which are inevitably imbued with historicity. Critically, while these relational networks, and the social practices that constitute them, exist through the ongoing, networked interactions of individuals, they constitute at the same time the discursive means by which individuals define and understand evaluative moments of politeness in the first place.

There are two key important aspects of 'field' as social space that distinguish it from classic accounts of society or norms in politeness research. First, there is the claim that 'the properties of the individual entity cannot be definitely established except in the *ba* ['field'] within which it is situated' (Ohtsuka 2011: 4). What this means for us is that what is experienced as 'individual' and what is experienced as 'social' in the human experience cannot be separated. In other words,

In the human experience, then, not only are individuals qua individuals dependent upon the nexus that is the social, but also the social qua social is dependent on individuals in nexus. What is individual in nature and what is social in nature are fully interdependent, while at the same time, individual phenomena and social phenomena are distinct and functionally contradictory poles of human experience. (Arundale 2009: 40–1)

This is important to note, because it means that we cannot fully understand politeness from the perspective of individual persons who are contributing to ongoing evaluative moments of politeness. We must also, at the same time, examine the 'field' or social space in which these evaluative moments arise. A practical consequence of this is that it is not sufficient to simply ask individuals whether they think something was polite, impolite and so on. Such evaluations must be situated relative to the social space or 'field' in which they arose. Rather than seeing this 'field' as static and fixed, however, what we find is that it involves multiple interpenetrating relational networks that vary in their degree of salience within particular, situated, evaluative moments of politeness.

Second, the field in which politeness as social practice arises is a *complex system*, which means it has both self-organising and emergent properties that go beyond the characteristics of the individual nodes which constitute that relational network. A language is an example *par excellence* of a social phenomenon that emerges through the interactions of individuals. We cannot trace a language to one single person, but rather to the self-organising properties of a complex system that form through ongoing interactions between persons over time and social space. In the same way, we cannot trace politeness as social practice to any single person, but rather to the self-organising emergent properties of a particular relational network over time. This means politeness as social practice is ultimately a characteristic of the complex system as a whole (relational networks), not of its parts (individuals). Yet this complex system cannot arise in the first place without ongoing interactions (whether direct or mediated) between those individuals. Moreover, no individual is fully subordinated to a relational network, as individuals have the opportunity to initiate changes in social practices, albeit depending in part on their place within the relational network. The study of politeness, then, involves understanding how evaluative moments of politeness are situated relative to both persons and relationships/relational networks. We address the way in which understandings of politeness are situated vis-à-vis persons and relational networks in Chapters 9–11.

It is essential, therefore, to acknowledge the relativity of individualism when it comes to evaluations of politeness. As sociological research, such as that of the renowned philosopher Michael Foucault (1973) illustrates, individualism is itself an ideology that we inherit in many societies, with this ideology being spread in various (sometimes aggressive) ways. His point is that social organisations are a natural constraint on individualism in itself, and people in societies or certain networks of societies always act in relation with others, no matter what their claims to being individualistic might be. In an important sense, then, even a seemingly antisocial act presupposes the acknowledgment of social standards, and it is in this sense that politeness is ultimately a socially *constructive* act.

A further reason why individualism is relative is that it is a dominant ideology in only *some* societies and networks. It is necessary to acknowledge that in other societies and networks hierarchy and interdependence, not individualism, underpin perceptions of norms of appropriate behaviour, and these understandings of persons thus influence practices and evaluations of politeness. Moreover, even in seemingly egalitarian societies there are inevitably groups that prefer hierarchical orders, a preference which manifests itself in their social practices. And there are also societies which not only refute the ideology of individualism, but in fact regard individualism itself as a recent 'invention', a point which becomes clear when we consider historical societies that valued power and communality.

Notions such as individualism must therefore be regarded critically and self-reflexively, otherwise researchers are likely to project their own understandings on understandings of politeness that differ culturally or diachronically. For example, let us imagine a medieval nobleman cursing a commoner who crossed the street in front of his horse. Although our immediate reaction might be that the given person is being 'rude', if we take into account the medieval belief that the nobleman is simply more valuable than the commoner, then we can see that his cursing is afforded by his social position, and thus it is unlikely that either the nobleman or the commoner regarded the cursing as rude by default. The relativity of individualism thus necessitates examining every particular evaluation of politeness in a situated way: by examining the field or social space in which it takes place.

As we shall discuss further in Chapter 10, understandings of politeness ultimately draw from conceptualisations of persons-in-relationships, which, in turn, draw from socially constituted understandings of cognition and emotion. And, as we shall see in Chapter 11, understandings of politeness can lie at the heart of the social constitution of both identities and cultures, and thus persons and relational networks are intimately interlinked.

4.6   Summary

In this chapter we have outlined an understanding of politeness as a form of social practice. We have suggested that politeness is thus ultimately located in evaluations of social actions and meanings by persons that are situated relative to both time and social space. However, given we include, but also go beyond, a traditional focus on *linguistic politeness* in conceptualising politeness as social practice, this approach necessarily calls for multidisciplinary perspectives on politeness. In other words, conceptualising politeness as social practice requires an appreciation that there are multiple ways of understanding politeness. It is to this problem of the multiple understandings of politeness, and how to situate them relative to each other, that we now turn in Chapter 5.

5   Understandings of politeness

5.1   Introduction

In Chapter 3 we introduced the distinction between first-order politeness and second-order politeness. A first-order perspective on politeness is generally thought to encompass the understandings of participants or lay users of language. A second-order perspective, in contrast, is thought to encompass a theoretical approach to politeness. However, while the first-order/second-order distinction has been useful in politeness research in stimulating a move to greater diversity in the ways in which we study politeness, this two-way distinction nevertheless masks a number of very different kinds of understandings. It has also been claimed that there are 'first-order' as opposed to 'second-order' approaches to politeness. We reject this kind of simplistic opposition. We suggest that not only does this set up an unproductive tension in the field, it is also a view that neglects the fact that *any* approach to politeness necessarily draws from multiple loci of understanding.

Let us consider for a moment the following interaction from the comedy *Seinfeld*. In example (1) Jerry has just noticed an unusual pen belonging to Jack, who is one of the neighbours in the retirement village where Jerry's parents live.

(1) Jerry: What kind of pen is that?
     Jack: This pen?
     Jerry: Yeah.
     Jack: This is an astronaut pen. It writes upside down. They use this in space.
     Jerry: Wow! That's the astronaut pen. I heard about that. Where did you get it?
     Jack: Oh it was a gift.
     Jerry: Cause sometimes I write in bed and I have to turn and lean on my elbow to make the pen work.
     Jack: Take the pen.
     Jerry: Oh no.

Jack: Go ahead.
Jerry: I couldn't
Jack: Come on, take the pen!
Jerry: I can't take it.
Jack: Do me a personal favour!
Jerry: No, I'm not . . .
Jack: Take the pen!
Jerry: I cannot take it!
Jack: Take the pen!
Jerry: Are you sure?
Jack: Positive! Take the pen!
Jerry: Okay. Thank you very much. Thank you. Gee, boy!
            ('The pen', *Seinfeld*, Season 3, Episode 3, 1991)

In this example, we see an instance of offering occasioned by Jerry showing
an interest in Jack's pen. But this is no ordinary offering, but rather one that is
repeated a number of times using direct imperatives, and which Jerry repeatedly
refuses before finally relenting and accepting Jack's offer. From the perspective
of the stereotyped version of Jewish American culture (see Chapter 11) in which
this scene plays out, these repeated, directly formulated offers are a way for
Jack to show his offer is sincere, while Jerry's repeated refusal is a way to show
his reluctance to accept Jack's offer unless it is truly sincere. It thus constitutes
a kind of recognisable social practice through which evaluations of politeness
are evidently occasioned. However, Jerry's acceptance of Jack's offer of the pen
results in a dispute between Jerry and his father Morty, on the one hand, and
Helen, his mother on the other, as we can see in example (2) which continues
on from example (1).

(2) Helen: (as soon as the door is closed) What did you take his pen
                 for?
       Jerry: What he gave it to me.
       Helen: You didn't have to take it.
       Morty: Oh my God! She's gotta make a big deal out of everything.
       Jerry: He offered it to me.
       Helen: Because you made such a big fuss about it.
       Jerry: I liked it. Should I have said I didn't like it?
       Helen: You shouldn't have said anything. What did you expect
                 him to do?
       Jerry: He could have said: 'Thank you, I like it too' and put it
                 back in his pocket.
       Helen: He loves that pen.
       Morty: Oh come on!

> Helen: He talks about it all the time. Every time he takes it out he goes on and on about how it writes upside down, how the astronauts use it.
>
> Jerry: If he likes it so much, he never should have offered it.
>
> Helen: He didn't think you'd accept.
>
> Jerry: Well, he was wrong.
>
> Helen: I know his wife. She has some mouth on her. She'll tell everyone in the condo now that you made him give you the pen. They're talking about it right now.

What is disputed here is whether Jerry should have accepted Jack's offer to give Jerry his pen. Helen criticises Jerry for taking the pen, arguing he should have never accepted it in the first place. She attributes the offer made by Jack as being a result of Jerry making a 'big fuss' about the pen, and so characterises Jerry as *soliciting* an offer from Jack. Underlying this characterisation there is a cultural assumption at play here, namely, that it is good to share things with others when they indicate they like it. Jerry and Morty, however, reject this interpretation, arguing that Jerry was simply complimenting Jack on his pen, and that if Jack was not truly sincere in making the offer he should not have made it in the first place. At the end of this example Helen worries about what Jack's wife will say to others in the retirement village; particularly that she will tell others that Jerry solicited an offer from Jack, putting Jack in the potentially embarrassing situation of not offering it when it seemed Jerry wanted it. It appears, then, that Jerry and Morty have evaluated Jerry's acceptance of the pen as quite acceptable (i.e. 'polite' or at least 'not impolite'), while Helen has evaluated it as impolite, at least in the eyes of Jack and his wife. Helen is also clearly concerned about the possible repercussions of this evaluation of impoliteness for their relationship with others in the community. What this kind of example shows us is that different understandings of politeness, impoliteness and the like can arise amongst participants.

Because there are multiple ways of understanding politeness we need to start talking of *understandings* of politeness rather than of any single understanding. In this chapter, we thus revisit the first-order/second-order distinction, which we discussed in Chapter 3, and introduce a framework which situates understandings of politeness relative to four key loci of analysis, not just two. Our point is that in order to effectively study politeness we must first begin to appreciate that there are different ways of looking at the same phenomena, and we need to be aware of how these different understandings are situated relative to each other.

One way of understanding the world is from the study of the nature of being, existence or reality, or what is called **ontology**. The word ontology comes from the Greek words ὄντος (*óntos*) and λόγος (*logos*) and literally means 'the study of that which is'. The ontological perspective we take here, namely, a *social realist ontological position*, necessarily assumes there is such a thing as politeness in the first place, and that it forms part of our social reality.

Understanding the world also involves the study of the nature and scope of knowledge, or what is called **epistemology**. The word epistemology comes from the Greek words ἐπιστήμη (*epistēmē*) and λόγος (*logos*), and literally means 'the study of knowing'. An epistemological perspective on politeness is somewhat different in that it involves the question of how we look at the world and make sense of it. Since the notion of politeness is itself a way of making sense of our social world, then an epistemological perspective involves the questions of *how* we come to such understandings in the first place, and importantly *whose* understandings are involved. Our basic position is that such understandings arise in the *interface* of those perceiving the world and the perceived social reality.

What the first-order/second-order distinction points to is that there are two quite different epistemological perspectives we can take in perceiving politeness as part of our presumed social reality: that of the *user* (first-order) and that of the *observer* (second-order). However, given any understanding is necessarily situated within a 'field' (*ba*) – a dynamic relational network which is imbued with its own historicity as well as ongoing interaction and emerging relationships, as we discussed in Chapter 4 – we propose that understandings of politeness are necessarily embedded in the 'field' of that user or observer. In other words, we adopt a *social constructivist* epistemology here, where understandings of politeness are situated relative to the 'field' in which they are perceived.

On the one hand, there is the view of the **participants** themselves: the people who are themselves involved in the evaluative moments through which politeness arises. Of course, human communication has for a long time been supported by various technologies, and we are not restricted to direct, face-to-face communication. Even in historical times there were various *mediated* forms of communication, as we argue in Chapter 8, although with the rise of more recent technologies, mediated communication has become increasingly widespread and influential. In relation to politeness, then, we must also consider the understandings of **metaparticipants**: people whose evaluations of politeness arise through vicariously taking part in the interaction by viewing it on television or on the internet, for instance. Both participant and metaparticipant understandings are first-order in the sense that they involve some kind of *participation* in the evaluative moment.

On the other hand, there is the view of those who *observe* evaluative moments through which politeness arises. The *lay observer* can observe such moments spontaneously in an ad hoc manner. We are all lay observers when it comes to politeness, because we all engage in social interactions with others, both as participants and as metaparticipants. However, there is another, more formalised way of observing that involves more systematic and evidenced interpretations of evaluative moments. An understanding that arises through systematic and evidenced observation is that of an *analyst*. Both lay observer and analyst understandings are second-order in that they involve *observation* rather than participation in the social world.

While the first-order/second-order distinction has generally been held to be between participant and analyst understandings of politeness, we suggest that this neglects a further two loci of understanding. Given evaluations of politeness are inevitably constituted within a 'field', we propose here that an additional first-order loci for understanding politeness that we need to consider is one rooted in the distinction between insiders and outsiders, while an additional second-order loci for understanding politeness that we must take into account is one rooted in the distinction between 'lay explanation' and 'theory'.

In Chapter 4, where we introduced an approach to politeness as social practice, we pointed out that politeness involves implicit appeals by members of a relational network to a moral order in the very evaluative moments in which politeness arises. But what do we mean by the term *member*? A **member** is an individual (or group of individuals) who assumes, or claims, an *insider* perspective on the backgrounded, and generally unnoticed, expectations that constitute a certain moral order. In particular, a member is a person who holds both themselves and others accountable to this moral order. Following the linguistic anthropologist Kenneth Pike (1967), the understandings of insiders are generally termed an emic perspective, and contrasted with the understandings of *outsiders* to a moral order, or what is termed an etic perspective. Emic understandings are not always made explicit, however, and indeed may remain tacit and understood amongst members to the extent they inform social practice. These are both first-order understandings because they each constitute a set of *expectancies* that practically *inform* the very evaluative moments that give rise to politeness.

It is worth noting that in making a distinction between two kinds of first-order perspectives, that between participants and members, we are deliberately opening up a way for analysts to account for the fact that not everyone from the same society necessarily agrees about what counts as polite, impolite and so on in particular, situated interactions. Of course, in many instances the perspectives of a participant and member are co-present in one and the same person. But as we shall see in this chapter, this is not always the case.

Second-order epistemological understandings of politeness also involve explicit accounts or attempts at rationalising the ways in which people are polite, impolite and so on, and how something counts as polite, impolite and so on in the first place. On the one hand, sociocultural accounts of interpersonal phenomena, such as politeness, can be developed and shared amongst ordinary users of a language. These constitute **folk-theoretic** understandings of politeness. Emic (or etic) accounts of politeness that are made explicit amongst members (and sometimes shared with non-members) thus constitute folk-theoretic understandings. On the other hand, explicitly defined and formalised accounts of politeness can be shared amongst scientific observers. **Theoretical** understandings of politeness (or what might be termed *scientific-theoretic* understandings) are thus restricted to a particular group: a community of practice of scientific observers or academics. Theoretical understandings are required – at least ideally – to be constructed in such a way that they can be consistently applied by different scientific observers. Both folk-theoretic and (scientific-) theoretical understandings are second-order in that they involve *conceptualisation* rather than actual participation in the social world.

To summarise, then, from a *user* perspective, there are four inter-related perspectives from which the nature of politeness, as an assumed part of our social reality, can be understood:

(i) *First-order participant:*   Participant understandings
                                  Metaparticipant understandings
(ii) *First-order expectancies:* Emic understandings
                                  Etic understandings

From an *observer* perspective, there are four inter-related ways in which we can account for how we evaluate something to be polite, not polite, impolite and so on in the first place.

(iii) *Second-order observer:*   Lay observer understandings
                                        Analyst understandings
(iv) *Second-order conceptualisation:* Folk-theoretic understandings
                                        Theoretical understandings

There are thus four, not just two as commonly thought, important loci that constitute the first-order/second-order distinction: participation (participant/metaparticipant) and expectancies (emic/etic), (the first-order loci of understanding), and observation (analyst/lay observer) and conceptualisation (theoretical/folk-theoretic) (the second-order loci of understanding). We thus propose a framework that situates understandings of politeness relative to these four key loci of the first-order/second-order distinction.[1] This framework is summarised in Figure 5.1.

We are not suggesting that all of these different loci of understanding are important all of the time. In some cases just a few loci of understanding may be salient. It depends on the nature of the questions being asked, and the nature of the interaction or discourse being observed. But it is also important to realise that one person can have multiple understandings of politeness at the same time. Indeed, if our aim is to grasp the nature of politeness then it is necessary to embrace the idea that we need to be talking more about multiple **understandings** of politeness.

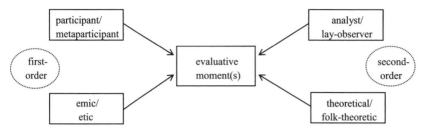

Figure 5.1 Loci of understandings of politeness.

We will now discuss, in turn, each of these four different loci of understandings of politeness in more detail. In particular, we will explain how each of these four different loci in fact encompasses a number of different ways of understanding in and of themselves.

5.2   Participant/metaparticipant understandings

A participant is an individual in interaction who takes up a particular position or perspective in relation to that talk or conduct. We generally first think of speakers and hearers when the question of who participates in interaction arises. However, we use the terms *producer* and *recipient* here, instead of speaker and hearer, to avoid confusion with these commonly used folk terms, as well as to allow that interaction can occur over multiple modes (not just through speech). It is now well known that there are various ways in which individuals – or indeed groups of individuals – can position themselves in relation to producing, interpreting and evaluating talk or conduct. These different positionings or alignments are what Goffman (1979, 1981) called *participation status*.

One key distinction that can be made in relation to participation status is between *ratified* and *unratified participants* (see Chapter 11 for further discussion of ratification in relation to identities and cultures). This is based on the intuitive distinction between *listening to* and *hearing* talk. When we *listen to* talk we are assumed to have some degree of responsibility, or in some cases even an institutionalised obligation, to attend to or participate in that talk. That responsibility makes us ratified participants. As ratified participants we are entitled to hold other participants (as well as ourselves) morally accountable for the social actions and meanings that arise through that talk. When we *hear* talk, however, while it is audible to us and we may (or may not) understand it, we are not expected to attend to or directly participate in that talk. If we are not expected to participate, then, we are unratified participants. As unratified participants, then, we do not have an entitlement to hold the producer morally accountable for the social actions and meanings that arise through that talk, although individuals may attempt, of course, to upgrade their participation status from unratified to ratified (and vice-versa) in the course of interaction. What we find, then, is that interactions can involve, on the one hand, more 'focused encounters' where all the individuals are ratified participants who are expected to jointly sustain and attend to the talk and conduct at hand (Goffman 1964). A conversation between two or three friends in a private setting is more often than not a good example of a focused encounter. On the other hand, interactions may involve larger gatherings where there are both ratified and unratified participants. A conversation between two or three friends in a public setting like a café or restaurant is often a good example of a broader social situation. In the latter situation others present, such as waiters or people at adjacent tables, may be able to hear what the friends are talking about, at least at times, but they are not generally considered ratified participants in that interaction.

Ratified and unratified participants can be further subdivided into different types. There are a number of different models for doing this, but we will start here by outlining the basic model proposed by Goffman (1979, 1981). A ratified recipient may either be an *addressee* or an unaddressed *side participant*. An addressee is a person (or persons) to whom the talk or conduct is (ostensibly) directed, while a side participant is not directly addressed as such. Both addressees and side participants have recognised entitlements to respond to the talk, although their degree of responsibility to do so varies (at least ostensibly). Unratified recipients, on the other hand, can be divided into *bystanders* and *overhearers*. The former is an individual (or group of individuals) that can be expected to be able to hear at least some parts of the talk, but are not ratified as a participant. An overhearer, on the other hand, refers to an individual (or group of individuals) that might be able to hear some parts of the talk. Overhearers include *listener-ins* (persons whom speakers and other ratified participants are aware can hear the talk) and *eavesdroppers* (persons who are secretly following the talk). The notion of participant is thus a complex one despite being represented as one locus for understanding politeness in Figure 5.1. These different types of participation status are summarised in Figure 5.2.

To appreciate the various different kinds of participation status, let us consider example (3), which happened, or perhaps was imagined to happen, at a U2 concert, when Bono, the lead singer, had taken the microphone to address the audience between songs.

> (3) At a recent U2 concert in Glasgow, Scotland, he asked the audience for total quiet. Then, in the silence, he started to slowly clap his hands, once every few seconds. Holding the audience in total silence, he said into the microphone,
> 'Every time I clap my hands, a child in Africa dies.'

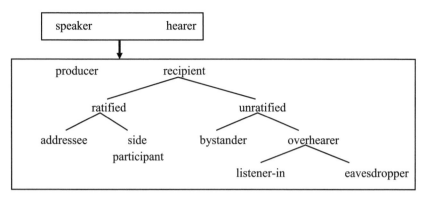

Figure 5.2 Types of participation status.

From the front of the crowd a voice with a broad Scottish accent pierced the quiet...
'Well, f – ckin stop doin it then, ya evil bastard!'
(http://phocks.org/stumble/bono/)

The response from the member of the audience here is an instance of deliberate misinterpretation of Bono's earlier claim being one of causation (i.e. his clapping is leading children in Africa to die) rather than what was evidently meant (the clapping is a chilling way of representing an estimate of a horrific number of deaths). However, deliberately misinterpreting Bono's point in this way projects an ironic evaluation of Bono. In other words, while the explicit denunciation of Bono is itself only mock censure, there is nevertheless implied censure of Bono for being self-righteous here, and a mocking attitude towards that sense of self-righteousness he is presupposed to have. We might ask the question as to whether this ironic evaluation from the audience is offensive or simply mock impolite. Or to phrase the question more carefully, for *whom* might this be considered offensive or simply considered mock impolite?

The *producer* here is the member of the audience that shouted out the remark, while the *addressee* is, of course, Bono himself. Whether he found (or would find) such a response offensive is open to question, but it's not entirely out of the question to think that he might. However, Bono is not the only party present. There are a large number of *side participants* here for whom the remark was most likely meant to entertain, namely, the audience at the concert, at least those ones who could hear the comment. For them it is clearly open to evaluation as mock impolite, that is, an evaluation of a potentially impolite social action (here, ironic censure) as non-impolite, although some in the audience could also be offended if they thought the remark made light of a very serious matter. There are also, arguably, a number of unratified participants here, including the other members of U2 who are positioned here as *bystanders*, and other members of the technical crew backstage who are essentially *listener-ins* in this situation. They are perhaps less likely to evaluate the remark as simply mock impolite than the side participants here, in part, because they are associated (to varying degrees) with the target of the ironic censure. The point being made here is that how this ironic censure is evaluated critically depends, in part, on the participation status of the person(s) concerned.

Example (3) is in fact an anecdote that went 'viral' on the internet, which is, of course, how it ended up in our email inboxes in the first place. As we briefly noted previously, the development of various technologies has meant there are increasing numbers of different kinds of mediated forms of communication where participation is vicarious, including more 'traditional' forms such as television, film and radio through to relatively newer 'digital' forms, such as social media, discussion boards and the like. The line between the two is increasingly becoming blurred though, as mediated forms of communication, such as messenger, Skype, SMS, social media and the like can involve direct participation, of course, and increasingly so. However, it is nevertheless clear that evaluations of politeness can arise through metaparticipants vicariously taking part in the interaction by viewing it on television or on the internet. Consider the following two responses to the posting of the above anecdote on a blogger's website.

(4) Barbara_jozsef
It is still funny, too funny XD

(5) Pamsplace7
your so cruel!! Cant believe this person come to see U2. EVIL man, pure evil.
We are talking about children! Dying![2]

In example (4) the first commenter evaluates the remark as mock impolite given she treats it as humorous. In example (5), however, the second respondent evaluates both the remark itself and its producer, and the first commenter's response to it as offensive. At this stage, whether or not the incident really happened starts to become immaterial, as metaparticipants start to evaluate the responses of others to the anecdote, as well as the original remarks themselves. The main point to take note of here is that we need to extend the model of different types of participation status to include not only evaluations that arise through co-present or mediated participation (i.e. by participants), but also evaluations of politeness that arise through vicarious participation (i.e. by metaparticipants). In relation to politeness, this is important, because often the understandings of metaparticipants can be just as important, and sometimes even more important, than those of the participants themselves.[3]

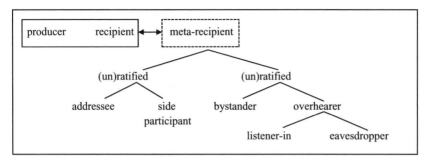

Figure 5.3 Types of recipient and meta-recipient participation status.

The extension of participation status to encompass the understandings of metaparticipants is summarised in Figure 5.3. Once again we can see that the loci of participation for understanding politeness are indeed complex when one considers things more carefully. One important difference to note between participants and metaparticipants is that in the case of the latter, the distinction between ratified and unratified recipients becomes less clear-cut. Meta-addressees and metaside-participants can be treated as unratified recipients, while metabystanders and meta-overhearers can be treated as ratified recipients. Viewers of film and television, for instance, are often treated as ratified overhearers (Dynel 2011).

Take example (6), which is from the American comedy *Seinfeld*. Jerry, Elaine, Kramer, George and George's new girlfriend Audrey are sharing a pizza at Jerry's apartment. At the point this excerpt begins, Kramer has just been talking about a reggae lounge he went to the previous night.

(6) Kramer: You wouldn't believe the women at this club. Ohh, man.
    Audrey: It's amazing how many beautiful women live in New York. I actually find it kind of intimidating.
    Kramer: Well you're as pretty as any of them. You just need a nose job.
    ((Audrey stops eating, Elaine looks up with a shocked look on her face, Jerry lifts his hand to his forehead in a sign of exasperation, and George chokes on his food))
    Elaine: Kramer!
    Kramer: What? What?
    Elaine: How could you say something like that?
    Kramer: What do you mean? What, I just said she needs a nose job. So what?
    Elaine: No no, there's nothing wrong with her nose! I'm so sorry, Audrey.

Audrey: No, it's ok.
Elaine: What did you have to say that for?
Kramer: Well, I was just trying to help out.
          ('The nose job', *Seinfeld*, Season 3, Episode 9, 1991)

Audrey's self-deprecatory comment about her looks occasions a compliment ('you're as pretty as any of them'), here a positive assessment, followed by some advice ('you just need a nose job') from Kramer. Embedded within this advice, however, is a negative assessment of her nose: namely, it is too big (a point about her looks, incidentally, about which George himself has been obsessing but has not been able to bring himself to say anything to her). This negative assessment, albeit presupposed in the context of friendly advice, is clearly evaluated as impolite by the others present. This is evident both through their non-verbal responses, and from the way in which Elaine holds Kramer to account for giving this advice, implying that it is very inappropriate ('How could you say something like that?'; 'What did you have to say that for?'), claims his negative assessment is improper ('there's nothing wrong with her nose'), and apologises to Audrey for Kramer's remark ('I'm so sorry, Audrey'). In other words, Kramer's advice, which is addressed to Audrey, is treated by the other side participants as an impropriety that demands a display of censure of both the comment and of Kramer for making it. Notably, Audrey who is the target and addressee of the advice, downplays the improper nature of it in responding to Elaine's apology ('no, it's okay'). Thus, it is the side participants who display evaluations of Kramer's advice as impolite or offensive here, rather than the addressee. Kramer, on the other hand, remains seemingly oblivious to the negative import of his advice, as he does not acknowledge that there was even an impropriety on his part ('What, I just said she needs a nose job. So what?'), and indeed seems to perceive it as simply friendly advice ('Well, I was just trying to help out'), and consequently is visibly frustrated by Elaine's negative response to it.

In terms of participant understandings, then, it appears we have at least three perspectives: the advice is evaluated as clearly impolite/offensive by the side participants (Elaine, George and Jerry); the advice is evaluated by the addressee (Audrey) as not being as offensive as Elaine claims; and the advice is evaluated by the producer (Kramer) as not at all impolite (and possibly even polite). There is, however, yet another understanding of politeness at play here, namely, the perspective of the viewers of this episode. We, the viewers, are ratified overhearers as the interaction here is clearly recipient designed for our entertainment. We vicariously experience interactions between characters, one of whom at least is seemingly oblivious to widespread societal disapproval – at least in mainstream Anglo-Englishes – of making negative comments about the appearance of others. Impoliteness thus becomes here a form of entertainment for metaparticipants (see also Culpeper 2005).

To understand politeness, then, we must first consider the different perspectives from which participants themselves may be evaluating social actions and meanings. It is not sufficient to talk only of speakers and hearers. There are multiple types of participation status, and although we have only just given a few limited examples of this here, it is important to bear in mind these multiple different types of participant understandings when analysing politeness. We will revisit and expand upon such issues in subsequent chapters (see Chapter 6). However, before doing so, we need to first consider more carefully on what grounds participants (and metaparticipants) evaluate social actions and meanings as polite, impolite, mock impolite and so on. In other words, how is it that people know (or think they know) something is polite, impolite, mock impolite and so on. It is to the second loci of understanding politeness, namely, the set of moral expectancies that inform such evaluative moments, to which we now turn.

5.3   Emic/etic understandings

As we discussed in Chapter 4, our view of politeness as social practice grounds evaluations of social actions and meanings, and by extension evaluations of those people held accountable for them, in the moral order. Evaluations are based on a set of backgrounded, and generally unnoticed, expectancies through which members know (or think they know) what social actions and meanings can count as polite or impolite in particular situated contexts. In attempting to better understand what we mean by this moral order, let us first consider a broad working definition of politeness developed by Culpeper:

Politeness involves (a) an attitude compromised of particular positive evaluative beliefs about particular behaviours in particular social contexts, (b) the activation of that attitude by those particular-in-context-behaviours, and (c) the actual or potential description of those in-context-behaviours and/or persons who produced as *polite, courteous, considerate*, etc. . . . Impoliteness, although its performance involves significant differences, can be defined along similar but contrary lines: it involves negative attitudes activated by in-context-behaviours which are associated, along with the person who gave rise to them, with impoliteness metalanguage (e.g. *impolite, rude, discourteous*, etc.). (2011b: 428, underscore added)

We have underlined three key words in this definition that point to the critical role of the moral order in how it is that people know (or at least think they know) something is polite, impolite and so on. The first is the claim that (im)politeness involves evaluative **beliefs**, specifically beliefs about what behaviour is *expected* in particular contexts. In characterising this set of expectations as constituting the moral order, what we mean is that these expectancies are themselves realised through interaction, and deviations from them thus result in social actions or meanings for which persons are held accountable in interaction.

The second important claim is that these beliefs are socially grounded: they are dispersed to varying degrees across various kinds of relational networks, ranging from a group of families and friends, to a localised community of practice, through to a larger, much more diffuse societal or cultural group (see also Chapters 7, 9 and 11). What is critical to note is that members can hold both themselves and others *accountable* to the moral order of this particular relational network. To be held accountable involves various real-world consequences, ranging from approval and social inclusion through to censure and social exclusion. The notion of *member*, in turn, presupposes two fundamentally different perspectives on the moral order, namely that of the insider (an emic perspective) and that of an outsider (an etic perspective).

The third important claim is that these beliefs have recourse to a set of (im)politeness **evaluators**: descriptors or **metalanguage** used by members to conceptualise their social world. What is interesting about politeness and impoliteness in English, and indeed many other languages, is that these evaluative beliefs have become institutionalised in the language itself. This is not to say that everyone who speaks a particular language will have the same set of beliefs about politeness, but rather that they can draw from a common set of (im)politeness evaluators in the evaluative moment. We thus suggest it is important to investigate what these (im)politeness evaluators mean to the members who use them, as well as the underlying set of moral expectancies that ground evaluative moments of politeness from the perspective of members; in other words, from an emic perspective. However, we briefly point out at the end of this section that we are inevitably required to examine politeness from *both* emic and etic perspectives if we are to understand the full range of contexts in which it arises given we are living in an increasingly globalised world.

The moral order is constituted, as we discussed in Chapter 4, through practices by which social actions and meanings are recognisable to members. These practices are inevitably open to moral evaluation – they can be assessed as good/bad, appropriate/inappropriate, polite/not polite, impolite/not impolite and so on by members. Evaluations of politeness are thus rooted in the expectations that constitute the moral order. Here, we expand on this point by suggesting that it is useful to think of the moral order as multilayered and dispersed in various ways and to varying degrees across relational networks. Michael Silverstein (2003), a linguistic anthropologist, suggests that expectancies (or what he terms norms) form **orders of indexicality**. This refers to the idea that sets of expectancies are *reflexively layered*. At the first layer (or *first-order*) of expectancies we find probabilistic conventions for evaluating social actions and meanings. These are formed for individuals through their own history of interactions with others, and so while they may be similar they are never exactly

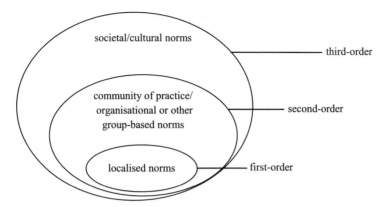

Figure 5.4 Reflexive layers of the moral order (cf. Holmes, Marra and Vine 2012: 1065).

the same across individuals (cf. 'habitus', Watts 2003); although they are likely to bear greater similarity in localised relational networks within which there are ongoing interactions between members over long periods of time (such as within families or between groups of friends). At the second layer (or *second-order*) we find semi-institutionalised conventions for evaluating social actions and meanings. In other words, sets of expectancies that are shared across identifiable communities of practice, organisational cultures or indeed any social group recognised as such by members. Finally, at the third layer (or *third-order*) we find sets of expectancies as they are represented in supra-local (i.e. societal) conventions for evaluating social actions and meanings. In being reflexively ordered, it should not be assumed that third-order expectancies will necessarily always take precedence over second-order ones and so on (although they often do), but rather that in invoking first-order expectancies we inevitably invoke second- and third-order ones as well.

The three reflexive layers of the moral order underpinning evaluative moments of politeness are represented in Figure 5.4. In this figure, it is suggested that localised sets of expectancies that develop for individuals in situated relationships are necessarily embedded (and thus interpreted) relative to communities of practice, organisational or other group-based sets of expectancies, which are themselves necessarily embedded relative to broader societal or 'cultural' sets of expectancies (see also Chapter 11). All three layers of the moral order are potentially relevant to understanding politeness.

These various layers of the moral order implicitly assume an insider's, or emic perspective. An emic perspective is often related to the study of 'cultures', but here we return to Pike's (1967) original treatment of emic as an understanding formulated in terms of conceptual schemes and categories regarded as meaningful and appropriate to 'insiders', i.e. 'members' of relational networks.[4] It is through members holding both themselves and other (perceived) members accountable to these sets of expectancies that they can claim an insider's understanding. An etic perspective, on the other hand, is an understanding formulated in terms of conceptual schemes and categories regarded as meaningful and appropriate to 'outsiders', that is, those who are treated as lying outside the relational network in question. It is important to note that an etic perspective is *not* synonymous with a theoretical one. An etic perspective is simply 'an approach by an *outsider* to an *inside* system, in which the outsider brings his own structure – his own emics – and partly superimposes his observations on the inside view, interpreting the inside in reference to the outside starting point' (Pike 1990, emphasis added). The system in question here is, of course, the moral order that grounds evaluative moments of politeness. In other words, we propose, consistent with Pike (1967), that the etic not be confused with issues of theory, and that the emic/etic distinction be used simply to refer to the distinction between insiders and outsiders relative to relational networks.

The sets of expectancies that constitute the moral order draw in important ways from sets of (im)politeness evaluators (descriptors or metalanguage used by members to conceptualise their social world). What an etic perspective offers is a way of systematically investigating the different ways in which the social world is conceptualised across different relational networks. In this way, we can appreciate differences, and of course similarities where they exist, across different emic perspectives on (im)politeness evaluators.

We therefore argue that it is important to tease out the emic worldviews that underpin (im)politeness evaluators. Otherwise we may fall into one of two traps: first, thinking we are talking about the same phenomena across languages and cultures when in fact we are not; second, generating analytical artifacts that are of no consequence for those people concerned through the imposition of tacit etic understandings that underlie (im)politeness evaluators in English when applied to the analysis of politeness phenomena in other languages (Haugh 2012a). In other words, to talk about 'politeness' in various languages without a consideration of emic or insider perspectives on the phenomena in question is akin to essentially bleaching out these important conceptual differences. We will revisit such issues again in subsequent chapters (see Chapter 9).

It is important to note, however, that we are not suggesting here that an emic understanding necessarily be privileged over an etic one. Indeed, in some instances, an interplay between emic and etic understandings lies at the very core of the evaluative moment of politeness itself. This becomes most obvious when one considers the issue of how to analyse evaluations of politeness in intercultural interactions where participants do not share similar insider perspectives on the moral order.

Consider example (7), an intercultural apology that arose subsequent to an Australian man (Wayne) and his wife not turning up to dinner to which he had been invited by a Taiwanese woman (Joyce) and her family. While Joyce tried to contact Wayne that night he did not answer his phone, and only later, the next day, sent a short SMS text to Joyce, saying 'Sorry I forgot I was busy with something.' The following evening, two days after the event, Joyce called Wayne having not received a follow-up call from him. The point at which example (7) begins is when Wayne offers an apology to Joyce (and her family).

(7) W: It's just, ah, I really apologise for not to you getting back the other day but we couldn't make it?

J: oh, that's okay. yeah, yeah, yeah. I- I just thought oh probably you are busy with something so you ah probably were easy to- to for(hhh)get it.

W: yeah we were pretty busy actually

J: oh, okay, yeah, yeah that's fine. I just want to call you, that- that- that's okay.

(Chang and Haugh 2011a: 420)

Wayne made no further apology in the remainder of the call, but rather repeatedly asked after Joyce and her family. The question, then, is how was this apology evaluated by Wayne and Joyce? From an emic perspective, Wayne appears to evaluate his own apology as sufficiently *polite*, an analysis that is evidenced by the fact that Wayne did not attempt to make any further apologies, but rather attempted to show *friendliness* towards Joyce and her family by asking questions about them (see the complete transcript in Chang and Haugh 2011a). Joyce, on the other hand, appears to evaluate his apology as 'impolite' (*mei-limao*), a finding that is indicated through Joyce repeating absolution of Wayne's offence at a number of different points in the conversation despite Wayne only ever offering an apology once in the interaction. What repeating an absolution (i.e. 'that's okay') should occasion, from Joyce's emic perspective, is an attempt to show sincerity (*chengyi*) through repetition of the apology or by giving a more detailed account or explanation.

Of course, what we need to bear in mind in this analysis is that from Wayne's point of view, Joyce's evaluation of his apology is one based on an outsider or etic perspective, while from Joyce's point of view, Wayne's evaluation of his apology is one based on an outsider or etic perspective. In other words, both Wayne and Joyce can be regarded as taking either an emic or etic perspective in their evaluations of the relative (im)politeness of the apology depending on whose understanding we are talking about in the first place (i.e. either Wayne's or Joyce's). We will revisit the particular challenges posed for understanding politeness in intercultural settings in Chapter 11.

5.4   Analyst/lay-observer understandings

Understandings of politeness can arise not only through participation but also through observation of evaluative moments. Whether we are lay persons or analysts, we all begin from the same point, making observations. The difference between understandings of lay observers and analysts lies in what is done with those observations of evaluative moments of politeness.

Lay observers are persons who do not have specialised knowledge of a particular field, in this case, the field of politeness research. What is done in lay observation, then, is to move straight from observation to interpretation. In other words, observations about a particular evaluative moment result in spontaneous accounts of it. These accounts seek to generalise and attribute motivations and the like, but are not based on any attempt to systematically build up evidence for those accounts. For example, if a friend, in an outburst quite out of character, yells at me in anger, I might attribute this potential impoliteness to him 'not feeling well' or being 'upset about something else'. I might then generalise from this incident to conclude that my friend is the kind of person who does or says impolite things when he is sick or upset. Lay observers thus generate spontaneous and less stringently evidenced understandings of politeness.

In the case of analysts, however, these observations are subject to two further processes before generating interpretations of those evaluative moments, according to the communication scholar Klaus Krippendorff (1970; see also Arundale 2013). The first is that these observations are formalised in some way. This involves systematic labelling, classifying or categorising these observations using technical terms or concepts. These processes result in 'formalised observations', or what is generally termed 'data' in the social sciences. The second set of processes involves inferential work where one detects possible relationships, order and structure in the data, thereby generating evidence for one's subsequent interpretations. Many of the studies of politeness we discussed in the previous two chapters involve exactly these kinds of processes. An analyst thus generates interpretations of evaluative moments of politeness through systematic and evidenced observation. What counts as 'systematic' and 'evidenced' observation varies, of course, according to the nature of the initial observations of evaluative moments and the means by which they are formalised into data.

The different pathways by which lay observers and analysts generate interpretations of their observations of evaluative moments of politeness are summarised in Figure 5.5. Lay observers move directly from making observations to interpreting those observations. Analysts, on the other hand, offer (or at least attempt to offer) systematic evidence for those interpretations through formalising those observations by generating data, and teasing out possible relationships, order and structure in that data.

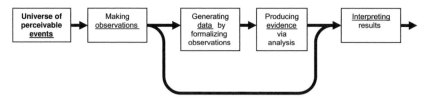

Figure 5.5 Procedures in interpreting observations of evaluative moments of politeness (Arundale 2013, after Krippendorff 1970: 242).

However, while the perspective of lay observers is considered marginal at best in the physical sciences, in the social sciences the situation is quite different. In studying politeness, we are in fact very interested in the understandings of lay observers. This is because the understandings of lay observers can constitute an important influence on what it is we are studying, the understandings of participants and metaparticipants. In other words, how people talk and think about politeness can influence the ways in which evaluations of politeness arise in and across moments of time in the first place, as we noted in Chapter 4. It is also important to remember that everyone, including the analyst, generates understandings of politeness from the perspective of a lay observer. There is thus the ever-present danger that lay observation masquerades as analysis in the interpretation of evaluative moments of politeness.

Thus, while we maintain that the understandings of politeness which arise through lay observation and analysis should be carefully distinguished, we are not arguing that one should be privileged over the other. Indeed, the understandings of lay observers can offer useful insights into evaluative moments of politeness if they are examined in systematic and evidenced ways by analysts. Let us return to the 'intercultural apology' we introduced in example (7). We noted that there was evidence from the interaction itself that while Wayne evaluated the apology as sufficiently polite, Joyce evaluated the apology as impolite (*mei-limao, bu-limao*). The question this analysis raises is whether these are idiosyncratic evaluations or they are legitimately invoking their respective moral orders. In other words, are we actually dealing with an intercultural difference here or is it simply that Wayne and/or Joyce understand this incident in ways peculiar to them? Chang and Haugh (2011a) thus systematically examined responses of lay observers, a group of twenty-five Australians and a group of twenty-five Taiwanese, in order to explore this question. The lay informants were first asked to report their evaluations of the apology after listening to the whole conversation, rating it on a five-point Likert-type scale, ranging from 'very impolite', 'impolite', 'neither polite nor impolite', 'polite' through to 'very polite'.[5] The results of this survey are summarised in Figure 5.6.

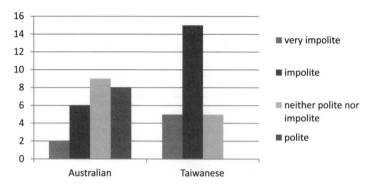

Figure 5.6 Overall ratings of the degree of (im)politeness by lay observers.

There are two points we can note from the responses of Australian and Taiwanese lay observers. First, overall the Australians tended to evaluate the apology as 'not impolite' (i.e. either 'polite' or 'neither polite nor impolite'), while the Taiwanese tended to evaluate the apology as 'impolite', a difference that was found to be statistically significant. Second, despite this overall trend there was some degree of intracultural variation, especially amongst the Australian lay observers. In other words, there was both intercultural and to a lesser extent intracultural variability in their evaluations of (im)politeness.

A subset of twenty-eight respondents were then asked in interviews to explain why they evaluated the apology in the way they did. Australian lay observers who evaluated the apology as 'polite' or at least 'not impolite' most often made reference to Wayne being 'friendly' towards Joyce in the course of their conversation.[6] In example (8), one Australian informant suggests the apology would have been much less polite if Wayne had not been friendly.

> (8) AM6: And um that when she suggested that they make another
> time he was keen for that, and he seemed concerned with
> her mother's issue and also with her and how she were, so
> I think if he didn't really want to speak to her, then he- he
> could have been a lot less polite.
>   I: Okay.

(Chang and Haugh 2011a: 427)

In other words, showing interest in Joyce and her family contributed to the overall evaluation of the apology as 'not impolite'. This indicates that evaluations of (im)politeness are holistically grounded, often being *discourse-based* impressions rather than utterance-based, a point we will revisit in Chapter 6.

Taiwanese lay observers who evaluated the apology as '(very) impolite', on the other hand, most often made reference to the notion *chengyi* ('sincerity').

Evaluations of an apology as 'sincere' (*chengyi-de*) and thus 'polite' (*limao*) are often occasioned through repetition of the speech act, by means of which one can also secure uptake of an offer of redress (i.e. another meeting at another time), another important means of displaying 'sincerity' (*chengyi*), as we can see in example (9) below from a Taiwanese informant.

(9) 8 TM3: 我感覺他一直想把電話掛掉,
'I feel he wanted to hang up the phone quickly,'
那我會覺得他不禮貌
'so I think he was not polite [*bu-limao*].'
((section omitted))

11 TM3: 他的道歉很短, 讓我覺得他是急著要掛電話,
'his apology was short, I think he was hurry to hang up the phone'
因為他説可以約下一次, 但是Joyce沒有回應,就講別的
'Because he said he would like to make it next time. But he continued talking about something else before Joyce said anything.'

(Chang and Haugh 2011a: 429–30)

The lay observer accounts for why he evaluated the apology as 'impolite' (*bu-limao*) by making reference to the perceived lack of 'sincerity' (*chengyi*) on Wayne's part in making the apology. First, the Taiwanese informant implies that the apology should have been repeated in suggesting that Wayne wanted to get the conversation, and thus his apology, over and done with quickly (turn 8). Second, he suggests that while Wayne made an offer of redress, namely, meeting at another time with Joyce and her family, the invitation lacked sincerity (*chengyi*) because he did not arrange a specific date for another meeting. What becomes apparent here, then, is that not only did the Australian and Taiwanese lay observers evaluate the apology differently, they offered different accounts for why they evaluated the apology in that way. In other words, they appealed to emic understandings of their own respective moral orders, one where *friendliness* was invoked, and another where *chengyi* ('sincerity') was emphasised. It can be inferred, therefore, that the respective evaluations of Wayne, who evaluated the apology as 'polite' or at least 'not impolite', and Joyce, who evaluated it as 'impolite' were grounded in the third-order cultural or societal expectancies that constitute their respective perceptions of the moral order.

Our point here, then, is that not only do we need to be careful to distinguish between the understandings of lay observers and analysts, but also that the understandings of lay observers can offer a useful resource for analysts in interpreting evaluative moments of politeness (see also Chapter 9).

5.5   Theoretical/folk-theoretic understandings

The final locus for understanding politeness involves the ways in which it is conceptualised. This can be either from a scientific-theoretic perspective or from a folk-theoretic perspective. A scientific-theoretic perspective involves the conceptualisation of politeness as an object of study. Some of the key characteristics of a scientific conceptualisation are that it is precise and accurate (e.g. there is no ambiguity in categorisation of phenomena), internally coherent (e.g. the same underlying epistemological and ontological foundations underpin all parts of the theory, or the absence of internally contradictory propositions), replicable (e.g. other analysts could generate similar interpretations with the same or similar data), and it has some degree of explanatory or predictive power. Most importantly, the conceptual schema/categories used to analyse and describe politeness must be regarded, according to the ethnographer James Lett, as 'meaningful and appropriate by the community of scientific observers' (1990: 131). In other words, scientific-theoretic accounts involve explicitly defined and formalised understandings of interpersonal phenomena that are shared amongst scientific observers. Brown and Levinson's (1987) politeness theory (see overview in Chapter 2), for instance, represents a conceptualisation that was previously regarded as 'meaningful and appropriate' by most politeness researchers, but nowadays is regarded in that way by only some. It is worth noting that not only do our views of scientific knowledge change, the key source of scientific theorising (at least in social sciences) is in fact emic and folk-theoretic perspectives on interpersonal phenomena.

A folk-theoretic perspective aligns to a large extent with the emic understandings of members, but refers specifically to the emic knowledge represented in conceptualisations of persons, relationships, social structures and the like, which tacitly underpin the moral order in question. For example, in folk-theoretic accounts of politeness shared amongst some English speakers, politeness is assumed to arise because we need to show *consideration* and *respect* to others. Other English speakers assume, however, that politeness arises as a way of showing one is of a higher social class than others. These both constitute folk-theoretic understandings of politeness. However, while different in scope, if we look a little deeper we find that in both cases a conceptualisation of persons as independent and autonomous individuals is presumed in such accounts.

Lying somewhere between scientific and folk-theoretic understandings of politeness are what Kádár (2007) terms 'proto-scientific' understandings. These arose in the work of scholars in the past where politeness was studied, not systematically in its own right, but rather as just one part of a more holistic record of customs and philosophical beliefs. In certain historical cultures such as the Chinese there is a long proto-scientific history of studying politeness and impoliteness for educational or moral purposes. Although such theories inevitably lack the methodological and terminological systematicity of their modern counterparts, they are invaluable as sources of understandings of politeness that go beyond folk theorising.

Once again, it is important to note that while folk or proto-scientific-theoretic understandings are considered marginal at best in many areas of research, since we are interested in the case of politeness in what is an inherently social phenomena, such understandings can potentially play a very important role in scientific theorising. However, we would emphasise here that a scientific theorisation should only ever be informed and never unduly constrained by folk-theoretic understandings of politeness. This does not amount to a claim that a scientific-theoretic understanding should be 'independent of the observer's culture' (Lett 1990: 131). We, like Pike, are doubtful that such observer-independent understandings are even possible. As he argues,

there are no observer-independent bits of knowledge of any kind – scientific or other...there is no observer-independent world view; there is no set of observer-independent data accessible to us; the scientific method does not eliminate that dependency'. (1990: 187)[7]

It is thus even more critical in our view that we carefully identify the loci of the understandings of politeness in question.

One very important consequence of the way in which we theorise politeness, whether one draws from a scientific-theoretic or folk-theoretic understanding of politeness, is that this conceptualisation both affords and constrains what count as observations, data, evidence and interpretations for the analyst. Arundale (2013) argues, for instance, that a conceptualisation of politeness as rooted in a view of persons as independent and autonomous individuals affords interpretations of politeness as a kind of strategic choice on the part of the speaker, as described in Brown and Levinson (1987). However, it constrains, at the same time, understandings of politeness as normative practice. Given that different theoretical conceptualisations not only afford but also constrain our understandings of politeness, in the remainder of this book we will make reference to a range of different scientific-theoretic and folk-theoretic conceptualisations of politeness. Our basic position is that due consideration should be given to emerging, alternative theoretical paradigms that afford new understandings of politeness alongside those that are more well established in the field.

5.6 Summary

In this chapter we've suggested that there are four key loci in which understandings of politeness can be grounded:

(i) Participant/metaparticipant understandings: *user* interpretations
(ii) Emic/etic understandings: *user* conceptualisations
(iii) Analyst/lay observer understandings: *observer* interpretations
(iv) Theoretical/folk-theoretic understandings: *observer* conceptualisations.

In other words, we have proposed that first-order understandings of politeness encompass the interpretations (participant versus metaparticipant) and conceptualisations (emic versus etic) of *users*, while second-order understandings of politeness encompass the interpretations (lay versus analyst) and conceptualisations (folk-theoretic versus theoretical) of *observers*. We've suggested that collectively these four key loci offer a more nuanced framework for understanding politeness than a simple distinction between the understandings of 'participants' and 'analysts' or 'non-scientific' and 'scientific' understandings.

What the framework also suggests is that there are no purely 'first-order' or 'second-order' approaches to politeness. Instead, any examination of politeness can be grounded in a number of different loci of understanding. Indeed, it is important to understand that any one person can have multiple perspectives on politeness. While analysts are very often metaparticipants, they are at times also participants themselves in evaluative moments of politeness. An analyst is also able to make observations grounded in a lay observer's perspective on those evaluative moments, and may draw from either folk-theoretic or theoretical conceptualisations of politeness. It follows, then, that it is important to carefully distinguish between what counts as an analyst's, as opposed to a lay observer's, understanding of politeness. It is also important to distinguish between the different kinds of participation status relative to which understandings of politeness are situated, and the emic/etic understandings that different persons may invoke in the course of the evaluative moment(s) of politeness.

There are a number of advantages in acknowledging that ultimately we should be talking about *understandings* of politeness rather than any one particular understanding. On the one hand, it affords a more nuanced range of approaches and methodologies to be drawn upon in furthering our understanding of politeness. This allows us to break free from the 'linguistic' constraint on studying politeness – the traditional focus on linguistic manifestations of polite behaviour such as politeness strategies and linguistic forms. In this way, we can further explore the inherent multimodality of politeness as a social practice, and also explore the various modalities in which such social practices are situated. On the other hand, it helps to integrate different perspectives into holistic – but nevertheless internally coherent – approaches to the study of politeness. When politeness is understood in this way, it can be approached from the perspective of various different disciplines, employing a wide range of approaches and methodologies. In other words, when we talk of understandings of politeness we mean both different *epistemological* bases (e.g. user versus observer) and different *disciplinary* bases (e.g. linguistic pragmatics versus corpus linguistics) for grounding the study of politeness. However, rather than surrendering completely to theoretical eclecticism, what this framework offers is a way of situating understandings of politeness in such a way that more meaningful comparisons can be made. In the remaining chapters in this book, we explore more fully the implications of conceptualising politeness as a social practice and appreciating the multiple loci in which understandings of it can be situated.

Part II

Politeness and time

6 Politeness in interaction

6.1 Introduction

It has long been recognised that time is fundamentally constitutive of social action in interaction. In the course of reconceptualising politeness as social practice in Chapters 4 and 5, we have argued that time both constrains and affords understandings of politeness in various ways. For this reason, it is important to analyse understandings of politeness as they arise in situated interactions. However, to situate politeness in interaction need not necessitate a narrow focus on micro-analyses of individual encounters. We have suggested that particular understandings of politeness in the here-and-now are inevitably interlinked with understandings of politeness in the there-and-then, both over the course of the relational histories of those participants, and across the multitude of interactions through which the relational network(s) and attendant moral order(s) that are involved are constituted. In other words, we assume here a view of interaction as a meeting point between time in the sense of the locally situated here-and-now, and time in the sense of the historically and socially relative there-and-then.

To illustrate what we mean by this, consider example (1), from the American film *Trains, Planes and Automobiles*. The interaction begins after Neal has been forced to walk a considerably long way back from the carpark having found his rental car was not there, adding to his numerous trials in trying to get back home for Thanksgiving after his flight was cancelled.

(1) 1   Agent: (smiling with a cheerful voice) Welcome to Marathon, may I help you?

    2   Neal: Yes.

    3   Agent: *How* may I help you?

    4   Neal: You can start by wiping that fucking dumb-ass smile off your rosey, fucking, cheeks! And you can give me a fucking automobile: a fucking Datsun, a fucking Toyota, a fucking Mustang, a fucking Buick! Four fucking wheels and a seat!

    5   Agent: I really don't care for the way you're speaking to me.

6   Neal: And I really don't care for the way your company left me in the middle of fucking nowhere with fucking keys to a fucking car that isn't fucking there. And I really didn't care to fucking walk, down a fucking highway, and across a fucking runway to get back here to have you smile in my fucking face. I want a fucking car RIGHT FUCKING NOW!

7   Agent: May I see your rental agreement?

8   Neal: I threw it away.

9   Agent: Oh boy.

10 Neal: Oh boy, what?

11 Agent: You're fucked!

(*Trains, Planes and Automobiles*, 1987)

This excerpt begins with an ostensibly polite greeting and a standard pre-offer of assistance used in service settings, 'May I help you?' (turn 1). While her offer literally seeks a yes/no response, it is normally expected that the customer will launch immediately into his or her request given the presumed service encounter interpretative frame at play here. Neal's literal response in turn 2 is thus the first indication that something is amiss. The agent nevertheless retains her (stereotypical) 'Pan-Am smile' and cheery tone of voice in formulating the offer of assistance itself in turn 3 subsequent to Neal's gratuitous go-ahead response. Neal responds by launching a long tirade where he repeatedly swears as he demands the agent stop smiling and that he be given a car (turn 4). The agent remains composed subsequent to this in indirectly requesting that Neal refrain from using such language through a mild complaint (turn 5). However, this occasions yet another long tirade of complaints from Neal where he once again repeatedly uses the word 'fuck' (turn 6). The litany of complaints is concluded with a forcefully worded demand that he be given a car immediately. Once again, despite the clear impolite attitude on the part of Neal, the agent retains a polite demeanour, as she continues using a 'cheerful' intonation and once again uses a formulation which is conventional for a polite service encounter frame (i.e. 'may I . . .') in requesting further information from Neal (turn 7). It is at this point that the tenor of the interaction begins to alter. Upon learning that Neal does not have a copy of his rental agreement, the agent concludes, employing a 'non-cheerful' intonation for the first time and without a smile, that Neal is 'fucked' (turn 11). The contrast between the polite demeanour of the car rental agent in continuing to adhere to the script for a polite service encounter and the overtly impolite responses of Neal thus becomes even more salient at this point in the interaction, when the agent switches into formulating her utterance with an overtly impolite attitude (albeit not quite as vehement as Neal).

What we can see from example (1) is that the polite attitude on the part of the agent and the consistently impolite attitude on the part of Neal, in the here-and-now of this particular interaction, are readily *recognisable* to the participants (and to us, the viewers) through their interdependence with understandings of politeness in the there-and-then in two key ways. First, in order to appreciate that the agent's attitude can be characterised as 'polite', while Neal's attitude can be characterised as 'impolite', it is necessary to invoke a particular interpretative frame, a set of expectancies in relation to mainstream North American service encounters, which constitutes the moral order at play here. This 'polite service encounter' frame is invoked by the agent through her classic 'Pan-Am smile', her 'cheery' intonation, and the use of various formulations conventionally associated with such a frame (e.g. 'may I . . .', 'I don't really care for . . .'). It is contested, on the other hand, by Neal through repeated use of an expression (i.e. 'fuck') that is considered taboo relative to this frame; although as we pointed out in Chapter 4, even this seemingly antisocial act presupposes the acknowledgment of social standards through which it is constituted as taboo in the first place.

Second, the impact of the agent's use of language that contests the 'polite service encounter' frame is increased because it stands in marked contrast to her prior polite attitude. In other words, our evaluation of her assertion that Neal is 'fucked' is made relative to evaluations of her prior demeanour. The pragmaticians Arin Bayraktaroğlu and Maria Sifianou (2012) describe this as an instance of 'the iron fist in a velvet glove', where an ostensibly polite attitude is progressively built up in an interaction to the point where an impolite attitude becomes even more devastating for the target than it otherwise would have been (and thus amusing for the viewers in this case).[1] The way in which Neal, and, perhaps more importantly, we the viewers, evaluate the agent's last assertion that Neal is 'fucked' thus draws from the relational history of these two characters that has been established in the course of this particular interaction, as well as from understandings of the 'polite service encounter' frame involved. In other words, we have a brief relational history at play here, which affords an evaluation of 'you're fucked' that is more marked than it might otherwise have been relative to this frame. It also illustrates how the analysis of politeness can go hand-in-hand with analyses of impoliteness, and thus ultimately we should be theorising them both within one overarching framework.

What becomes apparent here, then, is that understandings of politeness, impoliteness and so on are *co-constructed* by two or more participants over the course of an interaction. To be co-constructed means that not only the speaker but also other participants can influence the *trajectory* of social actions/meanings and the evaluations of politeness they reflexively occasion as they develop in interaction. The upshot of this is that politeness must be analysed as situated in interaction, although it is important to note here that we conceptualise interaction not as isolated moments of the here-and-now but rather as inextricably linked to understandings of politeness in the there-and-then. In this chapter we thus consider more deeply the various ways in which interaction in this broader sense, whether it be direct or mediated, both constrains and affords understandings of politeness.

6.2   Key concepts

Incrementality and sequentiality

Politeness has traditionally been analysed as a discrete, independent evaluative moment on the part of either the speaker or the hearer at the utterance level (see Chapter 2), which assumes, in turn, a *punctuated* view of time. However, as we discussed in Chapter 4, a key finding from more recent research is that understandings of politeness are cumulative: they build on one another, both within and across interactions. In other words, evaluations of a particular utterance of turn at talk vis-à-vis politeness are invariably understood relative to both prior and forthcoming evaluations, rather than simply retrospectively (see Eelen 2001). While those evaluations that arise adjacently to each other, or what is sometimes termed contiguously, tend to be most tightly interlinked, the retrospective/prospective sense of a present occurrence can, of course, go beyond adjacent turns at talk, and indeed may go beyond a single interaction located at a particular point in time and space. This latter perspective on politeness as cumulative assumes, in turn, a perspective on time in the here-and-now as *emergent*.

In order to analyse emergent understandings of politeness in interaction alongside punctuated understandings, there are two key inter-related analytical notions that we need to consider: **incrementality** and **sequentiality**. *Incrementality* refers to the way in which speakers adjust or modify their talk in the light of how the progressive uttering of units of talk is received by other participants. In other words, the fact that social actions and meanings are produced incrementally in interaction means they are inevitably subject to ongoing evaluation as they are produced, and so can be adjusted accordingly in real time. *Sequentiality*, on the other hand, refers to the way in which current turns or utterances are always understood relative to prior and subsequent talk, particularly talk that is contiguous (i.e. immediately prior to or subsequent to the current utterance). This means that next turns are a critical resource for participants in reaching understandings of the evaluations of others, including understandings of other's understandings of one's own evaluations. It also means that not only participants, but we analysts as well, have access to a record of what John Heritage characterises as 'publicly displayed and continuously up-dated intersubjective understandings' (1984: 259) when examining understandings of politeness in interaction. It is very important to remember, however, that next turns constitute an *indirect* record from which both participants and analysts can only make inferences. A response in next or subsequent turns rarely provides proof of how a prior turn has been understood except in those relatively few cases where participants utter explicit metacomments about that turn (a point which we will discuss further in Chapter 9). Instead, responses in next turn provide some evidence for participants, and thus for analysts, to make inferences about the current speaker's understanding of the prior turn.

To illustrate the ways in which incrementality both constrains and affords understandings of social actions and meanings, and thus (im)politeness, consider for a moment example (2), from the film *There's Something About Mary*. Here, Ted (a 'nerd') is inviting (or attempting to invite) one of the 'cool' girls at school (Renise) to go to the senior prom.

(2) 1 Ted: ((taps Renise on the shoulder as she is smoking)) Hey,
                Renise.
    2 Renise: ((as she slowly turns around to face Ted)) Hey.
    3 Ted: So what's up?
    4 Renise: ((looks away)) Er, I dunno.
    5 Ted: Cool. (looks away)
    6 Ted: ((long pause: Ted nods twice with body oriented
                towards Renise but not gazing directly at her; Renise
                orients her body at right angles to Ted and does not
                return his gaze at any point))
                So I was wondering, I don't, I don't know uh, if may-
                maybe you wanted to,
                ((Renise turns her gaze further away from Ted looking
                at something in distance))
                or not, if you don't want to you don't have to, I mean,
                I don't, I, I was just wondering if maybe you'd go to
                the prom and, or uh, if you felt like that maybe you
                wanted to go, with me, or I mean whatever, if, if you
                didn't.
    7   ((pause))
    8 Ted: Did you take that bio test? Cos that was like-
                            (*There's Something About Mary*, 1998)

What is notable here, of course, is the way in which Renise deploys gaze and the orientation of her body to signal disengagement with Ted's talk. This evident disengagement, in turn, occasions the incremental development of an invitation where the structurally *preferred response* to the invitation is initially acceptance, but which is subsequently transformed into one where rejection is projected. **Preference** is a technical term from the field of conversation analysis, which refers to the non-equivalent ordering of actions. A *preferred action*, according to Anita Pomerantz (1984), is one that is performed with a minimum of delay early in the turn, or with some kind of upgrade, while a *dispreferred action* is one that is performed after some delay later in the turn and may be qualified or hedged. Acceptance of the invitation (as well as the invitation itself) is initially structured as a preferred action by Ted in turn 6 as it is launched with the conventional form for making tentative invitations ('I was wondering if') early in the turn. However, this trajectory is subsequently abandoned as both the invitation (and acceptance of it) is progressively transformed into a dispreferred action through hesitations, hedges ('I don't', 'I mean'), qualifications ('I if may-maybe you wanted to'), to the point that a refusal is evidently the structurally preferred response ('or not, if you don't want to you don't have to', 'or I mean whatever, if, if you didn't'). Indeed, at the conclusion of his long-winded invitation, Ted attempts a topic shift in turn 8 before Renise has even responded (at least verbally), perhaps because he is anticipating a refusal from her.

Whether or not Renise's evident disengagement in this interaction would be evaluated as impolite is an open question, especially given this is meant to be an interaction between high school students. However, Renise is arguably indexing at least a non-polite attitude here because she does not display any visible sign of interest in either Ted or his invitation. That Ted picks up on this non-polite attitude is evident from the way in which he progressively adjusts the preference structure of the invitation in the course of his talk. In other words, we can find evidence of a particular understanding of politeness (i.e. a non-polite attitude on the part of one of the participants) through close examination of the incremental development of a social action, in particular, the **transformation** of the preference structure of Ted's invitation from a preferred to a dispreferred action.

Renise's subsequent response is not, however, the structurally preferred rejection, as we can see in the continuation of the dialogue in example (3). This, in turn, muddies the waters somewhat in relation to how her attitude towards Ted might be evaluated.

> (3) 8 Ted: Did you take that bio test? Cos that was like-
>   9 Renise: ((moves her head to gaze at Ted)) Look, I heard this rumour that this guy, like, was gonna ask me. ((moves her gaze away)) So I'm gonna wait and see what happens there. ((pause)) But that sounds great ((torques her body to face Ted)), yeah.
>   10 Ted: Okay.
>   11 Ted: ((turns away to leave, and then turns back)) So, is that like-, is that like a yes or a no or?

12 Renise: ((turns to face Ted)) I thought I made it perfectly clear, ((starts moving away)) if everything else falls apart, ((torques body to face Ted as she is leaving)) maybe.
13   ((Renise walks off))
14 Ted: (towards Renise's back as she walks away) I'm gonna hold you to that.

(*There's Something About Mary*, 1998)

Instead of flatly refusing, Renise follows her implied refusal (in indicating there is someone else she is hoping will ask her) with an upgraded appreciation ('but that sounds great'). On the one hand, this affords an evaluation of her response as at least not impolite, if not polite. On the other hand, it creates ambiguity in interpreting pragmatic meaning. That is, in relation to the *content* of her response, is she refusing Ted's invitation or conditionally accepting it? This ambiguity is oriented to by Ted who pursues a less equivocal response from Renise, albeit with a tentatively formulated question. At this point, however, not only does Renise's meaning here become clear (accepting Ted's invitation is a last resort that she might consider if no other invitations were forthcoming), but it becomes clear that Renise is once again indexing a non-polite, if not outright impolite, attitude here. The humorous intent of this interaction becomes clear for the viewer, of course, when Ted indicates that he is taking her highly conditional 'acceptance' of his invitation seriously. But what is important to note here is that Ted's understanding of Renise's immediately prior talk (i.e. turn 9), as well as her evaluative attitude towards him and his invitation, is dependent on her current turn (i.e. turn 12). This illustrates the critical importance of taking into account the sequentially situated nature of understandings of politeness. In this way, we can see how the inherent sequentiality of dialogic interaction can also both afford and constrain understandings of politeness. It is also in this sense that we can talk about the 'retrospective/prospective' nature of understandings of politeness.

What is meant by the 'retrospective/prospective sense of a present occurrence', according to Schegloff, is that retrospectively, current turns offer indications of the current speaker's understanding of a just prior turn, while prospectively, current turns set 'some of the terms by which a next turn will be understood' (2007: 16). The way in which current turns are inevitably understood relative to both prior and forthcoming talk is thus a critical normative force that both affords and constrains understandings of politeness. It is also the simultaneously retrospective and prospective operation of current turns of talk that can ultimately confer *emergent* properties on understandings of politeness.

We briefly introduced the notion of emergence in relation to perspectives on time in Chapter 4. Here, we will define the notion of emergence more formally.

In order to do so, let us consider the way in which the following request sequence develops in an episode of the television series, *Desperate Housewives*. Example (4) begins when one of the characters, Susan, goes across to see her neighbour, Mrs Greenberg.

(4) 1 Greenberg: Susan. Long time no see.
    2 Susan: Mrs. Greenberg. Do you remember those two eggs I let you borrow last Christmas?
                  ((She opens up her carton of eggs and motions to two empty spaces in the container which is otherwise full of eggs))
    3 Susan: I need those back.
    4 Greenberg: Well gosh, honey, I'm fresh out, but if you want, I could run to the store.
    5 Susan: Oh, forget about it, it's not that important.
    6   But since I'm here, do you still have that old hatchback sitting in your garage? Can I borrow it tomorrow?
    7 Greenberg: You wanna borrow my car?
    8 Susan: Just for a couple of hours.
    9 Greenberg: Well, I'm not sure. Do you know how to drive a stick?
   10 Susan: Yes, I think so. I learned in college. It's like riding a bike, right?
   11 Greenberg: I'm not sure, dear. ((moves to shut the door))
   12 Susan: It's no big deal. It's just for a couple of hours.
   13   I let you borrow my eggs for a whole year.
                  ('Running to standstill', *Desperate Housewives*, Season 1, Episode 6, 2004)

Susan launches straight into a pre-request in turn 2, after a perfunctory greeting, through a recognition check that orients Mrs Greenberg to the possibility of a forthcoming request. However, rather than waiting for a go-ahead response, Susan moves immediately into the request itself in turn 3, which is formulated here as a directive, thereby displaying high entitlement to have her request to borrow eggs granted. While Mrs Greenberg offers to purchase more eggs, after indicating she does not have any eggs at present (turn 4), Susan dismisses the offer (turn 5), and instead moves immediately into a check of availability of Mrs Greenberg's car (turn 6). This check of availability is interpretable as a pre-request, an understanding which is subsequently confirmed when, once again without waiting for a go-ahead response, Susan issues a second request: this time to borrow Mrs Greenberg's car. When Mrs Greenberg responds with an expression of surprise, and thus equivocally to the request (turn 7), Susan attempts to downgrade the imposition ('just for a couple of hours') over the course of the next few turns – or what Brown and Levinson (1987) have termed the degree of negative face threat (see Chapter 2) – before offering a justification for this request in turn 13, namely, that she lent eggs to Mrs Greenberg for a whole year. While this is somewhat ridiculous from the perspective of the viewer, and it is this that lends humour to the sequence, it also becomes apparent why Susan drew attention to the borrowed eggs in the first place, namely, she equates her lending two eggs to Mrs Greenberg with borrowing the latter's car. In other words, a possible understanding emerges here that Susan was asking to borrow eggs from Mrs Greenberg in order to justify asking to borrow the latter's car. Whether or not Susan's reasoning or assumption here is accepted by Mrs Greenberg (and by we viewers) is consequential, in turn, for the understandings of politeness at play in this interaction.

One question we can consider, for instance, is how Susan's declination of Mrs Greenburg's offer in turn 5 might be evaluated vis-à-vis politeness. As we noted, in formulating the request with a directive ('I need those back'), and in not waiting for a go-ahead response from Mrs Greenberg subsequent to the recognition check pre-request, Susan displayed a high entitlement to having the request granted. In other words, Mrs Greenburg was being put on the spot, as it were, in that no contingencies in granting the request were oriented to by Susan in the formulation of her request, and thus a refusal to grant the request was projected as the dispreferred response here. Yet in spite of this, there was no indication in Mrs Greenburg's response that she evaluated Susan's request or the formulation of it as impolite, or at least she did not display an evaluation of it as impolite. And indeed she offers to go to buy some eggs in turn 4, a display of concern that is interpretable here as polite given this goes beyond what might be normally expected from one's neighbours. This display of concern is reciprocated when Susan refuses Mrs Greenberg's offer in turn 5. Since Susan treats the granting of her request that Mrs Greenberg return the two eggs as no longer 'important' in her declination of Mrs Greenberg's offer to buy some eggs, the declination is itself interpretable as polite, since she has ostensibly relinquished a high entitlement to have her request granted.

However, Susan's declination of Mrs Greenberg's offer is cast in a somewhat different light as the interaction progresses. In particular, it is shifted in part through Susan's subsequent request in turn 6 to borrow Mrs Greenberg's car, and Mrs Greenberg's initial equivocal response in turn 7. It shifts even further when Susan responds to Mrs Greenberg's subsequent implied refusal in turn 11 by downgrading the request in turn 12, and justifies her request to borrow Mrs Greenberg's car by reminding Mrs Greenberg in turn 13 that Susan previously lent her two eggs. In the light of this, then, Susan's declination of Mrs Greenberg's offer is evidently less polite than it first appeared, given this is being used as a means to persuade Mrs Greenberg to lend her car to Susan. We can

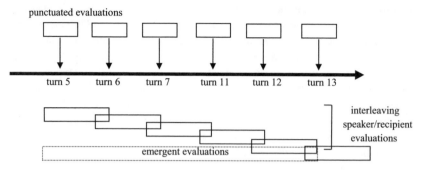

Figure 6.1 Punctuated versus emergent understandings of politeness.

see from this that the way in which Susan's declination in turn 5 is evaluated vis-à-vis politeness can be revised in the light of the social actions/meanings that arise through subsequent turns, in particular turns 6–7 and 11–13. Ultimately, then, the evaluation of turn 5 vis-à-vis politeness is formally dependent on what subsequently occurs in the interaction (as well as what precedes it).

This is displayed schematically as illustrated in Figure 6.1. The arrow pointing from the left to the right side of the page in Figure 6.1 represents the ongoing movement of time in the here-and-now. The individuated boxes above the main time arrow represent punctuated evaluations of politeness at each turn. The interleaving boxes under the main time arrow represent the interleaving of speaker and recipient evaluations of politeness across contiguous turns. The dotted box underneath the interleaving boxes represents an instance of an emergent evaluation of politeness. The difference between understandings of politeness represented above the time arrow (representing those derived via punctuated evaluations) and those representations below the time arrow (representing those derived emergent evaluations) is that the former are formally *independent* of each other while the latter are formally *interdependent*. The most important thing to note here, then, is that understandings of politeness cannot always be tied to single utterances or turns at talk. In cases where they are cumulative across an interaction, this means evaluations of politeness are interdependent or intertwined with prior and forthcoming evaluations of politeness, and thus an evaluation of current utterances or turns cannot be formally examined without considering prior and forthcoming utterances or turns. In other words, politeness must be analysed as incrementally and sequentially situated in the here-and-now of dialogic interaction, or what is termed 'talk-in-interaction' in conversation analysis.

One final point to note is that since incrementality and sequentiality both afford and constrain understandings of the social actions and meanings that occasion evaluations of politeness in the here-and-now, we must inevitably allow for what Schegloff terms **possible understandings**. It is evident that in many cases participants pursue possible understandings of actions along multiple lines, and thus, 'they are therefore prepared to recognise even ones arrived at by others that might have been thought elusive' (2006: 147). The multiple lines along which participants pursue understandings of social actions and meanings, and thus evaluations of politeness which are reflexively occasioned by these understandings, is an important characteristic of politeness in interaction. One key upshot of this is that understandings of politeness are inevitably tinged with some degree of contingency. In other words, participants, and thus analysts, can only be as sure in our understandings of politeness as the prior and subsequent turns allow.

Accountability

In Chapter 4 we briefly noted that evaluations of politeness, impoliteness and the like can have significant consequences for those parties involved. The real-world consequentiality of understandings of politeness is a function of the way in which participants can be held *accountable* for social actions and meanings, and thus the evaluations that are reflexively occasioned by them, in interaction. **Accountability** is a notion that was first introduced in the work of the ethnomethodologists Sacks (1992 [1964–72]) and Garfinkel (1967). It refers to the degree to which a person (or group of persons) is taken to be committed to or responsible for the real-world consequences of their social actions and meanings. Accountability arises in two key ways in interaction. On the one hand, participants are *normatively accountable* for their evaluations of themselves and others. This is accountability in the sense of what Heritage refers to as 'the taken-for-granted level of reasoning through which a running index of action and interaction is created and sustained' (1988: 128). On the other hand, participants can be held or hold themselves *morally accountable* for how they are taken to be evaluating something or someone, in the sense of 'overt explanation in which social actors give accounts of what they are doing in terms of reasons, motives or causes' (Heritage 1988: 128). In both cases however, participants are drawing from a perceived moral order in attributing or claiming accountability for particular understandings of politeness.

Let us consider example (5), an interaction from a documentary investigating race relations in Australia, where four Indians are being taken around various communities in Australia. In the example, two of them are talking with an Aboriginal elder about the experiences of indigenous Australians. It begins here with Radhika asking the elder why indigenous Australians have struggled to improve their lives. Here we use a slightly more complex set of transcription conventions so that we can examine paralinguistic and prosodic aspects of the interaction alongside what is said.[2]

(5) 1	Radhika:	So do they lack motivation? Why do they lack [motivation?]
2	Elder:	[some do] because of, uh, the sss- so I think because they've been so suppressed, you know if you kick a dog so much and call 'em a dog he'll stay there [so that-
3	Gurmeet:	[so >there there there< should be uhm, educational institutions, uh specific educational institutions for Aborigines [then,] after that there [will be no ( )]
4	Elder:	[there is] [there is a lot of that] here there is a lot of that here.
5	Gurmeet:	then what are the complaints.
6	Elder:	((cocks her head)) uh uh, beg your pardon?
7	Gurmeet:	why are you complaining then.
8	Elder:	((steps back)) ↑am I complaining?=
9	Radhika:	=n::o.
10	Gurmeet:	((smiles)) heh [heh]
11	Elder:	[I'm] answering questions that they asked. I'm not complain-
12	Gurmeet:	but but [you are] saying
13	Elder:	[you don't] you don't live in my country, you don't- this is my country, ((points her finger at Gurmeet)) Kamilorau is my country. I see what happens here, whatever happens in your country.
14		We complain about some of our governments=
15	Gurmeet:	=yeah=
16	Elder:	cos are they making right decisions for us? You know this is what we've gotta ask questions about. And why can't we complain.

(*Dumb, Drunk and Racist*, Episode 4, 2012)

The issue of accountability starts to come to the fore at turn 5, when Gurmeet asks what the elder's complaints are about, having been told that there are specific educational institutions to support Aborigines. This is evidently taken to be more than simply an information-seeking question by the elder, as we can see from her response in turn 6, where she asks that Gurmeet reformulate his question, thereby implying dissatisfaction with the formulation of his current talk, as well as displaying puzzlement at the terms of the question through cocking her head. However, despite the indications that something is amiss, Gurmeet nevertheless pursues a response from the elder in turn 7, once again asking her to justify her complaints. In doing so, Gurmeet is implicitly challenging the elder's right to complain, invoking the moral claim that if one does not have grounds for complaining, one should not complain. It then becomes evident from the elder's response in turn 8 that the way in which Gurmeet has cast the elder's prior responses as *complaining* is potentially causing offence. In other words, the elder evaluates Gurmeet's casting of her responses as *complaining* as 'not polite' or even 'impolite'. The elder steps back, thereby metaphorically indicating relational separation from Gurmeet, while the prosodic contour of talk also indicates astonishment or surprise at this pursuit of a response, both through the raised pitch and the emphatic stress on 'complaining'. While the question is ostensibly addressed to Gurmeet, it is Radhika who offers the preferred response here, namely, that she is not complaining, in the subsequent turn. Gurmeet then displays recognition of the possible offence by displaying embarrassment through smiling and two laughter particles (turn 10), and this offence is confirmed through the elder's subsequent response in turn 11, where she challenges the casting of her prior talk as complaining by Gurmeet, and recasts it as simply 'answering questions'. Yet despite his recognition of the possible offence, Gurmeet nevertheless pursues his line that the elder is complaining in turn 12, although he abandons his turn when the elder moves to cast Gurmeet as an *outsider*, and herself as an *insider*. In doing so the elder invokes her right to judge the situation of indigenous Australians in turn 13. Ultimately the elder concedes in turns 14–16 that she does complain about the government, but ends by claiming the right not only to judge but also to complain. What appears to have caused offence here, then, on the part of the elder is that Gurmeet as an *outsider* has challenged her (insider's) right to complain, and this breaches her expectations vis-à-vis what is considered an allowable and would thus count as a polite assessment.

A complaint, as we discussed in Chapter 4, involves constituting the moral character of the conduct (whether it be verbal or nonverbal) through that talk itself, since particular talk or conduct is never inherently a transgression, impropriety, offence, fault and so on. In challenging the elder's grounds for complaining, Gurmeet is implicitly positioning himself as having the right to evaluate the moral character of her conduct vis-à-vis discussions of problems facing indigenous Australians. In essence, he is appealing to a perceived moral order and positioning himself as an *insider* alongside the elder in relation to this moral order. It becomes evident by the end of this example that it is this positioning that causes offence. From the elder's emic perspective, Gurmeet does not have the (moral) right to challenge her (moral) right to judge and complain, and thus his line of questioning constitutes a transgression or impropriety that grounds her offence. More specifically, she treats the evaluative character of Gurmeet's line of questioning as in breach of her understanding of what counts as polite by positioning Gurmeet's perspective as one that is etic, that is, an *outsider's* perspective. In this way, we can see how understandings of politeness can intersect with issues of culture and identity, a point we will discuss further in Chapter 11. The point we are making here, however, is that this interaction clearly illustrates the importance of accountability for understandings of politeness in interaction. It is notable that such expectations become particularly salient when there is perceived to have been a breach of the moral order, and thus expectations vis-à-vis politeness. On the one hand, we can see that Gurmeet is holding the elder morally accountable for complaining in that he seeks an overt explanation or account for why she is complaining. On the other hand, we can also see that not only is the elder holding Gurmeet morally accountable for how he is being taken to be evaluating her, but that she also treats Gurmeet's attempts to hold her morally accountable as offensive. Thus, in order to examine the way in which understandings of politeness and impoliteness arise through participants holding others (and themselves) accountable to a perceived moral order, we must carefully examine how participants orient to the moral order itself in interaction.

The moral order, as we noted in Chapter 5, is multilayered. It consists of localised sets of expectancies that develop for individuals in situated relationships (first-order) which are embedded (and thus interpreted) relative to communities of practice, organisational or other group-based sets of expectancies (second-order), which are themselves embedded relative to broader societal sets of expectancies (third-order). Participants can thus be held accountable to different layers of the multiple sets of expectancies that constitute the moral order. Let us explain what we mean by this by first considering an interaction between Chinese participants of an online discussion board focusing on animation, which is taken from a study of 'doing deference' by Haugh, Chang and Kádár (2013). The thread from which example (6) is taken was initiated by Angele, who began by apologising to everyone in a group of net-friends for a transgression; namely, reposting pictures that others had previously posted. This apology thread is occasioned by Angele being held accountable by others to the set of expectancies for posting in this particular relational network. Since her transgression is of the expectations of a relational network that has formed through ongoing contact around a common interest (namely, discussing animation) it constitutes a transgression of second-order moral expectancies. We pick up this thread at the point Angele is apologising for the third time having had her two previous apologies rejected by Alice. We provide here just a translation of the original Mandarin Chinese (see Haugh, Chang and Kádár 2013 for the original text).

(6) Post 8, 16:21 (Angele)
[I] apologise for this: I posted some pictures on 'Mr A and Ms A's sweetheart little shop' (newbie > <)'. I really don't know my behaviour [of posting pictures] makes me an idiot~~~) [I] here apologise to everyone. [I] hope you can forgive me... [I] will never do this again... [I am] sorry everyone...

Angele structures her apology in a particular way, starting with an announcement that explicitly **indexes** her current post as constituting an apology through a performative verb ('[I] apologise for this'). She then describes the offence, namely, posting some pictures on an area belonging to Mr A and Ms A, as well as casting herself as a newbie (*xinshou*), and displays her frustration with this newbie status through an emoticon representing 'closed eyes' (> <). This casting of herself as a newbie is offered as an account for this offence, as she acknowledges that by infringing upon this norm she has made a fool of herself. She then repeats her apology, asks for forgiveness, promises forbearance (i.e. that it will not happen again), and then apologises yet again. In repeating her apology in this way, Angele is orienting to a broader societal set of expectancies in relation to apologies in Chinese, namely, that one indexes sincerity (*chengyi*) through repetition of an apology expression (a point we noted in Chapter 5). In doing so, Angele is also displaying a markedly deferential line, thereby opening up her apology to evaluation as 'polite' (*limao*). However, she is also orienting to the expectancies of this particular relational network, or what can be termed a community of practice. In other words, Angele is simultaneously orienting to both second-order (group-based) and third-order (societal) norms that constitute the moral order being invoked by these participants.

In the following three posts, however, we can observe how first-order norms (localised sets of expectancies that develop for individuals in situated relationships) can intersect with second-order and third-order sets of expectancies, and thus also play a part in understandings of politeness that arise through interaction. Example (7) begins when another participant (Juziheng) intervenes in the thread.

(7) Post 9, 16:22 (Juziheng)
That... Miss A... your apology has no format >/////<. [I am] afraid you have to apologise one more time >/////<

Post 11, 16:23 (Alice)
Sigh... Miss A is a newbie... Her membership was created by me a few days ago. She is a little fart kid who doesn't know anything. Over!

Post 12, 16:25 (Juziheng)

Oh Miss A . . . we encourage each other to go through things. I've been here for a long time . . . [I] also don't understand anything either >//////<

>/////< [blushing, embarrassed]

In post 9, Juziheng complains that Angele's apology does not follow the correct format expected by members of their group (thereby orienting to a second-order norm), and demands yet another apology from Angele, although the illocutionary force of this complaint and directive is softened somewhat by the emotive stance of embarrassment that Juziheng displays through an emoticon that represents blushing. This display of embarrassment about continuing to hold Angele accountable for the formulation of her apology mitigates to some degree a potential evaluation of her post as 'impolite' (*mei-limao, bu-limao*).

At this point, however, Alice intervenes to defend Angele as seen in post 11. Specifically, she casts Angele as a 'little fart kid' (*xiao-pihai*) who does not know anything (specifically about the rules on reposting prior posts and the correct format for apologies), and thus implies that Angele cannot be expected to know everything. She also identifies Angele as a newbie who has just joined their group at Alice's invitation. In being posted subsequent to Juziheng's attempt to hold Angele accountable, Alice holds Juziheng accountable for a post that she considers inappropriate (i.e. too harsh), and thereby implies Juziheng does not have moral rights to be making such an evaluation of Angele. In other words, Alice asserts that while *she* can hold Angele accountable for transgressions, Juziheng does not have such rights. Alice's post thus invokes a localised sets of expectancies vis-à-vis her own situated relationship with Angele that contrast with the set of expectancies vis-à-vis the situated relationship between Juziheng and Angele, and in this sense, we can see how first-order sets of expectancies that develop for individuals in localised, situated relationships can also play a part in understandings of politeness in interaction.

The invoking of these first-order norms by Alice is subsequently ratified by Juziheng in post 12, when the latter expresses empathy for Angele through claiming to have had similar experiences or feelings, and displays embarrassment through a 'blushing' emoticon. In other words, Juziheng implicitly acknowledges her transgression or impropriety in attempting to hold Angele accountable for transgressions, thereby orienting to the sets of expectancies that have developed for the localised relationships that have developed between these various participants.

To analyse understandings of politeness in interaction, then, we must carefully examine the ways in which participants orient to or invoke (whether implicitly or explicitly) the reflexively inter-related layers of the moral order. Invoking the moral order can also involve, as we have seen, explicitly casting participants as either members relative to this moral order, and thus insiders, or as non-members who are inevitably seen as taking an outsider perspective on it. Attributing or claiming an insider versus outsider perspective on the moral order can be highly consequential for how understandings of politeness, impoliteness and so on develop in interaction, because what participants can be held accountable for can be traced, in part, to perceptions of the moral order and the (perceived) status of participants vis-à-vis that moral order.

Footing

In Chapter 5, we introduced the notion of participation status. We pointed out that when examining politeness in interaction we consider the different perspectives from which participants themselves may be evaluating social actions and meanings. In particular, we argued that understandings of politeness must be situated in relation to various different possible types of participation status. However, closer examination of the perspectives of participants in interaction indicates that there is yet another phenomena we need to take into account – what the sociologist Erving Goffman (1979, 1981) called **footing**. The notion of footing refers to four distinct sets of roles and responsibilities that Goffman suggested were conflated in the folk notion of speaker. According to Goffman there are four different speaker footings: animator, author, principal and figure. An animator (or utterer) is the one producing talk, an author is the entity that creates or designs the talk, a principal is the party responsible for that talk, and a figure is the character portrayed within the talk.

In example (8), taken from the film *Four Weddings and a Funeral*, we can see how the person serving in the shop exploits these footings in making suggestions that would be conventionally understood as polite, but given the ironic framing here, are open to evaluation as not polite (and even perhaps as impolite).

(8) (Charles is going to buy a gift for Carrie's wedding to a rich Scotsman)
    1 Charles: Do you have the wedding list for Banks?
    2 Server: Certainly, sir. Lots of beautiful things for around about the £1,000 mark.
    3 Charles: What about things around the sort of £50 mark? Is there much?
    4 Server: Well, you could get that Pygmy warrior over there.
    5 Charles: This? Excellent!
    6 Server: If you could find someone to chip in the other 950 pounds. Or our carrier bags are £1.50 each. Why don't you just get 33 of them?

7 Charles: Well, I think I'll probably leave it. Thanks very much.
              You've been very ...
                             (*Four Weddings and a Funeral*, 1994)

What we can see here is that the server maintains the same seemingly 'polite' demeanour throughout the interaction consistent with expectations invoked by the service encounter frame relative to which the two participants co-construct the social actions, meanings and evaluations here (cf. example (1)). However, it becomes apparent that this demeanour is only a polite veneer on the surface of the interaction, in which Charles is ultimately left in no doubt as to the server's true attitude towards him. It thus constitutes a prototypical instance of what Leech (1983) terms 'mock politeness'. It can be characterised as 'mock' (as opposed to 'genuine') because seemingly helpful suggestions (which are consistent with a polite service encounter frame) actually mask a negative assessment of Charles' request that she suggest something much cheaper than she initially canvassed. This negative assessment is masked because it is achieved through ironic detachment, which is achieved, in turn, through the server invoking a complex set of footings.

There are two suggestions made by the server in response to Charles' request. While the suggestion that he buy a 'pygmy warrior' in turn 4 appears at first to be a genuine one, and towards which Charles expresses an appreciation (in turn 5), it becomes apparent in her subsequent turn that the suggestion is an entirely unrealistic one given Charles' budget. Another suggestion (to buy carrier bags) is also made in the same turn, which although formulated in the conventional manner of a polite suggestion in a service encounter, is nevertheless also clearly unhelpful. Charles is left with no option but to leave the shop, leaving it unsaid what he thinks of the service he has just received (in turn 7).

If we consider this interaction from the perspective of Goffman's notion of footing it becomes evident that while the server is the animator and is seemingly committed as the principal of these suggestions, she is not the author. Instead, the server is animating the kinds of things a helpful and polite server might suggest. In this way, she detaches from being a 'fully committed participant' to a 'detached observer', as argued by the conversation analyst Rebecca Clift (1999). In the footing of a 'detached observer' she is able to imply an evaluation of these suggestions, namely, that they are absurd, thereby implying that Charles' request that she suggest gifts that cost around £50 is also an absurd one. In other words, she is implying a negative assessment of Charles' request, which in the context of a service encounter frame is clearly not polite (and perhaps even interpretable as impolite). Moreover, through the ironic frame invoked here, she takes a footing relative to the implied negative assessments as a fully committed participant: she is the animator, author and principal of these negative assessments, and thus her negative evaluations may also be perceived as hostile towards Charles. In this respect, it is open to evaluation as impolite. She also implicitly invites Charles to share in this ironic frame, although this is obviously difficult given he is the target of the negative assessments. However, we, the audience, as ratified overhearers, clearly can share in the irony. Ultimately, then, it is this clash between the ostensibly polite demeanour of the server, the implied negative assessments that are not polite relative to a service encounter frame, and the hostile attitude towards Charles that is potentially open to evaluation as impolite, which gives rise to what can be termed 'mock politeness'. Notably, these different understandings of politeness arise simultaneously through the complex set of footings invoked by the server.

In Goffman's framework only the speaker has a complex range of footings available to him or her. Yet clearly recipients can also take various footings. It is thus proposed by Haugh (2013c) that in the notion of speaker – or what we term here *production* – footing needs to be complemented by the notion of recipient (or reception) footing. While the animator (or utterer) is completed by the (meta)recipient, as we discussed in Chapter 5, it is further argued that the role of the author who constructs the talk has a counterpart in the *interpreter* who perceives and evaluates the social actions and meanings that arise through that talk. The role of the principal who is socially responsible for those meanings or actions is necessarily complemented by the *accounter* who (explicitly or tacitly) holds the principal responsible for those social actions and meanings. And, finally, the production role of figure, namely, the character depicted in the talk, is also a potential *target* when the character depicted is co-present, or when an utterance is attributed to someone other than the speaker. The complex array of participation footings proposed here are summarised in Figure 6.2.

From Figure 6.2 it becomes apparent that understandings of politeness need to be situated not only simply vis-à-vis speakers or hearers, but relative to a complex array of production and reception footings. To examine how this complex set of participation footings can underpin multiple understandings of politeness in interaction, let us return to the example of the interaction between two visiting Indians and an Aboriginal elder talking about the experiences of indigenous Australians, which we discussed earlier. The relevant part of the interaction is reproduced in example (9) below.

(9) 5   Gurmeet: then what are the complaints.
    6   Elder: ((cocks her head)) uh uh, beg your pardon?
    7   Gurmeet: why are you complaining then.
    8   Elder: ((steps back)) ↑am I complaining?=

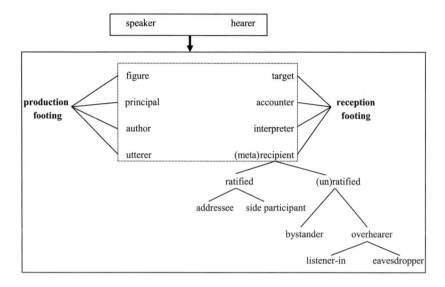

Figure 6.2 Types of participation footings.

9 Radhika: =no::
10 Gurmeet: ((smiles)) heh [heh
11 Elder: [I'm answering questions that they
              asked. I'm not complain-
12 Gurmeet: but but you are saying
                        (*Dumb, Drunk and Racist*, Episode 4, 2012)

As we previously discussed, the elder appeared to take offence at Gurmeet holding her morally accountable for 'complaining' about the situation of indigenous
Australians, as seen in turns 5, 7 and 12 in example (9). This was apparent from
the way in which the elder held Gurmeet morally accountable for how he was
being taken to be evaluating her in holding her morally accountable for complaining, as seen in turns 6, 8 and 11. We would go further here though, and
argue that this interaction involves a complex array of participation footings
on the part of Gurmeet and the elder. In suggesting that the elder is unjustified in complaining (in turns 5, 7 and 12), Gurmeet is clearly taking the
participation footing of animator, principal, author, with the elder as the figure. The reception footings that are invoked through Gurmeet's talk, on the
other hand, involve the elder as the addressee and figure, as well as interpreter and accounter. This array of participation footings is largely mirrored in
the elder's responses (in turns 6, 8 and 11), where she takes the participation

footing of utterer, principal and figure. However, the authorship of her utterances is in fact attributable to Gurmeet (given he is the one who suggested she is complaining). This interactional detachment from the author footing is how, in part, the elder signals her potential offence at Gurmeet's line of questioning.

There are, moreover, more than two participant loci in relation to understandings of (im)politeness in this interaction. There is, for instance, the host of the documentary as well as two other visiting Indians who do not directly contribute to this particular interaction, but are nevertheless co-present, and so are positioned in the reception footings of side participants and interpreters. There is also yet another layer of participation footings; namely, we, the viewing audience, who are ratified overhearers to this interaction, and thus can also form our own evaluations of politeness relative to this interaction. But most importantly for the trajectory of this particular segment of their interaction is the solitary contribution of Radhika. While the elder's question in turn 8 is ostensibly directed at Gurmeet, the presence of side participants, including Radhika, allows Radhika to step into the addressee footing in turn 9. In endorsing the elder's implicit rejection of Gurmeet's suggestion, or what the conversation analyst Tanya Stivers (2008) terms an *affiliative* response, Radhika not only takes up a reception footing as accounter and interpreter of the elder's prior turn, she also takes up a reception footing as accounter of Gurmeet's prior talk. In other words, she implicitly holds Gurmeet accountable for his potentially offensive suggestion. The fact that Gurmeet moves to reiterate his stance once again after this (in turn 12), however, suggests that he does not have the same understanding vis-à-vis impoliteness as the elder and most likely Radhika. It also remains an open question what understandings the host and the other two Indians might have had. But this multiplicity of possible understandings is, we would argue, the whole point. When examining politeness in interaction the question should not be 'is this talk or conduct polite or impolite?' and the like. Instead, the question should be 'for *whom* is this (potentially) polite or impolite for?' There is no reason to think that there should be only one answer to the question of how interactions are evaluated vis-à-vis politeness. This is not to suggest that participants always have diverging understandings of politeness, but rather to simply point out that we need to relinquish the oft implicit assumption that everyone has the same understanding of politeness in interaction.

Interactional multimodality

Throughout the analyses in this chapter we have been alluding to yet another key feature of how understandings of politeness arise in interaction, namely, multimodality. We will consider the issue of multimodality further in Chapters 7

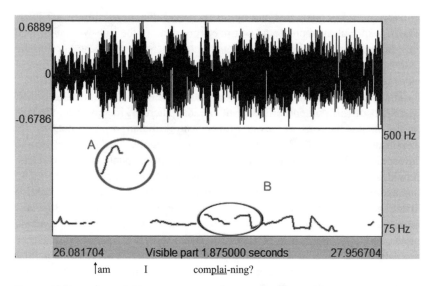

↑am   I   com<u>plai</u>-ning?

Figure 6.3 Instrumental analysis of 'agitated' pitch contour.

and 8. Here, we will thus only briefly consider what might be termed **interactional multimodality** – the way in which multiple modes can be drawn upon in forming understandings of politeness in interaction. In the case of *direct* interaction, apart from talk (i.e. what is said), it is now well established that prosody, essentially *how* something is said, can be enormously influential on understandings of politeness, as pointed out in an instructive survey of prosodic dimensions of impoliteness by Culpeper (2011a) (see Chapter 3). The prosody of talk involves a complex interplay of factors such as timing, loudness, accent, pitch and voice quality. While the more detailed transcription conventions of conversation analysis pick up on many of these features, as we saw in our analysis of example (5), an instrumental analysis of prosodic features can further ground systematic analyses of the role of intonation in reaching particular understandings of politeness. We suggested earlier, for instance, that the elder displayed astonishment at Gurmeet's repeated request that she provide a justification for complaining about the situation of Aboriginal Australians through both a raised pitch and emphatic stress on 'complaining' when responding '↑am I com<u>plaining</u>?'. The former markedly raised pitch is clearly visible in an instrumental analysis of the pitch contour of this particular utterance, as illustrated in Figure 6.3.

At the beginning of her utterance, the elder's local pitch on 'am' is markedly higher and rising relative to her global pitch register, as seen in the contour labelled A in Figure 6.3. This was represented by an upward arrow (↑) in the conversation analytic transcription. At the end of the 'complaining' her pitch is also visibly rising, albeit at a lower pitch as seen in the contour labelled B in Figure 6.3. This was represented by a question mark (?) at the end of the word in the transcription. The conversation analyst Margaret Selting (1996) describes this kind of intonation contour as displaying 'astonishment', through which the elder signals that Gurmeet's pursuit of a response is unexpected. In other words, through this intonational contour the elder implies that Gurmeet's question is inapposite (i.e. inappropriate or unjustified) (Couper-Kuhlen 2012). The 'astonished' or 'surprised' intonational contour also signals that the preferred response to her question is in fact denial of her question. As well as displaying agreement with her astonishment, an affiliative response that is subsequently provided by another participant, Radhika, is signalled through a fall-rise pitch on an elongated 'no'.

The advantages of this kind of instrumental prosodic analysis is that it is relatively objective and accessible given it is a visual representation of pitch movement rather than being based on various different kinds of transcription systems, as well as being more finely nuanced. However, ultimately, the main advantage of such an analysis is that it draws the attention of researchers to examine the important role intonational patterns can play in the interactional achievement of understandings of politeness, which might otherwise go unnoticed in our analyses of politeness.

It is also becoming increasingly apparent that non-verbal modes can also be critical in constituting understandings of politeness in interaction, as we have observed in a number of the examples in this chapter. These modes include gesture (i.e. an expressive movement that has a clear boundary of onset but does not result in any sustained change of position), facial expressions (i.e. movements of parts of the face, such as the mouth, nose, eyebrows), gaze (i.e. the organisation, direction and intensity of looking), proxemics (i.e. the distance that individuals take up with respect to others and relevant objects) and posture (i.e. the way participants position their bodies in a given interaction) (Norris 2004). In example (5), for instance, the elder steps back as she utters '↑am I complaining?'.

In example (10), an insurance agent (Lan) in Taiwan has been asking about whether a long-term customer (Chen) has renewed his car insurance with them. At the point this excerpt begins, the insurance agent topicalises unmet expectations, namely, that he had expected the case to go to them because the customer's mother had said it would (turn 3). This is followed by a denial of knowing what his mother had promised by the customer, and admitting that the case is being dealt with by someone else (turn 4). An interpretation of Chen's response as displaying embarrassment is evident from close examination of not only his pausing and use of hesitation markers, but also from an analysis of his gaze, as illustrated in the figure in example (10), which is adapted from Chang and Haugh (2011b).

(10)   IR-4

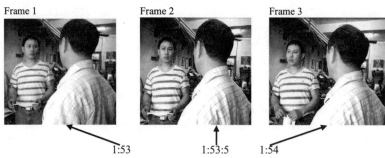

Frame 1   Frame 2   Frame 3

1:53   1:53:5   1:54

3 L: *lín bú   a tsit-leh kóng bé ho guá °bé ho guá°=*
   your mum PRT once say want give me want give me
   "Your mother once said she wants to give it to me"

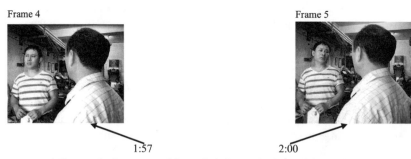

Frame 4   Frame 5

1:57   2:00

4 C: *=>ah tshia< e:::guá hit tai huètshia* (1.0) *ah ↓ guá hit tai huètshia*
       PRT car PRT I t hat C van   PRT I that C   van
   ho guán giap-bū-a   pān   lah
   give our business agent handle PRT
   "How do I know. Er, that van. Ah, that is being dealt with
   by my business agent"

As Lan's utterance in turn 3 (whereby he implies a complaint) progresses we can observe how Chen's line of gaze moves from being directed at Lan (frame 1) to being askew of Lan (frame 2) through to being directed at something else in the distance (frame 3). In other words, Chen cuts his line of gaze towards Lan as the implied complaint becomes apparent. In his subsequent verbal response in turn 4, Chen frowns as he first claims a lack of knowledge about the details of the case, thereby doing 'recalling' (frame 4), before returning his line of gaze to Lan when he begins to offer an account for these unmet expectations on the part of Lan (frame 5). Through cutting his line of gaze with Lan at this particular point in the interaction, commitant with the hesitation markers and pausing, Chen thereby displays 'embarrassment' (*buhao-yisi*) in response to Lan raising the issue of unmet expectations. This display of embarrassment is important because through it Chen displays his evident discomfort and sense of impropriety at not being able to met Lan's expectations vis-à-vis the insurance case. Thus, while Lan's topicalising of these unmet expectations is open to evaluation as 'not polite' (*bukeqi*, lit. not holding back), Chen does not display offence, but rather displays embarrassment, thereby indicating an evaluation of Lan's stance here as 'not impolite' (*bushi bu-limao*).

Finally, it is worth noting that both prosody and non-verbal modes of interaction are not restricted to direct (i.e. face-to-face) interaction, as we also observed the way in which emoticons, for instance, can influence understandings of politeness in mediated interaction, such as in online discussion boards or messenger services and the like in examples (6) and (7).

6.3   Key studies

In a series of articles on the so-called Conjoint Co-Constituting Model of Communication, Arundale (1999, 2006, 2008, 2010b) offers a theoretical grounding for much of what we have discussed in this chapter. In this theory, three key principles are proposed, drawing from work in conversation analysis, namely, the Sequential Interpreting Principle, the Recipient Design Principle and the Adjacent Placement Principle. These are claimed to lie at the heart of all understandings of social action, meaning and evaluations in interaction, and so are arguably critical to our understanding of politeness in interaction.

Along similar lines, Haugh (2007c, 2013d) develops an approach to situating politeness in interaction, with a particular focus on how participants' understandings of politeness can be situated vis-à-vis the analyst, on the one hand, and how understandings of politeness are tightly interwoven with interpretations of social actions and meanings, on the other. Both these approaches fall under the general purview of interactional pragmatics, an approach to pragmatic phenomena that is informed by research and methods in conversation analysis.

Readers who are interested in how conversation analysts themselves might approach the analysis of politeness (although it has not been a core interest in conversation analysis to date), would be well advised to consult an article by Ian Hutchby (2008) where he outlines both the potential contribution that conversation analysis can make to studies of politeness, as well as its natural limitations.

A range of approaches to analysing politeness in interaction that are broadly discursive can be found in a special issue on *Politeness as a Discursive Phenomenon* edited by Kasper (2006a). It features papers by Locher (2006), Haruko

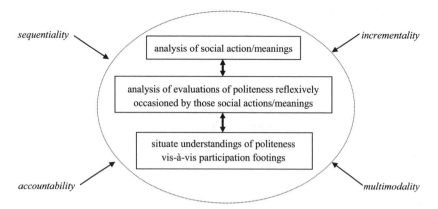

Figure 6.4 Key steps in analysing understandings of politeness in interaction.

Cook (2006) and Kasper (2006b) herself, which offer different ways in which politeness can be analysed in interaction.

Finally, for an approach to analysing politeness in discourse that remains more faithful to the Brown and Levinson (1987) original model of politeness, see Usami's (2006) introduction to *Discourse Politeness Theory*. In this approach, Usami draws from corpus-informed approaches to analysing politeness in discourse, arguing that politeness involves an holistic evaluation of discourse rather than remaining at the level of individual utterances.

6.4   Summary

Ultimately, no matter whether we choose to focus exclusively on linguistic dimensions of politeness, or aim to broaden our analytical scope to include multimodal elements as well, the general approach that we have suggested here remains the same. This general approach to analysing evaluative moments of politeness in interaction is summarised in Figure 6.4.

In order to analyse understandings of politeness in interaction we must first start with an analysis of the social actions and meanings that arise in this interaction. From there we can start to build our analysis of the incremental and sequential development of understandings of politeness, which are invariably constituted through multiple modalities. In particular, we need to focus on how participants can be held accountable for those social actions and meanings, and the evaluations of politeness they reflexively occasion. In doing so, however, it is critical to remain cognisant of the various possible participation footings taken up by participants. In this way, we can go beyond the overly constraining view that there is only ever one understanding of politeness in interaction.

6.5   Exercises

I. Answer the following questions:
  1. Can you think of instances where what appeared at first to be impolite talk or conduct turned out to be not as impolite as you first imagined? If so, why might that have been the case?
  2. Have you ever experienced situations where different people in a group had very different understandings about whether something was polite or impolite? If so, why might that have been the case?
  3. Do you feel differently when watching someone being teased in a joking manner as opposed to being teased yourself? If so, why?
II. Consider the following questions and analyse the politeness phenomena occurring in them. Compare your analysis with the brief annotations below:
  (a) (Flora is sitting by herself in a local teahouse when Mr Mybug comes and sits down)
      Mybug: Do you know what D. H. Lawrence said?
      Flora: I do actually, yes.
                ((pause))
      Mybug: He said, 'There must always be a dark, dumb, bitter belly tension between the living man and the living woman.'
      Flora: Mr Mybug, do tell me about the book you're writing.
                                                  (*Cold Comfort Farm*, 1995)

  (b) (Kat is talking with her mother Lesley. They are discussing Kat's plans for coming home from university)
       1   Les: Anyway when d'you think you'd like to come home ↓love.
       2   (.)
       3   Kat: Uh:m (.) we:ll Brad's goin' down on Monday.
       4   (0.7)
       5   Les: Monday we:ll ah-:hh .hh w: ↑Monday we can't manage because (.) Granny's ↓coming Monday?
       6   (0.4)
       7   Kat: Oh;,
       8   (0.5)
       9   Kat: Could- (0.3) Dad↑couldn't pick me up from:: (.) ee-even from Westbury could he
      10   Les: .hh I ↑CAN'T HEAR you very well cz of this damn machine that's attached to this telephone ↑say it again,
      11   Kat: Would it be possible: for Dad to pick me up from Westbury on [Monday.
      12   Les: [Ye:s yes ?THAT would be ↓alright
                                  (adapted from Curl and Drew 2008: 146)

In example (a), we can see how what is normatively expected by the conversation opener 'Do you know . . . ?' is flouted by Flora in order to imply she is not interested in the topic. While it is a recognisable pre-telling, in other words, the preferred response here is 'yes', which therefore acts as 'go-ahead' for Mybug to launch his telling, Flora neglects this preference structure in issuing a bald 'no' that blocks the progressivity of that telling. It is thus open to evaluation as impolite. However, Mybug is not at all deterred and launches his telling nevertheless, to which Flora responds by attempting a topic-shift. Thus, while we the audience (who are ratified overhearers) can see Flora is being potentially rude to Mybug, he seems blissfully unware.

In example (b), we can see how Kat changes the formulation of her request from an 'indirect proposal' in line 3, whereby she nevertheless displays a relatively high entitlement to be able to come home when she likes, to a more tentative formulation ('couldn't . . . could he?') in line 9, and finally to a formulation ('would it be possible . . .') in line 11 that displays a much diminished estimation of entitlement to come home as and when she likes. This reformulation of the request, and the degree to which it orients to her entitlement to have that request granted thus develops incrementally over the course of this interaction in response to her mother's orientation to the problematicity of Kat's request.

7   Politeness, convention and rituality

7.1   Introduction

The present book has so far analysed politeness as it emerges and develops in a given interaction. Indeed, in many cases understandings of politeness come into existence 'on the spot', as the interactants draw from certain sets of expectancies in co-constructing interaction in localised, situated contexts. If we put politeness on a time scale, it can be argued that evaluative moments of politeness in the here-and-now represent a cycle of participant actions and reactions, which come into existence in either the punctuated or emergent sense of the present moment. However, understandings of politeness are not always completely localised in this way. A certain interaction is often the continuation of a previous one, and so the interactants construct politeness in the light of understandings formed in prior interactions. Even more importantly, many contexts do not necessitate such localised understandings. In many settings, perhaps most typically formal or institutionalised ones, understandings of politeness are arguably less localised in the here-and-now given the interactants are expected to follow certain 'scripted' expectations. In such contexts politeness tends to follow certain underlying **schemata**: pre-existing patterns of thought or behaviour used in recurrent ways that are readily recognisable to members. These schemata reduce uncertainty in the formation and interpretation of linguistic politeness for the simple reason that by relying on them the interactants can follow pre-existing ways of understanding politeness. It can be argued that, if localised understandings of politeness arise in the here-and-now of time, such schemata represent a pre-existing frame for understanding politeness in the here-and-now.

Indeed, if we observe various interactional datasets it becomes evident that we are often less original than we would normally think. There are certain situations and acts, which seem to 'speak for themselves', in a sense that they evoke relatively little ambiguity (see Chapter 5), due to the fact that the interactants, unwittingly or not, utilise schematic forms or social practices. A reliance on schemata should definitely not be imagined as a robotic process of copying of models of politeness: pre-existing patterns of politeness can be

137

made use of by members as **discursive resources**, to use a term which is widely used in discourse analysis (see e.g. Thornborrow's (2002) study for a detailed analysis, as well as Taylor (2007). To draw upon schemata in projecting understandings of politeness is an inherently social practice, which can be utilised to successfully cope with difficult situations, or even to politely gain the upper hand in a conflict, as the interaction in example (1) below illustrates.

> (1) Sheriff: 'We are looking for a man who might be around here.'
>
>   . . .
>
> Colonel Ludlow: 'What is he wanted for, sheriff?'
> Sheriff: 'That would be of a private nature.'
> Colonel Ludlow: 'A private nature? That's a public office you hold, isn't it Sheriff?',
>   ((awkward silence))
> Colonel Ludlow: 'Gentlemen . . . '
>
>   (*Legends of the Fall*, 1994)

Example (1) takes place between a retired colonel who works on his land and a company led by a corrupt sheriff who is pursuing a fugitive, who is in fact hiding at the colonel's property. This interaction represents a case where a recurrent social practice, namely, the use of the form of address 'Gentlemen' to address others 'politely', is utilised to conceal aggression. In other words, a particular interpretative schema is being drawn upon here as a discursive resource to accomplish a particular end. The noteworthy element in this interaction is that the colonel's final utterance, which follows a long and awkward silence and is made with a rising pitch, does not leave any doubt with regard to its meaning: it politely but very determinedly signals the end of the interaction. That this is understood is evident from the pursuers indignantly leaving at that point. The form of address 'gentlemen' could have various readings in the present context. For example, it could function as a polite imperative for the sheriff to answer the colonel's question. However, as 'Gentlemen' sets up schematic interpretation of a marker of leave-taking in this particular social setting, the sheriff and his companion can have little doubt with regard to the meaning of the colonel's utterance.

As a matter of course, the interaction in example (1) represents a prototypical situation where a schema is being deployed and understood according to what appears to be the speaker's plan. However, ambiguity is an inherent feature of understandings of politeness, and even those understandings that draw from schemata are not completely exempt. This claim has been confirmed by anthropological research (e.g. Rasmussen 1992), which claims that schematic behaviour and ambiguity are not at all contradictory phenomena. One could argue that a particular schema tends to generate a default understanding, but then it depends on various factors whether this understanding actually arises in a particular communicative interaction or not. There are cases, for instance, when seemingly polite patterns just do not seem to function as such, as we can see illustrated in example (2). This interaction takes place between Veek, an alcoholic French vicomte (nobleman), and his friend 'Packy', an American millionaire, at a train station, while Packy's high-class English fiancée, Beatrice, who is known for being a prude, stands next to them.

> (2) He chuckled amusedly and turned to Beatrice, all smiles, as one imparting delightful news.
> 'When last I see this old *farceur* it is in New York, and he is jumping out of the window of a speakeasy with two policemen after him. Great fun. Great good fun. Do you remember, my Packy, that night when . . . '
> 'Are you off somewhere, Veek?' asked Packy hastily.
> 'Oh yes. But do you remember . . . ?'
> 'Where?'
>
> (P. G. Wodehouse, *Hot Water*, Chapter 2, 1963)

When Veek begins to retell stories from Packy's stormy past the latter attempts to silence him by changing topic and inquiring about the other's plans, which is often interpreted as a polite sign of discomfort. However, Veek does not seem to get the hint, and after perfunctorily answering Packy's question, restarts the telling of the story, and so Packy needs to interrupt him yet again. While the schema used by Packy here is not understood by the vicomte in the way it would normally be, and it is this that creates the comical situation here, this humour could not come into existence should the reader not perceive the failure of this schema in the first place.

Examples (1) and (2) illustrate that there are certain pre-existing patterns which are associated with politeness and which are understood by most people. This would imply that these patterns operate according to rather simple principles, that is, they are generally understood by all members of a society, having been learnt by everyone through socialisation, and thus only socially incompetent people like the vicomte in example (2) fail to understand them properly. However, as this chapter will illustrate, the situation is considerably more complex than this, because patterns of politeness are often not socially but locally constituted, and so they can remain invisible, and thus are often a source of ambiguity and confusion, for the external observer.

7.2   Key concepts

This section overviews the role of schemata in understandings of politeness by looking into two major types, namely, **conventions** and **rituals**.

Conventions

Schemata come into operation due to their *recurrent* nature. A certain linguistic form or behaviour becomes schematic for a group of people if it is used and used again, and so in this sense it also becomes a social practice. **Recurrence** is an important factor behind the way in which we structure both information and pragmatic meaning. Although utterances come into existence in the course of the discursive co-construction of interaction, they tend to be formed according to certain recurrent forms and practices, for the aforementioned reason that it is economic to rely on schemata. As Garfinkel (1967) notes, a large proportion of our everyday speech activity is recurrent, or what he defined as **routine** language usage. Routine language activities have the following representative properties:

- They are often left unspoken.
- They involve continuous references to the biography and prospects of an ongoing interaction.
- They are often hidden from the external observer.

Routine is a relatively broad category, as it covers the recurrent ways in which information and actions are organised in discourse in general. To provide a simple example, when a mother habitually asks her child 'How was it today?' after school, she can use the anaphoric 'it' because both she and the child know, from the context created by a series of (often similar) previous interactions, that the topic here is 'school'.

Certain routines specifically regulate social interaction (i.e. the ways in people negotiate, maintain and, in some cases, renegotiate their relationships). Those forms of recurrent schematic behaviour which follow patterns associated with understandings of politeness, as well as humour, sarcasm and so on, are defined as *conventional*.

Examples (1) and (2) are both cases of politeness arising through conventions exactly because they represent language usage that is meant to be understood by everyone. As Terkourafi (2001) explains, conventional politeness is typically understood on the basis of not only what is actually said but what is left unspoken, because conventions 'encode particular illocutionary forces' (Copestake and Terkourafi 2010). For instance, the indirect utterance 'I was wondering if you could open some windows?' is a conventionally encoded request to open the window, and this interpretation would be clear to almost everyone, even if strictly speaking the request is not made in a direct way.

The conventions that underpin politeness often involve certain forms, such as honorifics, politeness formulae, nicknames, or any form which is standardly regarded as polite (e.g. 'please', 'thank you'). This relationship between convention and form has been described by Searle:

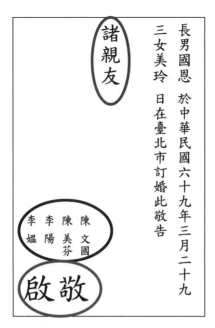

Figure 7.1 A Taiwanese invitation letter written in Chinese.

I am suggesting that *can you*, *could you*, *I want you to*, and numerous other forms are conventional requests... but at the same time they do not have an imperative meaning. (1975: 76)

Importantly, 'form' in our understanding does not necessarily cover a simple dictionary lexeme; in other words, it is not simply a word which is polite (in fact, we would argue that no word is in itself polite or impolite). In order for a form to become conventionally polite, it must involve social actions and pragmatic meanings that are regularly associated with evaluations of politeness. That is, once a certain form occurs and recurs together with a social action which regularly occasions evaluations of politeness it becomes a 'polite form', but of course only as long as the convention is recognised as such within a society or smaller relational network.

The relationship between a certain form and the polite meaning associated with it can be complex. As we could see in the case of 'Gentlemen' in example (1), the interpretation of this schema as a polite convention for leave-taking not only depends on lexical meaning but also, for example, on prosodic properties. Some other, written, conventional forms associated with politeness are represented through elaborate graphic ways, as illustrated in Figure 7.1. This figure is a schematic Chinese invitation card (for a detailed analysis of such cards see: Kádár 2011). The translated text is given in example (3) below.

(3) Our first son Guo'en
and our third daughter Meiiling
will have their engagement ceremony on March 29th, the 69th year
of the Republic of China (i.e. 1980), in Taipei. We would like to
notify about this matter, with sincere respect all our relatives and
friends.
Chen Wen-kuo, Chen Mei-ling, Li Yang and Li Ao
respectfully report this.

According to the traditional Chinese conventions for 'polite' invitations, one needs to denigrate oneself and elevate the other. Notably, this convention is actually represented by the graphic characteristics of those Chinese texts. That is, in Figure 7.1 the reference to others (諸親友 *zhu-qinyou*, i.e. 'all our relatives and friends'; circled at the top centre) and an honorific form which elevates the recipients (啓敬 *qijing*, 'respectfully report this'; lower left circle) are written with big characters, which thus expresses elevation, while the senders' names (upper left circle) are written with small characters, which thus expresses self-denigration. Obviously, such graphic conventions, which can become considerably more elaborate than we can observe in Figure 7.1, have a default reading as polite because they are associated with a specific action; that is, inviting. It is also necessary to note that conventional forms are not limited to lexical items, and longer utterances, such as those used in traditional courting etiquette, can also count as 'conventionally polite'.

Conventions come into the existence through conventionalisation – the process during which a form recurs until what it implies becomes accepted as a default meaning. Conventionalisation can be captured perhaps most clearly in historical contexts where its development process can be traced through the years. As Culpeper and Demmen (2011) argue, certain stereotypical forms of politeness, such as indirect requests in Anglo-Englishes, actually came into existence through a long process of conventionalisation. Conventionalisation is often not an arbitrary procedure because it tends to follows social needs, as well as changes in social values. For example, it has been argued that the rise of conventionally indirect requests reflects a strong emphasis on individualism, which grew in significance during Victorian times or even earlier (see Wierzbicka 2006).

Conventions can be more societal or more 'local' in scope. Cultural norms and changes in such norms, which give rise to new polite conventions, are always constituted within a distinct group. Various groups within a society orient to different cultural values, and so it can be argued that a given culture is constituted by an aggregation of subcultures (see more on this question in Chapter 11). Approaching this claim from a different perspective, a society is constituted through multiple intersecting and overlapping relational networks within which different values can develop. Although polite conventions often reflect dominant social values, as in the case of conventional indirectness noted in Figure 7.1 and example (3), they can reflect subcultural values as well. To provide an example, recently many Hungarian teenagers have adopted a conventional form of acknowledgement, *köszike*. This word counts as 'cute' to many in Hungarian because it is doubly diminutive (in a rather ungrammatical way): that is, the standard form *köszönöm* is modified with the diminutive suffix *-i* (*köszi*), which is then modified with the diminutive suffix *-ke*. This form has supposedly developed amongst female teenagers, and so it reflects a certain subcultural convention: a convention of a relational network of a certain age (i.e. teenagers) and gender (i.e. females).[1] Such conventions, which can gain popularity as happened also with *köszike*, often become the subject of social debates and criticisms, as they do not fit into the normative interpretation of 'appropriateness'. In other words, societal conventions are usually regarded as normative, and conventions particular to relational networks, insofar as they significantly differ from societal ones, are often disregarded and are criticised by those who do not identify as members of that given network.

What, however, makes convention a complex phenomenon is that even the seemingly non-controversial category of societal conventions may also have different interpretations across relational networks within that society. For example, in 2004, a British author, Charles Purdy, wrote a popular book entitled *Urban Etiquette*, in which he argued:

When I tell nice people that I write about etiquette, I can see from their faces that I am metamorphosing into Great Aunt Vivian before their very eyes: I have brought etiquette to a perfectly pleasant cocktail party. I am there to stop the fun; impose meaningless, archaic rules; and worst of all; to strongly disapprove.

But I would like you to forget about Great Aunt Vivian's misinterpretation of etiquette (although the dear lady does have her uses as a disciplinarian, and she knows many things we would be wise to keep in mind). Let's leave her to her sugary sherry and her often incorrect interpretation of *etiquette*. (2004: 2)

This folk description of politeness is rather illustrative with regard to the interpretation of societal conventions. While 'etiquette' is generally understood as a collective term for polite social conventions – or, more precisely, social conventions comprise the norms of etiquette (see Brody 1970) – the above discussion shows that such conventions are perceived differently by many. The author, by positioning Great Aunt Vivian's 'version' of etiquette as being 'incorrect' and 'old-fashioned', makes it clear that he (and the readers he presumes to speak for) have different interpretations of what counts as socially conventional politeness in modern times. However, such differences cannot be put under the umbrella of changes over time. For example, as Purdy notes about business etiquette:

Some people automatically practice social manners at the office – but, for example, a gentleman's racing to a table to hold a woman's chair for her is generally incorrect at a strictly business lunch . . . If they so desire, ladies can greatly help confused gentlemen and set a proper professional tone by saying something like: 'Please don't get up' if someone does so when she leaves the conference-room table, for example. (2004: 83)

That is, there are different understandings of societal conventions constituted across different relational networks and groups, and the way in which these societal conventions are held to differ intersects, in part, with the ways in which individuals, and groups of individuals, identify themselves in terms of age, gender and professional status, for instance (see more on such factors in Chapter 11). And, as the above-cited example illustrates, there are even conventional linguistic and non-linguistic means to handle situations in which different societal conventions conflict with each other, that leave evaluations of politeness open to contestation.

It should also be noted that polite societal and network conventions co-exist, and the choice and the interpretation of a given convention depend on one's 'footing' in a given context (see Chapters 4 and 6). For example, many workplaces, which Wenger (1998) argues can involve one or more *communities of practice* where a group within the workplace (or sometimes the whole workplace) is focused on some common task, tend to develop their own conventions, and this impacts upon understandings of politeness. A larger workplace is constituted by different communities of practice, which have their own, potentially different, conventions vis-à-vis evaluations of politeness, but when members of different communities of practice interact with each other, they may invoke societal conventions.

Every convention has a specific history of development. As we saw in the case of the Anglo-English convention of indirectness, and its association in many contexts (although not all) with politeness, it can be major social changes that generate the birth of certain – in fact, often a set of – societal conventions, as social changes transform the ways in which people work out their relationships with each other. Since such changes take place at the societal level, the conventions which they evoke reflect dominant societal values which are perpetuated through socialisation (and sometimes even explicit education). Such conventions are thus often transparent to anyone who observes a conventional interaction, even though they are subject to challenge and variation as we could see in the case of Purdy's examples. However, in relational networks that tend to be closed, conventions are often evoked by 'local histories'. These local histories, which should be defined as **relational history**, refer to the way in which members of the given network recurrently, and then, through conventionalisation, interact with each other in ways that are both constrained and afforded by those schemata. Network conventions thus evolve through relational histories that reflect both the biography and evolving prospects of the network, which can be somewhat hidden to the external, or non-member, observer (see Garfinkel 1967). More precisely, conventions which are developed in a distinct group are often not intentionally hidden, but it is simply that they are constituted in ways that only make sense for those who belong to the network. Although some conventions which are associated with politeness within certain relational networks, like the Hungarian teenager greeting *köszike* above, may be open to the researcher, in that they make sense to anyone irrespective of age (even though they may sound strange to many), there are some other conventions, created by smaller networks – often a group of few or just two people – which can be understood only with some explanation.

Example (4), cited from Gaëlle Planchenault's (2010: 99) study of a French language transvestite website, illustrates this point.

> (4) Bonjour à vous toutes je suis très émue à la pensée de me trouver parmi vous et d'être la copine de la semaine je ne l'aurais jamais imaginé... Merci de vos témoignages à toutes qui me donnent aussi la force d'être et un merci tout particulier à Isabelle pour son site.
>
> 'Hello to all[f] of you[f] I am very moved[f] to be among you and to be the girlfriend of the week. I would never have expected it... Thanks to all[f] of you for your life stories; they give me the strength to be myself and a special thank you to Isabelle for her website.'

According to Planchenault, the posters at this website conventionally use feminine French grammatical forms (marked with 'f'),[2] and also apply markedly polite forms and avoid any rudeness in their interactions. These behavioural schemata are considered atypical in comparison to many online interactions, and so may appear unusual from the etic perspective of a non-member of the network. The localised conventions for this relational network become understandable, however, if one reads the webmaster's description for newcomers, which prescribes conflict avoidance and a 'soft' style for posters, in order to generate a harmonious style, which is needed by many in the socially disadvantaged group of transvestites. In other words, what we can see here is a particular convention vis-à-vis politeness being 'codified' by a network as the 'insider' or emic understanding of politeness, in a somewhat similar way to etiquette manuals that codify social conventions. However, unlike social conventions these codified conventions are acquired only by those who join the network.

Example (4) represents a network convention, which is somewhat hidden but which can be 'decoded' by the observant because (a) it is codified in writing, and (b) because the above-mentioned 'soft' behaviour is a stereotypical marker of femininity, which is then associated with transvestitism. There are, however, some other conventions, which are not formally codified and, even more importantly, do not make any sense to outsiders (i.e. from an etic perspective) unless one clearly understands the specific relational history of a network. As a simple representative example, let us refer to one of the authors' personal story. When Kádár lived in Taiwan he used to go to martial art exercises on a daily basis and during the training he made friends with a young Taiwanese who attended a Chinese chef school. As this person was eager to speak about the new recipes he learnt and also frequently gave advice to Kádár – who he probably regarded as a foreigner who needed to be educated in Chinese culture – as to which Chinese dishes he should try, the latter asked him a schematic question (example (5)) whenever they met:

(5) 今天該吃什麼?
Lit. 'What do we need to eat today?'

This question, a symbolic request for the young Taiwanese's advice with regard to what to eat, became an in-group convention, which functioned as a greeting. From a participant perspective it was associated with politeness as it appealed to the Taiwanese person's professional identity as a chef (despite the fact that he was a student at that time). For network outsiders, and in isolation (i.e. without knowing the interactants' relational history and the identities they have in the given network) this utterance does not make much sense because it differs from conventions of greeting in Chinese. In other words, this convention is not transparent to the observer.

As we can see, conventions have different degrees of opacity – or, perhaps, we should say 'transparency' as they are not intentionally hidden – depending on the size and type of the network, which creates a given convention. This difference also determines the life-cycle of polite conventions: social conventions are likely to last for a very long time, until major social changes invalidate them, while network conventions cease to exist when a network dissolves. Semi-hidden conventions of larger networks like the Hungarian teenagers' form *köszike* above are more likely to survive for a longer period than hidden ones, simply because they are more likely to be 'inherited' by new networks. For example, while new groups of teenagers have developed their own conventions, *köszike* continues to be in use as a pragmatic 'heritage' inherited from previous generations of teenagers. Also, *köszike* has been adopted by other network-types such as males who often use this form in a new sense, i.e. as a source of humour (see more in Kádár 2013).

The above-discussed open or less transparent nature of recurrent behaviour is the so-called **visibility** issue, which is related to expectations. That is, as has been noted already, members of a network do not usually hide their conventions as such (although there are intentionally hidden forms of recurrent behaviour like secret rituals), but simply take them for granted as they constitute expected linguistic behaviour.

Expectations do not only differ across societal and relational networks. There is also an important distinction that can be drawn between recurrent forms or practices (a) which network members evaluate as *likely* to happen (sometimes called 'empirical norms'), based on their personal experiences and relational histories, and others (b) which they regard as *should* happen (sometimes called 'moral norms'); see Eelen (2001), Haugh (2003) and Culpeper (2008). In other words, there are conventions, which we simply expect to 'be there', and we tend to regard a breach of these expectations as grounds for evaluations of impoliteness. For example, an utterance which does not use feminine French grammatical forms in the aforementioned transvestite website (see example (4)) is open to being interpreted as impolite, irrespective of whether the person who has produced it means to be impolite or not. There is, however, another type of overtly moralistic expectation. This expectation occurs when conventions, in particular societal ones, are not followed in the way in which and the extent to which one would prefer them to be followed, as we could see in the case of Mr Purdy's claim, and which also manifests itself in grumpy complaints about the manners of the youth. For example, the British writer Thomas Blaikie has written books and articles about the lack of civility among the younger generations. In an article published in the *Telegraph* he argued,

Young people have always been rude, far ruder than anybody else. It goes back at least as far as Jane Austen... Even the Queen, aged 19, knocked off a policeman's helmet on VE [Victory in Europe] Day, so she once told the writer Hammond Innes.

But the young of today are worse than preceding generations. This is the depressing conclusion of a survey by the Left-wing think tank Demos. (www.telegraph.co.uk/culture/3653126/Why-are-the-youth-of-today-so-rude.html#)

As this example illustrates, moral expectations inevitably involve contestation. Thus, it can be argued that conventions, in particular those which are more societal in scope, are open to being challenged by members of certain social networks. Such challenges are less likely to emerge in the case of more local conventions. That is, conventions which are societal in scope are accessible to various networks with potentially different values, and this is obviously a source of different understandings of a given convention as '(in)appropriate', as well as debates that arise from such different understandings.

To sum up, the operation of conventions is bound up with expectations, both empirical and moral. Conventions remain unnoticed insofar as they conform with expectations, but they become visible, often in the form of debates and complaints, once expectations are breached.

So far we have discussed the conventional aspect of schemata, and the roles they play in understandings of politeness, with a particular emphasis on **conformance** (i.e. the need to conform to network expectations) to the sets of expectancies of societal or relational networks. There is, however, another important way in which recurrent schemata can operate in interaction: namely, when such schemata are *performed*. These are termed *rituals* to distinguish them from the conventions we have discussed thus far.

Rituals

Ritual is a fundamental notion in anthropological studies. As the renowned anthropologist and sociologist Durkheim (1915) argued, ever since the dawn of humankind ritual has been a key factor because it has aided, and continues to aid, humans to form social or relational networks, by providing a powerful way in which people's social dependence can be expressed. For example, a tribal religious ritual of dancing has an important role in reinforcing the bonds of the tribe, as it provides a joint experience which is recurrent (usually ritual events take place in prescribed times), and also it **symbolically** codifies the roles of the dancers, as well as their relationship with the performance. That is, to stick to the example of the ritual act of dancing, it codifies certain roles like 'chief dancer', 'subordinate dancer', 'leading musician' and so on, as well as the relationship between the performance and the external world. For instance, the group performs particular dances in order to commemorate the story of a particular deity. Thus, the act of dancing symbolically 'encodes' the social order of the community, as well as the community's values (respect towards that deity). This symbolic value can give rise to politeness as well, which in itself has a symbolic value. Similar to conventions, then, not every ritual is polite. However, politeness is arguably one of the most representative manifestations of ritual behaviour.

Ritual plays an important role not only in tribal societies but also in modern ones: there are socially coded rituals, and also families, workplaces and all other networks form their own ritualistic practices. For example, 'Welcome on board!' is a widely spread polite rite of passage (see more on such rites in van Gennep 2004), which signals acceptance in a network. It is not simply a convention because in terms of politeness behaviour a ritual like 'Welcome on board!' does not simply conform to expectations. By uttering these words the speaker symbolically *changes* the addressee's status, by providing her or him with membership in the network. Uttering these words in a specific institutional setting is a powerful act because the speaker does not speak for him or herself, but instead she or he animates the voice of the network or institution; in a way this is not so different from the leader of a tribe who provides adult membership for a young warrior who has passed through a rite of passage. In other words, the above ritual animates the voice of the network, and the person who utters it is undertaking a *performance*, something which is often referred to as **mimesis** in the anthropological literature (see Wallace 2007 for a useful description).

So how does ritual come into existence and how is it related to convention? A likely explanation is that once a convention is adopted by a social network, and when it takes on mimetic functions, it becomes ritual. That is, a conventional practice becomes a ritual one if it is recognisibly performed, a process which is described as ritualisation (note, however, that our interpretation of ritualisation differs to some extent from the way in which anthropologists like Bell 1992 describe it). The phenomenon of ritualisation implies that every ritual is convention(alised) but not every convention is ritual(ised). In order to illustrate this difference, let us briefly analyse example (6).

(6) Queen Gorgo: Spartan!
King Leonidas: Yes, my lady?
Queen Gorgo: Come back with your shield, or on it.
King Leonidas: Yes, my lady.

(*300*, 2006)

Example (6) is cited from the action film *300* which retells the Battle of Thermopylae in an epic way. In this interaction Queen Gorgo – wife of the Spartan King Leonidas – bids farewell to the king, leader of 300 Spartans who set off on a suicidal mission to protect their kingdom from the Persian army.

The queen's farewell includes two rituals, which neatly represent the difference between ritual and convention. First, Queen Gorgo addresses her husband in the third person as 'Spartan!' and then she utters 'Come back with your shield, or on it'; this latter utterance refers to the habit that it was a symbol of defeat if a Spartan lost his shield in war. With the context in mind, it is obvious that these utterances are more than simply conventional acts, as the queen goes beyond conforming with contextually situated expectances. While it would be proper for the queen to address a Spartan commoner as 'Spartan' and remind him of his duties, and in such a context these would be regarded as conventional, she interacts here with her superior ranked husband to whom she bids farewell forever. The rationale behind this seeming discrepancy resides in the mimetic ritual nature of these utterances. That is, in addressing the king by taking a 'Spartan' (i.e. rather puritanical) convention, instead of choosing a more emotive form of greeting, the queen seems to emphasise, more precisely mimetically re-evoke, the heroic, stereotypically Spartan, spirit of their relationship, which is reinforced by the king's brief and seemingly emotionless responses to the queen, as they *co-construct* the ritual. In other words, the queen plays a certain role here and convention becomes a ritual through this situated performance.

The reason why this performance functions effectively is related to its **emotive value** (see also Chapter 10). In general, politeness and emotions are interconnected, and this connection usually resides in the relational history of a network. That is, it can be argued that a particular usage of politeness evokes emotions, if it is formed in a way that reflects on the given network's history, often referred to as a network **ethos**. In other words, in many networks politeness involves an emotive experience, which is constructed through interactions (see more on this matter in Chapter 10). This emotive function is particularly salient in the case of ritual actions, due to their 'staged', mimetic nature (even though mimesis is arguably a matter of degree, i.e. certain ritual practices are more theatrical than others, see Kádár 2013). For example, the interactional rituals of farewell in example (6) come into operation through the pathos of the utterances: the strength of saying goodbye in a seeming emotionless and heroic tone when weaker people would weep, which reflects the queen and king's ingroup ethos of being representatives of the Spartans. This seeming emotionless performance is what seems to generate emotions in the given context for both participants and observers of this interaction.

The emotive function of ritual should not be understood as autotelic (i.e. having within itself the purpose of its existence or happening), and it is not a coincidence that it is referred to as 'function'. Emotions often address interactional needs, as they have a psychological effect on those who participate in the ritual. As noted by Manfred Kienpointner (1997: 262), ritual acts create an atmosphere in which states of mind alter, an atmosphere which 'cannot be endangered even by seemingly rude utterances'. This state of mind is often referred to in the field as the **ritual moment**. Jan Koster notes that the ritual moment has a key communicational function because it creates 'a temporary destruction of awareness of the wider meaningful relations of one's individuality and the reduction of the self to the immediate physical experience of the here-and-now' (2003: 219). This physical experience is a 'recurrent here-and-now' (see Section 7.1), in the sense that ritual language use ties one into all of the other times such a ritual schema has been used. That is, the moment is experienced through looking into and relying on a series of events, or in other words the utterance is connected to another time and place and potentially even another context. In the case of example (6), speaking in a ritual heroic way supposedly results in a state of mind in which saying goodbye becomes easier.

The ritual moment, evoked by mimesis, is indeed a key element of ritual practice. Often by means of ritual practice the interactants can playfully defy 'regular' behaviour: they act beyond societal conventions. As we discussed in the section on conventions, relational network conventions often differ from societal ones, and the same also applies to ritual, but the difference between convention and ritual resides in the mimetic value of ritual practices. That is, ritual can not only provide an alternative behaviour to conforming to conventions, but performers of ritual can also intentionally display difference and uniqueness through the ritual act. This illustrates that a seemingly polite act of ritual can be **creative** in spite of its schematic nature, not only because it is often co-constructed by the interactants (see example (6)), but also because ritual is often a playful act. The potential playful **creativity** of ritual vis-à-vis politeness is illustrated by example (7), drawn from Chinese:

(7) 陳遵尺牘, 名震當時。然高自位置, 惜墨如金, 不肯輕投一札, 足下殆亦有此癖!

'Chen Zun [of old] gained a great reputation amongst his generation for [his expertise in] letter writing. However, he formed an overtly high opinion of himself and he spared his ink as if it was gold, not willing to send a letter to anyone [if it were not necessary]. [I wonder,] sir, whether you are not on the edge of falling into the error of his conceit?'

(Cited from Kádár 2010a: 140)

Example (7) is cited from the correspondence of a group of Chinese men of letters, who developed extravagant ritual practices in order to distinguish themselves from others and reinforce their in-group solidarity. These ritual practices, among other things, prescribed that network members express politeness in most unusual ways in order to display their high intelligence and extensive education. In this fragment, the author writes to a close friend of his, and draws an analogy between the behaviour of Chen Zun 陳遵, a renowned historical man of letters, and that of the addressee. This reference expresses a seemingly 'negative' meaning, that is, the author – longing for the correspondent's letter – symbolically reprimands him for sparing his ink like Chen Zun, and wonders whether the correspondent has not 'fallen into the error of Chen's conceit'. However, at the same time the author emphasises the great expertise of Chen in epistolary art, and so by symbolically scolding the addressee for behaviour that resembles that of Chen Zun, he conveys a secondary elevating meaning by comparing the correspondent's talent to that of Chen.

It is pertinent to note in passing that, because ritual performance constitutes an alternative reality, rituals are adopted by different types of networks. Ritual, just like convention, can be constituted at a societal or a network level. For example, example (6) represents a societal convention being used ritually in a particular relational network, and example (7) is a case of ritual formed at the level of a particular relational network. However, rituals associated with politeness are often formed by another, noteworthy type of network, namely the network of the individual and the unseen world. More specifically, there are certain rituals – defined in the field as the so-called 'covert rituals' – which are performed by individuals towards imagined/spiritual entities (see more details in Kádár 2013).[3]

7.3   Key studies

Key studies on schematic forms of politeness describe convention and ritual from an outsider or etic perspective. The rationale behind this approach is that the words 'convention' and 'ritual' have very different implications across cultures. For example, 'ritual' can mean a potentially negative and superficial action in Western cultures, while in East Asian cultures it refers to a pre-dominantly positive phenomenon. 'Ritual' also carries connotations from a diachronic perspective, as in many cultures it is associated with the past rather than the present. Thus, a technical instead of a lay definition of ritual brings us closer to understanding the mechanisms of this phenomenon. In terms of analytic methodology, key theories of convention and ritual adopt first-order loci: they analyse the participants' evaluations with reference to conventions and rituals.

Watts (2003) is a groundbreaking study on conventions vis-à-vis politeness, which examines the ways in which conventionalised utterances convey politeness in schematic ways. In order to describe this phenomenon, Watts uses the label EPM ('expression of procedural meaning') to describe 'a linguistic or paralinguistic expression that is focused on instructing the addressee how to process the propositional content of the utterance' (p. 274). Watts argues that EPMs are conventionalised expressions, many of which are regarded as normative 'politic' behaviour. Through this analysis, Watts integrates conventions into a wider framework of politeness. Watts' volume is fundamental reading for those who are interested in the relationship between conventions and illocutionary force.

An article by Bax (2010a) provides an insightful conceptualisation of the historical development of rituality. As Bax, relying on evolutionary research, argues, ritual is one of the most ancient manifestations of linguistic politeness, and diachronic changes of rituality greatly influenced the development of politeness across cultures. Bax provides a useful overview of rituality research and he gives a framework by means of which rituals (also vis-à-vis politeness) can be categorised.

Kádár's (2013) monograph, *Relational Rituals and Communication*, provides a framework dedicated to conventions and rituals. This is a general framework, which aims to describe conventions and rituals in their own right, and it regards politeness as one of the many possible manifestations of these phenomena. Kádár defines convention and ritual by using the aforementioned concepts of 'conformance' and 'performance', and he uses these concepts to elaborate a complex theory of relational ritual. In terms of polite usage, Kádár examines the way in which 'ritual' interrelates with politeness, and integrates this relationship into a theory of relational ritual.

7.4 Summary

In certain contexts, the interactants are expected to follow certain 'scripted' expectations. In such contexts politeness tends to follow pre-existing patterns of thought or behaviour used in recurrent ways that are readily recognisable to network members. We have distinguished two types of such schematic thought/behaviour, namely conventions and rituals. Performance of conventions presupposes a particular emphasis on conformance, i.e. the need to conform to network expectancies, and that of rituals presupposes performance. Understandings of conventions and rituals are influenced, among other factors, by the societal vs. more 'local' scope of a given pattern as well as the transparency that this scope implies.

In order to analyse convention and ritual, it is necessary to approach these phenomena from a technical instead of a lay perspective. Such a perspective brings us closer to understanding the mechanisms of these phenomena, which have very different implications and definitions across cultures.

7.5 Exercises

I. Answer the following questions:
   1. Can you identify polite societal conventions in your native language? Can you find specific polite conventions used within your family or group of friends/colleagues? If yes, how do these conventions differ from societal ones?
   2. Can you list the relational networks within which you interact daily? Do these networks have different expectations with regard to politeness?
   3. Is there any polite ritual which you perform on a regular basis? If yes, can you describe and analyse this ritual?
II. Read the following examples, which represent increasingly complex cases, and analyse the politeness phenomena occurring in them. Compare your analysis with the brief annotations below:
   (a) On occasions when any little group of men and women are gathered together, nothing spoils the evening more than the absence of introductions. The perfect hostess will always attend to this branch of her duties first of all. Miss Putnam lost no time in making her identity clear.
   'Presenting Kate Amelia Putnam, of the James B. Flaherty Detective Agency of New York', she said amiably, holding the pistol in her hand

on a steady line with Mr Carlisle's pelvis. 'Drop that gun. And you', she added to Packy, 'keep your hands up.'
Mr Carlisle's automatic dropped to the floor. Miss Putnam seemed well content.
'Now we're all set', she said. 'Mrs G., might I trouble you to step across and pick that cannon ...'

(P. G. Wodehouse, *Hot Water*, Chapter 17, 1963)

(b) (Conversation between lovers)
Chad: Is it the eggs?
Dylan: It's not the eggs.
Chad: Is it the boat?
Dylan: No, it's not the boat, I have to go though.
Chad: Is it the Chad?
Dylan: It might be the Chad.
Chad: The Chad ... It's the Chad!
        ((Chad falls into the water))
        . . .
Chad: Starfish, I would just like to say that I'm honored, honored to see you taking an interest in my work and I also think you're very pretty and ...
        ((sees girls getting scuba gear on))
        Starfish? Where are you going? Starfish are you going swimming? Where are you going? Where are you going again Starfish? Was it the Chad?
Dylan: No, the Chad was great.
Chad: The Chad was great.

(*Charlie's Angels*, 2000)

Example (a) represents an instance of humour, the source of which is a stylistic discrepancy. This discrepancy roots in the contrast between the conventionally polite act of self-introduction and the context in which it occurs. The detective Ms Putnam introduces herself 'amiably', and so she follows a socially coded convention of politeness, yet she threatens the addressees with a pistol.

Example (b), from the film *Charlie's Angels*, represents the complex and often hidden way in which in-group rituals operate. What the reader can observe here is an indirect, step-by-step ritual confirmation of one's love emotions, which Brown and Levinson (1987) would supposedly define as 'positive politeness', as there is a 'face-threat' operating here (Chad might be disliked by Dylan). However, this confirmation takes place through an unusual, romantic and playful performance, which makes sense if one knows that in the network of Dylan and Chad it is a *ritual practice* to talk about Chad in the third person (*the* Chad), as an adored entity. What happens in these two interactions is that Chad wants Dylan to confirm that she loves him, and so he involves her in a ritual game of talking about him. In the first interaction Dylan has to leave and Chad inquires as to why she needs to leave. While Dylan obviously loves Chad, she teases him and she hints that 'It might be the Chad' as the reason why she leaves. However, she makes this utterance vague, hence minimising the face-threat (and keeping the door open to Chad to continue courting). In the next interaction, Dylan and Chad continue to talk about 'the Chad', this time in a very flattering way. What these interactions illustrate is that rituals are often jointly co-constructed in localised relational networks.

8   Politeness and history

8.1   Introduction

The norms and manifestations of politeness are historically **relative**. Relativity means that what is understood as appropriate is not only relative to social space, which is more often emphasised in the literature to date (e.g. norms differ across cultures), but perhaps even more importantly it is relative to time. With the passing of time, understandings are subject to change.

Changes evoked by time are particularly salient if we observe understandings of norms. There are certain polite usages that people once regarded as normative, but which now appear to be anachronistic, and even potentially nonsensical, to a contemporary observer. For example, medieval knightly challenges, studied by the historical pragmatician Bax (1999), may sound somewhat unusual, as the challenge in example (1) (made in Dutch) illustrates:

(1) Sprac hi te lancelote saen: *He spoke to Lancelot right*
                                          away:

     'Riddere, nv doet mi verstaen   *'Knight, enlighten me now*
     Van ere dinc die ic begere,   *On a matter that I desire to*
                                          know about,

     Oft wacht v iegen min spere   *Or beware of my lance.*
     . . .   . . .
     Bericht mi, ridder, bi vwer trouwen, *Tell me, knight, upon your*
                                          honour,

     Anders maget v wel berouwen,   *Or   otherwise   you   will*
                                          regret it,

     Die beste waerheit die gi wet   *As truthfully as you can*
     Dat ic v sal vragen ende nine let.' *What I will ask you, and do*
                                          not fail to respond.'

     Doe seide min her lanceloet: *Then said Sir Lancelot:*
     'Ic ware mi vele liuer doet   *'I would fain be dead,*
     Dan mi een ridder dwingen soude   *Than suffer a knight to*
                                          force me

156

Van dies ic doen nine woude.'	*To do something against my will.'*
. . .	*. . .*
Die swarte hi en hilt niet stille,	*The black [knight] did not remain standing still,*
Die op lancelote was erre;	*He who was angry at Lancelot.*
Hi omhaelde sinen loep verre	*He made his horse take a good run-up*
Ende verrechte sijn spere	*And couched his lance*
Alse die te vechtene heuet gere.	*Like one who enjoys combat.*

(Bax 2010b: 70–1)

This conversation represents a schema which was associated with the knightly code of appropriate behaviour in many parts of medieval Europe (see Chapter 7). That is, the knight Moriaen challenges the knight Lancelot by using a schematic practice (a pre-existing pattern of behaviour) as he makes an inquiry. This is not a 'harmless' inquiry: according to the knightly custom, upon challenging the other, instead of directly stating 'We will fight to death, knight' one was expected to make the challenge indirectly, by 'forcing' the other to answer a question, who in turn is expected to decline this request, which gives a green light to the fight.

It is obvious that the schema in example (1) does not exist anymore, at least not in the form represented above. Politeness, just like any other linguistic phenomenon is subject to diachronic change. This is why we can say that the 'appropriateness' of a manifestation of politeness is essentially relative: we cannot be sure, for example, whether a certain understanding of politeness which we take for granted will be understood by our grandchildren as well. Who could have imagined just a few decades ago, for instance, that such a thing as 'netiquette' (descriptions of norms of politeness in online interactions) would have come into existence?

It might seem tempting to brush historical politeness aside as an area which is perhaps interesting but essentially irrelevant to those who intend to examine politeness in the contemporary world in which we live. Obviously, medieval knights do not have much to offer, insofar as our aim is to understand how politeness is used in a modern urban life, for instance. Or do they? We can attempt to look beyond Sir Moriaen's and Sir Lancelot's archaic style – indeed, nobody would say 'I fain be dead' in a brawl – and look at the practice underlying this interaction. What these knights are essentially doing is using polite forms and expressions to conceal aggression. But does this not happen in our day? Ritual challenges continue to exist, as example (2) illustrates:

(2) Mark Darcy: Would you step outside please?
    Daniel Cleaver: I'm afraid it's not possible.
    Mark Darcy: Look, are you gonna step outside or do I have to
                    drag you?
    Daniel Cleaver: I think you're gonna have to drag me.
                    (*Bridget Jones II: The Edge of Reason*, 2004)

This interaction, which is a fictional representation just like the interaction in example (1), represents a contemporary British gentlemanly challenge made by Mark Darcy for the honour of a 'lady', the protagonist Bridget Jones. The source of humour in example (2) is that this challenge is refused in a clearly cowardly tone by Daniel Cleaver who knows that Darcy is stronger than him. Just as we saw in Sir Moriaen's inquiry, Darcy's question 'Would you step outside please?' is not a neutral question or proposal: in a similar way as in example (1), there is an expected (or *preferred*, to use a technical term, see e.g. Drew 1997) response to this turn, that is, acceptance of the challenge. When, however, a different answer is given by Cleaver, the schematic nature of Darcy's question becomes clear: Cleaver is not being given a real choice to refuse this challenge. In other words, while Cleaver makes an indirect response ('I am afraid it's not possible'), which could be understood as appropriate in other settings, it is definitely not acceptable here from the participants' perspective.

In brief, the appropriacy of certain forms and practices of politeness are temporally relative, and the actual language used in examples (1) and (2) is arguably different. However, as the comparison of these interactions illustrates, studying the pragmatic features of historical texts can nevertheless shed light on certain properties of politeness as social practice in contemporary interactions.

With this interconnection in mind, in this chapter, which is dedicated to historical politeness, we will not only focus on **historicity** but, more importantly, also on the implications of historicity for understanding politeness. Historicity is a complex philosophical concept (see sources of this notion in Martin Heidegger 1991 [1927]; and Foucault 1970[1966]), and it is sufficient here to limit its interpretation to saying: all actions (and things) in the world have their place and time, and so every action is part of history. The way in which we see the world, also in terms of politeness, is thus historically situated, and human behaviour can often be properly explained if we attempt to distance ourselves from assumptions.

That is, we will study historical politeness not simply out of pragma-philological interest (see e.g. Jacobs and Jucker 1995) to understand historically situated usages of politeness, but also in order to identify various key features that are significant for the analysis of contemporary politeness data. In fact, one could rightly argue that any theory of politeness, irrespective of the data it studies, must include historicity as a core concept, and **relativity** as the key to understanding this concept. In other words, every attempt to theorise linguistic politeness should represent the data studied as *relatively* polite in terms of time. If the key question for social space is 'To whom and in what context does utterance X express politeness?', then the question we need to ask ourselves when it comes to time is 'To whom and when does utterance X express politeness' (and also, 'Whose politeness does a historical text represent?', see below). In a sense it does not even matter whether a text is 'really' historical or not, even though studying old texts has its own advantages because the relativity of politeness becomes fairly obvious to the analyst when one examines interactions that occurred a long time ago. But arguably any utterance which does not emerge at this very moment is historical to some extent. To provide a simple example, even our personal understandings of politeness or impoliteness can change with the passing of time. Moreover, some utterances such as metapragmatic comments (see Chapter 9), which generally reflect on past events, include elements of historicity. An analysis which is based on this broad definition of 'historical' can include various data types: for example, an email written some time ago can be regarded as 'historical' as a medieval codex. In terms of politeness and time, if understanding of politeness in localised interactions (Chapter 6) represents the 'here-and-now', and evaluations of politeness occasioned through convention and ritual (Chapter 7) represent the 'recurrent here-and-now', then historical politeness constitutes the realm of 'there-and-then' that provides a fundamental link to the broader social spaces in which understandings of politeness arise.

In sum, the question we pursue is not so much how we define 'historical', but rather how we can incorporate historicity (and the notion of relativity) into research on politeness. The relativity of historicity is an issue that can challenge theoretical understandings of politeness, since as Kádár and Culpeper (2010) argue, historical politeness is an important 'testing ground' for politeness theories. In this respect, historical politeness is very close to intercultural and cross-cultural data in that assumptions that we take for granted often turn out to be invalid in historical settings. Thus, no theory of politeness that fails to include at least some recourse to historical analysis can be considered truly comprehensive.

8.2   Key concepts

Comparability and representation

The relativity of understandings of politeness manifests itself in a fundamental problem for the researcher, namely, **comparability**. That is, upon examining historical politeness phenomena, it becomes evident that it is often difficult to compare contemporary and historical data. This difficulty manifests itself in basic terminology. Just as conventions and rituals have different meanings across space and time (see Section 7.3), the very word *politeness* is problematic as in many historical cultures it does not have any direct counterpart, or practice that would equate to what early modern or modern British etiquette manuals describe as *politeness*. As discussed by Kopytko (1995), the English word *politeness*, which originates in the Latin *politus* ('refined', 'elegant'), and which was borrowed from the French, appeared in the sixteenth century, and it spread in the contemporary sense of *courteous* from only the eighteenth century onwards. Before the term *politeness* had entered into general usage, the French loanword *curteisie* was used in English to refer to manifestations of normative behaviour (see below, in the present section). Yet this brief analysis of *politeness* represents a historical development in a single culture only. While in many European languages the equivalent of *politeness* stems from *politus*, similar to English, in many other languages *politeness* has a different lexical origin, as in the case of the German term *höflichkeit*, the Hungarian notion of *udvariasság*, not mentioning non-European cases such as the Japanese concept of *reigi*, and the Chinese term *limao*, a point we will return to consider in more detail in Chapter 9. That is, the historical politeness researcher needs to examine a phenomenon which is not only labelled differently across languages and cultures (and defined differently by various networks of a single culture, see Chapter 11), but also differently over time. And, obviously, different metalanguage may involve different conceptualisations of politeness.

This problem calls for a careful consideration as to how we use the word *politeness* in the field when it comes to historical issues, considering that politeness can be grounded in various different loci of understanding (see Chapter 5). As far as we take the perspectives of relativity and historicity as key concepts, it is evident that politeness should be preferably used as a technical term, partly because it is a recently coined expression from a diachronic perspective.

In terms of methodology, it is difficult to reconstruct historical states of mind with full precision, even if reconstruction to some extent is possible in the case of certain text types. What makes it difficult for the researcher to get a grip on language users' (first-order) views on a historical term is that these views themselves would be mediated indirectly through sources, i.e. they are represented (see **representation** later in this section). Thus, it is relatively difficult to access an emic (i.e. insider's) understanding when it comes to historical data, and so our analyses inevitably are grounded in an etic (i.e. outsider's) understanding. However, we argue that one should try to tease out the participant's perspective whenever there is an opportunity to do this. Considering that we often do not know what a specific manifestation of politeness meant in a given setting, our politeness interpretations need to be guided by the evidence in the text – the hearer's/recipient's evaluations of certain utterances – and not by our intuitions, because those intuitions are likely to reflect our present-day assumptions. So the analysis of historical data necessitates studying evaluations, as well as conducting careful examination of historical facts. We are forced to make deductions about the interactants' motivations, not only because the interactants themselves cannot communicate to us (as in the case of an interview), but also because their reasons for a certain action might be entirely different from what we would assume on the basis of our contemporary understanding of politeness.

In order to illustrate this point, let us analyse the historical Chinese extract in example (3):

(3) 少游微微冷笑道: 「別個秀才來應舉時, 就要告命題容易了。
下官曾應過制科...」
丫鬟道: 「俺小姐不比尋常盲試官...他的題目好難哩!...」

Shaoyou said with a cold smile: 'When any other graduate [of the first degree][1] takes part in the exam, as soon as he receives the task, he will answer it easily. I, this worthless official (*xiaguan*) have already passed the exam...'
The servant girl said: 'My Madame is not like those blind exam officials... her tasks are quite difficult!'

(*Xingshi hengyan* 醒世恆言, Chapter 11)

Upon approaching the first utterance in this conversation, from a seventeenth-century Chinese novel, the analyst cannot safely make any deductions without examining the following points:

(i) the socio-pragmatic context (i.e. the historically situated communicational norms);
(ii) the interactants' reactions (i.e. the hearer's evaluation of an utterance, and her or his reaction in the course of constructing the interaction); and
(iii) narrow-sense contextual factors (i.e. the relationship developed through the actual interaction).

Without distancing ourselves from contemporary understandings of politeness, a most plausible explanation for the self-denigrating form 'I, this worthless official' (*xiaguan* 下官) is that the speaker uses this honorific form in order to express politeness in a form that Brown and Levinson (1987) would define as 'negative politeness'. Such a view is supported by the fact that in East Asian societies the appropriate usage of honorifics is a marker of one's level of education (see e.g. Ide 2005). However, the situation is more complex than this. As Kádár's (2007) historical pragmatic research on Chinese data shows, historical Chinese honorific forms displayed (or *indexed*, to use a technical term, see e.g. Silverstein 2003) the rank of both the speaker and the addressee, and the form used in example (3) is an honorific used by officials, specifically. What does this imply? Let us consider each of the three analytic points above to answer this question.

First, the form above is *not* polite in the sense in which politeness is interpreted in many contemporary cultures, but instead it displays the speaker's rank, which is understandably important in a hierarchical society like the Chinese. Thus, this utterance is not necessarily *other-focused* but instead it is potentially *self-focused*.[2]

Second, a discursive analysis of the hearer's evaluation confirms this claim. The servant girl does not seem to be too enthusiastic about the young official's language usage, which also illustrates that even in a society that is described as hierarchical, norms of hierarchy do not always operate in interaction. She responds to the official's utterance – words referring to his recent result in an imperial exam – by describing officials who conduct examinations as 'blind exam officials' (*mang shiguan* 盲試官). She also avoids using honorific forms as it is only the higher ranking official who applies ostensibly 'polite' lexical items.

Third, examination of narrow-sense contextual factors reveals that the servant girl has the necessary power to act in the way she does. That is, when the interaction in example (3) takes place, the servant girl is 'guarding' her lady's door; the lady is the newly wed wife of the official, and she makes playful 'exam questions' for the young man, who is told that he can only spend the night with her if he can answer the questions.

To sum up, due to the issue of comparability we must be careful to avoid projecting our contemporary assumptions about politeness onto the data studied. Yet we should also recall the point that the notion of historicity does not inherently imply many years: in fact, most of the institutions in our societies are historical, as Foucault argued (1970[1966]). Indeed, the 'order of things' as we often perceive them, also in terms of politeness, can often be properly explained if we attempt to distance ourselves from assumptions, and in this respect the above-discussed methodological stance is arguably valid for politeness research in general.

The above-discussed analysis of participants' understandings and evaluations in historical data has its obstacles. Historical texts are problematic in comparison with contemporary data as they provide a textual representation of speech rather than the speech itself. Because of this, historical texts sometimes offer less analytical affordances for the researchers than interactions which have been audio- or video-recorded. This makes it difficult for the analyst to examine the interactants' evaluation of certain utterances. As Culpeper (2009a: 182) notes,

Whilst researchers do have recourse to research conducted by social historians, it must be remembered that much of that research is (a) itself underpinned by written documents, and (b) often insufficiently detailed to assist in understanding the rich dynamics of particular situations.

That is, the fact that datasets are less rich from the analyst's perspective is an important aspect of historical politeness research, which manifests itself in the comparability issue as well (one cannot compare historical and contemporary texts, simply because they offer different degrees of detail in the datasets). Due to this problem, historical pragmaticians divide evaluation into the following forms of behaviour:

   (i) Metapragmatic comments (e.g. 'you're so polite')
   (ii) Follow-up politeness behaviours (e.g. 'thank you so much')
   (iii) Challenges to inappropriate talk signalled in the co-text (e.g. 'no, wait a minute, take that back!').

Dividing evaluations in this way helps the analyst to examine evaluations in relatively limited historical datasets (see also Chapter 9).

An alternative and useful way of exploring politeness in historical texts is the so-called 'corpus method', which has been developed, for example, by Culpeper and Kytö (2010). This method encompasses the reconstruction of politeness behaviour through the comparison of several corpora. The corpus method is particularly suited to texts that do not have any personal interactional history or other sources for the analyst to draw upon in interpreting evaluative moments of politeness in that dataset.

The approaches which have been discussed so far represent methodologies by means of which historical politeness can be described without taking a prescriptive view. However, there are two sources for forming prescriptive views on politeness: we can project our prescriptions on historical data, but it can also happen that prescriptive views are projected back on us through historical data. The comparability issue is present in another problem: representation in historical data means that historical texts are prone to represent politeness in a biased way.

Some of the limitations of historical data have been noted already. When we venture into the analysis of historical texts, the perhaps most challenging question is not so much whether a certain source is in a good condition or not, or even how it represents interaction. Of course, problems like missing parts of a text due to the dilapidation of a manuscript are sometimes painful realities for the researcher (see e.g. Kádár 2010b), not to mention the lack of interactional dynamics in historical materials. However, the most problematic question we always need to ask ourselves is 'whose politeness does the text represent?' It can be argued that the majority of historical texts have been written by highly educated people (writing was a privilege of the powerful in most historical societies), and so the understandings of politeness that arise in historical data reflect dominant views and ideologies (see e.g. Iggers 2007), often even in cases when they animate the language usage of lower classes.

There is not much the researcher can do about this problem, apart from adding disclaimers about the extent to which the politeness phenomenon being studied is socially representative. To put it simply, it is dangerous to claim that 'historical politeness was like X, and this was the only way to express politeness in the period Y', due to this issue of representativeness – we often simply don't know how the masses understood politeness in a historical society. Taking this train of thought further, if we consider that historicity is relative, it is in fact possible to also project this problem onto contemporary data. Indeed, we often represent understandings of politeness from the perspective of well-educated classes, and thus inadvertently exclude other understandings of politeness, such as working-class interpretations of this phenomenon (see more on this issue in Chapter 11).

The fact that any text can potentially represent certain dominating values implies that practically any interaction – which does not take place in front of us or in a setting that makes it possible to study the dynamics of an interaction (e.g. video-recording) – is in a sense biased (see more on this problem in Culpeper and Kytö 2000). In other words, when a polite interaction is *reported* to us, some degree of caution is inevitably due. In such reports representations often inadvertently become mispresentations, a transformation that can go unnoticed. For example, we tend to automatically disregard diachronic differences when instances of historical politeness are represented to us, because we take it for granted that politeness in certain periods nevertheless operates similarly with our time. This phenomenon becomes salient when we observe representations of historical language usage in popular genres such as films, as seen in examples (4) and (5).

> (4) The Emperor of China: I've heard a great deal about you, Fa Mulan. You stole your father's armor, ran away from home, impersonated a soldier, deceived your commanding officer, dishonored the Chinese Army, destroyed my palace, and . . . you have saved us all.
>
> *(Mulan*, 1998)

> (5) D'Artagnan: WAIT!
> Cardinal Richelieu: You object to losing your head?
> D'Artagnan: Yes, I like it where it is!
> Cardinal Richelieu: Then tell me what I want to know, and maybe you will keep it a while longer!
> D'Artagnan: I don't know where they are.
> Cardinal Richelieu: And if you did?
> D'Artagnan: I wouldn't tell you . . .

Cardinal Richelieu: I admire your courage, D'Artagnan. You
might have made a great musketeer. But now
we'll never know – will we?

(The Three Musketeers, 1993)

In example (4), cited from the animated film *Mulan*, the Emperor of China
addresses the protagonist, the young heroine Mulan, in front of a crowd, by
using mock scolding in order to express politeness. While this utterance represents behaviour what *we* would expect from a good emperor, and which looks
nicely 'majestic', this utterance reflects a contemporary egalitarian view on
the way in which a high-ranking leader (e.g. the President of the US) should
communicate with a young girl who has saved the country. In historical China
such a manifestation of politeness would have been unimaginable, not only
because the emperor would have not spoken with a commoner (especially not
in public) irrespective of her merits, but also because even if this interaction
had taken place he would have displayed his own rank (cf. example (3)) instead
of expressing 'politeness' *towards* Mulan (it is another question whether the
very fact that someone can communicate with an emperor occasions the feeling
of being honoured).

The same phenomenon arises in the second example from the film *The
Three Musketeers*, in which the protagonist, the young French swordsman
D'Artagnan, interacts with the infamous Cardinal Richelieu. Their style
represents the clash of good and bad, and it fits our expectations with regard to
the way a young hero should speak with a corrupt cardinal who aims (according
to the plot of the story) to betray his king. The cardinal seems to reward
D'Artagnan by politely noting that he admires his courage, which seems to be
appropriate in the present context. However, in historical France (as anywhere
in Europe) interactions with high-ranking people necessitated considerably
more sophisticated and ritualised exchanges than represented in example (5),
and it is likely that in a real situation D'Artagnan would have been killed or
tortured for breaching these norms. The noteworthy aspect in these interactions
is not so much that they mispresent historical politeness through the currently
dominating ideology of egalitarianism (which is perhaps not surprising given
these are essentially American films), but rather that such mispresentations are
likely to pass unnoticed. Supposedly, *dramatisation* has an important role in
this unnoticedness: due to the dramatic effects, the involved observer is less
likely to notice that something is amiss in these interactions.

Representation has yet another dimension of interest, namely, the area where
metapragmatics (discussed in Chapter 9) intersects with historical politeness
research. As it has been noted already, practically any time lag can transform
an interaction into the state of being 'historical'. This implies that representation is a potential problem when we retrospectively examine understandings

of politeness in an interaction that has taken place before, because such retrospection can generate equivocality or additional possible understandings (Chapter 5). Retelling a story often raises debates about the actual, historical intentions of interactants (de Berg 1995), and the way in which these intentions are reattributed to the interactants in representing the narrator's views in subsequent discourse, as the following case illustrates.

Recently, an email written by a mother-in-law, a certain Carolyn Bourne, has received a significant amount of publicity in the British press. This person wrote an email to her daughter-in-law-to-be, in which she 'educated' her about 'good manners', with this 'education' being 'wrapped' up in ostensibly 'polite' discourse. The text of the email itself is available online, but if one intends to analyse it, it becomes essential to get a grip on the background of this interaction. In other words, some form of retrospective inquiry is needed, and we unavoidably need to rely on sources such as the following one:

(6) Meeting Carolyn Bourne is a prospect many people might find somewhat intimidating. After all, she is the woman who has widely been described as 'the mother-in-law from hell' following the now notorious email she sent to her stepson Freddie's fiancée. In it, she attacked Heidi Withers's 'staggering uncouthness and lack of grace' before suggesting she attend a finishing school at the earliest opportunity to correct her 'bad manners'.
. . .
However, *The Mail on Sunday* has learned from a close family friend in London that the couple have been worried about Freddie for three years, believed to be a result of his relationship with Heidi.
The email is understood to refer to several incidents over the period in which Heidi's behaviour upset the Bournes and other members of the family.
. . .
It would be easy to accuse Carolyn of being anachronistic and snobby. She and Edward enjoy a privileged lifestyle, with a sprawling home set in grounds that contain a beautifully land-scaped garden, stables for their horses and greenhouses for Carolyn's plant nursery, Whetman Pinks.
The walls of their five-bedroom house are adorned with photographs of Edward rowing at Cambridge, and Victorian advertisements for his family's former business, Bourne and Hollingsworth, which was once an upmarket department store in London's West End.

But Carolyn insists her attitude towards etiquette has been mis-interpreted. And, much as she wishes the email had not been made public, she stands by its fundamental message.

'Manners are not a class thing, they are about treating others with consideration,' she says. 'It doesn't matter if you're a tramp in a hedgerow, if you know how to behave towards people, to be polite and kind, that's a great gift.'

(www.dailymail.co.uk/news/article-2013020/Carolyn-Bourne-mother-law-hell-hits-Politeness-greatest-gift-tramp-hedgerow.html#ixzz20PqCUTcS)

Example (6), cited from the online edition of the newspaper *The Daily Mail*, reveals that there are several discourses on the appropriateness of the email in existence, and also the mother-in-law retrospectively evaluates (narrates) her own behaviour in a way that positions her understanding vis-à-vis these discourses. One of these is, of course, the discourse on politeness as a marker of exclusion from the middle or upper classes in British society, and it is this discourse to which Carolyn orients. But the most important issue from the perspective of the historical pragmatician is the way in which the mother-in-law's behaviour is represented by the narrator of this article. It is first mentioned that 'It *would be* [our emphasis] easy to accuse Carolyn of being anachronistic and snobby', and hints are made to extenuating circumstances, such as the parents were actually worrying about their son, due to several 'incidents' that had previously occurred with the daughter-in-law-to-be. In other words, the mother-in-law's email is contextualised (that is, *represented*) in a way that motivates the reader to regard it as appropriate if not polite. Representing the mother-in-law as a person fond of 'anachronistic' politeness implies that her intention was to constructively educate her prospective daughter-in-law, and so the politeness in her email was indeed genuine. We will return to such issues in Chapter 9.

Transformation and continuity

Politeness is not a constant phenomenon: it goes through extensive changes over time, and during these changes it is in what might be termed a transitional state. The historical politeness researcher's goal is to provide explanations for changes in politeness in a society, both as a whole or within one or more of the relational networks through which that society is constituted. The key question is: why and how do understandings of politeness, and the language and practices involved in achieving politeness, change over time? In fact, this is a question one should also pose whenever one analyses data with any dimension of historicity (which we would in fact argue is relevant to essentially any discourse or interaction). The norms of politeness in a network imbued with any kind of relational history tend to go through changes as evaluative moments of politeness intersect and are recycled, revisited or invoked in the ongoing chain of interactions that constitute this relational network. Due to this, it can be argued that these norms are always in some degree of flux, or at least they are inevitably likely to transform with the passing of time, even if flux might be minimal in practice. Indeed, some norms are often inherently conservative in the sense that it can take a long period of time for certain norms to change. This phenomenon is defined as the so-called transformation issue.

In order to obtain a most representative example to illustrate the diachronic change of politeness phenomena, a glimpse at the history of politeness in English is quite sufficient. As historical pragmatic experts Thomas Kohnen (2012) and Jucker (2010, 2012) argue, politeness has gone through extensive transformations as Old English (used by the Saxons, in the period spanning roughly the fifth to the twelfth century) developed into Middle English (used in the period spanning roughly the late twelfth century to the late fifteenth century), and then into Early Modern English (used from the late fifteenth century to the late seventeenth century).

In the Germanic tribal Anglo-Saxon society where Old English developed, the secular value of heroism played an important role. Due to this, self-assertion, self-praise and even provocation (which is often referred to as 'flyting' in the technical literature) were recurrent practices, as historical records reveal. As Kohnen (2008: 142) notes,

the fabric of society depended very much on mutual obligation and kin loyalty, a tie which seems to have been especially pervasive with regard to the bond between man and lord. Apparently, it was only this bond which could guarantee a relatively normal life in society because it implied protection and safety.

In this society, politeness was predominantly expressed by forms of self-display (see example (3)) and other forms which reinforced bonds between superordinate and subordinate. Consequently, directives were more frequently used than in Modern English. In order to illustrate this, let us refer to example (7), which is from Kohnen (2008: 30):

(7) Ic bidde eow þæt ȝe ȝymon eowra sylfra, swa eowere bec eow wissiað.

I ask you to take care of yourselves, as your books teach you.

Accordingly, in many social settings, directness rather than indirectness was preferred. However, phenomena resembling indirect or so-called 'negative politeness' in a modern sense can be traced in Old English data, as example (8) illustrates:

(8) Ic þe nu ða, brego Beorhtdena, biddan wille, eodor Scyldinga, anre bene, þæt ðu me ne forwyrne, wigendra hleo, freowine folca, nu

ic þus feorran com, þæt i̱c mote ana <ond> minra eorla gedryht,
þes hearda heap, Heorot fælsian.

'Now, therefore, sovereign lord of the glorious Danes, prince of
the Scyldings, I want to beg a single favour from you: that you
do not deny it me, refuge of warriors, noble friend of the people,
now that I have thus come from far away, that I be allowed to
cleanse Heorot alone, without even my retinue of noble soldiers,
this troop of hardy men.'

(Beowulf, cited from Kohnen 2012: 243)

The interaction in example (8), which takes place between the hero Beowulf
and King Hrothgar, represents language usage which resembles a contemporary understanding of politeness, more specifically, that of the first wave
of approaches to politeness (see Chapter 2) as an indirect form of communication. That is, Beowulf combines praise and humbleness *(þæt ðu me ne
forwyrne... þæt i̱c mote* 'that you do not deny it me... that I be allowed'), in
order to express a request, and thus it can be considered an indirect speech act.
This usage might be taken to prove that Old English politeness had indirectness
as part of its inventory. However, this is a relatively rare usage in Old English
data, which is usually limited to religious texts (the heroic epos *Beowulf* is
a noteworthy exception in this sense). That is, apart from a few exceptions
like the one in example (8), we have little evidence that indirect speech acts
regularly occurred in Old English.

During the period of Middle English, the above situation changed dramat-
ically as a new conceptualisation of politeness gradually took shape that was
much closer in many respects to contemporary emic understandings of politeness in Britain. Indirectness as means of projecting politeness started to spread
as a normative practice in English. This development took place as a new dominating social value, *curteisie* ('courtesy') entered into emic understandings of
the British under the influence of the French court. *Curteisie* is a concept that is
relatively close to politeness. However, it describes an understanding of politeness 'in which the linguistic forms are chosen on the basis of interactional status
rather than on the ranking of imposition' (Jucker 2010: 196). This shows that
in Medieval English society, politeness was perceived as a less individualistic
phenomenon than in contemporary Britain. If one observes Middle English data
it becomes evident that this understanding manifests itself in the tendency for
interactants to choose certain forms of politeness in accordance with the *perceived* interpersonal relationship, instead of imposition. This poses a warning
for the researcher: although we can understand many Middle English sources
even without using a dictionary, and the politeness phenomena which occur in
these sources often seem to 'make sense', it is still as problematic to project
our preconceptions on these datasets as it is in the case of the more 'alien' Old

English sources. That is, if we interpret Middle English data through the lens of 'imposition' then we are distorting it, as we represent what is essentially an etic understanding as if it were an emic one.

The change of norms and practices has brought about various changes in English, such as the spread of the 'plain' and 'honorific' pronominal forms *thou* and *you* (see the so-called 'T/V forms' in Chapter 2). An examination of the pragmatic usage of these new forms is insightful for the researcher because they reflect the function of linguistic politeness in the Middle English period, namely, that it was bound to the above-mentioned importance of interactional status of relationships. This is illustrated by example (9):

(9) 'What do ye, hony-comb, sweete Aliusun,
     My faire byrd, my sweete cynamone?'
     . . .
     'Why, nay,' quod he, 'God woot, my sweete leef,
     I am thyn Absolon, my deerelyng.
     Of gold,' quod he, 'I have thee broght a ryng.
     My mooder yaf it me, so God me save;
     Ful fyn it is, and therto wel ygrave.
     This wol I yeve thee, if thou me kisse.'
                          (cited from Jucker 2010: 191, 192)

     The modern rhyming 'translation' of this section is as follows:
     'What do you, honeycomb, sweet Alison.
     My cinnamon, my fair bird, my sweetie?'
     . . .
     'Why no,' quoth he, 'God knows, my sweet roseleaf,
     I am your Absalom, my own darling!
     Of gold,' quoth he, 'I have brought you a ring;
     My mother gave it me, as I'll be saved;
     Fine gold it is, and it is well engraved;
     This will I give you for another kiss.'
                          (Trans. A.S. Kleine, available online at
                          www.poetryintranslation.com/PITBR/English/
                          CanterburyTalesIII.htm)

This interaction, which is drawn from *The Canterbury Tales*, represents a funny tale of the lovers Absolon and Alison. Absolon, who wants to make Alison his lover, first uses inflectional variants of 'you', but as the story unfolds he switches to variants of 'thou', which indicates changes in the way he perceives his relationship with Alison. That is, first he seems to evaluate his relationship with Alison as one that necessitates deference, while later he switches to a more intimate style.

Finally, politeness in Early Modern English had a fairly similar shape to its contemporary counterpart. However, the comparability issue is still lurking there: although politeness in Early Modern texts is really not unfamiliar for the contemporary reader, these texts are nevertheless products of a world which is somewhat different from ours. As Watts (1999) has insightfully pointed out, for a long time in England a proper command of politeness, which resulted in the state of being a 'gentleman', was regarded as an exclusive property of higher social classes. That is, the ideology behind politeness in Early Modern texts does significantly differ from the contemporary, generally more egalitarian, conceptualisations of politeness in modern English. Nevertheless, such a discourse does still pervade British conceptualisations of politeness to some extent as we saw from the above controversy over the email sent by Carolyn Bourne in example (6), with the difference being that it is now a contested rather than hegemonic ideology.

To sum up, change is an ever-present prospect for understandings of politeness, which is thus always in a state of a relative transition. There are, of course, many changes which are of a considerably smaller scope than the ones described above, such as the way in which politeness practices transform as the relational history of a group develops. But even in such settings awareness of issues of comparability should enter our analyses: it cannot be taken for granted that something which counted as polite yesterday will be evaluated in the same way today, as both relationships within networks and perceptions of contextual factors are open to change.

The fact that politeness is subject to (sometimes extensive) change raises an important challenge for researchers, namely, the **continuity** issue. It is not pre-evident that this development takes place in a gradual way, which in turn influences the relationship between different stages of development of politeness within a society or a relational network. In some cases the development of politeness can be abrupt if not brutal, and such transformations may result in conceptualisations or discourses of politeness that do not resemble at all their previous state. A representative case of this phenomenon can be provided through an examination of the history of politeness in Chinese.

Pan and Kádár (2011) argue that politeness in Chinese has undergone extensive changes in its recent history. The practices that constituted so-called 'polite communication' in Chinese underwent a dramatic transformation during the nineteenth and twentieth centuries in Mainland China. In the course of this period, which is relatively brief from a diachronic perspective, the historical norms of deferential communication practically disappeared from Chinese society and were replaced by a new set of politeness norms. The extinction of these historical norms has resulted in the disappearance of the extensive historical Chinese lexicon of honorifics, which in total included several thousand words. More precisely, some honorifics survived into modernity, but their number is extremely limited and they are used in a few special contexts only. This large-scale change is a noteworthy phenomenon, because it resulted in the birth of a 'new' emic understanding of politeness amongst Mainland Chinese which is considerably different from its ancestor.

From the perspective of continuity, this phenomenon raises an interesting question: what were the factors which might have provoked these changes? Various historians argue that these large-scale transformations in Chinese have taken place due to ideological changes. Historical Chinese honorifics developed in such a way that they were perceived to encode and reinforce the historical social order on China (cf. example (3)), and so during the nineteenth century, when traditional understandings of societal structures were being replaced with a new model in a response to attempts by the Western powers to colonise China, such traditional forms of language usage were 'doomed' to disappear. This is, in some respects at least, a convincing explanation, which can be supported with a variety of different sources of evidence. Yet it does not answer an important question: how it can be that no similar change has taken place in other languages in which politeness has undergone major changes? It is enough only to think about North Korea where traditional honorifics continue to be used, irrespective of the fact that the extremist Communist regime has implemented large-scale social and linguistic transformations. The answer resides in grammaticalisation: unlike honorifics in many other languages, Chinese honorifics had never become part of the grammar, due to which their disappearance was a relatively straightforward process.

Continuity, just like transformation, comparability and representation, is a concept which connects historicity with research into contemporary data. In fact, abrupt changes can take place in the practices of relational networks within a short period. While more 'local' changes influence the lives of fewer people than the ones described above, they tend to stir public interest and debates, similarly to changes in more 'social' practices. For example, there was a recent online discussion[3] on the question as to why suddenly customers who were reputedly 'rude' turn to being more unusually 'polite' when they have to pay for a customer support service. In fact, changes in practices can be initiated by a single person. This can be particularly the case (and such changes become salient) when it is the behaviour of a person who has power and, consequently, 'voice' in the given network that changes. Such abrupt changes, e.g. when a boss of a company or a politician changes their practices, are often contested, as example (10) illustrates:

(10) Changes in Attitude? Fenty Suddenly Seems So Polite
     Is the mayor playing nice or is his arrogant side playing possum?
     WASHINGTON – D.C. Mayor Adrian Fenty seems more polite
     and less abrupt than we're used to.

In recent months, Fenty attracted criticism for seeming arrogant, dismissive, petty and even infantile. The mayor says that's not him.

The usually supportive *Washington Post* editorial page decried his 'infantile' and 'petty' refusal to share city baseball tickets with the D.C. Council. In recent weeks, Fenty also has been criticized for letting a private friend and contractor drive his government issued car and for allowing a $75,000 heater to be installed in a public pool Fenty uses.

Fenty apologized for the pool heater Thursday, saying he knew it was being installed and he should not have let that happen, though he noted that the city is in the process of upgrading all public pools that need it.

The new burst of humility – and the fact that he turned the baseball tickets over to the Council – is prompting questions about an apparent change in attitude.

'Well, I think when you make a mistake, I think part of being a professional is admitting it and learning from it and getting past it,' Fenty said.

Fenty's talked to a lot of big city mayors who told him that you've got to roll with the punches and not have a lot of pent up anger when you're mayor.

(www.nbcwashington.com/news/local/
Changes-in-Attitude-Fenty-Suddenly-Seems-Polite.html)

As example (10) illustrates, although Mayor Fenty explains why he acts 'politely', as the title and text of this article suggests, this change is regarded critically by the author of the above text (Fenty's 'politeness' is ostensible) and perhaps also by the wider public.

Thus far we have discussed general concepts that should underpin an examination of the ways in which understandings of politeness are imbued with historicity. In what follows, we will focus on the interrelation between historicity and contemporary research at the level of data, by studying the issue of multimodality, which we briefly introduced in Chapter 6, but which has in fact played and continues to play an important role in communication in both the past and the present.

Historical multimodality

A property of certain text types and genres, which seems to be a continuous source of creativity, is **multimodality**. *Multimodal interaction* is an expression that originates in computer science, and it describes the option of inputting data through multiple channels. For example, a blog is multimodal because it allows the writer to make use of textual and graphical methods at the same time to convey a message (on multimodal issues see also Chapter 1). This expression is not commonly used with respect to historical communication, even though in historical texts many of the properties of multimodality operate, albeit in a technically less-developed way than in their contemporary counterparts (see e.g. Ong 1984). For example, multimodality is a key feature of historical epistolary genres (i.e. different genres of letter writing).

Examining multimodal dimensions of politeness is a topic of great interest because it represents an interface between historicity and modernity. Furthermore, historical multimodal genres also have a noteworthy value from the perspective of the politeness researcher. In this chapter, we have so far discussed the difficulties that a researcher of historical texts needs to cope with. Nevertheless, it can be argued that multimodality in historical texts provides some important analytical clues, which can aid us to reconstruct the way in which certain meanings and actions have been produced and interpreted.

The operation of politeness through textual multimodality was illustrated in Figure 7.1, the Taiwanese invitation letter written in Chinese. In historical and contemporary traditional Chinese texts, the arrangement, size and style of certain characters conventionally conveyed and continue to occasion evaluations of politeness. It is not only the text itself, but the way the message is reinforced by the graphic features of the message, which can express politeness. There are also conventional extra-textual tools that are commonly associated with 'politeness', such as the choice of certain colours, paper types, drawings and paintings on papers and so on. Such tools are not only popular in Chinese culture but were also widely spread in many European epistolary cultures (see a detailed description of this issue in Kádár 2010b, and see also Dury's 2008 study on handwriting and epistolary communication).

While textual features of multimodality in themselves provide an innovative area to explore as they bring an unusual, artistic element into politeness research, there is another aspect of multimodality, which has theoretical significance. More specifically, multimodality is useful for observing the way in which historical documents, in particular letters, have been transmitted, as well as the way in which this transmission influenced the wording of texts, because it reveals how communication – in particular written communication – was regarded in terms of privacy. As the examination of historical epistolary documents reveals, in historical writings, politeness was often framed with different types of audience in mind, thereby providing a noteworthy case of footing in text-based discourse (see Chapters 4 and 6).

In historical societies letters were often transmitted in ways that are quite different from our sense of private exchange, as is argued in the book edited by Terttu Nevalainen and Sanna-Kaisa Tanskanen (2007). Since there was no modern sense of privacy, the courier of the letter not only gave the document to the recipient but he also often read the text aloud to her or him, even in cases when the recipient was literate. In some other cases, a local person was supposed to read aloud the text for the recipients. The document – unless, of course, its content was really confidential as in the case of secret plans – was read aloud in front of kin and followers of the recipient, that is, the message was transferred via at least two channels, writing and speaking.

Since the writer knew that their letter would be read aloud, they had to formulate the letter vis-à-vis politeness with different audiences (i.e. both the addressee and the overhearers) in mind. The group of overhearers also included the courier, who in turn provided feedback to the writer with regards to the reception of the message. Quite understandably, the multiple reception footings in the audience resulted in practices addressing the multiple understandings of politeness that could consequently arise, as example (11) illustrates:

(11) 四弟, 六弟考運不好, 不必掛懷。

The luck of Fourth and Sixth Brothers in the examination was not good, but there is no need to worry about this.
                                                      (cited from Kádár 2010b: 57–8)

This is a fragment from a letter written by a renowned Chinese statesman Zeng Guofan to his parents, in 1842. In the section cited above he reflects on the fact that his younger brothers have failed to pass their imperial examinations (in historical China people could only be appointed as officials after passing state examinations). There is a noteworthy relational issue here: Zeng addresses the letter to his parents – to whom he expresses utter deference – and so he is not supposed to be tactful when it comes to a source of shame about which the whole family is aware. Yet despite this, Zeng uses the euphemistic expression *kaoyun-buhao* 考運不好 (lit. 'luck in the examination was not good'). The obvious reason for this careful formulation is that Zeng was aware that his brothers would be present when the letter was read aloud, or at least they would be informed about its contents by some of the overhearers. Historical evidence shows that the genre of family letters in China was one that was both read and shown to members of a wider clan, and so Zeng's awareness of multiple possible recipient footings is understandable. What is interesting to note in connecting historical and contemporary forms of multimodality and the participant footings they afford is that this phenomenon bears more than a passing resemblance to issues facing users of social media networks, such as Facebook and the like, where the producer needs to bear in mind a potentially complex set of participation footings vis-à-vis understandings of politeness.

8.3   Key studies

Readers who are interested in historical pragmatics in general are recommended to consult the article of Jacobs and Jucker (1995). This provides an excellent overview of the main methodologies of historical pragmatics, and due to its relative brevity is a useful starting point for those who intend to further themselves in this field.

An overview of the field of historical politeness research can be found in the article 'Historical (im)politeness: an introduction', written by Kádár and Culpeper (2010). This paper benchmarks the birth of historical politeness research as an independent field, and it introduces the main theoretical and methodological challenges of examining politeness in historically situated data. Furthermore, it argues for the importance of revisiting descriptive, first-wave approaches, such as Brown and Levinson (1987), to historical politeness from a discursive perspective.

The edited volume of Taavitsainen and Jucker (2003) includes a series of in-depth specialised analyses of terms of address. Research on terms of address is one of the most common fields within historical politeness research, and this volume offers examination of this phenomenon in a great variety of languages and historical periods.

The article by Watts (1999), 'Language and politeness in early eighteenth century Britain', has a most illustrative discussion of the way in which the notion of politeness can transform within a society. Among other issues, Watts discusses inequality in the social distribution of politeness, which was once regarded as a 'property' of high social classes.

Pan and Kádár (2011) cover issues related with continuity, which have been discussed in this chapter. Relying on an extensive interactional database, Pan and Kádár reconstruct the way in which historical Chinese politeness has transformed into its contemporary state. Importantly this research merges historical pragmatics with cross-cultural research.

8.4   Summary

Ultimately, history is an area which cannot be ignored by any theory of politeness. This chapter has argued that the norms and manifestations of politeness are historically relative, i.e. what is understood as appropriate is relative to time. Furthermore, understandings of politeness are influenced by historicity: with the passing of time, understandings and practices, as well as particular interactions, become historically situated, which has an impact on the ways in which they are understood. Historical situatedness poses various challenges for the researcher, such as comparability and representation, as well as transformation and continuity. Whilst these challenges may seem to be specific to historical data, as a matter of fact practically any time lag can transform an interaction into the state of being 'historical', and so arguably the challenges discussed here are also present when one sets out to analyse any interaction that does not occur in front of our eyes (or which cannot be replayed like a video-recording).

In this chapter we have devoted special attention to the point that 'historical' and 'modern' should not be treated in a dichotomic way, as any 'modern' understanding and practice of politeness is liable to become 'historical'. We have also discussed the importance of studying 'real' historical interactions, such as historical manifestations of multimodality, which have important value for research on contemporary data.

8.5   Exercises

I. Answer the following questions:
1. Can you think of cases where you use politeness in order to display your perceived rank rather than to express politeness towards the other? If yes, compare these cases with example (3) above.
2. Can you identify any significant change in the practices of politeness in your society? If yes, describe these changes in detail.
3. Have you ever experienced any situation when your language usage has been represented or mispresented by others?
4. Think about cases when you formed a certain utterance cautiously, out of awareness of multiple audiences who might have overheard your message. How does this situation compare with the case represented by example (9) above?
II. Read the following examples, which represent increasingly complex cases, and analyse the politeness phenomena occurring in them. Compare your analysis with the brief annotations below:
(a) Xerxes: But I am a generous god. I can make you rich beyond all measure. I will make you warlord of all Greece. You will carry my battle standard to the heart of Europa. Your Athenian rivals will kneel at your feet if you will but kneel at mine.

King Leonidas: You are generous as you are divine, O king of kings. Such an offer only a madman would refuse. But the, uh, the idea of kneeling, it's – you see, slaughtering all those men of yours has, uh, well it's left a nasty cramp in my leg, so kneeling will be hard for me.

(*300*, 2006)

(b) King Louis: You look beautiful.
Queen Anne: Thank you.
King Louis: Is something wrong?
Queen Anne: Cardinal Richelieu.

King Louis: Yes?
Queen Anne: He is an evil man.
King Louis: Do not believe every rumour you hear. He is powerful.
Queen Anne: I ride through the countryside every day, I've seen the uses of his power.
King Louis: Power sometimes frightens.
Queen Anne: Here in the Palace I have seen it too.
King Louis: I know.
Queen Anne: What shall we do?
King Louis: I don't know, but we will do it together.

(*The Three Musketeers*, 1993)

Example (a), in spite of the fact that it is a modern reproduction of a historical interaction instead of being an authentic historical source, neatly represents the use of politeness in a self-oriented rather than an other-oriented way, which was illustrated in example (3). King Xerxes, leader of the Persian army which is attemping to invade Greece, refers to himself as being a 'generous god', and his interactant King Leonidas acknowledges this rank deferentially (but in a somewhat mocking tone), by uttering 'You are generous as you are divine, O king of kings.'

Example (b) is a typical case of mispresentation. It seems to us natural that the French King and Queen, who are young lovers, exchange words of plain adoration, and that they promise to each other that they will go through difficulties together. However, this is simply not the way in which politeness worked in many societies of that age. The king and the queen of a country like France were assumed to interact with some degree of formal etiquette, for example, by using formal terms of address, and it is likely that they rarely interacted in private (that is, without courtiers being around), which would have thus influenced the ways in which understandings of politeness arose given the presence of 'overhearers'.

Part III

Politeness and social space:
from mind to society

9 Politeness and metapragmatics

9.1 Introduction

Politeness is something that we can all talk and think about. This talk about politeness ranges from specific comments we might make to, or about, participants in interactions through to whole books on etiquette or appropriate social behaviour. Indeed, in some cultures we can find discourses on politeness and related phenomena stretching back thousands of years, a point we noted in Chapter 8. Such talk comes under the umbrella of metapragmatics, which can be broadly defined as the study of *awareness* on the part of ordinary or *lay observers* about the ways in which they use language to interact and communicate with others.

In order to start thinking about how we might study the metapragmatics of politeness, let us first consider example (1), from the movie *Borat*, where the British comedian Sacha Baron Cohen plays the character of Borat Sadiyev, a fictitious journalist from Kazakhstan who is travelling through the United States interacting with real-life Americans. Here, Borat is receiving instruction on how to act appropriately at a dinner party from a professional etiquette coach (Kathie). He then takes what he has 'learned' and subsequently applies it with members of a Dining Society at a dinner party in the Magnolia Springs Manor in Helena, Alabama. The participants in both of these interactions were not aware at the time that Borat was a fictional character being played by an actor.

(1) Scene 1: Etiquette class with professional etiquette coach, Kathie Martin.

Borat: ((walks in and shakes hands)) Hello. Nice meet you.

Kathie: Hello, it's so nice to meet you. Welcome to America.

Borat: Will you please teach me how to dine like gentlemen?

Kathie: Of course, I'll be happy to.

Borat: ((sitting at table)) Should I pay compliments to the peoples?

Kathie: Yes, but only if you truly agree with that compliment.

Scene 2: Six people from the Dining Society are holding a dinner party with Borat at the Magnolia Springs Manor. Borat is seated between two ladies, Cindy and Sarah, with another lady, Sally, sitting at the end of the table opposite her husband, Cary.

Borat: ((orienting to Sarah)) You have a- very gentle face and very erotic physique.

Sarah: ((softly)) Thank you.

Jared: You're correct.

Cindy: ((laughs))

Cary: Yes, that's a very good observation.

Borat: She is your wife?

Cary: No, that's my wife ((points to his wife, Sally, at the end of the table))

Borat: In my country they would go crazy, for these two ((gestures to Sarah and Cindy))
          ((laughter from several participants; Sarah and Cindy smile))

Borat: Not so much . . . ((gestures to Sally))
          ((laughter drops off))

Cary: ((stares stonily at Borat))

(Borat: Cultural Learnings of America for Make Benefit Glorious Nation of Kazakhstan, 2006)

In the first scene, Borat learns that it is good to compliment others in the context of a 'polite' dinner party, which is explicitly invoked here through Borat's reference to dining 'like gentlemen'. The etiquette coach advises, however, that his compliments should be *sincere* (or at least should be seen to be so). Insofar as this is explicit talk about how to be a gentleman (i.e. 'polite'), it constitutes a very clear sign of awareness on the part of both of these participants that there are certain expectations in relation to 'polite' dinner parties in the US, or at least in the Southern States such as Alabama where these interactions took place.

In the second scene, Borat applies what he has 'learnt' by complimenting Sarah on her good looks. Despite the potentially inappropriate formulation of his compliment in referring to her 'erotic physique', Sarah herself thanks Borat for his compliment, and the other guests express agreement. Through this reciprocation, it is evident they are treating Borat's compliment as a polite one (albeit perhaps in an attempt to accommodate Borat's apparent *outsider* status in this interaction). However, Borat's apparent good work comes undone when he implies that while Sarah and Cindy are very attractive, Cary's wife Sally is not particularly attractive. At this point it becomes apparent from the marked drop in laughter in the group and the 'stony' expression on Cary's face that this latter implicature has caused offence. What we can observe in this second scene is that **metapragmatic awareness** is not always limited to talk about politeness. Here Borat is implicitly held accountable by the other participants, in particular by Cary, for having an impolite attitude towards his wife. In attributing this attitude to Borat, Cary and the others demonstrate *reflexive* thinking, where one thinks about what others think one thinks and so on. In this case, Cary (and the others) think that Borat thinks it is allowable to indicate that he does not think highly of Cary's wife, in particular, her looks. This attitude is characterisable as impolite through an implicit appeal to the moral order, namely, the set of expectancies around 'polite' dinner parties, including the expectation that one will avoid negative assessments of the physical appearance of others. While Borat is initially given leeway in that he is treated as an outsider, and thus is treated as having an etic perspective on the moral order assumed by the other participants, he is ultimately held accountable to the emic understandings of these participants as to what constitutes impoliteness in 'polite' society in Alabama – and more than likely amongst many Anglo-Americans (and many other societies) more generally. The expectation that one avoids negative assessments is here constituted through their responses, and thus it contributes to perpetuating this expectation as part of the moral order of this particular relational network over time.

In this chapter, we outline why a metapragmatic perspective on language use and communication is of particular importance to the study of politeness. As you will recall, we have proposed that lying at the heart of understandings of politeness is the notion of *social practice*. We have suggested that politeness constitutes a social practice because it involves evaluations (implicitly) appealing to a moral order, which are occasioned by social actions and meanings. In other words, evaluations of politeness are not idiosyncratic, but are constituted through the practices by which social actions and meanings are recognisable as 'familiar scenes of everyday affairs', and are thus open, because of this, to moral evaluation. However, as the pragmatician Verschueren (1999) points out, social practices cannot be separated out from the understandings of participants themselves without losing sight of what we have set out to understand as analysts in the first place:

in social life, *conceptualisations* and *practices* are inseparable. Consequently, there is no way of understanding forms of behaviour without gaining insight into the way in which the social actors themselves habitually conceptualise what it is they are doing. Preconceived theoretical frameworks just do not suffice. (1999: 196, emphasis added)

What Verschueren is arguing here is that we cannot understand the social practices by which politeness arises without investigating the ways in which participants generally conceptualise their own behaviour. In other words, we need to systematically analyse the *moral order*, through which evaluations of politeness are constituted, as an object of study in its own right.

The moral order is constituted, as we discussed in Chapters 4 and 5, through practices by which social actions and meanings are recognisable to members, and are thereby open to moral evaluation. The sets of expectancies through which the recognisability of these practices is constituted can be divided into three interleaving layers, where first-order expectancies (i.e. localised norms) reflexively invoke second-order expectancies (i.e. group-based norms), which can, in turn, reflexively invoke third-order expectancies (i.e. societal norms) (see Figure 5.4 in Chapter 5). In this chapter we thus attempt to outline how we can tap into politeness vis-à-vis all three layers of the moral order by examining various forms of metapragmatic awareness.

9.2   Key concepts

Reflexivity and meta-awareness

The prefix *meta*, which comes from Greek μετά meaning 'above', 'beyond' or 'among', is normally used in English to indicate a concept or term that is *about* another concept or term. For example, 'metadata' is data about data, while *metalanguage* is language about language. The term *metapragmatics* was first coined by the linguistic anthropologist Michael Silverstein (1976, see also 1993), and defined as 'reflexive pragmatic functioning' (1976: 36). In other words, it involves the study of reflexive awareness on the part of participants and observers of interaction about the ways in which language is used. The notions of **reflexivity** and *awareness* are thus critical to understanding metapragmatics.

Reflexivity arises when one level of interpretation or analysis is interdependently related to another. In the case of politeness this means a circular relationship invariably exists between what occasions an evaluation of politeness and the evaluation itself. An action or meaning counts as polite because it is *recognisable* to participants as polite, but it is recognisable to participants as polite because it is *recognised* by at least some participants as polite. In example (1), for instance, the way in which Borat implies Cary's wife is not attractive is recognisable as not polite (or even impolite) in part because Cary recognises it as not polite through his non-verbal response (i.e. his 'stony' stare and silence). However, Cary can only recognise it as not polite because it is recognisably not polite with reference to the set of expectancies these participants have vis-à-vis *polite* complimenting at dinner parties. The recognisability of politeness, impoliteness and so on is thus dependent on participants recognising social actions/meanings as occasioning politeness, impoliteness and so on, but recognising politeness, impoliteness and so on depends in turn on the recognisability of this politeness, impoliteness and so on. In other words, the recognition of politeness, impoliteness and so on (i.e. the evaluation) by participants is interdependently or reflexively related to the recognisability of politeness, impoliteness and so on (i.e. what occasions the evaluation).

This circular relationship between what occasions an evaluation of politeness and the evaluation itself means that this evaluation enters into the past, current ongoing and future evaluative moments of the person(s) to whom an evaluation can be traced. In other words, these reflexive evaluations are also fundamentally **recursive** across relational networks or social spaces. What we mean by *recursive* is that these evaluations reoccur or are repeated in a self-similar way over time and across social spaces, as we discussed in Chapter 7. For instance, Borat's remarks are recognisable to Cary and the other participants as impolite or offensive, because they are not consistent with their taken-for-granted expectancies in relation to compliments vis-à-vis this interpretative frame – in other words, the *conventions* in that relational network as to what counts as a polite compliment (cf. Chapter 7). Evaluations of politeness are thus *potentially* recursive in the evaluative moment of the here-and-now in the sense that Cary's evaluation of Borat's remarks as impolite rests in part on Cary's assumption that others present (excluding Borat) may evaluate Borat's remarks as impolite, and thus Cary might expect that the others would expect him to evaluate Borat's remarks as impolite, and furthermore that the others present might expect that Cary might expect that the others might expect him to evaluate Borat's remarks as impolite and so on.

In practice, of course, evaluative moments of politeness cannot be infinitely recursive, but they can readily reach a third or fourth degree of recursivity as we can see, for instance, in the additional layers of metapragmatic understanding that subsequently emerged when the interaction itself became the subject of discussion in the local media. Comments from the unwitting participants were elicited by reporters after they found out they had been misled by Sacha Baron Cohen (i.e. the comedian playing Borat). Cary Speaker, for instance, was quoted as saying in a local news report, 'Hey, he fooled us; it's funny. Watching this, I'm sure it's funny [to some people]', but nevertheless admitting that 'It was just not funny that night.' In other words, Cary alludes to the offence he took at Borat's remarks about his wife at the time, although in retrospect serious offence did not last beyond the here-and-now of that particular moment. Sarah Moseley, the lady who was 'complimented' by Borat, was quoted as saying, on the other hand, 'He insulted all of us', thereby alluding to a sense of broader offence at being misled by Sacha Baron Cohen. This talk about politeness and offence thus became part of a broader intergroup concern, namely, the way in which movie goers more generally view people from Alabama subsequent to witnessing this scene, something which became most apparent in Sarah's reported comments, 'I don't want our city and our state to be embarrassed.' A local reporter reassured readers, however, that 'they did Alabama proud', as it was only Borat who acted offensively, not the local Alabamans. In this way, we can also observe how the evaluations of participants vis-à-vis politeness can vary depending on their awareness of the extent to which the interaction in question is being witnessed by others.

The question, then, for us as analysts is how do we open up the circularity inherent in the recognition and recognisability of evaluative moments of politeness? One option is to tap into the reflexive awareness of such evaluative moments on the part of participants (and observers) themselves. Metapragmatic awareness varies both in its degree of accessibility and level of salience to participants. This means that while some indicators of metapragmatic awareness may be easily accessible and/or highly salient to users, others may not. This should not be taken to suggest, however, that metapragmatic awareness can be equated with levels of consciousness. The folk linguists Nancy Niedzielski and Dennis Preston (2009) suggest that there are at least four distinct modes of awareness:

a. Unavailable: phenomena that users will not, or perhaps cannot, comment on
b. Available: phenomena that are discussed only if they are carefully described
c. Suggestible: phenomena that are seldom initiated by users, but nevertheless are commented on without elaborate description
d. Common: frequent public topics of folk linguistic discussion.

(Niedzielski and Preston 2009: 147)

On this view, participants may not always be able to articulate their reflexive understandings of politeness, despite such understandings being inherent in that very same usage. It is also apparent that such awareness may become more or less salient in different situated contexts. In example (1), Borat's impolite attitude towards Cary's wife was highly salient. However, in other instances, metapragmatic awareness on the part of participants can be much more subtle, as we shall see.

Given that participants may not always be able to articulate their reflexive understandings of politeness, then, a focus on the metapragmatics of politeness is not simply a matter of analysing the talk of insiders (an emic perspective) – or outsiders (an etic perspective) – about politeness. In fact, there are four key forms of reflexive awareness that are relevant to understanding politeness:

(i) **metalinguistic awareness**, which involves reflexive *representations* of evaluations of politeness, impoliteness and so on. A representation is essentially a generalised interpretation of the world (including our social reality) that we find displayed in or through natural language terms or expressions. Essentially this involves the different expressions or *metalanguage* we can use in various languages to talk about politeness, impoliteness and so on, such as *polite* and *courteous* in English or *teinei* and *reigi* in Japanese.

(ii) **metacommunicative awareness**, which refers to reflexive *interpretations* and *evaluations* of social actions and meanings. This includes explicit

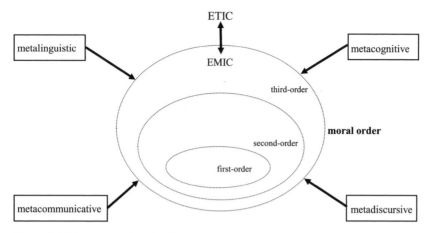

Figure 9.1 Metapragmatics of politeness.

comments that participants make in interactions using terms such as *polite* or *courteous*. Interpretations and evaluations lie at the core of politeness as social practice, as we have discussed in the preceding chapters.

(iii) **metadiscursive awareness,** which refers to reflexive *social discourses* on politeness that are constituted (and contested) at a societal or cultural level. A social discourse encompasses a *persistent frame of interpretation and evaluation* that has become objectified in ongoing metapragmatic talk about politeness.[1] This includes, for instance, talk about *politeness* or *courtesy* in the popular media.

(iv) **metacognitive awareness,** which involves reflexive *presentations* of cognitively grounded states, such as attitudes, expectations and so on, through discourse or pragmatic markers.

In Figure 9.1 these four key types of metapragmatic awareness are summarised as ways in which the moral order itself is constituted not only in particular evaluative moments of politeness, but over time and across social spaces. In this chapter, we suggest that an examination of these different forms of metapragmatic awareness vis-à-vis politeness gives us, as analysts, a window into the reflexive layers of the moral order we introduced in Chapters 4 and 5. At the top of Figure 9.1 we have also added that these various forms of metapragmatic understanding of the moral order can be situated vis-à-vis emic (or insider) understandings, or vis-à-vis etic (or outsider) understandings. This interplay between emic and etic understandings of the moral order is an ongoing theme that emerges when examining these different forms of metapragmatic awareness, as we shall see. We will now move to outline the first three types of metapragmatic awareness in the remainder of this chapter, (i.e. metalinguistic, metacommunicative and metadiscursive awareness), leaving our discussion of metacognitive awareness to Chapter 10, where we focus more specifically on cognition and emotion in relation to politeness.

Metalanguage

In order to describe and conceptualise our social reality, which includes politeness among many other things, we need to use language. However, since our social reality is itself constituted through language, the terms or expressions used to describe politeness involve a particular kind of reflexive language use that is termed *metalanguage* – essentially language which focuses on language itself. What this means is we can examine the conceptual underpinnings of politeness through careful analysis of the metalinguistic representations that are constituted through politeness-related terms and expressions. As we noted in Chapter 5, the sets of expectancies that constitute the moral order draw in important ways from inter-related arrays of (im)politeness evaluators (the metalanguage used by members to conceptualise their social world). It is thus important to systematically investigate the metalanguage of 'politeness' across different relational networks. In this way, we can tease out the emic worldviews that underpin '(im)politeness' metalanguage. In the following discussion of (im)politeness evaluators, then, we will use quotation marks to indicate where we are using 'politeness' in the etic sense (i.e. to discuss '(im)politeness' evaluators across languages), and italics when we are referring to them in the emic sense (i.e. to discuss how they are understood by speakers of those languages).

An important point to note, however, when setting out to examine the metalanguage of 'politeness' across language and relational networks is to appreciate that such terms do not exist in a conceptual vacuum. As Mills argues:

politeness only makes sense in relation to other terms within its semantic field, and the meanings of these terms are defined in a complex process of being set apart from and being conflated with other terms and playing off the meanings of those terms. (2009: 1055)

This means that we cannot study a term such as *politeness* in English in isolation. Inevitably any discussion of *politeness* involves appeals (albeit implicit) to understandings of *impoliteness*. It is for this reason we have not excluded 'impoliteness' and so on from our analyses in this volume. However, the interplay of these different metalinguistic expressions is not restricted to the reflexive conceptual underpinnings of *politeness* and *impoliteness*. Consider for a moment example (2), from an interview with an informant about his views on how he would rate a particular apology (which we discussed in Chapter 5) vis-à-vis *politeness*.

(2) AM4: 5:13
   69 A: maybe it'd- he'd be placing towards the neither polite nor impolite or <u>verging</u> (.) on the polite, cer- certainly not very polite?
   70 W: mhm?
   71 A: not obsequiously polite or not any not- not- not- overly polite in any other sense, but (.) nor was he particularly impolite, I thought.

The main point to note here is that the informant tries to characterise how he would evaluate the apology in terms of both how it might be evaluated (*verging on polite*), as well as how it would not be evaluated (*not polite, not obsequiously polite, not overly polite, not particularly impolite*). These metalinguistic terms in English are thus relativised within a **semantic field**: a set of related words that denote a segment of presumed social reality (i.e. 'politeness'). This semantic field is occasioned through his localised talk in order to clarify what is meant by his evaluation of the apology as *neither polite nor impolite*.

In Figure 9.2 we outline a basic framework through which we can represent the ways in which we necessarily draw from both emic and etic perspectives in understanding politeness across languages and relational networks. Some of the basic evaluators that are used in politeness research, where English is predominantly used as a scientific metalanguage, feature in the middle box (cf. Figure 4.1). These go beyond simply 'politeness' and 'impoliteness', since these do not exist in a vacuum, but within a larger semantic field, as we observed in example (2). The various lexemes featured in the circles on both sides of the middle box illustrate examples of emic '(im)politeness'-related evaluators in a selection of four different languages: English, Japanese, Spanish and Chinese. These are not meant as equivalents or translations of each other, but rather to illustrate lexemes that occupy a similar conceptual space or semantic field in those languages. What is important to note here is that *(im)politeness* evaluators in English are treated on a par with those in other languages from an emic perspective. From an etic perspective, however, they are necessarily privileged given this book is itself written in English. Another point to note is that we are only representing 'politeness' metalanguage at the 'societal' or 'cultural' level (which are third-order normative understandings), but the metalanguage itself may carry different connotations within different first- and second-order relational networks.

While a consideration of all these different metalinguistic terms inevitably goes beyond the scope of this chapter, what Figure 9.2 is meant to suggest is that rather than treating the metalanguage we use to describe politeness, impoliteness and the like as simply a given, we need to make more serious attempts to tease out the worldviews that underpin this analytical metalanguage.

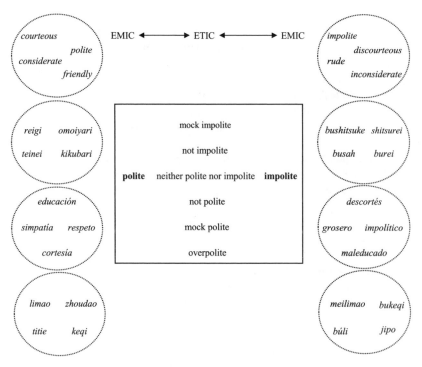

Figure 9.2 An emic/etic model of 'politeness' evaluators.

Otherwise, as Haugh (2012a) argued, we may fall into one of two traps: first, thinking we are talking about the same phenomena across languages and cultures when in fact we are not; second, generating analytical artifacts that are of no consequence for those people concerned through the imposition of tacit worldviews that underlie the metalanguage we use. It is thus important to properly analyse and to understand the 'politeness' metalanguage of the language that is the focus of analysis.

Take, for instance, two languages that have been characterised as 'negative politeness' cultures by Brown and Levinson (1987): (British) English and Japanese. The word *polite* in (British) English is often associated with terms such as *courteous, respectful, friendly, pleasant, thoughtful, cheerful, calm, gracious, charming and quiet* according to Culpeper (2012). In Japanese, in contrast, there are at least four possible 'equivalents' for *polite*: *teinei* (lit. 'warm/kind-hearted'), *omoiyari* (lit. 'consideration'/'empathy'), *kikubari/kizukai* (lit. 'attentiveness') *and reigi* (lit. 'manners') (Fukushima 2004, 2011; Haugh 2004). However, if we look more closely at the conceptual underpinnings of just one of these, take for instance *reigi*, we find an evaluator

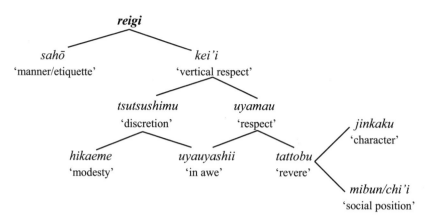

Figure 9.3 Semantic field of *reigi* in Japanese.

which has a rather different conceptual scope to that encompassed by the notion of *polite* in English.

Consider the analysis of the conceptual underpinnings of one of these terms, *reigi*, presented in Figure 9.3. What we find associated with the '(im)politeness' evaluator *reigi* in Japanese are notions such as 'status-oriented respect' (*kei'i*), 'discretion' (*tsutsushimu*), 'revere' (*tattobu*) and 'social position' (*mibun/chi'i*). What becomes apparent from this broad attempt at representing an emic under-standing of a key 'politeness' evaluator in Japanese is that we are dealing with a concept quite different to that encapsulated by *polite* in English.[2] What we can see is that the emic concept of *reigi* embodies a whole set of assumptions about personhood, relationships and social structure that deserve much closer atten-tion. The notion of *reigi* emphasises, for instance, a view of persons as defined in part through their social 'place' (both the 'place one stands' and the 'place one belongs'), and a view of social structure as involving vertical, hierarchical relationships. What becomes apparent, then, is that we are not dealing with *equivalent* notions here but rather with *analogous* conceptualisations. To put it more simply, there is little point in examining how understandings of politeness arise in Japanese using an implicit notion of *politeness* in English, or even a technical or operational definition of politeness that is meant to encompass both, because they involve quite different sets of underlying assumptions.[3] It is therefore essential that analyses of politeness are informed – although not overly constrained – by these emic conceptualisations.

How, then, might we study the metalanguage of politeness across different relational networks or social spaces more broadly? In Table 9.1 we briefly summarise three main approaches which have been utilised by politeness researchers to date, and some exemplary studies that can be consulted for

Table 9.1 *Approaches to analysing the metalanguage of politeness.*

Approach	Exemplar studies
1. Corpus analysis	Culpeper (2009b)
2. Lexical/conceptual mapping	Ide *et al*. ([1992] 2005)
a. Statistical	Pizziconi (2007)
b. Qualitative	Wetzel (2004)
	Watts (2008)
3. Metapragmatic interviews/questionnaires	Bolívar (2008)
	Gagné (2010)

further details on how to operationalise these approaches. Corpus analysis involves studying the relative *frequency* of metalinguistic expressions and the ways in which they *collocate* (i.e. co-occur) with other terms in a corpus, which is generally a large, representative and structured collection of texts sampled from various types of discourse. Given the method of choice in lexicography (i.e. the study of word meanings) is considered to be corpus linguistics (Culpeper 2009b), it is clear that corpus analysis offers a firm ontological basis for understanding 'politeness' across languages and relational networks. For instance, Culpeper analysed the 'impoliteness' lexicon in English using the Oxford English Corpus, a two-billion word corpus encompassing different varieties of English. An important finding was that *rude* is much more common than *impolite*, and indeed the latter has a more 'formal' or 'highbrow flavor' (p. 77). In other words, *rude* is the term of choice for ordinary speakers of English, while *impolite* is the term of choice for academics. What this indicates is that those interested in understanding the metalanguage of 'impoliteness' in English should be focusing on teasing out the conceptual underpinnings of the expression *rude* in the first instance rather than treating *impolite* as interchangeable with *rude*.[4]

However, while analyses of the metalanguage of 'politeness' through corpora is an analytically powerful approach, it inevitably needs to be complemented with other approaches for two reasons. One problem is there are not appropriate corpora in existence for all languages or language varieties, and certainly not many that can address differences in metalinguistic awareness across the different relational networks that constitute the broader community of speakers of a particular language. A second possible limitation is that corpus analysis does not necessarily always allow for in-depth analysis of the conceptual underpinnings of this metalanguage; in particular, the ways in which 'politeness' metalanguage inevitably forms semantic fields.

A second approach to analysing metalanguage that allows for the latter kind of analysis is through lexical or conceptual mapping. Here, the focus is on elucidating the conceptual network or field formed through metalinguistic expressions through either statistical or qualitative means. Ide *et al.* (2005 [1992]), for instance, undertook multivariate analysis of 'politeness' terms in American English and Japanese. A key finding was that *friendliness* was associated with *politeness* in American English, but not with *teinei* in Japanese. And Pizziconi (2007) has employed another statistical method, multidimensional scaling, to examine and compare the 'politeness' lexicon in British English and Japanese, with her results independently confirming (as well as elaborating on) the earlier findings of Ide *et al.* Other studies have used more qualitative means to develop conceptual maps or networks of metalinguistic expressions. Wetzel (2004), for instance, utilised discourse analysis in examining the 'politeness' lexicon in etiquette books about honorifics in Japanese, with a key finding being that many of them are oriented to the notion of 'vertical respect' (*kei'i* 敬意) and 'place' (*tachiba* 立場). Methods from cognitive linguistics have also been employed, with Watts (2008), for instance, using the 'mental spaces model' to analyse the 'impoliteness' lexicon in (British) English, with a particular focus on how these mental spaces are 'blended' in the course of interaction.

Finally, metapragmatic interviews and questionnaires have also been utilised to offer further insights into the metalinguistic awareness of cultural insiders or members. Adriana Bolívar (2008), for instance, examined perceptions of 'politeness' in Venezuelan Spanish using a questionnaire. She reported that her informants offered a wide range of words as somehow related to or equivalent to 'politeness', but the tendency was for women to associate it with *amabilidad* ('kindness') and *educación* ('education/good behaviour'), while men felt more inclined to associate it with *norma* ('norms') as well, the latter reflecting the perceived need to act as *caballeros* ('gentlemen'). And in a rather thought-provoking study, Gagné (2010) examined further elements of the Japanese '(im)politeness' lexicon through the analytical lens of the etic (in this case theoretical) notion of negative face. What she found in interviews was that while the informants could recognise negative face (the desire that one's wants be unimpeded) as an independent idea, they did not view it as naturally arising in request situations. Instead, they reinterpreted their hesitancy or avoidance of requests in some contexts in terms of the presumption they are *shakaijin* ('adult members of a society') who understand that it is expected one does things by oneself to cause as little *meiwaku* ('trouble') to others as possible. Crucially, it was claimed that a *shakaijin* is someone who avoids *meiwaku* because he or she can 'independently recognise the importance and conditions of one's social embeddedness, and act according to it' (p. 131). In other words, it was to their *relationships* with each other that the informants oriented in conceptualising 'polite' requests.

Metacommunication

In the same way that metalanguage is language that focuses on language itself, **metacommunication** involves communication about communicative events themselves, in other words, communication that focuses on the interpretation and evaluation of social actions and meanings in interaction. While the term **metadiscourse** is sometimes also used to refer to this (see Culpeper 2011a), we are reserving that term for a discussion of discourse in the more technical sense of persistent frames of interpretation or ideologies in the subsequent section. Various terms are used to describe instances where metacommunication surfaces in language use, including *metapragmatic comments, metalinguistic comments, metadiscursive comments*, or simply *metacomments*. These terms are largely interchangeable, but since they generally reflect the home discipline of the analyst (e.g. pragmatics, (socio)linguistics or discourse analysis), they can carry with them an implicit set of theoretical assumptions, a point which is important to bear in mind in situating different studies of politeness relative to each other (see Chapter 5). Since spontaneous or naturally occurring instances of metacommunication can, as Jaworski, Coupland and Galasiński point out, 'influence and negotiate how an utterance is or should have been heard, or try to modify the values attributed to it' (2004: 4), they should be studied in the locally situated context in which they occur. However, as Mills (2003) warns, even metacommunication which is elicited by analysts when trying to tease out participant and/or emic understandings of politeness itself constitutes a locally situated context, and so should also be treated as such.

Underlying such instances of metacommunication is, of course, metacommunicative awareness on the part of (meta)participants. This refers to our (implicit) awareness in communication that not only do we interpret and evaluate what we ourselves say and do, and what others say and do, but we also reflexively interpret and evaluate these social actions and meanings through the eyes of others. In other words, we include the perspective of others in our interpretations and evaluations of politeness. This kind of perspective-taking is what underpins metapragmatic comments, and thus what makes them so potentially useful to furthering our understanding of politeness.

For instance, in example (3), from the film *Gran Torino*, we can see how a young Vietnamese-American is being enculturated into a particular set of practices through such metapragmatic comments. The film is set in Detroit and the norms for interaction amongst males that are discussed in the example reflect a (perceived) slice of American male blue-collar values. The example involves Walt (a gruff Polish-American who has retired from the Ford factory) trying to teach his young neighbour, Tao, how he should talk to guys. After performing some 'guy talk' for Tao, where both Walt and the barber (Martin) insult each other, with much of this insulting having a strong undertone of racial stereotyping, Tao takes these instructions somewhat literally and begins his performance of 'guy talk' by calling the barber an 'old Italian prick'. They then go on to explain to Tao the norms vis-à-vis politeness underlying this kind of masculine talk.

(3) Walt: You know you don't just come in and insult a man in his own shop. You just don't do that. What happens if you meet some stranger? You get the wrong one and he's gonna blow your gook head right off.

Tao: What should I have said then?

Barber: Yeah kid. Why don't you start with um 'hi' or 'hello'?

Walt: Yeah just come in and say, 'Sir I'd like a haircut if you have the time.'

Barber: Yeah, be polite but don't kiss ass.

Walt: In fact, you could talk about the construction job you just came from. And bitch about your girlfriend in your car.

Barber: Uh, son of a bitch, I just got my brakes fixed, and those sons of bitches really nailed me. I mean they screwed me right in the ass.

Walt: Yeah, don't swear at the guy. Just talk about people who are not in the room. You could bitch about your boss making you work overtime when it's bowling night.

Barber: Right, or my old lady bitches for two goddamn hours about how they uh don't take expired coupons at the grocery store. And the minute I turn on the fucking game, she starts crying how we never talk.

Walt: You see? Now go out and come back and talk to him. And it ain't rocket science for Christ's sake.

Tao: Yeah, but I don't have a job, a car, or a girlfriend.

Barber: Jesus, I should have blown his head off when I had the chance.

(Gran Torino, 2008)

A number of key features of this form of 'guy talk' emerge in the course of example (3), as Walt and then also the barber (Martin) attempt to instruct Tao. One key 'rule', according to Walt and the barber at least, is that you don't *insult* someone unless you know them well (as do Walt and Martin), but rather you insult others who are *not* present. A second key 'rule' is that a balance needs to be maintained between being sufficiently respectful (i.e. *polite*) but

Table 9.2 *Approaches to analysing (im)politeness metacommunication.*

Approach	Exemplar studies
1. Naturally occurring	
a. Face-to-face interaction	Holmes, Marra and Vine (2012)
b. Computer-mediated interaction	Graham (2007)
c. Fictional interaction	Paternoster (2012)
2. Elicited	
a. Interviews	Spencer-Oatey (2011)
b. Diary/report method	Culpeper (2011a)

not overly polite (what is colloquially termed *kissing ass*). A third key 'rule' is that a common topic of conversation is complaints (or what is colloquially termed *bitching*). Complaining about others, particularly your boss or wife, or about the services offered by others, is deemed by Walt and the barber to be an acceptable way of making conversation. What is notable about this example is not that it can be used to make any claims about blue-collar workers in Detroit actually speaking like this *per se*, but rather that it illustrates, on the one hand, how metacommunication can provide insight into the (localised) moral order that grounds evaluative moments of politeness, and how non-members or outsiders can be introduced to such emic understandings, on the other.

There are various ways in which we can study this underlying moral order through the analysis of metacommunicative awareness on the part of participants and observers. Here we focus particularly on the analysis of metapragmatic comments vis-à-vis politeness. In Table 9.2 we summarise the key approaches to collecting metapragmatic comments, and exemplar studies that can be consulted for further details on how to operationalise these approaches. The main key distinction to be made is between metacommunication that is naturally occurring versus that which is elicited by the analyst. Naturally occurring metapragmatic comments can arise in either face-to-face, computer-mediated or fictional interactions, and may, in turn, be directed at evaluative moments of politeness situated in the here-and-now or past evaluative moments of politeness situated in the there-and-then. Metapragmatic commentary may also, in some cases, be directed not only at pragmatic meanings or social actions, but also at aspects of moral order itself. The focus in analysing naturally occurring metapragmatic comments is thus on their locally situated functions, as well as on what light they shed on the moral order to which they are appealing.

Holmes, Marra and Vine (2012), for instance, report on the explicit negotiation of politeness norms in European (termed Pākehā) and Māori ethnolects of New Zealand English. The former has traditionally been considered dominant or mainstream in New Zealand society, but in workplaces where

Maori predominate, such assumptions can be challenged. In example (4) we can observe a clash between Pākehā and Māori interactional norms that surfaces in the form of metalinguistic commentary. The exchange occurs in one of the regular meetings of Kiwi Consultations, where only three out of the regular participants are Pākehā.

(4) 1 Steve: we have capability development um
     2   the g m oversight here
     3   ((overlapped by a quiet conversation involving Frank
               and Daniel))
     4   is from Frank with Caleb the manager
     5   in charge budget of a hundred and eighty seven k
     6   ((pause)) obviously key area we want to ensure that
               um
     7   one of the important: things in communication is
     8   not to talk when others are talking
     9   ((loud laughter))
    10 Steve: I hope that the cameras picked up (that)
    11   ((loud laughter))
    12 Frank: Steve this indicates a need for you to be out in hui
    13   ((laughter))
    14 Frank: one of the things that you learn very quickly
    15   is that a sign of respect is that other people are talking
    16   about what [you're saying while you're saying it]
    17   [((laughter))   ]
               ((laughter))
    18 Steve: I see I see
                            (Holmes, Marra and Vine 2012: 1070–1)

In example (4), Steve asserts a third-level moral norm (for Pākehā New Zealand English speakers), namely, that one should not speak while others are speaking (lines 7–8). However, this is treated as an inappropriate assertion by Frank, another Pākehā. Frank implies that Steve is not sufficiently acquainted with Māori New Zealand English ways of speaking by suggesting that he needs to attend more *hui* (i.e. traditional Māori meetings). By doing so it is suggested that Steve would gain an appreciation of the Māori English taken-for-granted understanding that 'a sign of respect is that other people are talking about what you're saying while you're saying it' (lines 15–16). By asserting practice as normative in the Māori moral order, Frank reframes Steve metapragmatic comment as inappropriate for that workplace because it involves an orientation to the assumed Pākehā moral order.

Analyses of metapragmatic comments in computer-mediated interactions also offer considerable promise in expanding our understanding of the moral order, in part because they are an increasingly common form of interaction in their own right. Sage Graham (2007), for instance, focused on how expectations about politeness and impoliteness were negotiated in email interactions that arose in ChurchList. While elements of this moral order were specific to the computer medium in question (e.g. the moral censure of 'blatting' to all members of the list), and to that community of practice (e.g. prayers as the preferred response to requests for support), she nevertheless found that evaluative moments of politeness in the here-and-now were influenced by expectations based on prior behaviour of members, suggesting that elements of historicity play out in online as well as face-to-face interactions.

Fictional or literary dialogues in novels, short stories, films and the like can also offer a rich source of metapragmatic comments on politeness, following what is termed the pragma-philological method (see Chapter 8). Paternoster (2012), for instance, studied instances where metapragmatic comments about overpoliteness and impoliteness arise in a series of books about two fictional police investigators, Edinburgh-based John Rebus and Sicilian Salvo Montalbano. The advantage of such data is that the attitudes of characters are sometimes commented on explicitly by the narrator even when the characters themselves do not explicitly express such attitudes. An important finding from this study is that characters who have identifiable overpolite attitudes – 'insincere' politeness in this case – tend to be sceptical when evaluating others vis-à-vis politeness. Of course, findings from fictional dialogues cannot be readily generalised to other forms of interaction, but they do provide an alternative means of tapping into 'thick descriptions' of politeness and how they relate to what people are thinking but not necessarily saying or indicating in interaction (see Chapter 10).

Metapragmatic comments can, of course, also be elicited by analysts. The first main approach to eliciting such comments is through interviews (see Chapter 3). In a study of workplace project partnerships between British and Chinese universities, Spencer-Oatey (2011) collected interview comments from both British and Chinese informants on the interactions that occurred in the course of developing their partnerships. Interviewees made a small number of evaluative comments in terms of politeness or impoliteness. Their evaluations of 'polite behaviour' were all attributed to others, while their evaluations of 'impolite behaviour' were largely attributed to self, generally involving self-deprecatory comments to the interviewer about the issue being discussed. This is also an interesting study in that the metapragmatic comments made in Chinese were arguably 'eticised' to some extent, since the analysis of the Chinese informants' perceptions of (im)politeness focused on the comments translated into English, not the original Chinese. While such a practice clearly aided comparability it also throws up other questions about how the analysis should be situated vis-à-vis emic and etic understandings.

A second approach to eliciting metapragmatic comments is through diaries or written reports from informants about events they regard as involving politeness, impoliteness and so on. Culpeper (2011a), for instance, uses metapragmatic comments elicited in this way to examine the various ways in which impoliteness arises in interaction, such as in example (5), where an informant reports that she felt the way an acquaintance acted when she walked up to her at the local pub was rude.

> (5) As I walked over to the table to collect the glasses, Sarah's said to Tim 'come on Tim let's go outside', implying she didn't want me there. This was at the pub on Sunday night, and I just let the glasses go and walked away. I didn't particularly feel bad, but angry at the way she had said that straight away when I got there. We aren't particularly friends but she was really rude in front of others.
>
> (2011a: 160)

What is notable here is that the informant's interpretation of Sarah having implied something here and thus her evaluation of it as rude rests, in turn, on her assumption about their respective participation footings, namely, that she is not a bystander but rather an indirect addressee. What is also quite interesting to note is that along with reporting her evaluation of impoliteness here, the informant also reports on her emotive stance (feeling *angry* although *not particularly bad*). The close inter-relationship between (im)politeness and emotivity is a theme we will explore further in Chapter 10.

While metapragmatic comments are a useful means for analysts to identify instances of politeness, impoliteness and so on, and also very often offer insight into the moral order through which evaluations of politeness are constituted, they are grounded in the understandings of lay participants and observers, and so reporting such comments does not constitute analysis in and of itself (see Chapter 5). As Davies, Merrison and Haugh (2011) point out in their epilogue, such metapragmatic comments have natural limitations about which analysts should be cognisant. First, the lack of metapragmatic comments vis-à-vis politeness in naturally occurring interactions cannot be taken as evidence that the participants have not made such evaluations. Not all evaluations of politeness necessarily surface in that way in interaction, as we shall discuss further in Chapter 10. Second, metapragmatic comments more often than not highlight 'problematic' talk where expectations have not been met, and thus tend to be primarily invoked in relation to impoliteness, overpoliteness and the like. In order to understand the metapragmatics of politeness, then, we need to tap into the other forms of metapragmatic awareness, including awareness of social discourses of politeness as we shall now consider.

Metadiscourse

While the term *discourse* can be used in an ordinary sense to refer to talk or written texts, it can also be used in a more technical sense to refer to a persistent frame of interpretation and evaluation that has become **reified**: treated as if it has an objective reality in and of itself. The reification of this persistent frame of interpretation and evaluation occurs through lay observers talking about or 'discoursing on' social, cultural and historical patterns of language use at a societal level to the point that they become accepted as encompassing conventional wisdom, and so no longer open to doubt or questioning. Discourse focusing on such discourses is termed *metadiscourse*: where lay observers focus on how people *should* behave. In the sense that metadiscourse constitutes explicit moralising about politeness norms, it also offers yet another window on the moral order. However, since they are located at a different layer to the localised, situated interactions in which evaluative moments of politeness generally arise, their relevance to the latter is generally open to contestation by participants. In other words, whether a particular discourse is judged to be applicable to a particular evaluative moment of politeness is a matter open to discussion (hence the possibility of metadiscourse). And while they are prototypically not open to doubt or questioning, they can also be contested at a societal level in some cases.

The metadiscourse on politeness in Japanese is illustrative in that respect. As Haugh and Obana (2011) argue, metadiscourse on politeness in Japan has long been associated with (neo-)Confucianism, in particular, the notion that one should occupy one's 'proper place in society'. While this was initially limited to the aristocratic classes where it sustained the system of *absolute honorifics* (i.e. expressions that locate a person relative to a particular social place no matter whom they are interacting with), this discourse began to have an influence on wider Japanese society during the pre-modern era from the seventeenth to the nineteenth century as the use of *relative honorifics* (i.e. expressions that locate persons in relationship to other persons depending on which parties are involved and the wider context) became more common. From the twentieth century onwards, this metadiscourse on knowing one's place in society was promulgated more widely through the Japanese education system and official language policies. As Pizziconi points out, then, stereotypical views of honorifics in Japanese have 'facilitate[d] explicit metapragmatic reasoning, the creation of reflexive models of social behaviour, discourses of appropriateness and even language policies that target issues of morality and civic education' (2011: 70). In recent years, however, it has emerged from various studies of politeness in Japanese that one's 'place' (*tachiba*) in interaction is much more dynamic and sensitive to locally situated contingencies than such traditional metadiscourses allow for. The metadiscourse on politeness in Japan is now heavily contested amongst academics at least, although it remains an open question as to the extent to which it is contested amongst lay observers.

Metadiscourses on politeness can also become politically and ideologically charged. It is often claimed through such metadiscourses that the behaviour of 'certain groups of people or individuals is not appropriate for a society', which in effect constitutes 'a judgment about them in terms of whether they "belong" to that language group or culture, or whether we value their culture' (Mills 2009: 1055). The 'Respect Action Plan' of the British New Labour Government was initiated by then Prime Minister Tony Blair, for instance, to address concerns about certain individuals and families not adhering to values that were asserted to be shared by almost everyone in Britain. These values were couched in terms of *respect* towards others that everyone 'knows' and so were treated as not open to doubt or questioning. As Haugh (2010c) points out, there are now ongoing metadiscourses about the lack of *respect* shown to others in public interactions in the media of many English-speaking societies. Similar campaigns to promulgate metadiscourses on politeness have occurred in other societies, such as the 'National Courtesy Campaign' in Singapore and the 'Smile campaign' in Mainland China prior to the Beijing Olympics, as well as a series of political campaigns in modern Chinese history (see Kádár 2007).

Metadiscourse is not, however, limited to societal-level communications via the media and the like. We can also observe at an interactional level how such metadiscourses can be explicitly oriented to by participants in interaction. In example (6), for instance, Ildika is orienting to a particular metadiscourse on gender and politeness.

(6) ERIK: 11:20
     323 I: I'm a independent woman you know I live alone you
              know I make my own way=
     324 E: =yeah=
     325 I: =but there's nothing wrong with opening the door I
              mean I'm not going to be insulted to me it's just
              good manne[rs that's all
     326 E: [yeah yeah
     327 I: you know oh I'd open the door for you?
     328   and you know who cares you know

Ildika first positions herself as an 'independent woman', and thus implicitly not bound by traditional 'ladies first' norms of politeness (turn 323). She then orients to such behaviour on the part of men as *not insulting* but rather a matter of *good manners* (turn 325). In this way, she implicitly contests metadiscourses

Table 9.3 *Approaches to analysing politeness metadiscourses.*

Approach	Exemplar studies
1. (Historical) documents/texts	Sugimoto (1998)
	Kádár and Pan (2011)
2. Media commentary	Lakoff (2005)
	Haugh (2008)

on gendered politeness that treat men opening doors for women not as *polite* but rather as demeaning to those women.

It is important to note, however, that the focus in analysing such metadiscourses is not primarily on whether they are objectively true as such, but rather on how they are perpetuated as dominant within societies, as well as on how they may be challenged or contested. There are a number of approaches by which we can start to investigate such metadiscourses. In Table 9.3 we summarise two key approaches for analysing metadiscourses on politeness, and exemplar studies that can be consulted for further details on how to operationalise these approaches.

One very useful window into metadiscourses on politeness can be gained through careful discourse-based analyses of historical documents, etiquette manuals and native speaker intuitions or introspections represented in personal testimonies and ethnographic or cultural studies. Naomi Sugimoto (1998), for instance, focused on stated norms of apology in a careful analysis of etiquette and conduct manuals published in Japan and the US. She found in this metadiscourse that while there was a preference for 'individualising' apologies in the American conduct manuals, there was a strong preference for 'relationalising' apologies in the Japanese ones. In other words, 'good' apologies in Japanese were represented as ones that were tailored to the types of relationships that existed between the speaker and the recipient(s) rather than the personal qualities of the individuals concerned. In another study, Kádár and Pan (2011) make use of various historical documents and texts to offer useful insight into changes in the metadiscourse of 'politeness' (*li*, 'propriety'), in particular, the decrease in emphasis on 'deference' due to political changes in Mainland China during the twentieth century.

A second useful window into metadiscourses on politeness comes from analyses of media commentary or debates that arise in the media. Lakoff (2005) examines debates playing out in the American media which reflect a changing metadiscourse on politeness, including a preoccupation with the apparent breakdown of various public taboos, such as sexual coarseness, cursing and other bad language, uncontrolled displays of hostility (so-called 'road rage' and so on), negative political advertising and so on, as well as the erosion of the boundary between public and private life and the attendant sets of expectancies associated with each. This can include analyses of (private) interactions that have undergone 'scale shifts' into broader societal debates about politeness or (in)appropriate behaviour more generally. In one such study, Haugh (2008) has examined how attempts by supporters to normalise 'offensive' comments made by a Muslim cleric during one of his sermons were resisted by others through invoking broader societal norms. In example (7), the interviewer (KS) frames the claim by one of the cleric's supporters (KT) that the cleric's comments had been decontextualised as 'unacceptable' in broader Australian society.

> (7) ('Keysar Trad defends al-Hilali', *Today*, Channel 9, 30 October 2006)
> 154 KT: Now to take that (.) into a different context and read it- and really n̲itpick a speech that's a really about mo̲desty and abstinence is v̲ery
> very un[fa:ir.
> 155 KS: [Ke̲ysar he described women as me̲:at. You ca̲:n't do that.
> 156   N̲o one accepts that that is ac̲ceptable.
>
> (Haugh 2008: 217)

Here we can observe that the interviewer is invoking a particular metadiscourse; namely, how one should (and should not) talk about women, and it is with reference to this metadiscourse that the cleric is held accountable and his comments are evaluated as offensive. This norm is invoked through the interviewer's claim that 'no one' regards the cleric's comments to be acceptable, thereby implying that 'everyone' thinks they are unacceptable (cf. Charlie Brown's response to Lucy in Figure 4.1). It is important to note here that it is also presupposed by the interviewer that this societal metadiscourse takes precedence over particular norms of religious teaching in a mosque. Such debates can thus be used in positioning certain individuals or groups as either lying within or outside 'normal' society, often in an attempt to disempower certain groups through exclusion. In that sense, then, the metadiscourse of politeness is highly charged and ideological in nature, a point we will return to in Chapter 11.

9.3   Key studies

Chapter 3 of Culpeper's (2011a) book *Impoliteness* is an excellent overview of how the metalanguage of 'impoliteness' in English can be teased out and better understood using techniques from corpus linguistics. Based on this work he maps out terms such as *rude, inconsiderate, verbally aggressive* and *hurtful* in a conceptual map that distinguishes between in-group and out-group orientation, as well as the degree of symbolic violence involved.

Haugh and Kádár's forthcoming monograph, *Politeness in Chinese and Japanese*, offers an in-depth study of how studying the metapragmatics of politeness can offer a useful window into politeness as social practice. They draw from studies of politeness metalanguage, metapragmatic comments and metadiscourses in China and Japan to see what light they can throw on the various practices by which politeness arises in discourse and interaction.

In an article theorising politeness at an individual versus social level, Mills (2009) argues that they need to be more clearly distinguished as distinct types of approaches or understandings of politeness. She suggests that norms of politeness can be examined at multiple levels, ranging from individual and community of practice norms through to wider hypothesised or actual societal norms.

The interplay of individual and societal norms in relation to evaluations of (im)politeness are examined by Haugh (2010a) in an in-depth study of perceptions of the offensiveness of an email sent by an academic to an international student that entered the public domain when the said academic was dismissed. Metapragmatic comments made in online blogs and discussion boards about the email were examined, with a key finding being that these exhibited significant variability and argumentativeness.

Finally, a thought-provoking study by O'Driscoll (2013) examines how a seemingly innocuous private email communication sent in Northern England about the placement of a recycling bin was transformed into a public communication that was deemed highly offensive. He draws from Goffman's notions of footing and frame (discussed in Chapters 6 and 7 respectively) to show how communications can be situationally transformed with reference to metadiscourses of civility in British society.

9.4   Summary

In this chapter we have proposed that analysing different forms of metapragmatic awareness on the part of users and observers can provide valuable insight into the moral order that lies at the heart of politeness as social practice. It also helps us break open the inevitable circularity in the recognition and recognisability of evaluative moments of politeness, given an action or meaning counts as polite because it is recognisable to participants as polite, yet it is ultimately recognisable as polite because it is recognised as polite by members. We have focused, in particular, on metalinguistic, metacommunicative and metadiscursive awarenesss in relation to understandings of politeness. And we have shown how a great variety of methodologies, ranging from corpus analysis and statistical analysis through to conversation analysis and discourse analysis can be utilised in teasing out these different forms of metapragmatic awareness. It is thus in the study of the metapragmatics of politeness that the truly interdisciplinary nature of politeness research becomes most salient.

9.5   Exercises

I. Answer the following questions:
   1. What expressions do you know that are somehow related to 'politeness'? Do you think they all mean the same thing? If you are a speaker of a language other than English, can you compare the meaning and implications of these words with their English counterparts?
   2. Do you think people are more likely to make comments about politeness or impoliteness? Why do you think that?
   3. Do people always talk about politeness in a positive way? Can you think of individuals or groups who contest generally accepted politeness norms in your society?
II. Consider the following examples relating to a radio interview with Justin Bieber that went wrong when the interviewer (Mojo) made a joke about Harry Styles and Bieber's mother, and analyse the politeness phenomena occurring in them. Compare your analysis with the brief annotations below:
   (a) (Justin Bieber is interviewed on *Mojo in the Morning*, a Detroit-based radio show, 28 June 2012)

       1 Mojo: Do you worry about Harry [Styles], uh, you know when he's around your mom, since it seems he likes older women?
       2 Bieber: Do I wonder (.) what?
       3 Mojo: Do you worry Harry around your mum, since he (.) u:h (.) he likes older women?
       4 Bieber: I think you should worry about yo- your mom bro.
       5 Mojo: .hhhHahhh I should worry about *my* mum?
       6 Bieber: ye:a(hh)h
       7 Mojo: Justin, my mum's d[ead so unfortunately (.) that wouldn't work.
       8 Bieber: [jeez
       9   (10.0)
       10   ((line goes dead))
   (b) ('Justin Bieber hangs up on radio interviewer after Harry Styles 'mum' joke goes wrong', Jo Usmar, *Mirror*, 30 June 2012)
       The radio folk wonder why Justin would get offended when even his girlfriend, Selena Gomez, has said Justin doesn't want Harry near his mum – but we don't reckon he's offended at that at all, he's offended by the 'dead' comment which can only have been made to make him feel

uncomfortable. Yes, the interviewer's mum is dead – but Justin clearly didn't know that and was just trying to make a joke.

(c) User comment, posted 5:27 a.m., 1/7/12

That was rude for him to say if he worries about Harry around his mom he is just a kid not an adult. Mojo was wrong with the question. U all r adults expecting kids to act like adults. Inappropriate question! Grow up Mojo.

In example (a) the interviewer, Thomas 'Mojo' Carballot, teases Justin Bieber about Harry Styles, as the latter was in the news at that time for dating older women. Bieber initially responds with a request for a repeat (turn 2), which is potentially indicative of him taking offence at the question, but then responds with a counter tease in turn 4. However, the interviewer points out the implausibility of Justin's tease in turn 7, given the former's mother has already passed away. At this point in the interview there is a long silence of 10 seconds before the line goes dead. Afterwards when they tried to call back Bieber the technican reported that 'He [Bieber] got a little upset with the question.' The question is whether Bieber was offended by the tease (turns 1 and 3) or by the interviewer's counter to Bieber's counter-tease (turns 5 and 7), namely, that the interviewer's mother is dead. According to Mojo the reason Bieber got offended was 'he's starting to take himself way too seriously', in other words, invoking the metadiscourse of 'not taking yourself too seriously' shared amongst (many) Anglo-English speakers (see Goddard 2009).

In example (b), we can see the news reporter offers a different perspective. She claims that Bieber was offended by the 'dead' comment rather than by the initial tease, since in her view Bieber was trying to make a joke (in turn 4). There is some evidence to support this line of thinking given there are laughter particles interpolated in Bieber's subsequent affirmation in turn 6.

In example (c), a user posts a comment after example (b), claiming that the question (i.e. the tease by the interviewer) was itself rude. She invokes a metadiscourse about what is appropriate behaviour around kids versus adults in justifying her evaluation of the incident.

10   Politeness, cognition and emotion

10.1   Introduction

While there are times when we may believe with absolute certainty that some-one has been polite or rude, politeness is clearly not an objective behaviour, but rather involves a perceived state of mind about behaviour. It involves an interpre-tation or evaluation of situated behaviour as meaningful in some way in regards to one's person or relationship with others in some way, and so inevitably any discussion of politeness leads us to a consideration of cognition. When we think of cognition we generally think of what is often termed **subjectivity**: the perceptions, feelings, thoughts, beliefs, desires and so on of an individual person. However, clearly politeness does not only involve the perceptions of an individual in isolation. At the heart of politeness lies a concern with what others think of us, and so inevitably it also involves what is termed **intersub-jectivity**: how we interpret or understand the perceptions, feelings, thoughts, beliefs, desires of others, and in some cases reach agreement or a common understanding about them. The way in which politeness resides in both sub-jectivity and intersubjectivity lies, we suggest, at the core of the variability and contestedness of politeness, alongside its oft taken-for-grantedness and seem-ing unseen-unless-noticed qualities (see Chapters 3 and 4). The relationship between politeness and cognition, both in the sense of subjectivity and in the sense of intersubjectivity, is thus a key area of interest for politeness researchers.

While in first-wave approaches to politeness the focus was firmly on cogni-tion as states of mind, in more recent years it has become widely accepted that politeness inevitably also encompasses issues of emotion, or what in ordinary talk might be termed states of heart. To see why this might be, let us consider the following example from the American film, *Jeepers Creepers 2*, where a horrific flying creature is attacking high school children on a broken-down bus.

> (1) (Two high school boys, Scotty who is a white American, and Deaun-dre who is an African American, are arguing over what to do about the creature)
> Scotty: You want to play cock of the walk, bro?

Deaundre: Why do I think you want to call me something else?
You want to call me something else, Scotty?
'Cause I don't think you get I can see you thinking it
whether you say it or not.

(*Jeepers Creepers 2*, 2003)

Example (1) begins with Scotty challenging Deaundre about the suggestions he has been making in regard to how they should try to survive the attacks. He uses the formulaic expression, 'cock of the walk', which here means a 'dominating or overbearing person in a group', thereby implying that Deaundre is being overbearing in making these suggestions. In doing so, Scotty also demonstrates awareness of a relational pecking order – a hierarchy of dominance or decision making – that is emerging in their group, and paints Deaundre's suggestions as an attempt to gain a dominant position in that pecking order. The use of the referring expression 'bro' by Scotty to address Deaundre thus frames this as a kind of baiting challenge or goad. From Deaundre's response, however, we can see that he *perceives* 'bro' to be implying something much more derogatory or offensive, as he attributes a particular mental state to Scotty (i.e. the desire to call Deaundre something worse), and becomes visibly upset. What is interesting here is that Deaundre treats it as independent of whatever Scotty is taken to *intend* to mean ('I don't think you get I can see you thinking it whether you say it or not'), yet Scotty is nevertheless held accountable for having an offensive (possibly racist) *attitude*, and the *desire* (albeit unrealised) to voice it. In attributing this attitude and desire to Scotty, Deaundre displays *reflexive* thinking, where one *thinks* about what others think one thinks and so on (see Chapter 9). In this case, Deaundre is asserting that he thinks that Scotty thinks that Deaundre won't realise (i.e. think) that Scotty has a particular covert or tacit attitude underpinning his use of 'bro'. It is also reflexive in that Deaundre indexes a particular social discourse on race relations in the US.

In light of the fact that Scotty (a white American) is addressing an African American, and given the common ground between these characters and the others witnessing the exchange with regard to their understanding of race relations in the US at the time the film was set, it is more than likely that Deaundre is alluding to the possible racist overtones attributed to this kind of referring expression according to that discourse. In other words, Scotty's attributed mental state is treated as a transgression not only of Deaundre's expectations, but of the perceived set of expectancies in wider society (i.e. the moral order), and in this sense implicitly indexes what Deaundre would consider polite. From this brief example, then, we can see that politeness involves a consideration of mental states as well as emotions from a lay perspective. It is thus important for us to carefully analyse understandings of politeness as being grounded in cognition and emotion.

In this chapter, we overview the key cognitive states and processes that have been held to underpin politeness in research to date, and argue that politeness not only involves rationality and states of mind, but is inherently emotive. We begin by first discussing the various cognitive or mental states and processes that we need to consider in examining politeness, highlighting the fact that these mental states and processes are inevitably directed (what is termed **intentionality**) and selective (what is termed **attention**). The concepts of *attitude* and *evaluation*, which we have referred to throughout this volume, are then discussed in more detail. We draw attention, in particular, to the ongoing tension between a conceptualisation of them as a relatively stable cognitive predisposition, as opposed to a form of social action or practice. The notion of *metacognitive awareness*: reflexive presentations of cognitive states of others, which we briefly introduced in Chapter 9 on metapragmatics, is then revisited and explained in more detail. We next move to the questions of **inference** and *intention* and the ongoing debates about what roles they play in understandings of politeness. Finally, we move into a discussion of *emotion* and its importance for analysing politeness.

10.2   Key concepts

Intentionality and attention

In our above discussion of example (1), where Deaundre evidently found Scotty's use of the expression 'bro' offensive, we referred either explicitly or implicitly to a number of mental states-processes. These include:
- perception/perceiving
- intention/intending
- attitude/evaluating
- belief/believing
- desire/wanting
- thought/thinking
- inference/inferring

These are generally referred to as *intentional* states: mental representations of objects, properties or states of affairs. This property of having content or being *about* something is generally referred as **intentionality**. The notion of intentionality stems from the Latin word *intendere*, which means to 'aim in a certain direction' or to 'direct thoughts to something'. However, not only are these mental states held to be directed or about something, but intentionality is conferred on linguistic acts as well (see Haugh and Jaszczolt 2012). In other words, social actions and meanings that are occasioned through linguistic forms and practices are assumed to have content: to be directed at something. Politeness is thus doubly intentional. On the one hand, it necessarily involves mental-state processes, given that it involves a subjective or intersubjective understanding, not an objective behaviour. On the other hand, it involves forms and practices that influence the mental states of others. The presumed intentionality of mental-state processes and linguistic acts is important, because alongside the presumed *agency* of speakers – the fact that we are presumed to be acting of our own volition within the (social) constraints of situated interaction – this presumed intentionality is what underlies why we are, or can be, held accountable for understandings of politeness that arise through discourse and interaction (see Chapter 6).

There are, of course, a massive number of mental-state processes that could arise in interaction. Deaundre and the other side participants present could have all sorts of thoughts or beliefs about Scotty, for instance, as a result of what he has said, and how it has been cast by Deaundre in the subsequent turn. The fact that these thoughts and beliefs are directed at Scotty (in particular, Scotty's attitude and alleged desire to voice that attitude), involves a second critical property of cognition, namely, *attention*. There are a potentially infinite number of things we can concentrate on in a situated context, including both physical objects as well as intentional mental-state processes. Attention or *attending* involves selectively concentrating on just some of these, although this ranges from being foregrounded to being backgrounded. From the perspective of cognitive scientists or mainstream psychologists, *attention* is generally taken to mean selective allocation of mental energy or processing resources, and so is understood to be a matter of subjectivity. From an interactional perspective, *attention/attending* is taken to mean that participants are orienting to, and thus demonstrably responsive to, social actions and meanings that arise through talk or conduct, and so is understood to be a matter of intersubjectivity. Understandings of politeness can, of course, arise as part of both subjective and intersubjective experience, but most importantly they only arise when we are attending to particular mental-state processes with particular content.

In Chapter 4, we attempted to broadly outline this content, suggesting that it involves valenced categorisations of persons and relationships with respect to some kind of normative frame of reference. We can now revisit this definition from a more cognitively grounded perspective, or what is sometimes termed *social cognition*. What we find is that the categorisation/categorising which lies at the core of understandings of politeness, is part of a much more complex set of inter-related intentional state-processes. We have summarised some of the key ones, and what underpins them, in Figure 10.1.

At the core of evaluative moments of politeness lies **categorisation**, which is ultimately grounded in our agency, rather than being a matter of blindly following norms or the perceived intentions of speakers, and which is also imbued with emotivity. Categorising naturally involves attending to or perceiving these categorisations, as well as the processes of inferring (based on

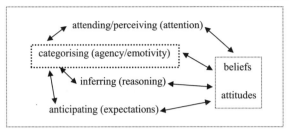

Figure 10.1 Key intentional state-processes in understanding politeness.

reasoning), and anticipating (based on our expectations). All of these draw, in turn, on dynamic and fluctuating sets of beliefs and attitudes. Rather than representing these intentional state-processes as related in a linear way, however, we have attempted to show is that these are interdependent and dynamically inter-related in Figure 10.1. It is also important to note that what is represented in Figure 10.1 summarises only what research has found to date, and thus it represents only a working model, not a definitive theoretical stance on our part. With that proviso in mind we now move to consider in more detail these various dimensions of social cognition, and the reflexive awareness of participants in relation to them, before returning in the final section to consider emotion.

Attitudes and evaluations

Attitudes are generally understood in fields such as social psychology and communication studies as a relatively stable intentional mental state that is located in the minds, or more specifically, cognitive-state processes of individuals. Although there is no one standard definition they are generally characterised as 'enduring and stable cognitive structures that evaluate a specific object, person or issue' (Augoustinos, Walker and Donaghue, 2006: 147). This builds on the so-called ABC model of attitudes as 'predispositions' to respond to certain classes of stimuli with particular affective, behavioural or cognitive responses. In a useful overview of the field, Augoustinos *et al.* go on to argue that

attitudes are therefore first and foremost *evaluations*. They convey what we think and how we feel about some object, or attitude referent. All attitudes have a referent, an 'object of thought', a 'stimulus object' ... By denoting the attitude-holder's 'orientation' to the referent, an attitude conveys that person's evaluation of the referent. (2006: 113)

Consistent with ordinary, lay understandings, then, attitudes are generally understood to encompass relatively enduring, valenced intentional mental states. By *intentional mental states* it is meant that attitudes involve beliefs or thoughts about a particular referent. By *valenced*, it is meant that they are inevitably expressed through evaluative language, such as 'good/bad' and 'like/dislike.' And by *enduring*, it is meant that such beliefs or thoughts are retained in the minds of individuals, and so can have an ongoing, persistent effect on their behaviour, including their behaviour towards others. Attitudes are thus understood to be cumulatively formed over periods of time, and to also vary in their degree of salience or accessibility to individuals.

A number of researchers have characterised politeness as a particular kind of interpersonal attitude, including Culpeper (2011a, 2011b), as we noted in Chapter 5, and Watts (2008, 2011) who has proposed that politeness arises with reference to a positively or negatively valenced *attitudinal cognitorium*. The term *attitudinal cognitorium* was originally coined by the social psychologist Milton Rosenberg (1968) to refer to 'a set of microconcepts that are associated with each other in varying degrees and that have, at any given moment, a certain level of activation' (Bassili and Brown 2005: 552). Watts claims that *polite* can be located within a positive attitudinal cognitorium, where it is more closely associated with micro-concepts such as *well-mannered, avoiding conflict, considerate, appropriate, courteous*; or in a negative attitudinal cognitorium, where it is more closely associated with micro-concepts such as *haughty, insincere, distant, standoffish, inappropriate* and the like. Whether politeness is located within a positive or negative attitudinal cognitorium is a function, in part, of the attitudes of the individual concerned. It is in this sense, then, that we can account for why particular individuals have a tendency to evaluate social actions and meanings, and the forms and practices through which they are accomplished, in certain ways vis-à-vis politeness. One issue that remains somewhat open to question, however, is just how enduring or stable such attitudes really are over time and across interactions.

Evaluations are conceptualised somewhat differently, for instance, in conversation analysis as a form of social action, such as an assessment, compliment, complaint, blaming, criticism and the like. An evaluative social action is recognisable to participants in the formulation of turns in talk and subsequent responses to that talk (and conduct more generally), as we discussed in Chapter 6. The focus in analyses of evaluations as a form of social action is thus on carefully tracing the participants' understanding of each other's conduct in talk-in-interaction. This approach is taken further by the discursive psychologist Jonathan Potter who argues that attitudes should be reconceptualised as 'evaluative practices which are used in different settings for different purposes' (1998: 259), such as blaming, excusing, justifying and rationalising. The main focus in this kind of approach, then, is on what is being done with evaluations in interaction by participants and the discursive resources that are used for constructing them. From this perspective it becomes clear that attitudes are not

always consistent across individuals within a particular social group or relational network, nor are they even consistent across the same individual over
time. This is variability is to be expected because, as Potter argues,

evaluations are flexibly constructed to mesh with specific ongoing practices. Variation is
[thus to be] expected as people perform different actions with their talk; for example, as
they respond to assessments, align themselves with friends and differentiate themselves
from enemies, and as they construct locally coherent versions of the social and moral
world. (1998: 244)

In other words, any attempt to aggregate data on evaluations of politeness must
be done in such a way that it does not inadvertently suppress this locally situated
variability.

Consider, for instance, example (2), which is from a conversation between
two Australians who are getting acquainted. Gary has been explicitly asked by
Natalie to ask her some questions just prior to this example, but he responds,
as we can see below, that he does not have any questions

(2) NJGR: 8:00
     210 G: U:M I haven't got any questions to ask you actually.
     211   (1.2)
     212 N: ↑you must be fun at parties.
     213 G: .hhh don't like parties
     214 N: No: I can imagine. ahe parties probably don't like you
               either(h)
     215   (0.6)
     216 G: I guess so. ↑OH NO. (0.8) people always like someone
               they can saddle up to (2.1) talk to.
               At least someone in the corner they can talk to.
                                                      (Haugh 2011: 178)

Natalie responds to Gary's apparent refusal to ask her some questions with an
ironically framed assessment in turn 212. While it appears she is saying he
would be 'fun at parties', it is hearable as sarcasm, as she places intonational
emphasis on 'you', thereby implying that Gary would not be fun at other
parties. In doing so, she also implies that Gary is socially inept. Gary responds
with a laughing in-breath and a claim that he does not 'like parties' in turn 213,
thereby implicitly affiliating with Natalie's negative assessment. This occasions
a further negative assessment that is upgraded from implicit to explicit ('parties
probably don't like you') in turn 214, with which Gary initially agrees in turn
216, although this is subsequently retracted and his response is reformulated
as qualified disagreement.

It becomes clear in the course of this interaction that Natalie and Gary have
reached a joint understanding that Natalie is evaluating Gary as not a very fun

person to have at a party, thereby implying he is socially inept. This negative assessment appears to be occasioned by Gary's refusal to ask questions despite Natalie's explicit request that he do so (data not shown here). The interactional achievement of this negative assessment (i.e. as a social action) thus constitutes evidence that Natalie is evaluating Gary's current behaviour – refusing to ask any questions – as impolite. In subsequent talk, Gary admits that he should ask questions 'to be polite', which constitutes evidence that he is evaluating his own behaviour as 'not polite', if not 'impolite'. It remains an open question, however, whether Gary evaluates Natalie's behaviour – her sarcastic negative assessment – as impolite. It is certainly possible, as Gary *could* have held Natalie accountable for this sarcasm as impolite, but he nevertheless didn't, at least not during the course of this interaction.

Evaluations of politeness, impoliteness and the like can thus surface to varying degrees in interaction, and so clearly an account of understandings of politeness must embrace in some manner interactional and cognitive perspectives on evaluations. The problem is that a very real epistemological tension continues to exist between them. Valenced categorisations, or evaluations, can be conceptualised, on the one hand, as interpersonal attitudes, which are relatively stable cognitive predispositions to respond to external stimuli (including the behaviour of others) in particular ways. On the other hand, they can be conceptualised as a form of social action, which varies according to the locally situated context in which they arise. Politeness researchers, to date, have tended to draw from both conceptualisations, despite this epistemological tension. One point that is certain, however, is that such attitudes or evaluations are not only socially distributed across participants, but also temporally distributed both within and across interactions. This calls for a range of different approaches vis-à-vis time in analysing politeness, as we discussed in Chapters 6–9.

Metacognition

In Chapter 9 we briefly introduced a fourth type of metapragmatic awareness, *metacognition* – intentional mental states directed at intentional mental states of others. We suggested that **metacognitive awareness** refers to reflexive *presentations* of cognitively grounded states, such as beliefs, thoughts, desires, attitudes and expectations, as we saw in example (1). It includes reflexive awareness of expectations of participants about what can, may or should happen (what is generally termed *deontic* aspects of the moral order), as well as about who knows what and how certain they are about it, and what counts as new or given information for participants (what is generally termed *epistemic* aspects of the moral order).

In example (3) we can observe the way in which participants can orient to particular *deontic* aspects of the moral order, thereby demonstrating how metacognitive awareness can surface in interaction. It is an exchange between an Anglo-Australian who was having dinner with a Taiwanese lady in Melbourne, witnessed and noted down by the second author. The lady was silent throughout the exchange, so here it is metacognitive awareness on the part of the man which is most salient.

(3) 1 A: ((pours himself tea from the teapot – the lady's cup is empty))
2 T: ((picks up teapot after he has finished))
3 A: Too sweet.
4 T: ((moving to pour herself tea))
5 A: Are you alright?
6 T: ((pours tea))
7 A: I thought it was too sweet. I would have poured you tea, but I thought it was too sweet for you.

The sequence began when the Australian man poured himself some tea, while the lady's cup remained empty. Straight after he put the teapot down, the lady picked it up, at which point the man asserted 'too sweet' (turn 3). The lady continued on to pour herself some tea, during the pouring of which the man inquired whether she was okay (turn 5), and then finally in turn 7 indicates through his account what he was orienting to, namely, her *expectation* that he would pour some tea for her. In other words, in attempting to justify why he didn't pour some tea for her, as well for himself, he was orienting to the expectation that it is 'polite', particularly from the lady's emic (i.e. Taiwanese) perspective, to pour drinks for others before serving oneself, or what is termed *titie* ('attentiveness') in Chinese. He thus orients to the possibility that she might be thinking he is 'impolite' having not met this expectation in this particular case. What is interesting to note is that at no point did the Taiwanese lady give any indication that she wanted the man to pour her some tea or that she thought he should.

We can also observe the way in which participants can orient to particular *epistemic* aspects of the moral order. In Chapter 5 we discussed at some length an example where diverging understandings of politeness arose when an Australian, Wayne, apologised to a Taiwanese lady, Joyce, and her family for not turning up to dinner despite having pre-arranged the dinner. We have reproduced this in example (4).

(4) 1 W: It's just, ah, I really apologise for not to you getting back the other day but we couldn't make it?
2 J: oh, that's okay. yeah, yeah, yeah. I- I just thought oh probably you are busy with something so you ah probably were easy to- to for(hhh)get it.

3 W: yeah we were pretty busy actually
4 J: oh, okay, yeah, yeah that's fine. I just want to call you, that-
       that- that's okay.
                   (Chang and Haugh 2011a: 420) [from Chapter 5]

Here we wish to focus in particular on how Wayne subsequently responds
in turn 3 to Joyce's attempt in turn 2 to 'accept' the apology through an
absolution ('that's okay') and her proposed account for him not showing up
(i.e. that he was busy and so it was easy for him to forget things such as their
arrangements for dinner). What we might notice here is that Wayne concludes
in his response in turn 3, where he appears to affiliate with what Joyce has said,
with a turn-final 'actually'. Clift (2001) suggests that 'actually' marks a stance
that is *contrary to expectations* when it occurs in an utterance-final position,
particularly when the prior turn is a question or involves the expression of
some kind of information or evaluation. In this case, it appears that Wayne is
orienting to aspects of the epistemic order, namely, that he knew what he was
doing, but that this is something about which Joyce cannot make any claims.
In other words, although from Joyce's (emic) perspective she appears to be
offering an account for Wayne's transgression, and this is open to evaluation as
'polite', from Wayne's disaffiliative response, it appears that from his (emic)
perspective her offer of a potential account is impinging upon his epistemic
domain, and thus is potentially open to evaluation as 'impolite'.

Close attention to linguistic or interactional markers of metacognitive awareness are thus arguably of potentially great import for analyses of politeness,
as we have seen in examples (3) and (4). This is an area that has been relatively neglected in politeness research to date, due in large part to much of the
focus being on examining two other dimensions of cognition: inferences and
intentions.

Inferring and anticipating

In the examples we have discussed thus far in this chapter, the participants'
understanding of the social actions and meanings that arise, and thus the evaluations vis-à-vis politeness they occasion, involves inference. An inference
generally refers either to some kind of conclusion or understanding reached
on the basis of evidence and reasoning, or to the *process* of reaching such a
conclusion. Here we will use the term *inferring* to make it clear when we are
focusing on the second sense. The philosopher John Woods (2010) describes
inferring as a basic form of reasoning whereby we draw the consequences that
a proposition logically has when the truth of the first proposition guarantees
the truth of further propositions, or alternatively the consequences that seem

necessary, permissible, or reasonable for one to draw. The latter type of infer-ring leads to inferences that are *defeasible*, which means they always allow for the possibility of error. In other words, they may not seem necessary, permis-sible, or reasonable in certain situations. Understandings of politeness arise, of course, through defeasible inferences. This is another reason why they are inevitably open to being contested (see Chapter 3).

Now let us consider example (5), where Yoko is inviting Mari to go along to karaoke.

(5) Yoko: *Osoku natta kedo, karaoke yotte ikanai?*
   'It's late, but do you want to go to karaoke?'
   Mari: *Ashita hachi-ji ni juyona kaigi ga haitte-iru no.*
   'I have an important meeting tomorrow at eight o'clock.'
   Yoko: *Wakatta. Ja mata kondo to iu koto de.*
   'Okay. Well next time then'

   (cited from Haugh 2003: 402–3)

Mari's response implies a refusal of Yoko's invitation, an understanding that is clearly jointly reached when Yoko subsequently responds that she understands and suggests they can make it another time. The Japanese relevance theorist Tomoko Matsui (2001) suggests that this implied refusal could be understood as 'polite' (*teinei*) since Mari gave a reason why she can't make it this time, and thus implicitly left open the possibility of joining Yoko for karaoke at another more convenient time. The evaluation of politeness here must be inferred by Yoko, because saying one has a meeting to attend the next day does not in itself count as a recognisably polite utterance.

However, understandings of politeness do not always arise through infer-ences. Marina Terkourafi (2001, 2005), in her frame-based approach to polite-ness, suggests that an important distinction can be drawn between politeness that arises through *particularised* implicatures and politeness that arises via *generalised* implicatures. The former encompasses instances where the expres-sion is not conventionalised for a particular use, while the latter involves instances where an expression is conventionalised for some particular use (cf. Chapter 7). Essentially this amounts to the claim that politeness can be either inferred or anticipated by participants (Haugh 2003). **Anticipating** thus involves presumptive forms of reasoning where inferences are grounded in experience and associative links. It is often characterised as a default form of reasoning, as opposed to the nonce or particularised reasoning that underpins inferring. Politeness arises through anticipating rather than inferring when 'the regular co-occurrence of particular types of context and particular linguistic expressions as the unchallenged realisations of particular acts . . . create the perception of politeness' (Terkourafi 2005: 248). For example, the expression '*I was wondering if* it is okay to open some windows' is conventionalised (i.e. a recurrent practice) in (British) English for orienting to contingencies in making requests (see Chapter 4). Terkourafi's claim is that based on prior experience in similar situations, the participants will already hold the belief that this request is polite, unless otherwise challenged. In this way, the evaluation of politeness is not inferred but rather can be seen to be regularly anticipated by the participants.

The way in which forms and expressions are identified as 'conventionalised for some particular use' in the frame-based approach is through examining the relative frequency of their occurrence in corpora (i.e. large datasets of naturally occurring texts and interactions). If a particular form or expression is found to regularly co-occur with a particular function relative to a particular minimal context, then it is conventionalised to some degree. A minimal context, or what Terkourafi (2001, 2005) terms a 'frame', involves the co-occurrence of the expression with social categories, such as the gender, age and social class of the participants, the relationship that exists between them (e.g. parent/child, teacher/student, boss/employee), and the setting of the exchange (e.g. formal, institutional, casual). A relatively high frequency of occurrence of such expressions means that when we encounter them in the minimal context in which their use is conventionalised, we can anticipate rather than having to infer (i.e. derive via reasoning) politeness.

A number of studies have focused on the ways in which understandings of politeness can influence inferences involved in person perception/impression management, as well as language production and comprehension more broadly. The social psychologist, Thomas Holtgraves (1998, 2000), for instance, has shown in a series of experiments how inferences of politeness necessarily arise in order for participants to make sense of indirect or implicit meanings. And more recently, the cognitive scientist Jean-François Bonnefon and colleagues have shown through a number of experiments how interpretations of politeness can enter into the interpretation of the very 'tool words' of rational decision making, such as quantifiers ('some', 'possibly') and connectives ('or', 'if'). In one study, Bonnefon and Villejoubert (2006) found that the more severe a medical condition was judged to be, the more likely participants were to interpret the use of 'possibly' as a hedge, and thus the more likely they would interpret the prospect of the medical condition arising. While 'possibly' is generally understood to mean something around 55% probability, it was found amongst many participants that they assessed the probability as rising to up to 70% when the medical condition was judged to be severe. Bonnefon and Villejoubert's (2006) conclusion was that the quantifier was being construed as a politeness marker rather than as an uncertainty marker by the participants.

There is some debate, however, as to whether traditional accounts of inferring and anticipating can account for the formal interdependence of at least some of the understandings of politeness that rise through interaction (see

Chapters 4 and 6). Arundale and Good (2002), for instance, argue that while traditional accounts of inference are necessary, they are not sufficient to account for this formal interdependence. They propose that a *dyadic* form of cognising needs to complement traditional monadic accounts of inferring and anticipating. They argue this is necessary because traditional accounts of inference cannot formally account for the inferential work involved in participants reciprocally affording and constraining understandings of politeness through adjacent placement of utterances that indicate their understandings of the interactional import of prior and forthcoming utterances. It would be fair to say, then, that the role of inferring and anticipating in understanding politeness is an area rich with possibilities for further research and theorisation.

Intention

In first-wave approaches to politeness it was assumed, following Grice, that participants are making inferences about the *intentions* of others (see Chapter 2). An intention is a specific kind of directed mental-state process which encompasses a person's plans or goals. The notion of intention is often confused with the notion of intentionality (see above). This is because when we talk of an act being *intentional* we can either be referring to the speaker having the *intention* to act in that way, or we can talk about the act itself having **intentionality** – having content and thus being directed at something. The basic idea shared by Brown and Levinson (1987), Leech (1983) and others is that a hearer understands the speaker to be polite when he or she infers that the speaker has the intention to be polite: that is, when the speaker is perceived to be *intentionally* polite. The assumption that politeness involves inferring the speaker's intentions has been extended to theories of impoliteness. There is now an ongoing debate as to whether a speaker has to have the intention to be impolite, or at least to be perceived to have the intention to be impolite, for some form or strategy to be evaluated as impolite, as discussed at length by Derek Bousfield (2010). The question, then, is the same whether we are talking about understandings of politeness, impoliteness, mock politeness, mock impoliteness and so on, namely, are we talking about 'real' intentions on the part of the speaker, or simply perceptions of these intentions by the hearer? As Locher and Watts point out, there are instances where participants do not recognise a speaker's (im)polite intention or attribute an intention to be (im)polite in spite of what the speaker claims.

A speaker may wish to be aggressive and hurtful, but still not come across as such to the hearer. Alternatively, a hearer may interpret the speaker's utterance as negatively marked with respect to appropriate behaviour, while the speaker did not intentionally wish to appear as such. (2008: 80)

In other words, the demonstrable existence of cases of so-called 'miscommunicated' impoliteness and 'unintended' impoliteness (and thus also 'miscommunicated' or 'unintended' politeness, mock politeness, mock impoliteness and so on) means that in analysing politeness we cannot simply make assumptions about the speaker's putative intentions, but must carefully examine how intentions vis-à-vis politeness are treated by participants. If we take into account the various participation footings that go beyond simply speakers and hearers (see Chapters 4 and 6), then the analysis becomes more nuanced. Just as there are multiple possible understandings of politeness that can arise in interaction because of the possibility of multiple participation footings, there are also multiple possible understandings of intentions vis-à-vis politeness.

However, there is a second complication when we are dealing with the issue of intention vis-à-vis politeness. As Haugh (2012b) points out, not only are there different *types* of intention, there are also various different theoretical understandings of intention, and thus different *usages* of intention prevalent in the field. In relation to understanding politeness the two most important types of intention are **communicative intentions**, as described by Grice (see Chapter 2), and **higher order intentions**. A *communicative intention* is an intention to communicate certain content to the audience that is fulfilled by its recognition (Grice 1957), which is generally associated with a particular utterance. A *higher order intention* refers to the prospective goals of participants, which can include particular social actions, activity types and the like, and so is generally, although not always, associated with longer stretches of discourse.

The recognition of communicative intentions is generally assumed to underpin how we understand particular linguistic forms and strategies as polite. For example, 'I was wondering if it is okay to open some windows' is understood as a polite request that the addressee open some windows because he or she recognises the speaker's communicative intention. This communicative intention is formulated as reflexive, as not only does the speaker intend that the addressee recognise that he/she has a certain *desire*, namely, that the addressee open some windows, but the speaker also intends the addressee to recognise that the speaker has the *intention* that the addressee recognise this desire. On this view, to recognise a polite communicative intention means the addressee perceives that the speaker not only intends that the addressee recognise that he/she has a certain *attitude*, namely, a polite attitude, but also that he/she intends the addressee to recognise that the speaker has the *intention* that the addressee recognise this attitude. The upshot of this attribution of a polite communicative intention to the speaker is that the hearer holds the *belief* that the speaker is polite (see Terkourafi 2005).

One challenge facing this view, however, is that evaluations of politeness are not limited to utterances. Throughout this volume we have illustrated how understandings of politeness arise over longer stretches of discourse or interaction. In some cases, evaluations of politeness are tied to higher order intentions. Consider the interaction in example (6), where the 'I was wondering' expression occurs not in a request *per se*, but in what is generally termed a *pre-request*: an utterance that indicates a request is possibly forthcoming (depending on how the addressee responds).

> (6) 1 A: Hullo I was wondering whether you were intending to go to Popper's talk this afternoon.
> 2 B: Not today. I'm afraid I can't make it to this one.
> 3 A: Ah okay.
> 4 B: You wanted me to record it didn't you heh!
> 5 A: Yeah heheh
> 6 B: Heheh no I'm sorry about that.
>
> (cited from Levinson 1983: 358)

The 'pre-request' in turn 1 is blocked in B's response in turn 2, and so A indicates understanding thereby moving to close this sequence in turn 3. What is interesting to note here is that in turn 4, B orients to A's intention to have B record the talk, an intention A acknowledges as having (turn 5), to which B responds with an apology (turn 6). This reciprocal display of concern here (i.e. through apology) indicates that B has evaluated A's request as polite. However, in evaluating A's request as polite, B has attributed a particular higher order intention to A, namely, to get B to make a recording. The attribution of particular communicative intentions in the case of each of these utterances, for example, the intention to check a contingency relating to making a possible request underpinning the pre-request in turn 1, depends, in turn, on B attributing this higher order intention to A. It is from the discourse as a whole that B evaluates A as polite, and thus this particular understanding of politeness is primarily related to a higher order intention that is explicitly oriented to by the participants in this interaction, not the various putative communicative intentions that an analyst might attribute to these participants.

The analysis of intentions vis-à-vis politeness is also complicated by the fact that there are different theoretical understandings of intentions. As we discussed in Chapter 5, politeness can be conceptualised in different ways according to different theoretical, proto-theoretical or folk-theoretical stances. The same range of understandings can be observed in relation to intentions and the ways in which they can be deployed by analysts in examining politeness:

Intention can be used definitionally ... without any necessary commitment to its psychological reality, and in that sense constitutes a *theoretical* construct only. Intention may also be assumed to constitute a crucial component of the cognitive activities involved in communicative interaction, and thus in that sense is a working *analytical* construct ... Finally, intention can be understood as a *discursive* construct, where the focus is on the normative work *intention* in the folk sense does in communicative interaction. (Haugh 2012b: 169)

It is thus critical that any discussion of intentions vis-à-vis politeness carefully situates the analysis both in terms of the type of intention involved (e.g. communicative versus higher order intention) and the implicit theoretical conceptualisation of intention by the analyst.

In the interaction in example (7) we can see how the participants are orienting to a higher order intention on the part of one of the characters, and thus, here, intention is being understood *discursively*. Example (7) also illustrates how an addressee can be arguably more hurt when they attribute an intention to inflict this hurt in evaluating the behaviour as impolite, as Culpeper (2011b) also argues.

> (7) Cuddy: Working with people actually makes you a better doctor.
> House: When did I sign up for that course?
> Cuddy: When did I give you the impression that I care?
> House: Working in this clinic obviously instills a deep sense of compassion. I've got your home number, right? In case anything comes up at 3 o'clock in the morning.
> Cuddy: It's not going to work. You know why? Because this is fun. You think of something to make me miserable, I think of something to make you miserable: it's a game! And I'm going to win, because I've got a head start. You are already miserable.
> ('Occam's razor', *House MD*, Season 3, Episode 1, 2004)

This interaction takes place between the grumpy doctor Gregory House and his colleague, Cuddy. House is reputed for his nasty remarks, and in the conversation in example (7) Cuddy interprets his words in light of the destructive intentions she attributes to him ('You think of something to make me miserable'). In other words, House's behaviour is evaluated particularly badly – and consequently it generates negative emotions – because Cuddy knows that his asocial behaviour is intentional. Although intention is generally more visible in the case of impoliteness than in that of politeness, in the following section on emotivity we will illustrate that it also plays an important role in the evaluation of politeness, as well as the consequent emotive reactions to an utterance.

Given that intention may be understood from the participants' perspective as a folk-theoretic, and thus a discursive construct, such intentions vis-à-vis politeness can become contested. In a study of the widespread offence over comments made in a sermon given by Sheikh Taj al-Din al-Hilali in a mosque in Sydney, for instance, Haugh (2008) focused on how al-Hilali's intentions to cause offence were disputed in media reports. For instance, in example

(8), from *60 Minutes*, Hilali's daughter Asama al-Hilali is talking about her understanding of her father's comments as 'not offensive', while the interviewer Ray Martin alludes to the way in which they were regarded as offensive by many in Australia.

(8) ('Defending the faith: Sheikh Taj al-Din al-Hilali', *60 Minutes*, Channel 9, 12 November 2006)

1 AH: I wasn't offended by the remarks (0.5) cause I under<u>stood</u> the meaning what what's be<u>hind</u> it.

2 RM: Well uncovered meat is the problem. That's pretty <u>spec</u>ific. Uncovered meat is the [problem.

3 AH: [Yeah. Because that was the a<u>na</u>logy that he used.

4 RM: Well the- the analogy has a <u>mean</u>ing and the meaning is that if you walk around without clothes on then you'll get raped.

(cited from Haugh 2008: 212)

Asama al-Hilali claims here to have 'correctly' understood her father's intended meaning (namely, that Muslim women should dress and behave modestly) and so was not offended (turns 1 and 3). The interviewer Ray Martin, on the other hand, claims that what was implied by his comments was women who dress inappropriately deserve rape (turns 2 and 4), and thus the cleric's comments were offensive. In doing so, Martin explicitly rejects the claim that the cleric could have intended something else by his comments (turn 4). In other words, *in spite* of the claims by Asama al-Hilali about her father's intentions, the comments are nevertheless treated as offensive. Cases of seemingly unintended offence can thus go beyond disputes about the speaker's putative intentions to attempts to invoke aspects of the moral order, as Martin does here.

Emotivity

First-wave theories – and, in fact, some second-wave theories – tend to describe politeness as a rational activity. Rationality on this view means that the interactional use of politeness operates by means of quasi-logical reasoning with reference to various intentional mental-state processes. As we discussed in Chapter 2, Brown and Levinson argue that rationality means 'the application of a specific mode of reasoning . . . which guarantees inferences from ends or goals to means that will satisfy those ends' (1987: 64). That is, the addressee recognises polite utterances as having been motivated by such rational and strategic states of mind. However, Brown and Levinson and other first-wave scholars did not claim that rationality excludes **emotive actions** and **reactions**, that is, cases where the usage of politeness is (at least partly) influenced by one's emotion rather than crystal-clear rationality. Due to the overwhelming focus on rationality, research on emotion has been relatively neglected in analyses of politeness until recent times.

In post-2000 research, a number of scholars – most representatively, Spencer-Oatey (2005), Locher and Langlotz (2008), Ruhi (2009) and Culpeper (2011b) – have argued that the emotive aspect of politeness and impoliteness should not be neglected. As Locher and Langlotz (2008) claim, politeness and emotions are interdependent because certain acts of politeness and impoliteness are meant to evoke emotions. On this interpretation, politeness and emotion become interconnected through intentions (cf. intentionality): a certain utterance generates a specific emotion as the 'interactants must be aware of the relative norms of a particular practice in order to adjust the relational work accordingly' (Locher and Langlotz 2008: 173). Putting it simply, the interactants follow or violate a particular practice with the other's feelings in mind.

Locher and Langlotz's claim that emotions can come into existence through the intentional usage of politeness clearly illustrates that emotions and rationality are not contradictory aspects of human cognition. This argument accords with recent findings in other areas, such as social psychology, where it is claimed that emotions evoked by the production and evaluation of social actions presuppose some degree of consciousness, and consequently they necessitate intentionality. As Schermerhorn *et al.* explain, it is necessary to 'differentiate between self-conscious emotions that arise from internal sources and *social emotions* [our emphasis] that are stimulated by external sources' (2011: 56). Social emotions are generated by external stimuli, such as an interaction, and they are cognitively of a higher order than self-conscious emotions (e.g. feeling sorrow for an unknown reason) because they 'require self-consciousness, a capacity that begins to emerge in the second year of life' (Goleman 2011: 131). They therefore necessitate more than simple reflexivity as they operate with 'heightened social consciousness' (Goleman 2011: 131). In other words, when following or deviating from a certain norm of politeness, we are often very much aware of the potential emotional consequences of our deeds.

Example (9) illustrates the interdependence between emotions evoked by certain usages of politeness.

> (9) 'Apparently, this was more intense than a little squabble, Love.' The way he ended the sentence made it sound as if there was more to say and he was uncomfortable about continuing. Doreen sensed this and was glad to see Glenn hadn't changed a bit. He was incapable of dishonesty, but that quality was often overridden by the desire to spare the feelings of those he cared for.

'I know you want to be kind, and I love you for it, but please tell me what happened. I'm all grown up now,' Doreen pleaded.
(http://voices.yahoo.com/father-where-part-v-10846943.html)

This interaction from a novella illustrates the emotion-evoking function of intentionally polite utterances. The protagonist Doreen senses that Glenn is being intentionally indirect, due to his 'desire to spare the feelings of those he cared for'. In other words, she orients to the intentions she attributes to him as underlying his behaviour. What is notable here is that this perceived intentionally polite behaviour generates positive emotions: Doreen 'was glad to see Glenn hadn't changed a bit'.

Although Locher and Langlotz's approach covers a key dimension of the emotive aspect of politeness and impoliteness, they treat emotions as bound to intentional actions. An important addition to this view has been made by Ruhi (2009) and Kádár (2013) who depart from intentional emotivity and argue that emotions should be studied in *every* manifestation of politeness. As both Ruhi and Kádár argue, human cognition is always in an emotional flux, and therefore one cannot be entirely emotionless, and the researcher cannot completely describe what is going on in terms of emotions, even though one can attempt to model the emotive process. While there are certain cases, as in example (9), in which intention is salient, one cannot generally predict the presence or lack of emotion in any interaction without examining the way in which (1) a given interaction is constructed, and/or (2) drawing from post-interaction interviews and the like to understand the emotive function and effect of a certain utterance. In other words, their view is that emotions should be studied irrespective of (perceived) intentions, in order to understand the interrelation between politeness and emotivity.

In principle, the researcher can attempt to capture emotion in any interaction type. However, it makes sense to focus on **emotively invested** actions, that is, practices of politeness, which tend to be emotive by their nature. A typical example for the category of emotively invested action is ritual (see Chapter 7). Ritual tends to primarily appeal to the speech partner's senses and emotions, as it operates as a mimetic performance. Consider the following interaction between three family members, for instance.[1]

(10) 1. D: ha (inaudible) ha kérdik az az iskolában (0.3) hogy ki az
          apád=
      N: =Grievous ↑tábornok
      K: már megint kezditek
     2. D: igen és aki= majd
      N: (.)   = >mit mond Grievous tábornok a buta (.)
          ↑gyerekeknek
      K:

3. D: (.2) ((altered bronchial voice)) bántottad a lányomat ezért
        megfizetsz te kis
   N:
   K: (inaudible)
4. D: rohadék   basszus
   N: folytatnád ezt szeretem
   K: @közön@ségetek van

1. D: if (inaudible) if they ask in the school (.3) who your
        father is=
   N: =General ↑Grievous
   K: you start it again
2. D: yes and who= then
   N: (.)   = >what does General Grievous say to the
        silly (.) ↑children
   K:

3. D: (.2) ((altered bronchial voice)) you've hurt my daughter
        and you will pay for this you little
   N:
   K: (inaudible)
4. D: bastard   shoot
   N: would you continue I like it
   K: you are having @gal@lery

This interaction in Hungarian took place among Kádár's daughter (N), his wife
(K) and Kádár himself (D), in front of his daughter's school. After his daughter
started to attend infant school and as many other children began to protest in
the mornings against going to school, she and Kádár formed a fairly complex
ritual practice. That is, Kádár's daughter, supposedly in order to ease morning
starts, invented imaginary conversations between herself and her otherwise real
friends who are the 'good children' and who voluntary agree to attend school,
and a group of imaginary 'silly children' who disagree to attend school and
who must be convinced that school is not a bad place. Their tacit agreement was
that Kádár's duty in these imaginary games was to put himself into the shoes
of book and film characters and help her convince 'silly children' to attend
school. In the interaction above, which took place after they watched the film
Star Wars, Kádár acted as the evil character General Grievous who needs to
teach the 'silly children' a lesson because they assaulted his daughter and her
friends after they attempted to convince them to go to school.

This relational ritual represents a case of politeness in the sense of involving
an evaluation of support for their relationship: Kádár behaved in a way that
was evaluated as positive (and supposedly supportive) by his daughter. This is
evident from Turn 4, at which point Kádár intended to stop this ritual when he

found that other parents were watching him with surprise, where his daughter requested him to continue, by evaluating the performance positively ('Would you continue, I like it.'). It is also clear that in such a performance – and its evaluation – the emphasis is on the positive emotions that arise through the influence of the emotively invested action of performance.

Both theories that focus on intentions and others that describe emotions on a more general level are still at an experimental stage, and the emotive aspect of politeness remains to be fully mapped out. Accordingly, while there are hypothesised models, such as that of Ruhi (2009), by means of which emotions can be described, the testing of these models is subject to future research. An important element in these models is the categorisation of emotions: the systematic description of different emotive states evoked by evaluations of politeness and impoliteness. A noteworthy categorisation is offered by Spencer-Oatey (2005: 116) who distinguishes the following emotive categories:

> emotional reactions (own and other)
> joy contentment/pleasure
> pride
> surprise surprise/amazement
> anger irritation/annoyance
> frustration
> disgust/disapproval
> sadness disappointment/displeasure
> shame/guilt
> embarrassment/insult/humiliation

Reliance on these categories is useful in helping researchers to describe manifestations of emotions in a systematic way. An important task for future research on politeness and emotions is to combine the analysis of linguistic politeness with that of facial expression, gestures and other non-linguistic and paralinguistic aspects of communication (see Chapter 6). As emotions are often evident in non-linguistic communication, this is a key area to examine. We would suggest such an approach would also accord with the treatment of politeness as social practice.

10.3   Key studies

Langlotz (2010) gives a very useful overview of different theories and frameworks for examining the relationship between cognition and politeness. He also draws attention to the ongoing tension between traditional approaches to cognition in social psychology and discursive psychology, and outlines attempts to bridge that gap.

In Chapter 2 of his book *Impoliteness: Using Language to Cause Offence*, Culpeper (2011a) develops an integrated socio-cognitive model for examining cognitive, normative and emotive aspects of impoliteness, which is applicable in many respects to politeness. The emotions associated with evaluations of impoliteness are empirically investigated, drawing from diary reports from informants who noted down salient events from their own perspective.

A paper by Holtgraves (2005) summarises a series of experimental studies on politeness and how it enters into processes of person perception and language comprehension. His work draws primarily from first-wave approaches to politeness, in particular, the model proposed by Brown and Levinson (1987).

The implications of drawing from a discursive approach to intention are explored in a chapter by Davies (2011). She examines how a statement from then Prime Minister Tony Blair, in which he expressed 'deep sorrow' about the past involvement of the UK in the slave trade, was treated in the media, in particular, the way in which they commented on his *intent* in issuing this apology.

Finally, a paper by Langlotz and Locher (2013), 'The role of emotions in a discursive approach to relational work', explores connections between relational meanings, under which politeness, impoliteness and the like fall, and emotional meanings. They propose that participants draw from composite emotional signals in integrating these socio-emotional meanings.

10.4   Exercises

I. Answer the following questions:
    1. What do you think are the key cognitive-state processes when examining politeness?
    2. Do you think behaviour which is regarded as intentionally polite or impolite is always regarded as more polite/impolite than behaviour which appears to be unintentionally polite/impolite?
    3. Have you ever encountered situations where someone being ostensibly polite made you feel bad? Why was that?
II. Consider the following examples and analyse the politeness phenomena occurring in them. Compare your analysis with the brief annotations below:
    (a) (Dominic does the washing-up, with help from four-year-old Sophie, and recounts how he helped an old lady cross the road earlier in the day)
        'She was saying 'It's very nice of you to do this.''
        And I said, 'Why it's just polite- ah it's just normal. You just do it.

If you see someone who needs help like that you just do it.'
She said, 'You're English, aren't you?'
I said, 'Well', I said, 'yeah'.
She said, 'Oh', she said, 'All Englishmen are gentlemen,' she said.
And that *made me feel good*. But that's one thing I'll always make time
for. I'm not blowing my own trumpet, I'm just saying what my personal
feeling about it. You go out of your way to help someone every now
and again like that you got more respect for yourself, not- As well as
for other people, you show respect for other people you got- *you got a
good feeling inside*, you got respect for yourself. And nobody can take
that away from you.

   (www.bbc.co.uk/videonation/articles/u/uk_politeness.shtml)

(b) ((Neal has been forced to walk a long way back from the carpark having
   found his rental car was not there))

Agent: (smiling with a cheerful voice) Welcome to Marathon, may I
       help you?
Neal: Yes.
Agent: *How* may I help you?
Neal: You can start by wiping that fucking dumb-ass smile off your
       rosey, fucking, cheeks! And you can give me a fucking automo-
       bile: a fucking Datsun, a fucking Toyota, a fucking Mustang, a
       fucking Buick! Four fucking wheels and a seat!
Agent: I really don't care for the way you're speaking to me.
Neal: And I really don't care for the way your company left me in
       the middle of fucking nowhere with fucking keys to a fucking
       car that isn't fucking there. And I really didn't care to fucking
       walk, down a fucking highway, and across a fucking runway to
       get back here to have you smile in my fucking face. I want a
       fucking car RIGHT FUCKING NOW!
Agent: May I see your rental agreement?
Neal: I threw it away.
Agent: Oh boy.
Neal: Oh boy, what?
Agent: You're fucked!

                           (*Trains, Planes and Automobiles*, 1987)

   In example (a), we can see how the narrator is recounting an experience
where an evaluation of him as *polite* made him 'feel good'. He is also
orienting to his belief that showing respect for others (i.e. being polite) is a
way of showing respect for oneself, and that this self-respect makes oneself
have 'a good feeling inside'. In this case, then, the informant associates
very positive emotions with evaluations of politeness.

In example (b), which we previously discussed in Chapter 6, we can see how Neal is projecting an impolite attitude in order to express his anger, while the agent express her displeasure through projecting a polite attitude. It is this contrast between projecting negative emotions through an impolite attitude by Neal, and an polite attitude by the agent, which gives her final utterance, where she projects an impolite attitude, a greater impact than it might otherwise have had.

11 Culture, identity and politeness

11.1 Introduction

For many, being polite is regarded as an important symbol of human culture. According to some, what distinguishes humans from other beings is that they can act in a 'civilised' way, by expressing politeness in different forms towards fellow humans. Within human civilisation, politeness is often regarded as a benchmark of civility, where a 'proper' command of politeness represents a certain type and level of culture, and so, politeness is claimed to distinguish certain individuals from others. The present chapter will not comment on the first point: opinions may differ across disciplines such as sociology, anthropology and ethnology as to whether politeness in the sense of relationality is a solely human property, even if there is no doubt that the abstract phenomenon of *linguistic* politeness is an absolutely human phenomenon. We will, however, consider in some detail the second point, by claiming that a treatment of politeness as a ruling norm, which is commanded by some and not by others, is an inherently biased and ideologically charged one: the association of politeness with 'standard' norms only reflects the view of the powerful classes and groups within a society.

If one ventures into politeness research, it is tempting to associate certain forms of behaviour with culture. This leads to simplistic essentialist views of culture and politeness. Certain researchers claim that politeness operates in binaries: in one culture it operates in form x, and in another culture it operates in form y. The above-mentioned distinction made between individuals who have civility and those who do not also presumes an essentialised binary view of politeness. Moreover, such essentialist views are not only present in research on politeness and culture but have also featured in traditional work on politeness and gender, for instance. According to the essentialist view, which will be challenged in a number of respects in the present chapter, culture manifests itself in one's identity, and consequently one's linguistic interpersonal behaviour is regarded as unavoidably driven by one's cultural identity. Since values, perceptions and the like appear to vary across cultures, politeness also seems to be a culture-specific phenomenon. This is often used to explain differences in norms of linguistic appropriateness behaviour. When people from different cultures interact, it is presumed that misunderstandings are likely to arise, as illustrated by example (1).

> (1) C: Teacher, how do you do?
>   B: How do you do? Where do you teach?
>   C: No, I'm not a teacher, I'm a student.

(Cited from Gu 1990: 250)

This interaction took place between a Chinese university student and a British lecturer. The Chinese student addressed the lecturer by using the job title 'teacher', which has a deferential implication in Chinese (since teachers, at least traditionally, have a respected social status). The British lecturer misunderstood this form of address as being a form of self-introduction, as 'teacher' is rarely used in English for this function. In other words, the interactants failed to properly understand each other because their interpretations of the meaning of this expression and the politeness occasioned by it – which to some extent reflect different worldviews (e.g. the social status of teachers) – differ. Thus, although the present chapter will illustrate that this is a vast overstatement, at first glance it might seem that people who come from different cultures are doomed to misunderstand each other in terms of their understandings of politeness, unless they are well-versed in the other's cultural norms.

Following this train of thought, and if we describe culture somewhat more broadly, it is possible to capture other oft-quoted examples of misunderstandings as well. For example, certain scholars, such as Deborah Tannen (1990), argue that men and women have different cultures. Differences in feminine and masculine 'cultures' manifest themselves in differences in gender identities, and thus in their communicative practices. Tannen argues that different gender identities are also held to be responsible for misunderstandings, as in example (2) by Tannen.

> (2) HE: I'm really tired. I didn't sleep well last night.
>   SHE: I didn't sleep well either. I never do.
>   HE: Why are you trying to belittle me?
>   SHE: I'm not! I'm just trying to show that I understand!
>   This woman was not only hurt by her husband's reaction; she was mystified by it. How could he think she was belittling him? By 'belittle me,' he meant 'belittle my experience.' He was filtering her attempts to establish connection through his concern with preserving independence and avoiding being put down.

(Tannen 1990: 51)

Since masculine identity is claimed to be dominated by status and power, the woman's attempt above to establish sympathy is argued to be doomed to fail. Males and females seem to speak different 'languages', and unless they are well-versed with the other's 'culture' (e.g. a male studying feminine speech styles), there is an inevitable 'intercultural' gap between them, which often leads to misunderstandings, in a similar way to the case of the Chinese student and the lecturer in example (1). Example (2) is used to support a claim that it is due to gender – and consequently cultural in the broad sense – differences that the woman's claimed polite intention was interpreted as impolite by the man.

Examples (1) and (2) both represent essentialist descriptions of language usage. The essentialist view has turned out to be problematic for researchers who regard culture critically, as a notion which is constructed in interaction (Chapter 4). This critical view questions notions that operate with binaries, such as male and female cultures. For example, in critical feminist research, Mills and Louise Mullany (2011) question the validity of the above-discussed representation of gendered language. By taking a non-essentialist and social constructionist line, Mills and Mullany argue that gender in discourse depends on context and negotiation: there are no pre-existing masculine and feminine cultures that control understandings of politeness in essentialistic ways.

This critical point, in our view, also applies to the relationship between culture and politeness more generally. Rather than operating as 'cultural dopes' who are 'controlled' by politeness norms of the culture in question, we take the view that we co-construct understandings of politeness as representative of cultural identities through discourse and interaction itself. In other words, the relationship between politeness and culture is constituted through discourse. However, in being taken-for-granted, our perceptions of cultural identities can of course, in some cases, be constitutive of evaluative moments of politeness in interaction as well, in the same way as the moral order which we discussed in Chapter 4.

Thus, in reality, understandings of politeness vis-à-vis cultural identities can be fairly complex. First, cultural identity is more often than not a locally situated phenomenon. Although it is tempting to regard differences in cultural identity as a source of misunderstanding, one's cultural identity is often deployed in a utilitarian way when it comes to politeness, as example (3) illustrates.

> (3) I looked up angrily. Over the wall, to my left, there appeared
>   a face. An egg-shaped head, partially covered with suspiciously
>   black hair, two immense moustaches, and a pair of watchful eyes.
>   It was our mysterious neighbour, Mr Porrott [the narrator makes
>   a typo here; authors' remark].
>   He broke at once into fluent apologies.
>   'I demand of you a thousand pardons, monsieur. I am without
>   defence. For some months now I cultivate the marrows. This

morning suddenly I enrage myself with these marrows. I send
them to promenade themselves – alas! Not only mentally but
physically. I seize the biggest. I hurl him over the wall. Monsieur,
I am ashamed. I prostrate myself.'
Before such profuse apologies, my anger was forced to melt.
(Agatha Christie, *The Murder of Roger Ackroyd*, Chapter 2, 1926)

This interaction is cited from a novel of the famous crime story writer Agatha
Christie. The protagonist, Hercule Poirot, is a Belgian detective who is a resident
in England. Poirot is known to be a very fluent, if not native, speaker of
English who has spent most of his life in England. Nevertheless, he tends
to utilise French lexical items, as well as a typical overexaggerated form of
'gentlemanly behaviour' which, as Christie tells us, the British associate with
his 'Latin-ness'. It is thus obvious that through this linguistic behaviour he
indexes, or represents, himself as 'alien'. However, this does not cause any
communication failure or misunderstanding, but in fact helps Poirot to cope
with certain problematic situations, as example (3) illustrates. He uses this
stance to gain advantage in different situations. For example, by displaying
his foreignness he can make indiscreet inquiries as, according to Christie, the
British tend to forgive foreigners certain failures which they would not forgive
themselves. Or, as in the case of example (3), he can use foreign Latin-ness
simply to make people sympathetic to him.

Due to the way in which identity is locally situated and intepreted, the
borderline between certain 'cultures' can also become rather blurred at the
level of social groups. To return to the example of gender in example (2), while
some men and women may speak differently, masculinity and femininity can
be observed to be utilised just as much as discursive resources by males and
females, alongside the essentialistic claims about them being practices inherent
in one gender. In fact, there are several alternative explanations for what occurs
in example (2), many of which would stem from prior interactions between
the couple. Without being familiar with communicative practices amongst
couples more generally, and the interactants' relational history, in particular,
we have no evidence at all for the claim that the wife protesting she has been
'misunderstood' by her husband has anything to do with their genders.

Second, politeness is often **discursively constructed**: the interactants continuously reflect on the interaction as it unfolds (see e.g. different studies in
Linguistic Politeness Research Group 2011). We can usually sense – especially
in longer interactions – if something begins to 'go wrong', and we can modify
our behaviour according to the situation. Thus, even in interactions in which
significant cultural differences apply, the interactants usually have opportunities
to recognise a given misunderstanding and to develop the trajectory of the given
conversation accordingly, hence decreasing communicational problems caused

by cultural distance. Example (4) illustrates this activity of interactional repair. This interaction took place in England between Kádár, a native Hungarian, and a British acquaintance of his.

(4) AC: You're all right?
    DK: Well, not really. We are still struggling to find a property.
    AC: [short surprised silence] Well, it's difficult to find an appropriate rental property in place X.
    DK: Yeah...

This person greeted Kádár by using the form 'You're all right?' This is a symbolic question just like 'How do you do?', and the preferred response is to give a brief positive answer. This is particularly applicable in the case of the present conversation because the interactants meet quite often, and the interaction reported in example (4) took place upon them passing each other at work. This norm, however, does not fully apply in Hungarian, in which questions like this are open to be interpreted as real ones. Kádár was not yet familiar with the proper usage of this English form, and, upon interpreting it as a genuine question, he gave a dispreferred (i.e. detailed) response. The dispreferred nature of this response was marked by a short silence, after which the British person reacted to Kádár's answer, by sympathetically affiliating with Kádár's complaint. That is, he recognised the misunderstanding and modified his response according to how he interpreted Kádár to be interpreting his initial question, hence smoothing over communicational discrepancy. This repair process was apparently facilitated by Kádár's perceived identity as non-British. To sum up, different perceptions of what counts as normative (and consequently polite) did not ultimately result in a communication failure due to AC's flexibility in accommodating to Kádár's interpretation of his utterance, and modifying the trajectory of the interaction accordingly.

The relationship politeness, culture and identity is thus clearly not a simple one, and so it cannot be described in terms of essentialised differences. In this chapter, we will outline how we can deal with this complexity in examining understandings of politeness vis-à-vis culture and identity.

11.2   Key concepts

Relativity, self-reflexivity and variability

As examples (3) and (4) in Section 11.1 have illustrated, national 'culture' is often more like a tool than an 'inherited' property – it is a *discursive resource*, to use a term which occurs in different discourse analytic works such as Thornborrow (2002) (see also Chapter 7). Therefore, it can be argued that 'culture' is a much more inclusive notion than simply referring to nationality.

Apart from nations such as the British, the Americans and the Chinese, certain groups within a society such as certain age groups, gender groups and different classes, constitute 'cultural groups' which participants can identify with, and with politeness practices which that cultural identity implies. Here we need to refer again to the notion of *network*, (see Chapters 4 and 7): a society is constituted by a network of social and relational networks, within which members can adopt different norms of politeness. This does not mean that there is not a single set of dominating norms, formed by those within a society who have the power to let their voice be heard, but it is likely that these norms do not universally apply to all the networks through which a society is constituted.

These normative differences represent themselves in debates on culture and (im)politeness, a point we briefly discussed in Chapter 9. Since extensive research on this topic has been undertaken in an article by Mills and Kádár (2011), in what follows let us refer to this research. As Mills argues in this work, within all cultures, there is not one single set of politeness rules that remains uncontested. Thus, if one does not recognise such rules are inevitably contested, one can easily form overly simplistic views of politeness at the societal level. Such overgeneralisations manifest themselves, most typically, in discourses on the politeness practices of certain marginalised groups such as working-class people and younger generations. To provide a most representative example, according to Lakoff (2005), politeness norms in American culture are changing from a so-called respect-based culture to a camaraderie culture. These changes manifest themselves, for example, in sexual coarseness in public contexts, violence in the media, agonism (the unwillingness to acknowledge a middle ground in debate), uncontrolled displays of hostility, negative political advertising; cursing and other bad language, flaming on the internet, the loss of polite conventions (such as 'please' and 'thank you'), invasions of privacy and the rise of conventional anti-formality (Lakoff 2005: 30–4).

The surprising aspect of this claim is that the author seems to be confident that she has the right and ability to claim that these changes are actually taking place, when she is drawing from metapragmatic evidence (i.e. what people are reporting) rather than close empirical examination of practices amongst Americans, and also that they are taking place at a cultural rather than at a sub-cultural level. But, as Mills demonstrates, there is an explanation for this confidence: the author tracks these changes down to social tensions over whose norms will hold sway, and to a discourse playing out in some parts of American society that identifies multiculturalism as the source of some of the ills of America. That is, there are 'Americans' who are threatened by incivility, and they are those Americans who are in a dominant position, that is white middle-class Americans. Lakoff outlines this emerging discourse as follows:

Americans have always been multicultural. But until very recently, those who were not white, male and middle-class and above had no access to public discourse, no way to compete for the right to make their own standards of meaning and language. Since the 1960s, more and more formerly disenfranchised groups have demanded, and to some degree received, the right to make language, make interpretations, and make meaning for themselves. The sharing of the right to make meaning turns America truly multicultural – and pretty scary for the formerly 'in' now moving toward the periphery. (2005: 36)

This description suggests that the 'new people' include African Americans, Hispanics and working-class Americans, whose supposed lack of civility is treated as problematic in this white, middle-class American discourse. She argues that what is problematic is that instead of 'respect' there is a growing 'camaraderie' that has gone too far in that that a 'good American' is increasingly:

one who is able to talk to anyone about anything, with nothing left unmention-able . . . [T]he sense of symbolic difference that permits the use of distance and deference politeness may be becoming too threatening in a society that is, in fact, increasingly diverse. (Lakoff 2005: 38)

Many readers may feel that this description overgeneralises, and indeed it does, because it reflects a metapragmatic discourse, not careful empirical examination of practices across interactions. But it also constitutes an overgeneralisation because the author treats her understanding of politeness as representative of American culture, thereby ignoring all the obvious diversity she alludes to in her discussion. It can rightly be argued that no researcher is exempt from representing politeness from her or his social group's or network's point of view. However, it is possible that the changes described above would be perceived as positive rather than negative by someone who belongs to a marginalised group. As Mills makes clear, the problem is that Lakoff has represented only one understanding of this discourse, treating it as uncontested, neglecting to acknowledge that it is more likely than not a highly contested discourse in American society.

From this discussion we can see that it is quite difficult to remain objective when it comes to discussing politeness vis-à-vis cultures. The perhaps most obvious way to address this problem is to conduct a **self-reflexive analysis** (on self-reflexivity see e.g. Baxter 2004). This means that the researcher should reflect on her or his own folk theory of culture and politeness in a critical way, acknowledging that any theory is likely to reflect a worldview that is rooted in the researcher's specific understanding of politeness, and which is inherited from the ideologies of the relational networks to which the researcher belongs. Such a self-reflexive approach necessitates that we do not confound politeness and culture. That is, we need to regard culture as a contested rather than normative notion. Culturally situated politeness practices are likely to be regarded as normative if a particular culture is associated with a 'standard' national culture – which inevitably means the dominant or 'mainstream' understanding of appropriate behaviour. For instance, in the discourse described above it is implicitly assumed there is only a single 'American culture', which allows for only one 'correct' usage of politeness.

In sum, a self-reflexive analysis requires us to acknowledge different understandings with regards to appropriate norms of politeness. The issue of variability in understandings of politeness is one we have noted throughout this volume. Our contention is that this variability in understandings reflects in many instances variability in perceptions of politeness norms. It is pertinent to note that variability does not always manifest itself in what are regarded as more or less 'standard' norms. As a recent study by the Chinese researcher Yun He (2012) has illustrated, some of the differences between network-specific understandings of politeness, such as generational ones, are so visible to members that one can rightly argue that there are different 'standards' in which different understandings of politeness are grounded within a single culture. In other words, when examining discourses of politeness at a societal level and relating these to practices across different social networks or groups with which individuals can identify, it is becoming increasingly clear that even lay understandings of norms acknowledge the existence of more than one set of expectancies or norms in relation to politeness within that culture. It is thus incumbent upon us as researchers to recognise the relativity and variability of politeness norms as well.

Identification: association and dissociation

The ambiguity of the notion of culture has some important implications when it comes to practices of politeness. When we engage in an interaction, it is possible to take certain stances with regard to the culture we represent, or we think we may represent in the eyes of others in a social network, and project our identity accordingly. As the sociolinguist Mary Bucholtz argues, **identification practices** – the processes by which identities are projected, negotiated and contested in interaction – manifest themselves in two ways.

Negative identity practices are those that individuals employ to distance themselves from a rejected identity, while positive identity practices are those in which individuals engage in order actively to construct a chosen identity. In other words, negative identity practices define what their users are not, and hence emphasize identity as an intergroup phenomenon; positive identity practices define what their users are, and thus emphasize the intragroup aspects of social identity. (1999: 211–12)

Negative and positive practices operate jointly in forming cultural identities: if one positions oneself as aligned with or taking up a certain cultural identity, one distances oneself from other cultures at the same time. Positive identity practices are often referred to as practices of **association**, and their negative counterparts as practices of **dissociation**. The question of what counts as dissociation or association is unavoidably relative, as it depends on the nature of a given network, and how individuals position themselves, or are positioned, as members or non-members. For example, detective Poirot's 'Latin' politeness in example (3) is recognisable as technique of dissociation, as he markedly emphasises his 'foreignness' in a British setting by using a practice that differs from local norms. Should he behave in the same way in a group of Belgians who use English as a lingua franca, his use of language could be interpreted as an example of association, provided, of course, that it is noted at all. In this sense, then, arguably both association and dissociation presupposes some degree of visibility: the speaker needs to clearly use certain forms or practices for occasioning politeness, which are associated with a certain cultural stance, in order for them to be recognised as associative or disassociative.

Association emphasises similarity. It often becomes most salient when a non-member, someone positioned as an 'outsider' relative to a particular relational network, attempts to associate him or herself with members or 'insiders' of that network. Consider example (5), for instance.

(5) DK: Well *dun*, as *we* Yorkshire people say!
    SL: [smiles and amiably hits DK's shoulder]

Our identities are constituted by many dimensions of indentifications, and national culture is only one. However, in some instances it can become highly salient with regard to understandings of politeness. This point is illustrated by example (5) in which the focus of association is a regional group (i.e. Yorkshire) within a nation, rather than a nation *per se* (i.e. Britain). This interaction took place between Kádár and his acquaintance SL in Yorkshire. Upon congratulating his acquaintance on an achievement, Kádár switched to a Yorkshire accent by pronouncing *done* as *dun*, and also markedly emphasised his association with Yorkshire identity through positioning himself as a member (albeit temporarily in this locally, situated interaction) through using an inclusive 'we' pronoun. It is clear from the reaction of SL, who is a native of Yorkshire, that this technique of association was interpreted as polite, an understanding that was confirmed in a post-event chat between Kádár and SL.

Normative differences among networks can manifest in practices of association and dissociation. Since groups and networks have different norms of politeness, manifestations of politeness often unavoidably associate the speaker with certain groups and networks and dissociate her or him from others. For example, in many parts of England, using stereotypically 'British' practices of politeness can be interpreted as the speaker associating him or herself with the upper classes, an identity with which others may dissociate. Recall, for instance, the description of 'politeness' offered by a local in northern England, which we discussed in passing in Chapter 4:

> (6) to him it was just another form of dishonesty, either used by 'wankers' who did not dare deliver a straight and honest message (he was probably indirectly referring to me and my rather pathetic attempts to order a drink), or by 'slimy bastards' whose mild manners concealed some devious ulterior motive.
> He was, on the whole, rather suspicious of polite people.
>
> (Deutschmann 2003: 23–4)

What we can see in example (6) is that perceptions of 'politeness' as positive or negative can be grounded relative to whether a person is associating or disassociating with the identity with which the practice is taken to be aligned.

It can be argued, then, that many of our linguistic choices can be interpreted as instances of association/dissociation. A most notable example of this can be found in Japanese, in which evaluations of politeness arise in part through the use of an elaborate system of honorifics. As the sociolinguist Shigeko Okamoto (1999) argues, in Japanese not only the choice to use honorifics, but also their omission indexes a certain stance: any usage represents the speaker's (claimed) sociocultural standing, as well as her or his claimed association with or dissociation from the interactant. Due to this, interactants may adopt certain forms, in order to 'manipulate' their social standing and their consequent relationship with the other.

It is pertinent to note that whether an act of association or dissociation is taken to be intentional or not itself constitutes an evaluation by participants, and so this too can be discursively disputed. Thus, whether association and consequent dissociation (or vice-versa) are taken to be unintended or deliberate, we are dealing with instances of identification, where one identifies oneself with recognisable groups. As the gender researcher Judith Butler (1990) argues, for a group to be recognisable it inevitably involves overgeneralisation and overhomogenisation. Obviously, it is makes no sense to attempt to claim membership with a group (and, automatically, distance oneself from others) if the given group is not known by the other. Thus, identification can often become charged with stereotypes, as example (7) from the American comedy *Rush Hour 3* (2007), which plots the adventures of a Chinese detective (Chief Inspector Lee) and his black American colleague (Detective James Carter), illustrates.

> (7) Carter: Well, for your information, I'm part Chinese now. That's right, Lee. For the last three years, I have studied the ancient teachings of Buddha, earning two black belts in Wu Shu martial arts, spending every afternoon at the Hong Kong Massage parlor. I'm half Chinese, baby!

Lee: If you're half Chinese, I'm half black. I'm your brother and I'm fly. You down with that, Snoopy? That's dope, innit?

Carter: Sorry, Lee. You can't be black. There's a height requirement.

(*Rush Hour 3*, 2007)

In this interaction, both of the interactants claim in-group relationship with the other's ethnicity, by listing characteristics they associate with the other. Detective Carter restricts his 'Chinese-ness' to activities which he thinks are stereotypically Chinese, such as earning black belts and going to massage parlors. On the other hand, Chief Inspector Lee attempts to associate himself with black Americans through the formulation of his utterances, such as 'You down with that, Snoopy' and 'That's dope, innit?', elements he thinks are from African American vernacular English.

The source of humour here is that both of these attempts to associate and claim insider status are quite obviously from non-members. This is made clear when Lee's attempts to associate himself with Carter's ethnic identity are rejected by Carter through an insult that invokes yet another stereotype (namely, the height of Chinese). While Carter's response might be evaluated as 'mock' impolite rather than genuinely impolite, it nevertheless indicates that he is disaffiliating from Lee's attempts to associate with him.

The real complexity of identification resides in its bidirectional nature. That is, we not only perform our identities, we also tend to attribute identities to others. For example, Hercule Poirot's words through which his identification with his 'Belgian-ness' is performed in example (3) pass by relatively unnoticed, while those of Chief Inspector Lee's become noticed as there are different values attributed to the speakers. It is represented as 'natural' that a Belgian uses French lexical items and expresses himself through a stereotypical 'Latin' temperament in Agatha Christie's book – even though this may be not at all 'natural' to many Belgians in reality. On the other hand, as we do not readily attribute the use of African American vernacular to native Chinese, Chief Inspector Lee's words are treated as marked.

Example (7) thus illustrates that a claim to association is subject to evaluation by others. In fact, it is not only an addressee who can evaluate a certain claim, but bystanders can also make evaluative comments (see Chapters 4 and 6). This is illustrated in example (8), which was observed by Kádár while he was guest teaching basic sociolinguistics for a group of Hungarian university students learning Japanese.

(8) Anita: Annyira *cuki*, hogy a japán női nyelvről egy férfi beszél! Én magamar is Harajuku-onna-nak tartom!

'It is so *cute* that a man speaks about Japanese female language. I also regard myself as a Harajuku-onna [Harajuku girl]!'

Bystander: (whispering to another) Atyavilág ...

'O gosh...'

When it came to a discussion of Japanese language and gender, the person who occurs here with the pseudonym Anita interrupted Kádár and attempted to associate herself with a stereotypical group of Japanese young women from Tokyo's Harajuku district who are called *Harajuku-onna* ('Harajuku girls'). This group of Japanese females is known for its habits of dressing in 'cute' ways, and indexing this 'cuteness' in language by using childish lexical items.[1] X accentuated her claimed similarity with Harajuku females by utilising the Hungarian word *cuki* (cute), in a stressed form. As *cuki* is a word associated with female teenager language, it functions as stereotypical Japanese 'cute' female language, i.e. as a means to narrow the intercultural difference between Harajuku females and the speaker. Anita's utterance was not directly evaluated, although Kádár felt slightly offended by being positioned in this way, but as he thought that Anita meant to be kind in her act of appraisal, he simply nodded and continued his presentation without commenting on this utterance. However, next to Kádár a student whispered Atyavilág ('O gosh') to his peer, thus indicating that he evaluated this attempt at association by Anita (and perhaps also her interruption of the lecturer) negatively. This negative evaluation might have been motivated both by Anita's attempt to associate with an 'exotic' foreign out-group and her consequent dissociation from her fellow students, because of the way she associated Kádár with this group.

The difference between the negative evaluations in examples (6) and (7) resides in the claimed role of the evaluating person: Detective Carter, as a black American, invokes the right to decide on the acceptability of Lee's claimed association, while the bystander student in example (7) simply communicated his negative opinion. Once a hearer has a recognised right to comment on a claimed cultural identity, he or she takes a positive stance on that identification, a process defined as **ratifying** (on ratification, see e.g. Selting 2009: 29). The function of ratifying was illustrated in example (5). The difference between examples (7) and (8) neatly illustrates the relativity of cultural identities in terms of politeness: neither Kádár nor Chief Inspector Lee are real culture insiders, and so the symbolic acceptance of their claims to insider membership depends on whether their indentification attempts have been ratified or not.

Cross-cultural versus intercultural

A very large body of work in politeness research has focused on comparing how politeness arises in a particular **languaculture**, such as (Mainland) Mandarin

Chinese, (British, American, Australian) English, Japanese, Turkish and so on, and then comparing that with how these forms or strategies differ with those in other cultures. This is generally termed **cross-cultural politeness** research, where interactions or other forms of data are 'obtained independently from different cultural groups' (Spencer-Oatey 2008 [2000]: 4). There are literally thousands of published studies, including dozens of monographs and edited volumes focusing on politeness from a cross-cultural perspective. Many of the earlier studies, inspired by the Cross-Cultural Speech Act Realization Project led by Blum-Kulka and colleagues, were focused on forms and strategies associated with polite expressions of speech acts across languages and cultures, with DCTs being the method of choice (see Chapter 2). While a much greater range of data types and methodologies are now used, the focus on speech acts when examining politeness across cultures remains a popular one (see, for example, an edited collection by Leyre Ruiz de Zarobe and Yolanda Ruiz de Zarobe, 2012), with the most popular speech acts in cross-cultural politeness research being requests, apologies and compliments/compliment responses.

While such studies clearly continue to be a mainstay of politeness research, and indeed have contributed a considerable amount to academic understandings of differences in the way politeness arises through different forms and practices across cultures, the assumptions underpinning such work have been largely inherited from first-wave approaches to politeness (see Chapter 2). This has (inadvertently) created two (unnecessary) constraints on cross-cultural politeness research. The first is the continuing reliance on basic assumptions in speech act theory, in particular, the narrow focus on social actions that are *labelled* in vernacular English, such as requests, apologies, invitations, refusals and the like. There are hundreds and hundreds of social actions, many of which are *not* labelled in the vernacular, but nevertheless are recognisable to participants (Schegloff 2007a). One such example is what Culpeper and Haugh (forthcoming), in their review of speech acts, term the generic act of 'soliciting', where another social action, such as inviting, complimenting, complaining or accounting, is embedded within a frame where the speaker is trying to get the recipient to undertake responsibility for the act in question. We all know there can be a big difference between inviting someone and, for instance, getting them to invite us somewhere. And this difference can be consequential for the ongoing relationship between those participants and for understandings of politeness.

The second is the relative neglect of *intra*cultural variation in cross-cultural politeness research. While it is often noted in passing by scholars that we should refrain from overgeneralising about politeness at the level of cultures, the fact that there have been thus far very few studies of variability in understandings of politeness amongst members of a culture (see Chapter 3), is rather telling, and indeed without it, cross-cultural politeness research continues to rest on rather shaky empirical grounds. However, it is worth noting such research is slowly beginning to emerge, with much of this is grounded in the *variational pragmatics* movement founded by Klaus P. Schneider and Anne Barron (2008), where five key macro-social identities that are displayed and perceived by participants in interaction have been recognised as particularly salient in that respect: namely, region, social class, ethnicity, gender and age. A special issue on 'Im/politeness across Englishes' edited by Haugh and Schneider (2012), for instance, represents one of the first attempts to move the variational pragmatics paradigm, and its attendant focus on intracultural (as well as cross-cultural) variability, into politeness research proper.

While it has been enormously popular to compare forms and practices that occasion politeness across cultural groups, it has been much less common for researchers to focus on examining understandings of politeness in interactions where the participants have different (socio–)cultural backgrounds claimed by or attributed to them. The latter is termed **intercultural politeness** research, where interactions or other forms of data are obtained when people from two different cultural groups interact with each other (Spencer-Oatey 2008 [2000]: 4).[2] Many, if not most, of these studies have focused on the ways in which divergent practices and expectations can give rise to discomfort or even offence in intercultural interactions. Differences in these practices are assumed to arise from *pragmatic transfer*, where particular lexical items, syntactic structures, pragmatic routines and the like used in the L1 (first language) of one (or more) of the participants are also used in their L2 (second language). There has been a much more limited amount of research focusing on how participants may in fact attempt to accommodate to these diverging forms and practices or expectations of the cultural 'other'. For instance, in recent work on understandings of politeness in English Lingua Franca (ELF) interactions, where none of the participants identify with English as their first language, the cross-cultural expert Juliane House (2008) found evidence that challenges the view that intercultural interactions inevitably give rise to perceptions of impoliteness or offence.

It is worth briefly considering why researchers have opted overwhelmingly to undertake cross-cultural studies of politeness as opposed to studies of intercultural politeness. One reason is that to date there has been no specific theorising of *intercultural* politeness. All the major theories of politeness that have been proposed have focused primarily on explicating how politeness arises within particular cultures, and then making comparisons of these so-called politeness forms and practices across cultures. This overwhelming focus on theorising politeness cross-culturally is arguably what has led to the rather unfortunate neglect of politeness in intercultural settings to date. Yet as Rehbein and Fienemann (2004) have argued, politeness in intercultural interactions involves a complex interweaving and emergence of localised, situated normative practices, not simply a transfer and possible 'clashes' of different sets of norms or expectancies. Such complexity poses a challenge for current theories of politeness, which have been developed largely for the study of politeness cross-culturally.

Stereotypical contrasting as a discursive resource

We have so far studied cases where a participant takes a certain cultural stance, which is either approved or refuted by others. There is, however, another important interactional situation, namely, when a certain cultural identity is positioned against other cultural identities in terms of politeness in order to reinforce relationships within a network. We refer to this situation as **stereotypical contrasting**. This phenomenon operates through overgeneralising and overhomogenising just as in the case of identification more generally, but it represents these features in a clear contrast with others. The function of stereotypical contrasting is illustrated by the following case, described by Kádár in Mills and Kádár (2011).

If one observes the way in which the Chinese describe their (in)directness, it becomes evident that it is a rather 'idealistic' concept. The Chinese stereotype their own cultural identity in different ways. The Chinese researcher Zhengdao Ye, for instance, comments that

The rules of 'being polite' are so different between Chinese and Anglo-Australian cultures that sometimes I find Aussies to be utterly impolite or *sans renqingwei* (human touch/interest) from the vantage point of Chinese culture. An honest response . . . simply leaves a Chinese with little *mianzi* (face). (2008: 57)

Here Ye is alluding to an 'honest response' as being one that is too direct. It is interesting to note that in other contexts Chinese authors describe the speech style of the 'Chinese nation' as a considerably direct one. For example, in 2007 a lengthy article was published in a rather nationalistic mainland Chinese website with the title: 日本人從來不直接説'不" – 曖昧文化讓人受不了 ('The Japanese never directly say 'no' – [Such an] ambiguous culture is difficult to get on with'). In this paper, the author characterises the Japanese culture as an overtly deferential and indirect one, in contrast to the way the Chinese are represented as preferring to be direct in communication. There is a thought-provoking contrast between this description and that of Ye, which demonstrates that the degree of (in)directness is an ideological judgement that can serve the maintenance of superiority in discourses on cultural identity. In other words, such stereotypical constrasting can function as a discursive resource. When compared to Westerners, the supposed Chinese indirectness is held to be a superior property, while in relation to the Japanese, the Chinese often represent themselves as a direct culture exempt from the decadence and social problems that are claimed to characterise the Japanese, and thus Chinese directness is treated as the superior notion.

Although stereotypes can conflict with each other, as in the case above, these different views provide useful materials for the researcher because they reflect the way in which politeness in one culture is contrasted with that in another culture. Although such differences must be treated critically, they inform the researcher about the most dominant attributes of discourse about politeness within a culture (see Chapter 9).

It is also pertinent to note that while stereotyping is often self-oriented, it can also be other-oriented, as illustrated in example (9), which takes place between the Hungarian Count Almásy and his colleagues, who are planning the details of an excavation in the Sahara.

> (9) Madox: Latitude 25, 33. Longitude 25, 16. We attempt to drive
> northeast of Kofer, we'll leave our bones in the desert.
> Almásy: I disagree.
> Madox: You're Hungarian. You always disagree.
>
> (*The English Patient*, 1996)

When Almásy disagrees with the others' ideas about how to remove the excavated bones, they dismiss his disagreement by labelling him a Hungarian. Hungarians are often stereotypically represented as people who do things differently from others. While this form of stereotyping appears mocking, it nevertheless can be evaluated as polite, or at least not impolite. Although it is potentially offensive to label others in such a way, here this stereotype helps to resolve a difficult situation: Almásy is not only a renowned academic but he also occurs in the film as a headstrong figure. Thus, this somewhat humorous stereotyping seems to allow a 'face-saving' way out for Almásy, as it dismisses his disagreement on a national cultural basis, rather than on a professional basis, while at the same time shifting the serious tone of the conversation into a humorous frame. In this way, then, we can see that stereotyping can be invoked in different ways in relation to politeness, and thus it is obvious that culture is often something that is *attributed* to participants rather than being a normative force that 'controls' participants when it comes to politeness.

11.3   Key studies

The paper 'Politeness and culture' by Mills and Kádár (2011) provides a general overview of culture and politeness. Mills and Kádár problematise the relationship between politeness and culture, arguing that homogenising views – such as 'the Australians prefer camaraderie' – are problematic because different social groups within a 'culture' have different interpretations of 'politeness'.

A complex account of culture, identity and politeness can be found in Mills' (2003) monograph *Gender and Politeness*. This volume as whole, and Chapter 5 in particular, provides insight into the complexity of culturally situating politeness by revisiting politeness stereotypes associated with gender, with the aid of a discursive framework. As Mills argues, traditional views that distinguish male and female politeness 'cultures', and which generally argue that females are more polite than males, must be regarded somewhat more critically. Gender, just as any other form of identity, is a complex one, and thus politeness can be perceived differently by members of the same gender.

A noteworthy description of the diversity of culturally situated politeness can be found in Okamoto (1999). In this paper, Okamoto revisits Japanese politeness, which is often described as homogeneous and highly regulated, by arguing that there are significant regional and social differences in the usage of politeness forms in Japan, just as in any other culture. Thus, this study de-exoticises claims about Japanese culture, which is often contrasted with Western cultures as being homogeneous.

Kádár and Francesca Bargiela-Chiappini (2010) address the problematic nature of culture, as well as the challenges posed by cross-cultural and intercultural research. As Kádár and Bargiela-Chiappini argue, 'culture' needs to be approached from innovative perspectives, in order for the field to depart from orthodoxic representations of culturally situated politeness.

Another interesting approach to culturally situated politeness is offered by Holmes, Marra and Schnurr (2008). This paper decontextualises culture by looking at workplace culture instead of other, more traditional, cultural contexts such as national culture. Furthermore, Holmes *et al.* examine the impact of ethnicity on 'cultural' differences in practices of politeness.

Haugh (2010c) offers a useful overview of intercultural politeness research to date. It also includes a critical consideration of methodological issues facing those wishing to undertake studies of intercultural politeness, and a proposal that intercultural research offers a potentially productive window in expanding our theorisation of politeness more generally.

Finally, the way in which multiple understandings of politeness can arise in intercultural settings is addressed in a thoughtful chapter by Noriko Inagaki (2011). She draws from Gadamer's work on understanding (what is called 'hermeneutical phenomenology') to argue that evaluations of politeness are always contingent because the basis of such evaluations is constantly in a state of flux. She illustrates these theoretical claims with an analysis of follow-up discussions after an intercultural dinner party where one of the participants asked a seemingly 'rude' question, arguing that these evaluations were mediated through their own personal and social histories.

11.4 Summary

Although culture can be approached from an essentialist viewpoint, this chapter has argued that culture and cultural identity are discursive phenomena. More specifically, as identity is locally situated and intepreted, it is difficult to make conclusive statement about culturally situated politeness. Furthermore, the borderline between certain 'cultures' can also become rather blurred at the level of social group. However, the construction of culturally positioned identity can be captured through the practices of association and dissociation, which position the individual within a given network.

The analysis of culture and politeness poses various challenges. Importantly, it is quite difficult to remain objective when it comes to discussing politeness vis-à-vis culture. Perhaps the most obvious way to address this problem is to conduct a self-reflexive analysis. This means that the researcher should reflect on her or his own folk theory of culture and politeness in a critical way, acknowledging that any theory is likely to reflect a worldview that is rooted in the researcher's specific understanding of politeness, and which is inherited from the ideologies of the relational networks to which the researcher belongs.

11.5   Exercises

I. Answer the following questions:
   1. Can you identify any stereotypical politeness practices in your nation? Is there any difference between these practices and other ones that are associated with your gender, ethnicity, age and other groups?
   2. Can you recall cases when the media or any other sources stereotyped usages of politeness?
   3. Have you experienced instances of feeling offended in intercultural situations? If so, do you think this is the norm in intercultural interaction?
II. Read the following examples, which represent increasingly complex cases, and analyse the politeness phenomena occurring in them. Compare your analysis with the brief annotations below:
   (a) Jonathan: I'm a vegetarian.
       Alex: You're a what?
       Jonathan: I don't eat meat.
       Alex: Pork?
       Jonathan: No . . .
       Alex: Chickens!
       Jonathan: No . . .
       Alex: And what about the sausage?
       Jonathan: No, no sausage, no meat!
       Alex: What is wrong with you?

                                      (Everything is Illuminated, 2005)

   (b) 'Still, you did get here, didn't you, Duke?' said Miss Putnam, smiling in a roguish sort of way. 'And how nice it will be for you, having somebody to talk to in your own language. I was saying to the Vicomte only just now that, however well you speak a foreign language, it is never quite the same.'

A somewhat strained pause followed the delivery of this dictum. For the space of perhaps a quarter of a minute the French aristocrats stared at one another dumbly. Here, you would have said, watching them, were two strong, silent Frenchmen.

Mr Carlisle was the first to rally from the shock.

'*Parfaitement*,' he said.

'*Alors*,' said Packy.

'*Parbleu!*'

'*Nom d'une pipe!*'

There was another pause. It was as if some theme of deep interest has been exhausted.

Packy indicated the sky, as something to which he felt the visitor's attention should be directed.

'*Le soleil!*'

'*Mas oui!*'

'*Beau!*'

'*Parbleu!*' said Mr Carlisle, rather meanly falling back on old stuff.

They paused again. Packy, except for '*O là là*' which he did not quite know how to bring in, had now shot his bolt.

But Mr Carlisle was made of a sterner stuff. If there is much to be said from a moral standpoint against Confidence Trickery as a profession, there is this to be urged in its favour, looking at it from a purely utilitarian point of view – that it undoubtedly breeds in its initiates a certain enviable coolheadedness and enables them to behave with an easy grace in circumstances where the layman would have been the first to confess a bad two minutes, he was his resourceful self once more.

'But really, my dear fellow,' he said, with a light laugh, 'all this is vairy delightful, but you must not tempt me, no. My English it is not good, and I promise my *instructeur* that always I would speak it only. You understand?'

(P. G. Wodehouse, Hot Water, Chapter 10, 1963)

Example (a) involves an interaction between a rather straight-laced American, Jonathan, and Alex, a native of the Ukraine where they are located over dinner. Here, Alex expresses disbelief about Jonathan's identity as a vegetarian, which results at the end of the exchange in an impolite – from Jonathan's perspective – negative assessment. The scene invokes a particular stereotype (from an American perspective), namely, that Ukrainians are (1) always meat-eaters and (2) always blunt when expressing their opinions to others. Such stereotyping is a common feature of representations of politeness in intercultural settings.

Example (b) represents a humorous case of constructing identity through identification. The interactants, Mr Carlisle and Packy, are in an unpleasant situation: both of them pretended that they are native speakers of French, and Miss Putnam, who suspects that they are lying, makes them interact in French. First they speak to each other by using conventional phrases, but when they run out of vocabulary, and this section is the most interesting from an analytic perspective, the coolheaded Mr Carlisle switches to a somewhat 'broken' English style, which he associates with 'Frenchness'. Furthermore, he, just as Hercule Poirot in example (4), intermixes English and French lexical items, by referring to his imaginary English language teacher as *instructeur*.

12 Conclusion

12.1 Politeness as social practice

If we were to ask someone what they think politeness is, they might mention things such as remembering to say 'please' and 'thank you' (e.g. in many varieties of English), using honorifics (e.g. in Japanese), or calling people by familial titles when greeting them (e.g. in Chinese). However, it is now widely accepted that politeness does not reside in particular linguistic forms or behaviours, but rather in evaluations of those forms and behaviours. In this volume, we have taken this idea a step further and proposed that politeness arises through evaluations of social actions and meanings. Social actions and meanings are recognisable to us because they draw on *practices*, regular or recurrent ways of formulating talk and conduct that are understood by participants as doing and meaning certain things. These regular ways of accomplishing social actions and meanings in interaction are constituted as part of what we take for granted in interacting with others. What is particular about these sets of expectancies is that because they are the means by which we constitute the familiar scenes of everyday life as familiar and everyday, they are inherently moral in nature. In other words, they are open to evaluation as good or bad, appropriate or inappropriate, and, of course, polite, overpolite, not polite, mock polite, impolite, not impolite, mock impolite and so on. Evaluations of politeness are thus not idiosyncratic but rooted in a moral order. It is in this sense that politeness can ultimately be understood as a form of *social practice*.

In characterising politeness as social practice, as not only constituted through a moral order but also as constitutive of that very same moral order, we have presumed that evaluations of politeness implicitly invoke a host of other potential evaluations. In other words, it is difficult to analyse politeness without considering other related evaluations with which it is inevitably interwined. Consider, for instance, example (1), which is from the film *Trains, Planes and Automobiles* (1987). The two main characters, Neal and Del, are waiting for their plane to depart. Del has been making conversation with Neal after realising he mistakenly stole Neal's taxi cab earlier that day.

> (1) Neal: Eh, look, I don't want to be rude, but I'm not much of a conversationalist, and I really want to finish this article, a friend of mine wrote it, so . . .
>
> Del: Don't let me stand in your way, please don't let me stand in your way. The last thing I want to be remembered as is an annoying blabbermouth. You know, nothing grinds my gears worse than some chowderhead that doesn't know when to keep his big trap shut. If you catch me running off with my mouth, just give me a poke on the chubbs.
>
> (*Planes, Trains and Automobiles*, 1987)

Neal is attempting here, rather unsuccessfully as it turns out, to break off the conversation with Del and get back to reading an article. This action of closing the conversation is accomplished through proposing two possible accounts or reasons for closing the conversation (i.e. 'I'm not much of a conversationalist' and 'I really want to finish this article [that] a friend of mine wrote') followed by a turn-final 'so', which not only explicitly marks the prior assertions as reasons, but projects that some upshot has been left unsaid. As the conversation analyst Geoffrey Raymond (2004) points out, in projecting an 'unstated upshot' the speaker is thereby anticipating some kind of response from the recipient. The upshot here, of course, is that Del will stop trying to make conversation with Neal. What is most interesting to note here though is that Neal, in attempting to break off the conversation with Del, makes explicit reference to the possibility of this action and the unstated upshot (i.e. a pragmatic meaning) being perceived as 'rude' (i.e. 'Eh, look, I don't want to be rude'). His turn is formulated, of course, to occasion the opposite evaluation, namely, that he is attempting to be 'polite' given he is drawing from recognisable practices for doing so (in English). Not only does this illustrate rather nicely how understandings of politeness are tied to evaluations of social actions (i.e. the closing of a conversation) and pragmatic meanings (i.e. the unstated upshot), but that any evaluation of politeness inevitably invokes the possibility of other evaluations (i.e. being rude).

The idea that politeness involves evaluations of social actions and meanings may seem counter-intuitive for languages where there are grammaticalised morphosyntactic forms that are regularly associated with politeness. In Japanese, for instance, it is claimed that there are so-called 'polite' forms (such as the *desu/masu* addressee honorific) that are 'socio-pragmatically obligatory' in particular circumstances (Ide 1989). However, more recent work examining the use of such honorifics in interaction has painted a much more nuanced picture. Okamoto (1999) and Cook (2006), for instance, have argued that such honorific forms do not invariably index politeness even in prototypical situations (e.g. conversations between teachers and students), where one might expect them to be used. Instead, they demonstrate how the use of addressee honorifics is mixed with so-called 'plain' forms (i.e. non-honorific) in order to accomplish different actions (e.g. questioning, asserting, co-constructing an idea, backgrounding information) and interpersonal meanings (e.g. deference, social distance, solidarity, personal conviction). It is these different social actions and interpersonal meanings that are open to evaluation as polite, impolite and so forth by participants, not the forms *per se*. However, it is clear that particular forms and expressions can be regularly associated with evaluations of politeness. It is for this reason we have characterised them as *discursive resources* that participants can draw upon in interaction.

In conceptualising politeness as social practice we have suggested that some of the key questions we need to start to consider include:

- *For whom* are these social actions or meanings polite?
- On what *grounds* are these social actions or meanings evaluated as polite?
- What *discursive resources* are drawn upon in recognising and evaluating these social actions or meanings?

In first-wave approaches to politeness the answers to such questions were relatively straightforward. It was assumed that what was identified as polite (or not) by the analyst, according to the underlying theoretical model and with reference to a set of particular forms and strategies, was polite. However, such views have been subsequently challenged, initially on cross-cultural grounds, but more recently on theoretical and methodological grounds. Throughout this book we thus have emphasised that politeness invariably involves multiple understandings.

In the first instance we have argued that we must make a distinction between the understandings of *users* and *observers*. This is the basis of the distinction between first-order and second-order understandings of politeness. However, we have taken this further in suggesting that the way in which this distinction is generally understood, namely, as a distinction between 'ordinary' and 'scientific' understandings of politeness, masks different loci that are important in examining user (first-order) and observer (second-order) understandings of politeness. In the case of first-order understandings of politeness, it is vital in many cases to make a distinction between *participant* versus *metaparticipant* and *emic* versus *etic* understandings of politeness. The former relates to the question of 'for whom' something is regarded as polite, while the latter relates to the question of 'on what grounds' something is regarded as polite. In the case of second-order understandings of politeness, we have argued that we need to distinguish between the perspectives of *analysts* versus *lay observers* and understandings generated through *theoretical* versus *folk-theoretic* perspectives. Once again, the former relates to the question of 'for whom' something is regarded as polite, while the latter relates to the question of 'on what grounds' something is regarded as polite. Since the questions of 'for whom' and 'on what grounds' something is regarded as polite can be answered from the perspective of both users and observers, it then becomes clear that first-order and second-order understandings are *not* mutually exclusive. Indeed, it has been our contention throughout this book that a comprehensive account of politeness necessarily draws on *both* first-order and second-order understandings. Approaching politeness as social practice thus means appreciating there are inevitably multiple understandings of politeness at play.

Another critical dimension of theorising politeness as social practice is that the understandings of users and observers are inextricably grounded with reference to *time* and *space*. As we have suggested, there are multiple senses of time relative to which understandings of politeness can be situated. Not only can such understandings be grounded with reference to the localised here-and-now, but also in the inevitable intertwining of understandings in the here-and-now with those in the there-and-then, as well as understandings in the there-and-then in their own right. We have further suggested that social space encompasses these multiple senses of time within a 'field' (*ba*), a dynamic relational network, which is not only imbued with its own historicity, given that there is no space without time, but is also imbued with ongoing interaction and emerging relationships. Critically, while these relational networks, and the social practices that constitute them, exist through the ongoing, networked interactions of individuals, they constitute at the same time the discursive means by which individuals (and groups of individuals) define and understand evaluative moments of politeness as social practice in the first place.

Consider for a moment example (2), which is from the comedy *Seinfeld*. Kramer is asking Jerry whether he thanked an acquaintance, Alec Berg, for giving them tickets to the ice hockey game they all went to the previous night.

(2) Kramer: Did you call Alec Berg and thank him for the hockey tickets?

Jerry: No.

Kramer: Oh, Jerry, what are you waiting for?

Jerry: What do I gotta call him for? I thanked him five times when he gave them to me, how many times do I gotta thank him?

Kramer: Oh, no no no, you gotta call him the next day, it's common courtesy.

Jerry: No, I don't believe in it. I'm taking a stand against all this over thanking.

Kramer: Jerry, good manners are the glue of society.

Jerry: Hey, if I knew I had to give him eight million 'thank you's, I wouldn't have taken the tickets in the first place.

> Kramer: Alright, you know what this is gonna do? He's gonna be
> upset because you didn't call him and we're not gonna
> get those tickets for Friday night.
>
> Jerry: Ah, you're out of your mind.
>
> ('The face painter', *Seinfeld*, Season 6, Episode 23, 1995)

This excerpt focuses on the question of whether Jerry should call up Alec to thank him for the tickets the day after watching the game. Jerry's position is that he already thanked Alec multiple times in their interaction when Alec made the initial offer of the tickets. He claims that to thank Alec yet again would be 'over thanking'. Kramer's stance, however, is that a 'day-after thank you' would be expected by Alec, and thus he is likely to be 'upset' if he does not get this call from Jerry. He explicitly invokes the moral order in claiming that making such a call constitutes 'common courtesy' or 'good manners', and casting these as 'the glue of society'. In other words, according to Kramer it is 'polite' to make 'day-after thank you' call to express appreciation, and thus Alec is likely to take offence or think it is 'not polite' or even 'impolite' if he does not receive the call, while Jerry considers making this call 'over polite'.

It is worth noting, however, that while Jerry was a participant in the prior interaction where he expressed strong, perhaps even deferential, appreciation for the tickets by thanking Alec multiple times ('Gee thanks! Thanks a lot!', 'thanks again', 'Really, thank you') and through positive assessments ('I'd love to'), Kramer was not present, and only received a second-hand report about the interaction from Jerry. The way in which a 'day-after thank you' is evaluated as 'polite' (by Kramer) or 'over polite' (by Jerry) thus arguably depends, in part, on their distinct relational histories with Alec. In other words, an evaluative moment of politeness in the here-and-now is interlinked with evaluations in the there-and-then of prior interactions. Evaluations of politeness must therefore be situated relative to both time and relational histories.

Kramer, on the other hand, invokes the moral order, as we have mentioned, thereby situating this evaluation in the broader 'field' through which this moral order is constituted by those who identify themselves as members. In example (3), a subsequent scene, Kramer finds out that Alec is indeed quite likely upset as he 'blanked' Jerry when they next met, and has not offered any more tickets. Kramer berates Jerry for this, and then demands that Jerry make the 'day-after thank you' call.

> (3) Kramer: I want you to get on this phone and give him his 'thank
> you'!
>
> Jerry: No. No, I can't!
>
> Kramer: Jerry, this is the way society functions. Aren't you a part
> of society? Because if you don't want to be a part of

society, Jerry, why don't you just get in your car and
move to the East Side!
('The face painter', *Seinfeld*, Season 6, Episode 23, 1995)

When Jerry refuses to do so, he is cast as an *outsider* by Kramer, someone who
is not 'part of society'. Kramer is also claiming that society itself is created
through such 'common courtesies' or 'good manners.' In other words, it is
through the 'unseen but noticed' sets of expectancies that constitute the moral
order that we can claim an emic or insider understanding of politeness. It is
thus our contention that to unpack the multiple possible understandings that
can arise in interaction, they must be situated with reference to both time and
social space.

In situating understandings of politeness in time and social space, we have
attempted in the course of this book to show the multiple temporal and spatial
loci in which these understandings can be positioned. From the perspective of
time, we have proposed that politeness can involve localised participant understandings that emerge within interaction, recurrent participant understandings
that arise across interactions, or representations of participant understandings
imbued with historicity interlinking the here-and-now with the there-and-then,
as well as the there-and-then in its own right. In relation to social space,
we have suggested that politeness can involve emic/etic understandings distributed across social networks, subjective/intersubjective understandings distributed across individuals, and understandings situated relative to identities
and cultures. We have linked these understandings to particular disciplines and
methodologies in order to show concrete ways in which such understandings
might be analysed. However, we hope it has also become clear that we see all
of these understandings as inextricably interlinked within the broader 'field'
(*ba*) *within* which politeness as social practice is reflexively *constituted*, but *of*
which politeness as social practice is also reflexively *constitutive*.

12.2   Looking forward

Our aim in this book has been not only to overview politeness research to date,
but also to map new developments in politeness research, in order to enable
readers to navigate an increasingly complex theoretical landscape. We have thus
focused on *concepts* rather than promoting or discussing merits of particular
theories. In doing so we have highlighted the many conceptual interconnections,
which are not always well recognised, between different areas of the field
of politeness research. We have proposed a framework in which to locate
these various conceptualisations that allows us to see how different approaches
compare with others, and thus to see how one's research relates to other parts of
the field. Our aim has thus ultimately not been to prescribe a particular theory,

given the obviously multifaceted and complex nature of politeness, but to enable those undertaking work in politeness to make informed decisions about choosing theories, data types, methodologies and analytical approaches that are congruent with the research questions one has. What we are suggesting, then, is that politeness researchers embrace multiple loci of understanding, multiple methodologies and multiple data types in order to move the field forward.

Of course we are not claiming to be completely unbiased in our presentation. In large part we have been emphasising a discursive-interactional approach to the analysis of politeness here. A discursive-interactional approach, as you will have seen, highlights the variable and contested, yet simultaneously taken-for-granted and unseen-unless-noticed qualities of politeness. We take as our founding assumption in theorising that there are inevitably multiple understandings of politeness. Yet we acknowledge without reservation that a discursive-interactional approach leaves open important questions in the field. It remains to be seen, for instance, how such an approach might impact on the natural tendency in the social sciences to aim to generalise and quantify, particularly given such an undertaking is much more complex than is often recognised. Our claim, of course, is that a convincing theory of politeness, whatever shape it might ultimately take, must take into account multiple perspectives. Our suggestion is that these understandings be clearly rooted in the various first-order and second-order loci of understanding we have outlined here, as well as rooted in multiple methodologies and approaches that investigating these multiple understandings inevitably entails. In this way, we can reach clearly positioned findings that build towards a more comprehensive whole, rather than generating scattered and unrelated findings that leave the field in an endless cycle of proposal and critique, although we acknowledge the latter still has an important role to play. In a sense, then, what we are calling for are self-reflexive analysts in politeness research, no matter what approach or theory they ultimately employ.

There is clearly much more to be done in politeness research. Given the scope of the field we have only been able to introduce small parts of it, and we must admit that there is much we have not able to give full justice to in our discussion here. However, the point here has been not to summarise all the findings in the field, but rather to develop a roadmap by which we might more successfully navigate, and thereby more clearly identify those areas which have been neglected or are in need of further research. In the course of this book we have alluded to just some of these, including the ongoing problem of how we can quantify something as complex as politeness without generating analytical artifacts that make little sense to participants themselves; how we can address the relative neglect of emotivity and multimodal dimensions of politeness given the apparent overemphasis on rationality and linguistic dimensions of politeness to date; and how we might shift politeness research away from its over-reliance on face as an explanatory metaphor to consider other alternative metaphors that could potentially enrich the field. Ultimately, then, we are suggesting that the field move forward in ways that avoid the ongoing bleaching out of emic perspectives that has plagued the field to date, yet nevertheless retains a coherent overall focus that does not splinter into disparate perspectives that cannot be reconciled. The framework developed here offers, we hope, a way forward in pursuit of an ever more comprehensive and nuanced understanding of politeness.

Notes

2 THE ROOTS OF POLITENESS RESEARCH

1 It was, in fact, initially published in a shorter form in 1978 as part of an edited book, but most references to Brown and Levinson's theory are generally to the book published in 1987.

2 Notably, the 'socially bound' application of honorifics and formal forms, which Ide defined as 'discernment,' is not limited to Japanese and other 'honorific-rich' languages such as Korean. For example, discernment is likely to step on the stage in hierarchical settings with strong power inequalities. It is enough only to think of a courtroom where it is likely that a defendant uses predetermined forms of politeness when interacting with the judge. However, what makes languages such as Japanese special is that honorific inflection is part of the grammar. That is, errors in the use of honorifics do not just have interpersonal implications but also grammatical ones. For this reason it is claimed that communal values are 'codified' both pragmatically and grammatically by Ide (1989).

3 See Walkers (1979).

4 Of course this is a potential advantage if one's explicit aim is to elicit perceptions of normative usage.

5 'Anglo-English' is a technical term borrowed from Wierzbicka (2006: 5) who, citing from Kachru's (1985, 1992) and Crystal's (2003) works notes that 'While there are many 'Englishes' around the world ... there is also an 'Anglo' English – an English of the 'inner circle' ... including 'the traditional bases of English, where it is the primary language: ... the USA, UK, Ireland, Canada, Australia, and New Zealand.' We argue that certain conventional relational phenomena such as indirect requests are typical Anglo-English phenomena, in the sense that they do not represent normative relational practices in certain non-Anglo-English countries such as Singapore.

3 RECENT DEVELOPMENTS IN POLITENESS RESEARCH

1 A detailed analysis of this example can be found in Mills and Kádár (2011).

4 POLITENESS AS SOCIAL PRACTICE

1 As Chapter 9 will illustrate, this manifests itself in different social 'standards' of politeness.

2 Haugh (2013c) discusses in more detail how the approach to politeness as social practice outlined in this chapter both builds on previous work by Eelen (2001) and Watts (2003), but also differs from it in critical ways.

3 We will introduce various different analogous terms for politeness in other languages in Chapter 9.

4 A simplified form of transcription is employed here where the square brackets represent overlapping speech, while the numbers on the left refer to the turn of talk in the overall recording. We will introduce more detailed forms of transcribing interaction in Chapter 6. This example is used with permission from Toby Richards.

5 *I-wonder*-prefacing is not restricted to requests, however, as it can also be used in displaying contingency and low entitlement in issuing invitations. For example, 'I was wondering if you fancy going to Ming's tomorrow evening' (BNC: PS05X).

5 UNDERSTANDINGS OF POLITENESS

1 Cf. an earlier version of this framework in Haugh (2012a).

2 Source: www.zmemusic.com/feature/wednesday-smilejerker/wednesday-smilejerker-bonos-an-evil-bastard/.

3 Our point here is that the importance of a given evaluation is determined partly by the participation status of the evaluator. For example, let us suppose that Pamsplace7 in example (5) was in fact uttering 'your so cruel' during the concert itself. While she could say this to her friend in the crowd, this evaluation would not count as an influential one in terms of the broader relational network because very likely nobody else would hear it. A posting, however, is different, as it is open to anyone via the Web, and so Pamsplace7's evaluation could become a relatively influential one.

4 Cf. the 'analysis of interaction in terms of conceptual schemes and categories regarded as meaningful and appropriate by native members of the "culture" being studied' (Lett 1990: 130).

5 Both the Australian and Taiwanese lay observers rated the apology using the same descriptors in English given the interaction they were rating was in English and the aim was to tap into intercultural rather than cross-cultural ratings of im/politeness.

6 A full copy of the conversation can be found in Chang and Haugh (2011a).

7 See also Krippendorff (1989: 11–36).

6 POLITENESS IN INTERACTION

1 The treatment of politeness as 'the velvet glove on the iron fist' can be traced to work on politeness in eighteenth-century Britain by Sell (1992) and Watts (1992).

2 The conventions, following standard Conversation Analytic practice, are listed in the order they appear in the transcript: '?' rising intonation; '[]' overlapping talk; ',' continuing intonation; '-' cutoff speech; '> <' markedly faster pace; '()' unintelligible talk; '.' utterance final intonation; '(())' descriptions of action; 'underlined' emphasis/stress; '::' elongated sound; '=' latched talk.

7 POLITENESS, CONVENTION AND RITUALITY

1 As far as we are aware, no historical pragmatic research has been conducted on the history of this form, and the claim here is based on some interviews with Hungarian language users. This form occurs briefly in a recent study by Bodor and Barcza (2011).
2 In French there are masculine and feminine inflections, and it is considered grammatically incorrect for males to use female inflection, and vice-versa.
3 Such rituals are formed by an individual, and they primarily serve the function of relating the individual to an imaginary entity. Thus, these rituals are codified in the closed and sacred individual world, and so they are covert ones, which means that they tend to be invisible for, and often *intentionally* hidden from, the external observer. While there are cases when covert rituals are revealed to the public, even in such cases they tend to be regarded as the 'property' of the individual. But usually they remain covert because they evoke shame, due to which the individual is likely to hide them.

8 POLITENESS AND HISTORY

1 In historical China, students became officials by passing examinations of different degrees.
2 Importantly, however, the self-focused display of one's rank does not necessarily imply that it cannot express politeness towards the other. For example, if two high-ranking persons interact in a self-displaying way, the display of ranks can imply that they acknowledge each other's social status.
3 See: www.techdirt.com/blog/casestudies/articles/20120813/14074420011/people-who-pay-service-are-lot-nicer-than-those-who-dont.shtml

9 POLITENESS AND METAPRAGMATICS

1 The term *discourse* is thus being used here in a technical sense rather than the ordinary sense of written or spoken communication.
2 See Haugh (2004, 2007b) for a more detailed explanation of emic understandings of 'politeness' evaluators in Japanese.
3 It is worth noting that the Natural Semantic Metalanguage (NSM) developed by Wierzbicka (2003) and Goddard (2006) may prove useful in representing these different emic understandings. However, given work in this direction has only just begun (Waters 2012; Ye 2004), further consideration of this possibility lies outside the scope of this book.
4 However, it is worth noting that because *impolite* is a low frequency term associated with formal contexts, any attempt to construct an analytical distinction based on these two terms is fraught with ontological difficulties (Bousfield 2010; Terkourafi 2008).

10 POLITENESS, COGNITION AND EMOTION

1 In the present transcription @ denotes laughter, ↑ describes high pitch, (.) a turn taking point, and > increased speed.

11 CULTURE, IDENTITY AND POLITENESS

1 See Miller (2004) for more details.
2 It is worth noting that the two terms 'cross-cultural' and 'intercultural' are sometimes used interchangeably. We are maintaining this distinction, however, consistent with Spencer-Oatey (2008[2000]) and Kecskés (2004).

Glossary

Accountability: The way in which a person (or group of persons) is taken to be committed to or (to varying degrees) responsible for the real-world consequences of social actions and meanings that are attributed to them.

Anticipating: Presumptive forms of reasoning whereby inferences are grounded in experiential and associative links.

Association: Aligning with or taking on a certain identity (or set of identities) in situated interaction. Realised through what Bucholtz (1999) terms 'positive identity practices' (cf. 'dissociation').

Attention: Attention or *attending* involves selectively focusing on particular elements of a situated context (including physical objects, persons, relationships, intentional mental state-processes and so on) out of the potentially infinite number of things we could be directing our attention towards. The degree of focus ranges from foregrounding through to backgrounding particular objects or elements of the situated context.

Beliefs: A specific kind of directed mental state-process which encompasses a person's (firmly held) assumptions or convictions about what is true. Beliefs relevant to evaluations of (im)politeness include beliefs about what behaviour is *expected* in particular contexts (see also 'intentionality').

Categorisation: The casting of persons and relationships into commonsense or ordinary knowledge classes or groups, based on which we make inferences about those persons and how we expect them to behave in context of those relationships.

Communicative intention: An intention to communicate certain content to the audience that is fulfilled by its very recognition. It is generally associated with the interpretation of a particular utterance.

Community of practice: A group of people that develops its own set of norms and practices through joint engagement in an activity or task. It is regarded as a key unit of analysis in discursive politeness research (see 'units of analysis').

Comparability: Degree to which sets of data or analyses can be regarded as equivalent. Examination of historical politeness phenomena indicates that it is often difficult to compare contemporary and historical data.

Computer-mediated communication (CMC): Interaction or discourse that is mediated through various forms of technology, such as email, SMS, social networking and blogs.

Conformance: Adapting to or meeting the expectations of the members of a particular relational network.

Contested: Refers to the way in which a particular understanding of politeness may be disputed or challenged by other participants in that interaction or by those observing it. Also referred to as 'argumentativity'.

Continuity: The degree to which the development of politeness practices in a particular society or relational group occurs more gradually, or in a more punctuated or radical manner.

Convention: Routinised social practice which specifically regulates social interaction; those forms of recurrent schematic behaviour which follow patterns associated with understandings of politeness, as well as humour, sarcasm and so on, are defined as conventional.

Conventionalisation: The process through which a form recurs until what it is taken to mean becomes accepted as its default meaning (i.e. what it is taken to mean unless otherwise indicated).

Cooperative Principle (CP): The claim that speakers can make available what they are meaning, although not necessarily saying, in a principled way, by breaching 'normative' expectations about communication.

Creativity: Creativity is a fundamental characteristic of politeness, which is present even in ritual in spite of its schematic nature.

Cross-cultural politeness: Where researchers compare culture-specific understandings of politeness by examining interactions or other forms of data from one cultural group that are obtained independently of another cultural group (cf. 'intercultural politeness').

Culture-specificity: The degree to which an understanding or conceptualisation of a particular social or interpersonal phenomenon can be regarded as limited to a particular cultural group. In politeness research it refers to those scholars who have an interest in emic concepts and 'insider' perceptions of linguistic politeness, who have generally refuted claims to universality in first-wave approaches to politeness (see '*emic*' and 'first-wave approaches').

Discourse completion task/test (DCT): A method of data gathering where normative responses are elicited through a one-sided situational role play designed by the researcher (see 'elicited data').

Discursive resource: A linguistic form or practice (or set of forms and practices) that can be drawn upon in indexing a particular interpersonal stance or evaluation, and which is often associated with the accomplishment of a particular goal or agenda in interaction.

Discursive turn: The methodological shift towards examining politeness situated in discourse and interaction, which is generally associated with the post-2000 turn in politeness theorisation.

Dissociation: Distancing from or rejecting a certain identity (or set of identities) in situated interaction. Realised through what Bucholtz (1999) terms 'negative identity practices' (cf. 'association').

Elicited data: Discourse or interaction that is prompted through the intervention of the researcher.

Emergent: Refers to an understanding that cannot be traced back to a single participant without remainder because it is mutually interdependent on the interlinked understandings of two or more participants.

Emic: An understanding of a member or cultural insider (cf. 'etic').

Emotive actions and **reactions**: Where an understanding or usage of politeness is (at least partly) influenced by one's emotion rather than rational reasoning.

Emotive value: The degree to which an evaluation of politeness evokes an emotive action or reaction.

Emotively invested: Refers to the way in which politeness practices tend to be inherently emotive rather than purely rational or strategic in nature.

Epistemology. The word epistemology comes from the Greek ἐπιστήμη (*epistēmē*) and λόγος (*logos*), and literally means 'the study of knowing'. An epistemological perspective on politeness involves the question of how we look at the world and make sense of it.

Essentialism: The claim that politeness operates in set ways in a particular culture. It most often leads to binaries, i.e. in one culture politeness operates in form x, and in another culture it operates in form y.

Ethos: The set of moral beliefs and values of a particular relational or social network. The ethos of social networks is what grounds the emotive value of politeness (see 'emotive value').

Etic: An understanding of a non-member or cultural outsider (cf. 'emic').

Evaluators: Descriptive metalanguage used by members to conceptualise their social world (see 'metalanguage').

Expectations: What is anticipated or taken for granted by members of a relational or social network in interpreting the behaviour of participants.

Face: Interpretations of persons-in-relationships as well as relationships-in-interaction by participants for which those participants can be held accountable. According to Brown and Levinson (1987, the most influential first-wave theory of linguistic politeness), the notion of face consists of two specific kinds of desires ('face-wants') attributed by interactants to one another: the desire to be unimpeded in one's actions (negative face), and the desire to be approved of (positive face) (see also 'negative politeness' and 'positive politeness'). First-wave approaches claimed that politeness is realised through facework, but this notion has been challenged in post-2000 politeness research.

Facework: The actions taken by a person to make whatever he is doing consistent with face (see also 'face'). In Brown and Levinson's (1987) model, facework is treated as essentially synonymous with politeness.

Field: A dynamic relational network, which is not only imbued with its own historicity, given that there is no space without time, but is also imbued with ongoing interaction and emerging relationships. It is a concept adopted from the term *ba* in Japanese (or *chang* in Chinese).

First-order politeness: An understanding of politeness that is grounded in the *interpretations* (participant versus metaparticipant) and *conceptualisations* (emic versus etic) of users (cf. 'second-order politeness').

First-wave approaches: A collective term for theories of politeness, which were developed before the post-2000 discursive turn and which attempt to model politeness at an abstract, theoretical level.

Folk-theoretic: Cultural accounts of interpersonal phenomena that are developed and shared amongst ordinary users of a language.

Footing: The four distinct sets of roles and responsibilities that can be occupied by a speaker according to Goffman: animator (the person producing the talk), author (the person designing the talk), principal (the person responsible for the talk) and figure (the person portrayed in the talk). Speaker footings are complemented by recipient footings: (meta)recipient (the person or persons hearing or observing the talk), interpreter (the person or persons interpreting and evaluating the talk), accounter (the person or persons holding the principal accountable for that talk), and target (a co-present person or set of persons portrayed in the talk).

Form: A meaningful unit of language, such as a morpheme, word, phrase or sentence. A focus on politeness forms entails an analysis of the linguistic structures by which politeness is conventionally accomplished.

Here-and-now: Refers to the way in which particular social actions and meanings are evaluated vis-à-vis politeness by participants in the very moment in which they arise.

Higher order intentions: The prospective or future-directed goals of participants, including the accomplishment of particular social actions, activity types and the like, which are generally, although not always, associated with longer stretches of discourse.

Historical politeness: Where politeness researchers examine politeness situated in the there-and-then in its own right. Historical politeness research has stirred interest in post-2000 politeness research due its explanatory nature: the examination of diachronically situated politeness can explain certain peculiarities of contemporary politeness usage, and as such it helps researchers to critically revisit certain prescriptive assumptions which are constrained by contemporary understandings of linguistic politeness.

Historicity: Refers to the way in which all actions (and things) in the world have their own place and time, and so every action is part of history; the way in which we see the world, also in terms of politeness, is thus in this sense always historically situated.

Identification practices: Processes by which identities are projected and attributed, negotiated and contested in interaction.

Identity: Where a person or group of persons is cast into a category with associated characteristics or features. Identities can be personal, relationship or group-related.

Indexicality: Refers to the way in which linguistic forms and practices can point to a state of affairs, in particular, to indicate particular stances or worldviews.

Incrementality: Refers to the way in which speakers adjust or modify their talk in the light of how the progressive uttering of units of talk is received by other participants.

Indirectness: As an analyst's category, indirectness refers to the relationship between two or more forms and functions. In speech act theory, it points to instances where a particular speech act is not achieved through its 'base' sentence type (e.g. a request achieved through an interrogative or declarative rather than an imperative form). As a participant's category, indirectness refers to instances where it is not entirely clear which speech act the speaker is projecting (i.e. illocutionary opacity), or the content of that speech act is not made entirely clear (i.e. propositional opacity), or to whom the speech act is directed is not made entirely clear (i.e. opacity of target) (see also 'speech act').

Inference: Refers either to some kind of conclusion or *understanding* reached on the basis of evidence and reasoning, or to the *process* of reaching such a conclusion.

Institutional discourse: Talk or interaction that is subject to particular functional or context-specific influences and specific practices and conventions. It includes interaction and discourse that arises in business workplaces, courtrooms, and classrooms through to broadcast interviews and parliamentary debates. It is generally contrasted with mundane or non-institutional discourse (e.g. conversations amongst family and friends). In politeness research, it is often associated with the study of the relationship between politeness and power.

Intention: A specific kind of directed mental-state process which encompasses a person's plans or goals.

Intentionality: The assumed property of social actions and meanings that are occasioned through linguistic forms and practices: that they have an object (i.e. they are directed at something). Intentionality is also a property of mental state-processes such as beliefs, intentions and desires.

Interactional multimodality: The way in which multiple modes can be drawn upon in forming understandings of politeness in interaction. A mode refers to the different ways in which interaction can be accomplished, including what is said (linguistic or verbal mode), how it is said (paralinguistic mode), facial expressions, gaze, gesture, body orientation and movement and so on. Multimodality in CMC research also refers to the various modes drawn upon in technology-mediated interactions, including the spoken mode, text-based mode, graphical mode and so on.

Intercultural politeness: Where researchers focus on examining understandings of politeness in interactions in which the participants have different (socio)cultural backgrounds claimed by or attributed to them.

Intersubjectivity: The way in which we interpret or understand the perceptions, feelings, thoughts, beliefs, desires of others, and in some cases reach agreement or a common understanding about them.

Interview: A method of data collection, by means of which the analyst can elicit metapragmatic information from the informant by requesting that the informant comment on a certain politeness-related topic (see also 'elicited data').

Languaculture: A term for a language and the attendant patterns of usage and associated behaviour and habits, as well as the underlying worldviews and values of its users.

Meaning representation: A reflexively intentional mental state-process (e.g. a belief, intention, desire, attitude) that is occasioned by talk or conduct on the part of a participant.

Member: A person who is recognised as affiliated with a particular social or relational network by other persons in that network. In relation to politeness, this refers to those persons who discursively maintain, change and challenge the moral order that underpins evaluative moments of politeness.

Metacognitive awareness: Involves reflexive *presentations* of cognitively grounded states, such as attitudes, expectations and so on, through discourse or pragmatic markers. In other words, linguistic forms through which participants index a particular cognitive state.

Metacommunication: Involves communication by participants about communicative events in which they themselves have been involved.

Metacommunicative awareness: Refers to reflexive interpretations and evaluations of social actions and meanings by participants. In other words, linguistic forms and expressions through which participants index a particular interpretation or evaluation of a social action or meaning.

Metadiscourse: Refers to talk by lay observers about how people should behave more generally, rather than in reference to particular situated, local interactions. These are also sometimes called 'social discourses'.

Metadiscursive awareness: Metadiscursive awareness refers to reflexive social discourses on politeness that are constituted (and contested) at a societal or cultural level.

Metalanguage: Language which focuses on language itself.

Metalinguistic awareness: Involves reflexive representations of evaluations of politeness, impoliteness and so on that are either tied to particular interactions, or behaviours more generally.

Metaparticipants: People whose evaluations of politeness arise through vicariously taking part in the interaction by viewing it on television or on the internet, for instance.

Metapragmatic awareness: A reflexive form of awareness about how language is used and what particular usages can index, which is drawn upon by both participants and observers in interpreting and evaluating social actions and meanings.

Metapragmatics: The study of awareness on the part of ordinary or lay participants and observers about the ways in which they use language to interact and communicate with others.

Mimesis: A term from the anthropological literature which refers to the way in which a person who engages in a ritual is undertaking a *performance*.

Moral order: The set of expected, background features of everyday scenes that members of a sociocultural group or relational network 'take for granted'. These seen but unnoticed features are imbued with morality (i.e. they are open to evaluation as appropriate/inappropriate, good/bad, polite/impolite) because they are familiar to those members through being sustained (and over time changed) by the practices of those members.

Multimodality: A collective name for the different modalities by means of which politeness is communicated (see also 'interactional multimodality').

Naturally occurring data: Language data that arises through spontaneous interaction amongst participants.

Negative politeness: An analyst's category used to refer to strategies that are directed at the hearer's negative face-wants, for instance, when the speaker avoids presuming, coercing and personalising, and emphasises the hearer's status (see 'face').

Normative frame of reference: The assumption on the part of members that others from the same (perceived) social group would evaluate a person or relationship in the same way.

Observer: A person who notices and thinks about evaluative moments through which politeness arises. Observers include both lay observers and analysts.

Observer coding: An approach to analysis where a system for categorising is established in advance on the basis of theory or research, and the analyst decides which category applies to each utterance or behaviour.

Ontology: The word ontology comes from the Greek words ὄντος (*óntos*) and λόγος (*logos*) and literally means 'the study of that which is'. An ontological perspective involves one's stance on whether there is such a thing as politeness in the first place in the sense of it forming part of our social reality, or being simply a reification of the perceptions of lay observers.

Orders of indexicality: This refers to the idea that sets of expectancies in the moral order are reflexively layered. In other words, the set of expectations invoked in a particular interaction is more often than not dependent on expectations assumed to hold across interactions over time in a particular social or relational network.

Paralinguistic features: Refers more broadly to non-lexical elements of speech, including laughter, breathing, cries and so on (cf. interactional multimodality).

Participant: A person who takes part in interaction. In relation to politeness, this refers to those persons who are themselves involved in the evaluative moments through which politeness arises.

Person: A person is an individual as conceptualised by other members in a social environment, and is thus an inherently socially constructed notion. What makes interpersonal evaluations interpersonal in the first instance is that they are directed at persons (see also 'relationships').

Positive politeness: An analyst's category used to refer to strategies that are directed at the hearer's positive face wants, for instance, when the speaker claims common ground with the hearer, conveys that they are co-operators, and when he fulfils a want of the hearer and so on (see 'face').

Possible understandings: Where participants hold to multiple incipient lines of understanding of social action and meaning in a particular interaction until such time that one or more of these incipient lines of understanding are confirmed or disconfirmed in subsequent talk.

Post-recording interviews: The method of conducting interviews with the participants in an interaction after that given interaction, in order to tap into their states of mind and claimed interpretations and evaluations during those interactions.

Pragmatic meaning: A meaning representation (encompassing both what is said and what is implied) that is recognised by participants and thus for which participants are routinely held accountable (see also 'meaning representation'; cf. 'social action').

Preference: A technical term from the field of conversation analysis, which refers to the non-equivalent ordering of actions in interaction. Next turns can be marked as preferred or dispreferred relative to prior turns in systematic ways by participants.

Prosody: Refers to aspects of the delivery of talk, including timing, loudness, accent, pitch and voice quality.

Punctuated: A view of politeness as involving a discrete, independent evaluative moment on the part of either the speaker or the hearer.

Questionnaires/surveys: A method of data collection where responses or evaluations are aggregated across a group of informants. It can be used to tap into evaluations by lay observers of a particular interaction vis-à-vis politeness (see 'elicited data').

Ratify: To confirm or support the stance or identity claim of another participant.

Rationality: Refers to decision-making based on logical reasoning rather than being influenced by emotion. In the Brown and Levinson (1987) framework, it is claimed that whenever a certain form of politeness is chosen to address the hearer's face needs (see 'face'), the speaker makes a rational choice as he observes the 'face-wants' of the hearer.

Recurrence: Where a certain linguistic form or behaviour becomes readily recognisable for a group of people as it is used again and again over time and across interactions within that relational network, and thereby forms a kind of social practice.

Recursive: Where an interpretation or evaluation reoccurs or is repeated in a self-similar way over time and across social spaces.

Reflexivity: Where one level of interpretation or analysis is interdependently related to another.

Reified: Where a social phenomenon noted by lay observers is treated as if it has an objective reality in and of itself.

Relational history: The history between and across members of a given relational network. In the case of conventions, this term refers to the way in which members of the given network recurrently, and then, through conventionalisation, interact with each other in ways that are both constrained and afforded by those schemata.

Relational network: Refers to sets of social links between persons that form the basis of an identifiable group to those persons who constitute that network. Relational networks range from a group of families and friends, to a localised community of practice, through to a larger much more diffuse societal or cultural group.

Relational shift: The increasing focus on interpersonal relationships in post-2000 politeness research.

Relationship: Refers to the establishment and maintenance of social connection between two or more otherwise separate individuals. What makes interpersonal evaluations interpersonal in the first instance is that they are directed at relationships (see also 'persons').

Relativity: The claim that norms of politeness are always dependent on both time and space. Relativity is particularly salient in historical settings (see 'time' and 'space').

Representation: Refers to the way in which a social or interpersonal phenomenon is described and presented to others. Historical texts are often prone to representing politeness in a biased way.

Ritual: A formalised/schematic, conventionalised and recurrent act, which is relationship forcing, i.e. by operating it reinforces/transforms in-group relationships. Ritual is realised as an embedded (mini-)performance (mimesis), and this performance is bound to relational history (and related ethos), or historicity in general (and related social ethos).

Ritual moment: Where the enactment of a ritual creates a temporary destruction of awareness of the wider meaningful relations of one's individuality and the reduction of the self to the immediate physical experience of the here-and-now.

Ritualisation: Where a convention becomes a ritual because it is recognisibly performed.

Routine: Refers to the way in which a great deal of our everyday activities is recurrent, and so these activities, including certain polite actions and reactions, are held to occur as a matter of course in interaction.

Schemata: Pre-existing patterns of thought or behaviour that are used in recurrent ways, and which are readily recognisable to members.

Second-order politeness: An understanding of politeness grounded in the *interpretations* (lay versus analyst) and *conceptualisations* (folk-theoretic versus theoretical) of observers (cf. 'first-order politeness').

Self-reflexive: Where the researcher reflects on his or her own folk theory of culture and politeness in a critical way, acknowledging that any theory is likely to reflect a worldview that is rooted in the researcher's specific understanding of politeness, and which is inherited from the ideologies of the relational networks to which the researcher belongs.

Semantic field: A set of related words that denote a way of representing an aspect of a presumed social reality.

Sequentiality: Refers to the way in which current turns or utterances are always understood relative to prior and subsequent talk, particularly talk that is contiguous (i.e. immediately prior to or subsequent to the current utterance or turn).

Social action: Where talk or conduct is recognised by participants as doing something that is real-world consequential for those participants, and thus something for which participants are routinely held accountable (cf. 'pragmatic meaning').

Social practice: A recurrent way of occasioning a particular set of inter-related social actions, pragmatic meanings and interpersonal evaluations that is both imbued with historicity and is situated within a particular social or relational network (see also 'time' and 'space').

Space: Social space refers to the relationship between the individual and the society in which he or she lives. It encompasses a dynamic relational network, which is imbued not only with historicity but also with ongoing interaction and emerging relationships. Social space ranges from the subjective understandings of the individuals that comprise a social space (e.g. social cognition) through to the intersubjective understandings that form across individuals in that social space (e.g. culture).

Speech act: Refers to the performative function of language – the way in which language is used to do things like requesting, offering, and inviting, rather than simply being a means of delivering information (cf. 'social action').

Stereotypical contrasting: When a certain cultural identity is positioned against other cultural identities in terms of politeness in order to reinforce relationships within a network.

Strategy: A plan or series of moves for obtaining a specific goal or result. In Brown and Levinson's (1987) approach, a focus on politeness strategies presumes that speakers have particular goals in mind, and employ rationale means-to-ends reasoning to formulate a series of moves in order to achieve that goal in a way that is considered 'polite', and that hearers must employ ends-to-means reasoning in order to figure out what that goal might be, as well as recognising the speaker's polite intention.

Subjectivity: The perceptions, feelings, thoughts, beliefs, desires and so on of an individual person.

Symbolic: Rituals are actions that symbolically 'encode' the social order of the community, as well as the community's values.

Theoretical: An explicitly defined and formalised account of a social phenomenon such as politeness that can be shared amongst scientific observers.

There-and-then: Refers to the way in which particular social actions and meanings are evaluated vis-à-vis politeness through ongoing linking with evaluations situated in other times and places. In other words, the way in which evaluations of politeness in the here-and-now are inevitably interlinked with evaluations in the there-and-then (i.e. over time), as well as the there-and-then in its own right (see also 'here-and-now').

Time: The claim that any understanding of politeness always arises relative to time, and so politeness in ongoing and historical interactions are necessarily interlinked.

Transformation: Where norms, social practices and the like are always in some degree of flux, or at least they are inevitably open to change with the passing of time, even if flux might be imperceptible in practice.

Understandings: The claim that politeness can arise through multiple ways of perceiving, interpreting or evaluating the very same moment.

Units of analysis: The scope of the analytical focus of politeness researchers. First-wave approaches have tended to use units of analysis focused at the level of languages, societies and cultures, instead of analysing politeness behaviour at the level of localised individuals and smaller groupings (see 'first-wave approaches').

Universality: The claim that linguistic politeness can be systematically described across languages and cultures using the same underlying theoretical framework.

User: A person who somehow contributes to evaluative moments of politeness either through being involved in those evaluations themselves, or by being implicated in them through their affiliation with the moral order that underpins those evaluations.

Utterance: A functionally meaningful unit of communication. Unlike units in descriptive linguistics, which traditionally span morpheme to sentence, an utterance is not defined by its size but rather with respect to its function: it is a communicative unit mostly produced by a single speaker.

Valency: Refers to the way in which scales vis-à-vis which persons and relationships are evaluated can range from good to bad, appropriate to inappropriate, like through to dislike and so on. Interpersonal evaluations thus involve not just any kind of categorisation, but rather categorisations that are valenced (see 'categorisation').

Variability: Refers to differences in the ways in which members from the same group may evaluate the very same event vis-à-vis politeness.

Visibility: Refers to the degree of hiddenness or opacity of a particular convention or ritual. This depends on the size and type of the network in which it is situated.

References

Arundale, Robert. B. 1999. An alternative model and ideology of communication for an alternative politeness theory. *Pragmatics* 9(1): 119–53.

2006. Face as relational and interactional: a communication framework for research on face, facework, and politeness. *Journal of Politeness Research* 2(2): 193–216.

2008. Against (Gricean) intentions at the heart of human interaction. *Intercultural Pragmatics* 5(2): 231–60.

2009. Face as emergent in interpersonal communication: an alternative to Goffman. In: F. Bargiela-Chiappini and M. Haugh (eds.) *Face, Communication and Social Interaction*. London: Equinox, 33–54.

2010a. Relating. In: M. A. Locher and S. L. Graham (eds.) *Interpersonal Pragmatics*. Berlin: Mouton de Gruyter, 137–66.

2010b. Constituting face in conversation: face, facework, and interactional achievement. *Journal of Pragmatics* 42(8): 2078–105.

2012. On understandings of communication: a response to Wedgwood. *Intercultural Pragmatics* 9(2): 137–59.

2013. Conceptualising 'interaction' in interpersonal pragmatics: implications for understanding and research, *Journal of Pragmatics* (forthcoming).

Arundale, Robert B. and David A. Good 2002. Boundaries and sequences in studying conversation. In: A. Fetzer and C. Meierkord (eds.) *Rethinking Sequentiality: Linguistics Meets Conversational Interaction*. Amsterdam: John Benjamins, 121–50.

Augoustinos, Martha, Iain Walker and Ngaire Donaghue 2006. *Social Cognition: An Integrated Introduction*. London: Sage.

Austin, John L. 1962. *How to Do Things with Words*. Cambridge MA: Harvard University Press.

Bargiela-Chiappini, Francesca and Michael Haugh (eds.) 2009. *Face, Communication and Social Interaction*. London: Equinox.

Bassili, John N. and Rick D. Brown 2005. Implicit and explicit attitudes: research, challenges, and theory. In: D. Albarracín, B. T. Johnson and M. P. Zanna (eds.) *The Handbook of Attitudes*. Mahwah, NJ: Lawrence Erlbaum Associates, 543–74.

Bax, Marcel 1999. Ritual levelling. The balance between the eristic and the co-n-t-ractual motive in hostile verbal encounters in medieval romance and early mo-dern drama. In: A. H. Jucker, G. Fritz, and F. Lebsanft (eds.) *Historical Dialogue Analysis*. Amsterdam and Philadelphia: John Benjamins, 35–80.

2010a. Rituals. In: A. H. Jucker and I. Taavitsainen (eds.) *Handbook of Pragmatics, Vol. 8: Historical Pragmatics*. Berlin: Mouton de Gruyter, 483–519.

2010b. Epistolary presentation rituals. Face-work, politeness, and ritual display in early modern Dutch letter-writing. In: J. Culpeper and D. Z. Kádár (eds.) *Historical (Im)politeness*. Bern: Peter Lang, 37–85.

Baxter, Judith 2004. *Positioning Gender and Discourse: A Feminist Methodology*. Basingstoke: Palgrave Macmillan.

Bayraktaroğlu, Arin and Maria Sifianou 2012. The iron first in the velvet glove: how politeness can contribute to impoliteness. *Journal of Politeness Research* 8(2): 143–62.

Bell, Catherine 1992. *Ritual Theory, Ritual Practice*. Oxford University Press.

Blitvich, Garcés-Conejos Pilar 2009. Impoliteness and identity in the American news media: the culture wars. *Journal of Politeness Research* 5: 273–304.

2010. Introduction: the *status-quo* and *quo vadis* of impoliteness. *Intercultural Pragmatics* 7(4): 535–59.

Blum-Kulka, Shoshana 1987. Indirectness and politeness in requests: same or different? *Journal of Pragmatics* 11: 131–46.

Blum-Kulka, Shoshana, Juliane House and Gabriele Kasper (eds.) 1989. *Cross-Cultural Pragmatics: Requests and Apologies*. Norwood, NJ: Ablex.

Bodor, Péter and Virág Barcza 2011. Érzelmi fejlődés és a kicsinyítő képzők elsajátítása [Emotional development and the acquisition of diminutives]. *Pszichológia* 31(3): 195–236.

Bolívar, Adriana 2008. Perceptions of (im)politeness in Venezuelan Spanish: the role of evaluation in interaction. *Pragmatics* 18(4): 605–33.

Bonnefon, Jean-François and Gaëlle Villejoubert 2006. Tactful or doubtful? Expectations of politeness explain the severity bias in the interpretation of probability phrases. *Psychological Science* 17(9): 747–51.

Bousfield, Derek 2010. Issues in impoliteness research. In: M. A. Locher and S. L. Graham (eds.) *Interpersonal Pragmatics*. Berlin: Mouton de Gruyter: 101–34.

Boxer, Diana 1993. Speech behavior and social distance: the case of indirect complaints. *Journal of Pragmatics* 19(2): 103–25.

Brody, Elaine M. 1970. The etiquette of filial behaviour. *The International Journal of Aging and Human Development* 1(1): 87–94.

Brown, Penelope 2001. Politeness and language. In: N. J. Smelser and P. B. Baltes (eds.), *International Encyclopedia of the Social and Behavioral Sciences*. Oxford: Elsevier Sciences, 11620–4.

Brown, Penelope and Stephen C. Levinson 1978. Universals in language usage: politeness phenomena. In: E. Goody (ed.) *Questions and Politeness*. Cambridge University Press, 56–311.

Brown, Penelope and Stephen C. Levinson 1987. *Politeness: Some Universals in Language Usage*. Cambridge University Press.

Brown, Roger and Albert Gilman 1960. The pronouns of power and solidarity. In: T. A. Sebeok (ed.) *Style in Language*. New York: MIT, 253–76.

Bucholtz, Mary 1999. 'Why be normal?': language and identity practices in a community of nerd girls. *Language in Society* 28: 203–23.

Butler, Judith 1990. *Gender Trouble: Feminism and the Subversion of Identity*. London: Routledge.

Chang, Wei-Lin Melody and Michael Haugh 2011a. Evaluations of im/politeness of an intercultural apology. *Intercultural Pragmatics* 8(3): 411–42.

2011b. Strategic embarrasment and face threatening in business interactions. *Journal of Pragmatics* 43(12): 2948–63.

Chomsky, Noam 1957. *Syntactic Structure*. The Hague: Mouton de Gruyter.

1965. *Aspects of the Theory of Syntax*. Cambridge, MA: MIT Press.

Clift, Rebecca 1999. Irony in conversation. *Language in Society* 28: 523–53.

2001. Meaning in interaction: the case of 'actually'. *Language* 77(2): 245–91.

Cook, Haruko Minagishi 2006. Japanese politeness as an interactional achievement: academic consultation sessions in Japanese universities. Introduction. G. Kasper (ed.), 260–91.

Copestake, Anne and Marina Terkourafi 2010. Conventional speech act formulae: from corpus findings to formalization. In: P. Kühnlein, A. Benz, and C. Sidner (eds.) *Constraints in Discourse* 2. Amsterdam: John Benjamins, 125–40.

Couper-Kuhlen, Elizabeth 2012. On affectivity and preference in responses to rejection. *Text and Talk* 32(4): 453–75.

Crystal, David 2003. *English as a Global Language*. Cambridge University Press.

Culpeper, Jonathan 2005. Impoliteness and entertainment in the television quiz show: *The Weakest Link*. *Journal of Politeness Research* 1: 35–72.

2008. In: D. Bousfield and M. Locher (eds.) *Impoliteness in Language*. Berlin and New York: Mouton de Gruyter, 17–44.

2009a. Historical sociopragmatics: an introduction. *Journal of Historical Pragmatics* 10(2): 153–60.

2009b. The metalanguage of impoliteness: explorations in the Oxford English Corpus. In: P. Baker (ed.) *Contemporary Corpus Linguistics*. London: Continuum, 64–6.

2011a. *Impoliteness: Using Language to Cause Offence*. Cambridge University Press.

2011b. Politeness and impoliteness. In: K. Aijmer and G. Andersen (eds.) *Sociopragmatics, Vol. 5: Handbooks of Pragmatics*. Berlin: Mouton de Gruyter, 391–436.

2011c. 'It's not what you said, it's how you said it!' Prosody and impoliteness. In: Linguistic Politeness Research Group (eds.) *Discursive Approaches to Politeness*. Berlin: Mouton de Gruyter, 57–83.

2012. (Im)politeness: three issues. *Journal of Pragmatics* 44(9): 1128–33.

Culpeper, Jonathan and Jane Demmen 2011. Nineteenth-century English politeness: negative politeness, conventional indirect requests and the rise of the individual self. *Journal of Historical Pragmatics* 12(1/2): 49–81.

Culpeper, Jonathan and Michael Haugh forthcoming. *Pragmatics and the English Language*. Basingstoke: Palgrave Macmillan, forthcoming.

Culpeper, Jonathan and Merja Kytö 2000. Data in historical pragmatics: spoken interaction (re)case as writing. *Journal of Historical Pragmatics* 4(2): 175–99.

2010. *Speech in Writing: Explorations in Early Modern English Dialogues*. Cambridge University Press.

Curl, Traci and Paul Drew 2008. Contingency and action: a comparison of two forms of requesting. *Research on Language and Social Interaction* 41(2): 129–53.

Davies, Bethan 2011. Discursive histories, personalist ideology and judging intent: analysing the metalinguistic discussion of Tony Blair's 'slave trade apology'. In: Linguistic Politeness Research Group (ed.) *Discursive Approaches to Politeness*. Berlin: Mouton de Gruyter: 189–219.

Davies, Bethan, Andrew John Merrison and Michael Haugh 2011. Epilogue. In: B. L. Davies, M. Haugh and A. J. Merrison (eds.) *Situated Politeness*. London: Continuum, 270–7.

de Berg, Henk 1995. A systems theoretical perspective on communication. *Poetics Today* 16(4): 709–36.

de Zarobe, Leyre Ruiz and Yolanda Ruiz de Zarobe 2012. *Content and Language Integrated Learning: Evidence from Research in Europe*. Bristol: Multilingual Matters.

Deutschmann, Mats 2003. *Apologising in British English*. Umeå, Sweden: Umeå University.

Drew, Paul 1997. 'Open' class repair initiators in response to sequential sources of trouble in conversation. *Journal of Pragmatics* 28(1): 69–101.

1998. Complaints about transgressions and misconduct. *Research on Language and Social Interaction* 31(3–4): 295–325.

Durkheim, Émile 2001 [1915]. Carol Cosman trans. *The Elementary Forms of Religious Life*. Oxford University Press.

Dury, Richard 2008. Handwriting and the linguistic study of letters. In: M. Dossena and I. Tieken-Boon Van Ostade (eds.) *Studies in Late Modern English Correspondence: Methodology and Data*. Berne: Peter Lang, 113–33.

Dynel, Marta. 2011. 'You talking to me?' The viewer as a ratified listener to film discourse. *Journal of Pragmatics* 43(6): 1628–44.

Eelen, Gino 2001. *A Critique of Politeness Theories*. Manchester: St Jerome Publishing.

Fienemann, Jutta and Jochen Rehbein 2004. Introductions: being polite in multilingual settings. In: J. House and J. Rehbein (eds.) *Multilingual Communication*. Amsterdam and Philadelphia: John Benjamins, 223–78.

Foley, William 1997. *Anthropological Linguistics: An Introduction*. New York: John Wiley & Sons.

Foucault, Michel 1966 [1970] *Les mots et les choses. Une archéologie des sciences humaines*. [The Order of Things: An Archaeology of Human Sciences]. Gallimard: Paris (English translation: New York, NY: Pantheon).

1973. *The Order of Things: An Archaeology of the Human Sciences*. New York: Vintage Books.

Fraser, Bruce 1990. Perspectives on politeness. *Journal of Pragmatics* 14: 219–36.

Fukushima, Saeko 2004. Evaluation of politeness: the case of attentiveness. *Multilingua* 23: 365–87.

2011. A cross-generational and cross-cultural study on demonstration of attentiveness. *Pragmatics* 21: 549–71.

Gagné, Nana Okura 2010. Reexamining the notion of negative face in the Japanese *Socio linguistic* politeness of request. *Language and Communication* 30(2): 123–38.

Garfinkel, Harold 1964. Studies in the routine grounds of everyday activities. *Social Problems* 11(3): 225–50.

1967. *Studies in Ethnomethodology*. Englewood Cliffs, NJ: Prentice-Hall.

Geyer, Naomi 2008. *Discourse and Politeness: Ambivalent Face in Japanese*. London: Continuum.

Goddard, Cliff 2006. Ethnopragmatics: a new paradigm. In: C. Goddard (ed.) *Ethnopragmatics. Understanding Discourse in Cultural Context*, 1–30. Berlin: Mouton de Gruyter.

Goddard, Cliff 2009. Not taking yourself too seriously in Australian English: semantic explications, cultural scripts, corpus evidence. *Intercultural Pragmatics* 6(1): 29–53.

Goffman, Erving 1964. The neglected situation. In: J. J. Gumperz and D. Hymes (eds.) *Ethnography of Communication, American Anthropologist* 66(6): 133–6.

1967. *Interaction Ritual: Essays on Face-to-Face Behavior*. New York: Anchor Books.

1979. *Footing. Semiotica* 25(1): 1–29.

1981. *Forms of Talk*. Philadelphia: University of Pennsylvania Press.

Goleman, Daniel 2011. *Social Intelligence: The New Science of Human Relationships*. London: Random House.

Graham, Sage Lambert 2007. Disagreeing to agree: conflict, (im)politeness, and identity in a computer-mediated community. *Journal of Pragmatics* 39(4): 742–59.

Grainger, Karen 2011. 'First-order' and 'second-order' politeness: institutional and intercultural contexts. In: Linguistic Politeness Research Group (ed.) *Discursive Approaches to Politeness*. Berlin: Mouton de Gruyter, 167–88.

Grice, Herbert Paul 1957. Meaning. *The Philosophical Review* 66(3): 377–88.

1989[1975]. *Studies in the Way of Words*. Cambridge, MA: Harvard University Press.

Gu, Yueguo 1990. Politeness phenomena in modern Chinese. *Journal of Pragmatics* 14(2): 237–57.

Harris, Sandra 2011. The limits of politeness re-visited: courtroom discourse as a case in point. In: Linguistic Politeness Research Group (ed.) *Discursive Approaches to Politeness*. Berlin: Mouton de Gruyter, 85–108.

2003. Anticipated versus inferred politeness. *Multilingua* 22(4): 397–413.

2004. Revisiting the conceptualisation of politeness in English and Japanese. *Multilingua* 23 (1/2): 85–109.

2007a. The co-constitution of politeness implicature in conversation, *Journal of Pragmatics* 39(1): 84–110.

2007b. Emic conceptualisations of (im)politeness and face in Japanese: implications for the discursive negotiation of second language learner identities, *Journal of Pragmatics* 39(4): 657–80.

2007c. The discursive challenge to politeness research: an interactional alternative. *Journal of Politeness Research* 3(2): 295–317.

2008. Intention and diverging interpretings of implicature in the uncovered meat sermon. *Intercultural Pragmatics* 5(2): 201–29.

2010a. When is an email really offensive?: Argumentativity and variability in evaluations of impoliteness. *Journal of Politeness Research* 6(1): 7–31.

2010b. Intercultural (im)politeness and the micro–macro issue. In: A. Trosborg (ed.) *Pragmatics across Languages and Cultures*. Berlin: Mouton de Gruyter: 139–66.

2010c. Respect and deference. In: M. A. Locher and S. L. Graham (eds.) *Interpersonal Pragmatics*. Berlin: Mouton de Gruyter, 271–88.

2011. Humour, face and im/politeness in getting acquainted. In: B. Davies, M. Haugh and A. Merrison (eds.) *Situated Politeness*. London: Continuum, 165–84.

2012a. Epilogue: the first–second order distinction in face and politeness research. Journal of Politeness Research 8(1): 111–34.

2012b. On understandings of intention: a response to Wedgwood. *Intercultural Pragmatics* 9(2): 161–94.

2013a. Disentangling face, facework and politeness. *Sociocultural Pragmatics* 1(1): 46–73.

2013b. Speaker meaning and accountability in interaction. *Journal of Pragmatics* 48(1): 41–56.

2013c. Im/politeness, social practice and the participation order. *Journal of Pragmatics*. Special issue on 'Interpersonal pragmatics', forthcoming.

2013d. *Im/politeness Implicatures*. Berlin: Mouton de Gruyter, forthcoming.

Haugh, Michael and Francesca Bargiela-Chiappini (eds.) 2010. Face in interaction. *Special issue of Journal of Pragmatics*, 42(8): 2073–171.

Haugh, Michael, Wei-Lin Melody Chang and Dániel Z. Kádár 2013. 'Doing deference': identities and relational practices in Chinese online discussion boards. *Language@Internet* 9.

Haugh, Michael, Bethan Davies and Andrew Merrison 2011. Situating politeness. In: B. Davies, M. Haugh, and A. Merrison (eds.) *Situated Politeness*. London: Continuum, 1–23.

Haugh, Michael and Kasia M. Jaszczolt 2012. Speaker intentions and intentionality. In: K. M. Jaszczolt and K. Allan (eds.) *Cambridge Handbook of Pragmatics*. Cambridge University Press, 87–112.

Haugh, Michael and Dániel Z. Kádár forthcoming. *Politeness in Chinese and Japanese*. Amsterdam: John Benjamins, forthcoming.

Haugh, Michael, Dániel Z. Kádár and Sara Mills 2013. Interpersonal pragmatics: an introduction. In: M. Haugh, D. Z. Kádár and S. Mills (eds.) *Journal of Pragmatics: Special Issue – Interpersonal Pragmatics*, forthcoming.

Haugh, Michael and Yasuko Obana 2011. Politeness in Japan. In: D. Z. Kádár and S. Mills (eds.) *Politeness in East Asia*. Cambridge University Press, 147–75.

Haugh, Michael and Klaus P. Schneider (eds.) 2012. Im/politeness across Englishes. *Journal of Pragmatics* 44(9): 1017–1133.

He, Yun 2012. Different generations, different face? A discursive approach to naturally occurring compliment responses in Chinese. *Journal of Politeness Research* 8(1): 29–51.

Heidegger, Martin 1991[1927]. *Being and Time*. New York: John Wiley & Sons.

Heritage, John 1984. *Garfinkel and Ethnomethodology*. Englewood Cliffs: Prentice-Hall.

1988. Explanations as accounts: a conversation analytic perspective. In: C. Antaki (ed.) *Analyzing Everyday Explanation: A Casebook of Methods*. London: Sage, 127–44.

Holmes, Janet, Meredith Marra and Stephanie Schnurr 2008. Impoliteness and ethnicity: Māori and Pākehā discourse in New Zealand workplaces. *Journal of Politeness Research* 4(2): 193–219.

Holmes, Janet, Marra Meredith and Bernadette Vine 2012. Politeness and impoliteness in ethnic varieties of New Zealand English. *Journal of Pragmatics* 44(9): 1063–76.

Holtgraves, Thomas M. 1998. Interpreting indirect replies. *Cognitive Psychology* 37: 1–27.

2000. Preference organization and reply comprehension. *Discourse Processes* 30: 87–106.

2005. Social psychology, cognitive psychology, and linguistic politeness. *Journal of Politeness Research* 1(1): 73–94.

House, Juliane 2008. (Im)politeness in English as lingua franca discourse. In: M. Locher and J. Strässler (eds.) *Standards and Norms in the English Language*. Berlin: Mouton de Gruyter, 351–66.

Hutchby, Ian 2008. Participants' orientations to interruptions, rudeness and other impolite acts in talk-in-interaction. *Journal of Politeness Research, Special Issue: 'Impoliteness and Rudeness'* 4(2): 221–41.

Ide, Sachiko 1982. Japanese sociolinguistics: politeness and women's language. *Lingua* 57(2–4): 357–85.

1989. Formal forms and discernment: two neglected aspects of linguistic politeness. *Multilingua*, 8(2–3): 223–48.

2005. How and why honorifics can signify dignity and elegance: The indexicality and reflexivity of linguistic rituals. In: R. T. Lakoff and S. Ide (eds.) *Broadening the Horizon of Linguistic Politeness*. Amsterdam: John Benjamins, 45–64.

Ide, Sachiko, Beverly Hill, Yukiko Carnes, Tsunao Ogino and Akiko Kawasaki 2005[1992]. The concept of politeness: an empirical study of American English and Japanese. In: R. J. Watts, S. Ide and K. Ehlich (eds.) *Politeness in Language: Studies in its History, Theory, and Practice*, 281–97.

Iggers, Georg G. 2007. Rationality and history. www.culturahistorica.es/iggers/ rationality_and_history.pdf

Inagaki, Noriko 2011. Unpacking the hearer's interpretation of situated politeness. In: B. Davies, M. Haugh and A. J. Merrison (eds.) *Situated Politeness*. London: Continuum, 147–64.

Jacobs, Andreas and Andreas H. Jucker 1995. The historical perspective in pragmatics. In A. H. Jucker (ed.) *Historical Pragmatics – Pragmatic Developments in the History of English*. Amsterdam and Philadelphia: John Benjamins, 3–36.

Jaworski, Adam, Nikolas Coupland and Dariusz Galasiński 2004. Metalanguage: why now? In: A. Jaworski, N. Coupland and D. Galasiński (eds.) *Metalanguage: Social and Ideological Perspectives*. Berlin: Mouton de Gruyter, 3–9.

Jucker, Andreas H. 2010. 'In curteisie was set ful muchel hir lest', politeness in Middle English. In: J. Culpeper and D. Z. Kádár (eds.) *Historical (Im)Politeness*. Berne: Peter Lang, 175–200.

2012. Positive and negative face as descriptive categories in the history of English. In: M. Bax and D. Z. Kádár (eds.) *Understanding Historical (Im)Politeness*. Amsterdam: John Benjamins, 178–97.

Kachru, Braj B. 1985. Standards, codification and sociolinguistic realism: the English language in the outer circle. In: R. Quirk and H. Widdowson (eds.) *English in the World: Teaching and Learning the Language and Literatures*, Cambridge University Press, 11–30.

1992. Teaching world Englishes. In: B. B. Kachru, (ed.) *The Other Tongue: English Across Cultures*. Urbana, IL: University of Illinois Press, 355–66.

Kádár, Dániel Z. 2007. *Terms of (Im)Politeness: On the Communicational Properties of Traditional Chinese (Im)Polite Terms of Address*. Budapest: Eotvos Lorand University Press.

2010a. Exploring the historical Chinese denigration/elevation phenomenon. In: J. Culpeper and D. Z. Kádár (eds.) *Historical (Im)Politeness*. Berne: Peter Lang, 117–45.

2010b. *Historical Chinese Letter Writing*. London: Continuum.

2011. A graphic–semiotic analysis of the Chinese multimodal elevation and denigration phenomenon *US–China Foreign Language* 9(2): 77–88.

2013. *Relational Rituals and Communication: Ritual Interaction in Groups*. Basingstoke: Palgrave Macmillan, forthcoming.

Kádár, Dániel Z. and Francesca Bargiela-Chiappini 2010. Introduction: politeness research in and across cultures. In: F. Bargiela-Chiappini and D. Z. Kádár (eds.) *Politeness Across Cultures*. Basingstoke: Palgrave Macmillan, 1–15.

Kádár, Dániel Z. and Jonathan Culpeper 2010. Historical (im)politeness: an introduction. In: J. Culpeper and D. Z. Kádár (eds.) *Historical (Im)Politeness*. Berne: Peter Lang, 9–36.

Kádár, Dániel Z., Michael Haugh and W. Chang 2013. Aggression and perceived national face threats in Mainland Chinese and Taiwanese CMC discussion boards. *Multilingua* 32(3): 343–72.

Kádár, Dániel Z. and Sara Mills 2011. Politeness in East Asia: an introduction. In: D. Z. Kádár and S. Mills (eds.) *Politeness in East Asia*, Cambridge University Press, 1–17.

(forthcoming). *Bluntness and Yorkshire Identity*.

Kádár, Dániel Z. and Yuling Pan 2011. *Politeness in China*. In: D. Z. Kádár and S. Mills (eds.) *Politeness in East Asia*, Cambridge University Press, 125–46.

Kasper, Gabriele 1990. Linguistic politeness: current research issues. *Journal of Pragmatics* 14: 193–218.

(ed.) 2006a. Politeness as a discursive phenomenon. *Multilingua* 25(3).

2006b. Introduction. In: G. Kasper (ed.), 243–8.

Kecskes, Istvan 2004. Lexical merging, conceptual blending, cultural crossing. *Intercultural Pragmatics* 1(1): 1–26.

Kienpointner, Manfred 1997. Varieties of rudeness: types and functions of impolite utterances. *Functions of Language* 4(2): 251–87.

Kohnen, Thomas 2008. Linguistic politeness in Anglo-Saxon England? A study of Old English address terms. *Journal of Historical Pragmatics* 9(1): 140–58.

2012. Understanding Anglo-Saxon 'politeness': Directive constraints with *ic wille / ic wolde*. In: M. Bax and D. Z. Kádár (eds.) *Understanding Historical (Im)Politeness*. Amsterdam: John Benjamins, 230–54.

Kopytko, Roman 1995. Linguistic politeness strategies in Shakespeare's plays. In: A. H. Jucker (ed.) *Historical Pragmatics. Pragmatic Developments in the History of English*. Amsterdam and Philadelphia: John Benjamins, 515–40.

Koster, Jan 2003. Ritual performance and the politics of identity. On the functions and uses of ritual. *Journal of Historical Pragmatics* 4: 211–48.

Krippendorff, Klaus 1970. On generating data in communication research. *Journal of Communication* 20(3): 241–69.

1989. On the ethics of constructing communication. In: B. Dervin, L. Grossberg, B. J. O'Keefe and E. Wartella (eds.), *Rethinking Communication: Paradigm Issues*. Newbury Park, CA: Sage, 66–96.

Kuno, Susumu 1973. *The Structure of the Japanese Language*. Cambridge, MA: MIT Press.

Lakoff, Robin T. 1973. The logic of politeness; or, minding your p's and q's. In: C. Corum, T. Smith-Stark and A. Weiser (eds.) *Papers from the Ninth Regional Meeting of the Chicago Linguistic Society*. Chicago Linguistic Society, 292–305.

Lakoff, Robin T. 1977. What you can do with words: politeness, pragmatics, and performatives. In: A. Rogers, B. Wall and J. P. Murphy (eds.) *Proceedings of the Texas Conference on Performatives, Presuppositions, and Implicatures*, Arlington: Center of Applied Linguistics, 79–105.

2005. Civility and its discontents: or, getting in your face. In: R. T. Lakoff and S. Ide (eds.) *Broadening the Horizon of Linguistic Politeness*. Amsterdam: John Benjamins, 23–44.

Langlotz, Andreas 2010. Social cognition. In: M. A. Locher, and S. L. Graham (eds.) *Interpersonal Pragmatics*. Berlin: Mouton de Gruyter, 167–202.

Langlotz, Andreas and Miriam A. Locher 2013. The role of emotions in a discursive approach to relational work. In: M. Haugh, D. Z. Kádár and S. Mills (eds.) *Journal of Pragmatics: Special Issue – Interpersonal Pragmatics*, forthcoming.

Leech, Geoffrey N. 1983. *Principles of Pragmatics*. Harlow: Longman.

Lett, James 1990. Emics and etics: notes on the epistimology of anthropology. In: T. N. Headland, K. L. Pike and M. Harris (eds.) *Emics and Etics: The Insider/Outsider Debate*. Newbury Park: Sage, 127–42.

Levinson, Stephen C. 1983. *Pragmatics*. Cambridge University Press.

2003. *Space in Language and Cognition*. Cambridge University Press.

Linguistic Politeness Research Group (ed.) 2011. *Discursive Approaches to Politeness*. Berlin: Mouton de Gruyter.

Locher, Miriam A. 2004. *Power and Politeness in Action: Disagreements in Oral Communication*. Berlin: Mouton de Gruyter.

2006. Polite behaviour within relational work: the discursive approach to politeness. *Multilingua* 25(3): 249–67.

2010. Introduction: politeness and impoliteness in computer-mediated communication. *Journal of Politeness Research* 6(1): 1–5.

Locher, Miriam A. and Andreas Langlotz 2008. Relational work: at the intersection of cognition, interaction and emotion. *Bulletin Suisse de Linguistique Appliquée (VALS-ASLA)* 88: 165–91.

Locher, Miriam A. and Richard J. Watts 2005. Politeness theory and relational work. *Journal of Politeness Research* 1(1): 9–33.

2008. Relational work and impoliteness: negotiating norms of linguistic behaviour. In: D. Bousfield, and M. A. Locher (eds.) *Impoliteness in Language. Studies on its Interplay with Power in Theory and Practice*. Berlin: Mouton de Gruyter, 77–99.

Mao, Luming R. 1994. Beyond politeness theory: 'face' revisited and renewed. *Journal of Pragmatics* 21(5): 451–86.

Matsui, Tomoko 2001. Kanrensei riron kara mita poraitonesu [Politeness from the Perspective of Relevance Theory]. *Gengo* 30: 52–9.

Matsumoto, Yoshiko 1989. Politeness and conversational universals – observations from Japanese, *Multilingua* 8(2/3): 207–21.

Miller, Laura 2004. You are doing *burriko*! Censoring/scrutinizing artificers of cute femininity in Japanese. In: O. Shigeko and J. Shibamoto-Smith (eds.) *Japanese Gender and Ideology: Cultural Models and Real People*. Oxford University Press, 148–65.

Mills, Sara 2003. *Gender and Politeness*. Cambridge University Press.

2009. Impoliteness in a cultural context. *Journal of Pragmatics* 41(5): 1047–60.

2011a. Discursive approaches to politeness and impoliteness. In: Linguistic Politeness Research Group (ed.) *Discursive Approaches to Politeness*. Berlin: Mouton de Gruyter, 19–56.

2011b. Communities of practice and politeness. In: B. Davies, M. Haugh and A. Merrison (eds.) *Situated Politeness*. London: Continuum, 73–87.

Mills, Sara and Dániel Z. Kádár 2011. Culture and politeness. In: D. Z. Kádár and S. Mills (eds.) *Politeness in East Asia*. Cambridge University Press, 21–44.

Mills, Sara and Louise Mullany 2011. *Language, Gender, and Feminism: Theory, Methodology, and Practice*. London: Routledge.

Milroy, Lesley and James Milroy 1992. Social network and social class: toward an integrated sociolinguistic model. *Language in Society* 21: 1–26.

Nevalainen, Terttu, and Tanskanen Sanna-Kaisa (eds.) 2007. *Letter Writing*. Amsterdam: John Benjamins.

Niedzielski, Nancy and Dennis Preston 2009. *Folk Linguistics*. Berlin: Mouton de Gruyter.

Nishida, Kitaro 1949. Basho [Place]. In: *Nishida Kitaroo Zenshuu* 4 [The Collected Works of Kitaro Nishida]. Tokyo: Iwanami Shoten, 208–89.

Norris, Sigrid 2004. *Analyzing Multimodal Interaction: A Methodological Framework*. London: Routledge.

O'Driscoll, Jim, 2013. Situational transformations: the offensive-izing of an email message and the public-ization of offensiveness. *Pragmatics and Society* 4(2), forthcoming.

Ohtsuka, Masayuki 2011. On *ba* (field) theory: *ba*-oriented language and thought. Paper presented at the 11th Korea–Japan Workshop on Linguistics and Language Processing, Waseda University, Tokyo, 10–11 December.

Okamoto, Shigeko 1999. Situated politeness: manipulating honorific and non-honorific expressions in Japanese conversations. *Pragmatics* 8(2): 51–74.

Ong, Walter 1984. Orality, literacy, and medieval textualization. *Oral and Written Traditions in the Middle Ages* 16(1): 1–12.

Pan, Yuling and Dániel Z. Kádár 2011. *Politeness in Historical and Contemporary Chinese*. London: Continuum.

Paternoster, Annick 2012. Inappropriate inspectors: impoliteness and overpoliteness in Ian Rankin's and Andrea Camilleri's crime series. *Language and Literature* 21(3): 311–24.

Pike, Kenneth 1967. *Language in Relation to a Unified Theory of the Structure of Human Behavior* (2nd edn). The Hague: Mouton.

1990. 'Pike's final response'. In: T. N. Headland, K. L. Pike and M. Harris (eds.) *Emics and Etics. The Insider/Outsider Debate*. Sage, Newbury Park, 184–201.

Pizziconi, Barbara 2007. The lexical mapping of politeness in British English and Japanese. *Journal of Politeness Research* 3(2): 207–41.

2011. Honorifics: the cultural specificity of a universal mechanism in Japanese. In: D. Z. Kádár and S. Mills (eds.) *Politeness in East Asia*. Cambridge University Press, 45–70.

Planchenault, Gaëlle 2010. Virtual community and politeness: the use of female markers of identity and solidarity in a transvestites' website. *Journal of Politeness Research* 6(1): 83–104.

Pomerantz, Anita 1984. Agreeing and disagreeing with assessments: Some features of preferred/dispreferred turn shapes. In: J. M. Atkinson and J. Heritage (eds.) *Structures of Social Action: Studies in Conversation Analysis*. Cambridge University Press, 57–101.

Potter, Jonathan 1998. Discursive social psychology: from attitudes to evaluative practices. *European Review of Social Psychology* 9: 233–66.

Purdy, Charles 2004. *Urban Etiquette: Marvelous Manners for the Modern Metropolis*. Tulsa, OK: Wildcat Canyon Press.

Rasmussen, Susan J. 1992. Ritual specialists, ambiguity, and power in Tuareg society. *Man* 27(1): 105–28.

Raymond, Geoffrey 2004. Prompting action: the stand-alone 'so' in sequences of talk-in-interaction. *Research on Language and Social Interaction* 37(2): 185–218.

Rehbein, Jochen and Jutta Fienemann 2004. Introductions. In: J. House and J. Rehbein (eds.) *Multilingual Communication*. Amsterdam and Philadelphia: John Benjamins, 223–78.

Rosenberg, Milton J. 1968. Hedonism, in-authenticity and other goals. In: R. Ableson, E. Aronson, W. J. McGuire, T. M. Newcomb, M. J. Rosenberg and P. H. Tannenbaum (eds.), *Theories of Cognitive Consistency: A Sourcebook*. Chicago: Rand McNally and Company.

Ruhi, Şükriye 2009. *A Place for Emotions in Conceptualizing Face and Relational Work*. Plenary lecture, International Symposium on Face and Politeness, Griffith University, Brisbane.

Sacks, Harvey 1992[1964–72]. *Lectures on Conversation, Vols. 1 and 2*. G. Jefferson (ed.). Oxford: Blackwell.

Schegloff, Emanuel A. 2006. On possibles. *Discourse Studies* 8(1): 141–57.

2007a. *Sequence Organization in Interaction: A Primer in Conversation Analysis, Vol. 1*. Cambridge University Press.

2007b. A tutorial on membership categorisation. *Journal of Pragmatics* 39: 462–82.

Schermerhorn, John R., James G. Hunt and Richard N. Osborn 2011. *Organizational Behaviour*. New York: Wiley & Sons.

Schneider, Klaus P. and Anne Barron 2008. *Variational Pragmatics: A Focus on Regional Varieties of Pluricentric Languages*. Amsterdam: John Benjamins.

Searle, John 1969. *Speech Acts: An Essay on the Philosophy of Language*. Cambridge University Press.

1975. Indirect speech acts. In: P. Cole and J. L. Morgan (eds.) *Syntax and Semantics, Vol. 3: Speech Act*. New York: Academic Press, 59–82.

Sell, Roger 1992. Literary texts and diachronic aspects of politeness. In: R. J. Watts, S. Ide and K. Erlich (eds.) *Politeness in Language. Studies in Its History, Theory and Practice*. Berlin: Mouton de Gruyter, 109–29.

Selting, Margaret 1996. Prosody as an activity-type distinctive cue in conversation: the case of so-called 'astonished' questions in repair initation. In: E. Couper-Kuhlen and M. Selting (eds.) *Prosody in Conversation*. Cambridge University Press, 231–70.

2009. Communicative style. In: S. D'Hondt, J.-O. Östman, and J. Verschueren (eds.) *The Pragmatics of Interaction*. Amsterdam: John Benjamins, 20–39.

Shimizu, Hiroshi 1995. *Ba*-principle: new logic for the real-time emergence of information. *Holonics* 5(1): 67–79.

Sifianou, Maria 1992. *Politeness Phenomena in England And Greece: A Cross-Cultural Perspective*. Oxford: Calendron.

2012. Disagreements, face and politeness. *Journal of Pragmatics* 44(12): 1554–64.

Silverstein, Michael. 1976. Shifters, linguistic categories, and cultural description. In: K. H. Basso, and H. A. Selby (eds.) *Meaning and Anthropology*. Albuquerque: The University of New Mexico Press, 11–56.

1993. Metapragmatic discourse and metapragmatic function. In: J. A. Lucy (ed.) *Reflexive Language: Reported Speech and Metapragmatics*. Cambridge University Press, 33–58.

2003. Indexical order and the dialectics of sociolinguistic life. *Language and Communication* 23: 193–229.

Spencer-Oatey, Helen 2005. (Im)politeness, face and perceptions of rapport: unpackaging their bases and interrelationships. *Journal of Politeness Research* 1(1): 95–119.

2008[2000]. Introduction: language, culture and rapport management. In: H. Spencer-Oatey (ed.) *Culturally Speaking*. London: Continuum, 1–10.

2011. Conceptualising 'the relational' in pragmatics: insights from metapragmatic emotion and (im)politeness comments. *Journal of Pragmatics* 43(14): 3565–78.

Stivers, Tanya 2008. Stance, alignment, and affiliation during storytelling: when nodding is a token of affiliation. *Research on Language and Social Interaction* 41(1): 31–57.

Sugimoto Naomi 1998. Norms of apology depicted in U.S. American and Japanese literature on manners and etiquette. *International Journal of Intercultural Relations* 22(3): 251–76.

Taavitsainen, Irma and Andreas H. Jucker 2003. *Diachronic Perspectives on Address Term Systems*. Amsterdam: John Benjamins.

Tannen, Deborah 1990. *You Just Don't Understand: Women and Men in Conversation*. New York: Bellentine Books.

Taylor, Stephanie 2007. Narrative as construction and discursive resource. In: M. Bamberg (ed.) *Narrative – State of the Art*. Amsterdam: John Benjamins, 113–22.

Terkourafi, Marina 2001. The distinction between generalised and particularised implicatures and linguistic politeness. In: P. Kühnlein, R. Hannes and H. Zeevat (eds.) *Proceedings of the Fifth Workshop on the Formal Semantics and Pragmatics of Dialogue*. Bielefeld: ZiF, 174–88.

2005. Beyond the micro-level in politeness research. *Journal of Politeness Research* 1(2): 237–62.

2008. Toward a unified theory of politeness, impoliteness, and rudeness. In: D. Bousfield and M. A Locher (eds.) *Impoliteness in Language: Studies on its Interplay with Power in Theory and Practice*. Berlin: Mouton de Gruyter, 45–74.

Thornborrow, Joanna 2002. *Power Talk: Language and Interaction in Institutional Discourse*. London: Longman (Pearson Education).

Truss, Lynne 2005. *Talk to the Hand: The Utter Bloody Rudeness of Everyday Life (or Six Good Reasons to Stay Home and Bolt the Door)*. London: Profile Books.

Usami, Mayumi 2006. Discourse politeness theory and cross-cultural pragmatics. In Asako Yositomi, Tae Umino, and Masashi Negishi (eds.) *Linguistic Informatics V: Studies in Second Language Teaching and Second Language Acquisition*. Tokyo: Center of Usage-Based Linguistic Informatics, Graduate School of Area and Culture Studies, Tokyo University of Foreign Studies, 9–31.

van Gennep, Arnold 2004. *The Rites of Passage*. London: Routledge.

Verschueren, Jef 1999. *Understanding Pragmatics*. London: Arnold.

Walkers, Joel 1979. Strategies for requesting in Spanish and English: structural similarities and pragmatic differences. *Language Learning* 9: 277–94.

Wallace, Mari I. 2007. Experience, purpose, pedagogy, and theory: Ritual activities in the classroom. In: C. Bell (ed.) *Teaching Ritual*. Oxford University Press, 73–88.

Wang, Changhuan 王昌煥, Song Yu 宋裕, and Li Cuiying 李翠瑛 2002. *Shiyong yingyong wen* 實用應用文 (*Practical Applied Writing*). Taipei: Wan-chuan-lou.

Waters, Sophia 2012. 'It's rude to VP': the cultural semantics of rudeness. *Journal of Pragmatics* 44(9): 1051–62.

Watts, Richard J. 1989. Relevance and relational work: linguistic politeness as politic behavior. *Multilingua* 8(2–3): 131–66.

1992. Linguistic politeness and politic behaviour: reconsidering claims for universality. In: R. J. Watts, S. Ide and K. Ehlich (eds.) *Politeness in Language. Studies in Its History, Theory and Practice*. Berlin: Mouton de Gruyter, 43–69.

1999. Language and politeness in early eighteenth century Britain. *Pragmatics* 9(1): 5–20.

2003. *Politeness*. Cambridge University Press.

2005. Linguistic politeness research: *quo vadis*? In: R. J. Watts, S. Ide and K. Ehlich (eds.) *Politeness in Language. Studies in Its History, Theory and Practice*. Berlin: Mouton de Gruyter, xi–xlvii.

2008. Rudeness, conceptual blending theory and relational work. *Journal of Politeness Research* 4(2): 289–317.

2011. A socio-cognitive approach to historical politeness. *Journal of Historical Pragmatics* 12(1/2): 104–32.

Watts, Richard J., Sachiko Ide and Konrad Ehlich (eds.) 1992a. *Politeness in Language: Studies in its History, Theory and Practice*. Berlin: Mouton de Gruyter.

1992b. Introduction. In: R. J. Watts, S. Ide and K. Ehlich (eds.) *Politeness in Language: Studies in its History, Theory and Practice*. Berlin: Mouton de Gruyter, 1–17.

Wenger, Etienne 1998. *Communities of Practice: Learning, Meaning, and Identity*. Cambridge University Press.

Wetzel, Patricia 2004. *Keigo in Modern Japan: Polite Language from Meiji to Present*. Manoa: The University of Hawaii Press.

Wierzbicka, Anna 2003 [1991]. *Cross-cultural Pragmatics: The Semantics of Human Interaction*. Berlin: Mouton de Gruyter.

2006. *English: Meaning and Culture*. Oxford University Press.

Wilson, Thomas P. 1970. Conceptions of interaction and forms of sociological explanation. *American Sociological Review* 35(4): 697–710.

Woods, John (ed.) 2010. *Fictions and Models*. Munich: Philosophia Verlag.

Ye, Zhendao 2004. Chinese categorization of interpersonal relationships and the cultural logic of Chinese social interaction: an indigenous perspective. *Intercultural Pragmatics* 1(2): 211–30.

2008. Returning to my mother tongue: Veronica's journey continues. In: M. Besemeres, and A. Wierzbicka (eds.) *Translating Lives: Living with Two Languages and Cultures*. Brisbane: University of Queensland Press, 141–51.

Index